D0797164

Introduction to
Reference Sources
in the Health Sciences
SIXTH EDITION

ALA Neal-Schuman purchases fund advocacy,
awareness, and accreditation programs
for library professionals worldwide.

MEDICAL LIBRARY
ASSOCIATION *Guides*

Introduction to Reference Sources in the Health Sciences

UPDATED, REVISED, AND EXPANDED

SIXTH EDITION

Compiled and edited by

Jeffrey T. Huber
Susan Swogger

Introduction to reference
sources in the health

Neal-Schuman

An imprint of the American Library Association

Chicago   2014

JEFFREY T. HUBER is Director, School of Library and Information Science, at the University of Kentucky. He completed his master's at University of Kentucky and earned his doctorate at the University of Pittsburgh and has been on the faculty in the School of Library and Information Studies at Texas Woman's University since 1998. He held a concurrent appointment as associate director for research at the Houston Academy of Medicine–Texas Medical Center (HAM–TMC) Library from 2001 to 2008. During that time he also was appointed adjunct associate professor in the School of Health Information Sciences at the Health Science Center at Houston, University of Texas.

SUSAN SWOGGER began her interest in libraries by repairing books as a student worker, eventually going to the University of Texas at Austin for library school. She spent some years as director of a psychology library in Phoenix before joining the University of North Carolina's Health Sciences Library as Collections Development Librarian.

Printed in the United States of America

18 17 16 15 14   5 4 3 2 1

Extensive effort has gone into ensuring the reliability of the information in this book; however, the publisher makes no warranty, express or implied, with respect to the material contained herein.

ISBNs: 978-0-8389-1184-6 (paper); 978-0-8389-1956-9 (PDF); 978-0-8389-1957-6 (ePub); 978-0-8389-1958-3 (Kindle). For more information on digital formats, visit the ALA Store at alastore.ala.org and select eEditions.

Library of Congress Cataloging-in-Publication Data
Introduction to reference sources in the health sciences / compiled and edited by Jeffrey T. Huber, Susan Swogger.—6th edition.
       pages cm
   Includes bibliographical references and index.
   ISBN 978-0-8389-1184-6 (print : alk. paper) — ISBN 978-0-8389-1956-9 (pdf) — ISBN 978-0-8389-1957-6 (epub) — ISBN 978-0-8389-1958-3 (kindle) 1. Medicine—Reference books—Bibliography. 2. Medicine—Bibliography. 3. Medicine—Information services. I. Huber, Jeffrey T., editor of compilation. II. Swogger, Susan, editor of compilation.
   Z6658.I54 2014
   [R118.6]
   016.610—dc23   2014004660

Book design in the Times New Roman and Avenir typefaces.

Cover image © Click Bestsellers/Shutterstock, Inc.

⊗ This paper meets the requirements of ANSI/NISO Z39.48-1992 (Permanence of Paper).

To
Fred W. Roper
who identified the need
for this textbook
and mentored
and guided the contributors
of the first four editions

Contents

PART I

Health Reference in Context

CHAPTER 1

PART II

The Reference Collection

CHAPTER 2

PART III

Bibliographic Sources

CHAPTER 3

CHAPTER 4

Figures and Tables

Figures

Tables

Foreword

The first edition of *Introduction to Reference Sources in the Health Sciences* was conceived and published more than thirty years ago, inspired by Fred Roper's need for a textbook to use with his health sciences classes at the University of North Carolina. He invited me to join him in this endeavor as a practicing health sciences librarian at the UNC-CH Health Sciences Library. The text was designed to be a selective guide to the most important reference resources in the health sciences, with sections on the Reference Collection, Bibliographic Resources, and Information Resources. The plan was presented to the Medical Library Association's Books Panel. Our proposal was accepted and the first edition appeared in 1980. Fred and I were extremely gratified by the overwhelmingly positive reviews and the enthusiastic acceptance that the health sciences library community gave the first and subsequent editions.

From the beginning, Fred and I sought out knowledgeable practicing health sciences librarians who had the expertise to address the topics covered in each chapter. It has always been a collaborative endeavor. Within the format we developed, each author was given the discretion to identify and describe the most relevant resources on their topics. This approach has proven to be very effective and has given a broad cross-section of Medical Library Association members an opportunity to share their expertise with several generations of library school students and colleagues new to the field of health sciences librarianship.

In reviewing the first edition with subsequent ones, the most significant change is the increasing importance of electronic resources and the pervasiveness of the Web. The first edition primarily focused on traditional print resources, with the notable exception being MEDLINE and early indexing and abstracting databases. The format, with three sections, remained the same. Additions and changes are most apparent in the resources covered in the Information Sources section. The first two editions have chapters on Audiovisual Reference Sources. The second edition (1984) added chapters on Grant Sources and Health Legislation Sources. With the third edition (1994) the chapter on Health Legislation Sources was dropped and the chapter on Audiovisual Sources was expanded to include Microcomputer and Multimedia Reference Sources. The fourth edition in 1992 dropped the chapter on Audiovisual, Microcomputer, and Multimedia References Sources, with online resources in all formats having primacy and representation in each chapter. A chapter on Consumer Health Reference Sources was also added in the fourth edition, recognizing the increasing importance of the information needs of that population and the health professionals that serve them. The sixth edition reflects the further evolution of health sciences reference resources and services. Addition of an introductory chapter on Health Information Seeking Behaviors and two new information chapters on Point-of-Care Sources and Global Health Sources show the expanding scope of the profession and the range of sources and services available.

Fred Roper and I started this publication without ever dreaming that it would endure and grow to become a standard textbook in health sciences librarianship. We are most gratified that our efforts and collaboration with this publication have continued and expanded. As Fred planned to retire, we invited Jeff Huber to join us in editing and compiling the fourth edition. Jeff was a great addition to our team as I took the lead with that edition. With the publication of the fifth edition, just prior to my retirement, Jeff and I invited Jean Blackwell to join our team. We achieved a smooth transition of the editorial responsibilities, without Fred's guidance. Jeff invited Susan Swogger to co-edit and compile the expanded sixth edition. They have engaged a remarkable list of continuing and new chapter authors to compile this edition. I am pleased to see that the transition of editors has been achieved so seamlessly and I am excited to see this latest edition in such capable hands. I look forward to the continued success of *Introduction to Reference Sources in the Health Sciences.*

I want to thank Fred Roper for inviting me to join him in developing and shaping this textbook. He has been a wonderful mentor over the course of my career. I have benefited from his expertise, knowledge, and vision for the training and continuing education of health information professionals. It has been a joy to have the opportunity to work with him on the creation and development of *Introduction to Reference Sources in the Health Sciences.* Our professional and personal friendship has enriched my life.

As Fred has stated earlier, I, too, am grateful that the Medical Library Association saw merit in the proposal for *Introduction to Reference Sources in the Health Sciences* when we submitted it to their fledgling publication program. That support and opportunity gave us the impetus to undertake an ambitious project and see it to successful completion. I had no idea what a rewarding adventure it would be, nor did I foresee that it would continue throughout most of my career!

Jo Anne Boorkman
Librarian Emerita
Carlson Health Sciences Library
University of California, Davis

Preface

Reference work is the cornerstone of public services in libraries and is fundamental to health sciences librarianship. Competent reference work is essential to locating relevant, accurate, and timely information in today's maze of print and electronic resources, especially given the common misperception that most information is now available and accessible on the Web. Assisting a medical student in determining best evidence related to a particular diagnosis, helping a nursing student identify a drug interaction, locating the correct bibliographic citation for a secretary in order to finalize a manuscript submission, demonstrating the differences between point-of-care resources to a group of residents, and showing a graduate student which databases to search for information on a research topic are just a few of the functions that fall within the broad purview of health sciences reference work. *Introduction to Reference Sources in the Health Sciences*, Sixth Edition, provides basic information on the nature of reference work and the authors' selections of some of the most important resources for gathering data and answering questions in the health sciences.

The chapters in this guide identify and describe both important types of reference resources: recommended general resources that serve as sources for answering bibliographic reference questions and authoritative reference sources specific to health sciences librarianship, which can be used to assist a library's clientele in finding information on medical topics. This text is designed to identify and describe the best resources available for answering questions from health professionals, students, researchers, and consumers interested in health information.

Every edition of *Introduction to Reference Sources in the Health Sciences* has included both print and electronic resources. In the first edition, most references cited and discussed were for print resources, with electronic resources focused on online bibliographic citation databases (e.g., MEDLINE and BIOSIS). At that time, these databases were primarily available to librarians who provided mediated searches for clientele. With the growth of the Internet, many resources became available via the Web, such as *The Merck Manual of Diagnosis and Therapy* and *Enzyme Nomenclature*. Other new resources that bring together the full text of books, journals, and other information under one aggregated resource (such as MD Consult) also became available, providing the power of searching across multiple sources for information on a particular topic. The Web has also allowed availability of a wealth of electronic-only resources that may or may not have had a print counterpart, such as the information from professional associations and organizations (e.g., Association of American Medical Colleges and the Malaria Foundation International), as well as collaborative ventures such as the Cochrane Library's databases with information on evidence-based medicine. These have all enriched the range of resources available to our libraries to answer reference questions for our clientele or assist them in answering their own questions.

Purpose and Scope

Our purpose remains the same—to discuss various types of reference and information resources and their use in reference work in the health sciences, regardless of format, but with an increased focus on highlighting electronic resources that have become such a fundamental part of reference services. Our library clientele has become familiar with searching the Web using search engines such as Google for all types of information, so their expectations have grown to include library support for desktop and mobile device access to information they need for their personal, patient care, research, and teaching needs as well.

Health sciences librarians are challenged to provide an expanding plethora of electronic versions of traditional print reference sources as well as new reliable electronic-only resources, thereby creating electronic reference collections that complement the print collection for use by their clientele directly with librarian assistance. In some instances, the expectation is to replace the print collection with electronic-only resources, allowing for greater mobility and access. The wealth of free quality information that is available via the Web can augment a small library's collection and the librarian's resources for assisting clientele in answering questions. On the other hand, many online resources come with restrictive licenses and hefty access fees that make it difficult or impossible for some libraries to make them available to their clientele.

This sixth edition of *Introduction to Reference Sources in the Health Sciences* explores these issues. We address questions librarians need to consider in developing and maintaining their reference collections in both the print and electronic environments, whether for use by their clientele directly or with librarian assistance. We have chosen those tools that librarians may use on a daily basis in reference work in the health sciences—those that may be considered foundation or basic works. Some major specialized works have also been included when appropriate. Emphasis is placed on U.S. publications and libraries, although an attempt has been made to address Canadian publications and needs.

The Arrangement of the Material

The major portions of the book again present the different types of bibliographic and informational sources. Chapter titles are the same as those used in the fifth edition. However, the sixth edition has been expanded to include chapters on point-of-care sources and global health sources. In addition, the sixth edition opens with a chapter on health information seeking behaviors in order to help provide context. Each chapter devoted to bibliographic and informational resources contains current content that reflects the realities of that particular area. Each of these chapters includes a discussion of the general characteristics of the type of source being considered, followed by examples of the most important tools in the area. The book is organized into four parts: *Health Reference in Context*, *The Reference Collection*, *Bibliographic Sources*, and *Information Sources*. Part I provides an overview of health information seeking behaviors with an emphasis on how the emergence of electronic resources has affected human behavior. Part II discusses the nature of reference and ways to organize and manage a reference collection. Part III covers bibliographic sources. Chapter 3 discusses sources for verifying, locating, and selecting monographs, while chapter 4 discusses sources for verifying, locating, and selecting periodicals. Chapter 5 focuses on the rich array of databases now available in the health sciences, providing the author's perspective on primary and secondary databases. Chapter 6 discusses U.S. government and technical report literature, and chapter 7 discusses resources for identifying conference proceedings, reviews, and literature in translation. Citations list availability of electronic access to print resources in addition to listing electronic-only resources.

Part IV focuses on information sources. Chapter 8 covers terminology and dictionaries, while chapter 9 discusses handbooks, manuals, and nomenclature sources. Chapter 10 discusses drug information sources, including databases. Chapter 11 discusses consumer health resources, which has become an important area of collecting and service in many health sciences libraries. Chapter 12 provides an extensive discussion on the types of medical and health statistics that are collected and resources where they can be found. Chapter 13 provides information on history sources, while chapter 14 discusses directory and biographical information sources. Chapter 15 provides information on grant sources. Chapter 16 discusses point-of-care sources. The final chapter, chapter 17, reviews global health sources. As with Part III, citations to print sources provide information regarding electronic availability as well as citations for electronic-only sources.

Since no consensus exists as to what constitutes "basic works," the materials represent the authors' candidates for such a list. In many instances, other equally appropriate examples could have been selected. For certain groups of sources (e.g., technical report literature), materials that are considerably broader in scope than the health sciences field alone have been included to help the reader gain a clear understanding of the use of these sources in reference work in the health sciences.

The URLs for Web resources are included with citations and were checked for accuracy at the time of manuscript submission; however, due to the ever-changing nature of health sciences publishing and the wide range of technical glitches that can occur, the authors cannot guarantee that these Web addresses will remain the same.

A Brief History of *Introduction to Reference Sources in the Health Sciences*

In 1979, Fred Roper approached the Medical Library Association's publications program about writing a text to support a course in health sciences reference that he taught at the University of North Carolina–Chapel Hill's School of Library Science, with the idea that it would be useful for others teaching similar courses at other library schools. The Medical Library Association expressed interest and suggested that there would be a broader audience for such a text among practicing health sciences librarians and for supporting MLA's CE course in reference resources. At that time, Jo Anne Boorkman was head of public services and head of reference at the Health Sciences Library at UNC–Chapel Hill. Fred asked her to join him as a coeditor in this endeavor. They invited several librarians, some of whom were relatively new to the field and others with a wealth of experience, to participate in this publishing venture. This mix of contributors proved to be a successful collaboration.

In 1980, the first edition appeared and was met with enthusiasm. It became a familiar text for both library school courses and MLA CE courses. It also gained a broader audience than the authors expected among practicing librarians from general academic and public libraries as well as health sciences libraries. The second edition followed four years later and continued to receive acceptance and recognition. Following major career moves for both authors to different parts of the country, their goal of regular updates slipped, and the third edition did not appear until 1994. A full ten years later, the fourth edition was published. With the fourth edition being completed as Fred prepared for retirement, Jeff Huber was invited to assist as one of the editors.

The reception of the first four editions of *Introduction to Reference Sources in the Health Sciences* has been most gratifying. It was the editors' intention to begin work on a fifth edition soon after publication of the fourth edition, to keep the publication up-to-date to reflect the changes brought on by the growth of the Web and expansion of electronic reference resources. Jo Anne's plans to retire provided further impetus to complete the fifth edition in a timely fashion. To assist with preparation of the fifth edition, Jean Blackwell was invited to serve as one of the editors and with the hope that she would continue with future editions of this book.

Jean Blackwell's plan to retire led to inviting Susan Swogger to serve as co-editor and assist with preparation of the sixth edition. A different mix of authors was invited to contribute to this edition for another successful collaboration that is in keeping with the idea originally promoted by Fred and MLA almost thirty years ago.

Many people have played important roles in the production of this sixth edition. The chapter authors have all shared their expertise, experience, and enthusiasm for their respective topics. New authors have revised several chapters from the fifth edition. As with previous editions, chapter authors for this edition are indebted to previous chapter authors. In addition, we gratefully acknowledge the production assistance of University of Kentucky Graduate Assistant Heather J. Burke. *Introduction to Reference Sources in the Health Sciences* truly is a collaborative endeavor.

Jeffrey T. Huber
Susan Swogger

PART I

Health Reference in Context

CHAPTER 1

Health Information Seeking Behaviors

Have Technological Advances Changed Health Information Seeking for Patients and Providers?

J. DAVID JOHNSON

There have been dramatic changes in the availability of information for both health professionals and their patients/clients over the past couple of decades, something explored in depth in the other chapters in this book. We have been contemplating the growth of information in our contemporary world since its very beginnings. Information technologists who focus on information retrieval systems essentially assumed that more information was always good.[1] So, normally we have seen big data, and even larger opportunities, but increasingly we also sense a flood that threatens to engulf us and our institutions.

Perhaps the historically unique feature of our contemporary world is the explosive growth of information coupled with the ready access instantiated on the Internet. Individuals have free access to an often bewildering wealth of information. They can choose from an ever-expanding array of information sources. There are literally millions of articles published every year in the technical literature, making it impossible for even the most dedicated individual to keep abreast of recent advances. For example, it has been calculated that physicians need to read an average of nineteen original articles each day to keep abreast of their fields.[2] More than 1 million articles are published every year in the biomedical and technical literature. Many patients do not receive state-of-the-art treatments, partly because physicians cannot keep up with the information explosion—a growing concern within the National Institutes of Health (NIH). The overload of information on health professionals today forces decentralization of responsibilities, with increasing responsibility passing to patients and their families if they are going to receive up-to-date treatment.[3]

What Kind of Change?

There is so much change, happening so rapidly, with such broad-ranging impacts that it is often argued that in our current era we are experiencing a revolution; that it is equivalent to one of the three historical revolutions in communication: the advent of writing, which allowed for the permanent storage of communication messages and their physical transport across time and distance; the Gutenberg revolution of moveable type, which permitted the mass production and dissemination of messages; and the telegraph, the so-called Victorian Internet, which started the electronic revolution that permitted messages to be instantly transferred over distances, which meant that their transfer was no longer equivalent to their physical transmission.

While most observers would seem to suggest that our modern communication era, often labeled the Information Age, represents a similar historical change in communication, others have reservations.[4] It has also been argued that the communication revolution is really part of a bundle of changes that have occurred in our society in general and health in particular. So, we have experienced the consumer movement in health; changes in the basic delivery of health services; changes in government regulations, especially regarding privacy; rapid development of a number of technological advances in imaging; the genomic revolution; and so forth.

Often what has happened with prior communication revolutions is the continuation of what has existed before with some modifications along with the rapid development of the new form; what Borgman has termed a process of coevolution.[5] People do not discard all their old habits, and, at least initially, they often treat the new as if it was the old, as when the first versions of word processors were treated as just a different kind of typewriter.[6] So, at least initially, a new technology is treated in much the same way as the one it supplanted, and some have gone so far as to argue there are many similarities between the Internet in its applications and the telegraph. Others suggest essentially a turbocharging view, in Ev Rogers's phrase,[7] that modern technologies essentially enhance what we had before.

For most individual information seekers the new technologies that we have seen emerge in the past several years probably do not constitute disruptive technological innovation, in Clayton Christensen's now classic concept.[8] However, for providers the same threats he outlined to their very existence are still playing out: institutions may be threatened with discontinuous, radical change as they adapt their services to a new generation of users and constantly emerging technology. For example, universities are currently confronted with massively open online courses (MOOCs) offered by elite institutions that are drawing hundreds of thousands of students from around the world. Distance learning, a traditional strength of library and information science education, is threatening the very foundations of higher education. It may also be the case that for hyperinformation seekers and cyberchondriacs the Internet has indeed changed everything, something we will return to when we discuss issues surrounding the digital divide.

Technology

The question of what kind of change we are experiencing is also linked to definitions of technology and specification of its properties. The proliferation of various forms of technology often masks a careful delineation of their underlying properties, so one focuses on e-mail rather than asynchronicity. This in part encourages a constant fascination with the new rather than a careful assessment of what kinds of attributes produce particular impacts.

At a fundamental level, technology may be defined simply as actions employed to transfer inputs into outputs. It can be viewed not just in the narrow sense of focusing on machines needed to produce physical goods, but in the broader sense of any systematic set of techniques, some of which can be associated with information-seeking tactics.

An example of a systematic approach to understanding individual information-gathering tactics has applied evolutionary psychology findings related to how humans gather food. Information foraging theory suggests that people will modify their strategies and the structure of their information fields to maximize their exposure to nutrients, in this case the rate of gaining valuable information. It develops three classes of models designed to describe how individuals adapt their information-seeking tactics to changes in their information environments. First, information patch models deal with the time allocated, filtering, and enrichment activities when information is detected in limited areas in an individual's environment. Increasing the proximity of individuals to information patches decreases their "down time" when they cannot forage. Second, information scent models address the cues individuals use to determine the value of information. Enhancing people's skill in detecting information scents also results in an easier time detecting the correct patches in which to forage. Third, information diet models focus on decision making related to the selection and pursuit of certain bits of information.[9] We can enhance the capabilities of foraging once individuals are in a patch by filtering and enrichment activities that mold the environment to fit available strategies. So, specialists focus on high density patches, while generalists gather information from a wide variety of patches.[10]

Technology, of course, has many benefits associated with enhanced information seeking. First, it increases access both in terms of electronic propinquity, bringing people closer together and in terms of scale with worldwide access to sources that are often intercultural and international.[11] Online support groups have built in homophily (at least on one dimension) and the additional benefit of ameliorating stigma and embarrassment.[12] Access entails not only the availability of a technology, but that it has the needed content and that it is usable.[13] Second, it provides unique context spaces for interactions (e.g., chat rooms) that often blend dialogue and dissemination.[14] These spaces promote interactivity and the possibilities of collaboration on common problems. Third, it can warp time in multiple ways: speeding it up, shifting it, making it asynchronous, and on and on. Fourth, because of the increasing flood of information available multiple means of delegation/gatekeeping have emerged that encourage disintermediation and the breakup of the stranglehold that the professions once held on health information.

Technology also provides us with an ever-increasing array of tools for on demand, real-time inquiry to pressing questions that people may have. These tools often have a wide range of properties and can activate many senses, increasing their social presence. The best information systems often have a game-like feel. This maxim has been directly translated by people interested in new technology into the development of games and apps that have health-related themes. Games can provoke engagement in users, encouraging self-administration and self-management of chronic diseases. Some games are also designed to reduce stigma, change an individual's self-concept, and enhance self-efficacy.[15]

A variety of games have been developed for traditional computer and Web platforms with Facebook especially receiving attention. Increasingly these games are being applied in the area of m-health with a number of smartphone games. It is estimated that at least 124 million people use smartphones for apps related to such things as logging exercises, tracking blood glucose levels, and even performing ultrasounds. There is almost an endless variety of these games: Elm City Stories aims at encouraging AIDS prevention; Massive Health's Eatery uses social media to encourage users to lose weight; Quit Now! estimates the money saved for each day someone has quit smoking; and Every Move shares users' activities on Facebook.[16]

M-health applications have the capacity to reach and follow individuals in real time across the multiple everyday contexts they inhabit in interactive and adaptive ways with impacts ranging from greater weight loss to greater adherence to scheduled appointments.[17] So someone who is concerned about nutrition and counting calories can get instantaneous feedback when selecting meals at a new restaurant.

Often these games have been developed with the specific input of health professionals. For example, Whyville has content provided by the CDC and is focused on the spread of epidemics.

As a result of these enhanced capabilities, health professionals increasingly turn to technology to facilitate their work. While traditionally slow to adopt new technologies, the adoption of e-health and, more recently, m-health is changing the world of health communicators. However, in spite of often rosy predictions, the impact of information-processing technologies has been a matter of some controversy, as has its relationship to productivity, profitability, quality, and competitive advantage. There is a consensus that eventually, often after a considerable lag time, new information technologies have payoffs, often by providing new ways of organizing represented by many of these properties and increasing the importance of the wisdom of crowds and third parties.[18]

Patients and Providers

There continues to be a shift from traditional models of medicine to ones where patients have a greater role in their own decisions, from treatment options, to involvement in clinical research, to actually initiating and driving research. The Internet has heralded many changes in our world, particularly in emerging social networks. There also has been a substantial evolution in the relationships between patient and providers, in part in response to these trends and the growing complexity of our health-care system. The simple dyadic model with the physician and client operating independently from the health-care system is increasingly outmoded; it is simultaneously being supplanted by forces contributing to disintermediation and pointing to the need for more collaborative relationships with other professionals.

The Simple Dyadic Relationship

For many people, face-to-face interpersonal interactions are still the gold standard for provision of health information with many of the properties of technology we discussed earlier used to reveal the extent to which they measure up to them. One truism of information seeking research is that people prefer to receive information from interpersonal sources.[19-21]

There are six core functions in the patient-clinician communication relationship: fostering healing relationships, exchanging information, responding to emotions, managing uncertainty, making decisions, and enabling patient self-management. This is a lot to accomplish in the typical seven-minute interaction a doctor has with a patient. Historically these relationships have been viewed from a deficit model with a focus on insufficient information as a result of lack of its provision by clinicians. More recent approaches have focused on a process model where a clinician monitors the amount of information being provided to patients and helps them interpret it so that they do not become overloaded and can truly participate in decision making.[22]

In the absence of considerable progress on the physician side, more and more attention, especially given our recent focus on patients as consumers, has been devoted to issues of patient self-advocacy and the active role that they can play in health-care decision making.[23-24] Patients who are more assertive in their information seeking are more likely to receive answers that allow them to make informed health-care decisions.[25] However, even the most dedicated patient can quickly become overloaded with the amount of information available through the Internet and other sources.[26]

Many problems exist in traditional physician-patient interactions. The difficulty of the task facing physicians, who are often operating under severe time constraints, of finding a definitive diagnosis with often scant information, should not be underestimated. Physicians are also under increasing financial and institutional pressure to shorten, not expand, the time they spend with any one patient. Sadly, it also may be the case that it is unrealistic to expect both high levels of medical competence and warm, empathic communication skills from a large proportion of physicians.[27]

Patients often do not receive the information they desire during consultation; lack of communication between doctor and patient has been found to contribute to decreased ability to recall information given by the caregiver, patient dissatisfaction, decreased adherence to prescribed regimens and other forms of noncompliance.[28-29] Physicians spend less than 10 percent of their time explaining things to their patients and health-care providers overestimate the quantity, completeness, and effectiveness of their explanations.[30] Though patients often have unresolved questions, they appear to be reluctant to ask doctors about them,[31] in part because of the status differences between them[32] and some are concerned with impression management.[33] So, patients engage in surprisingly little information seeking with physicians, particularly question asking.[34-35] Patients only directly voice their concerns one-quarter of the time.[36] Physicians then interpret this lack of question asking as a sign of apathy, which indicates to them that the patient does not want more information.[37]

The traditional physician role is viewed as having the central place in a patient's treatment, often adopting a more patriarchal approach to patient-client interactions assuming the role of decision maker and the person who absorbs uncertainty. In terms of human information behavior, including searching, seeking, and exchange of information with the patient, they often have a minimalist approach, resting their judgments on their long experience and training in the medical profession.

Patients are not expected to perform their own information seeking in this traditional approach. Health care reform will place increased importance on the stated satisfaction of clients, but traditionally physicians have, in spite of considerable evidence to the contrary, assumed that satisfaction is determined by their professional medical advice. As we have seen, this traditional approach resulted in very low compliance rates and, as a result, poorer medical outcomes. In sum, there are many problems with the classic physician-patient model, leading people to seek information elsewhere.

Disintermediation

Professionals' exclusive control over information resources is steadily declining, raising concerns about self-administration of medical information. The emergence of the Internet as an omnibus source of information has apparently changed the nature of opinion leadership; both more authoritative (e.g., medical journals and literature) and more interpersonal (e.g., support or advocacy groups) sources are readily available and accessible online. This is part of a broader trend that is referred to as "disintermediation," or the capability of the Internet to allow the general public to bypass experts in their quest for information, products, and services.[38] Heavy users of the Internet are more likely to disintermediate, bypass, or downplay physician's authority and gatekeeping status by going directly to a source.[39] Health professionals, in effect, have lost control of the message and they can't set the agenda of what the public will attend to as seen in the recent controversies surrounding vaccination and autism.

The past several decades have seen a shifting of normative expectations, with individuals adopting proactive approaches to health, going so far that individuals see their bodies as a project. So we have information-rich consumers who rely on multiple sources of expertise, and a diminishing role for health professionals. Information seeking becomes a key tool in overcoming the traditional passivity of the sick role in favor of action: reducing guilt and imparting to individuals the sense that they are still serving society. They have the responsibility to seek out information to restore the self to the status of functional efficacy.[40] However, knowledge is intimately related with credentialing and training and the formal (and often legally, state enforced) differentiation of specialties in societies generally and organizations specifically.[41] The natural reluctance to share professional knowledge is further exacerbated by the more general reluctance to share knowledge with others if they are thought incapable of understanding it; a key problem in the highly health illiterate U.S. population.[42] However, never has secret, professional knowledge been more accessible to those who are interested in it.

Policy Implications

We have given a lot of thought to the role of information systems and professionals, but we have given much less attention to the role of patients/clients and how they actually process and seek information and ultimately how successful they are in negotiating our increasingly Byzantine health-care system. Collaboration among patients means enhanced knowledge sharing, and the citizen researcher can leverage collaborative research via the wisdom of crowds to quickly correct erroneous information[43] and to supplement the wisdom of experts with that of laypersons.[44] Participation online is often asymmetrical, with up to 41 percent having consulted peers online, but less than 6 percent actively contributing.[45]

Growing Digital Divide

The concepts of an "information gap" and the "information poor" have been advanced as important policy issues, generally in terms of their broad societal ramifications.[46-49] This is coupled with a growing interest in our federal agencies in health disparities. In general, it has been argued that there is a growing difference in access to information between different segments of our society and that increasingly this gap also reflects other demographic classifications, such as socioeconomic status.

Creating rich information fields through such practices as "self-serving" to information from databases, for example, should make for more informed consumers, who are likely to consume less time of health professionals "being brought up to speed" on the basics of their disease and its treatment, since they can self-administer. Developing a wide range of delivery systems one can choose from and facilitating access has become a popular strategy for encouraging people to regulate their own doses of information.

The risk here, however, is that individuals can quickly become overloaded or confused in an undirected environment. In essence, while the goal may be to reduce uncertainty or help bridge a knowledge gap, the actual effect can be increased uncertainty and, ultimately, decreased sense of efficacy for future searches. A focus on promoting health information literacy, then, would mean helping people gain the skills to access, judge the credibility of, and effectively utilize a wide range of health information. Increasing health literacy by encouraging autonomous information seekers also should be a goal of our health-care system.

Do patients have the health literacy to survive? The consumer movement in health assumes individuals are increasingly sophisticated and can understand issues ranging from the fundamentals of genomics to psychosocial adjustment to resulting family dynamics. Individuals have free access to a world of health information. This very capability to navigate an increasingly complex health-care system becomes an important element of health literacy. The public's lack of health knowledge about causes, prevention, detection, and treatment is also a significant problem, since limited health literacy is associated with higher rates of hospitalizations, poorer health, and higher mortality.[50–51]

Even more disturbing than the information gap is the understanding gap that is developing between individuals who have access to a rich array of diverse information sources and the resources necessary to synthesize information.[52] "[B]ad ideas spread more rapidly among the ignorant than among the informed, and good ideas spread more rapidly among the informed than the ignorant."[53] The very proliferation of new technologies, and the speed with which they operate, may result in the further marginalization of those most disadvantaged by our current health-care system.[54] Few people receive formal training in information seeking and one of the things that distinguishes experts and novices is that the former persist in searching whereas the latter all too readily give up when confronted with obstacles.[55] In a variant of the classic phrase only the strong survive, only the most knowledgeable can fully utilize our current health-care system.

Motivations

The efficacy of information systems relating to health is often dependent on the motivations, incentives, and capabilities of users.[56] People often want to minimize the intrusiveness and impact of the health-care options they choose; they often want to maintain hope in the presence of despair, and they often spurn effective treatments (e.g., minimizing calorie intake while increasing exercise for controlling weight). All of these factors are associated with the relatively low levels of information seeking and the lack of persistence in information seeking often demonstrated in empirical studies. While all humans have some appetite for food, there is still individual variation in what kinds of nourishment they seek, and as we have seen, the information seeking literature suggests that not all individuals have a drive to forage for information, in spite of characterizations of the human species as informavores.[57]

On the other hand, there are the outliers, who dominate our imagination, who doggedly pursue answers to the questions that interest them. They have been labeled hyperinformation seekers and cyberchondriacs and they expand the boundaries of information available to the public at large. The most recent manifestation of this group comes in the area of m-health and the growing possibilities through apps and sensors to have a quantified self. These quants, for short, religiously track biometrics indicators ranging from blood pressure to blood sugar levels to the number of miles they run.[58] Their results often contribute to citizen science movements that try to accumulate, then analyze, biomedical data of various sorts.

The resulting data then enhance the possibilities for collective political action, which has never been greater, but one must be careful about the intentions of those who offer help. There is an underlying commercial motivation for many websites that have an increasing emphasis on the monetization of their various services. Agencies want to decrease overall costs and encourage and facilitate the dissemination of information, in part to increase the demand for more effective services among patients. Advocacy groups often act on behalf of larger political agendas that may be hidden from their clients.[59] Too often we focus on the rational and normative when the dark side of health information seeking is what really needs to be addressed.

Collaborative Opportunities for Informaticians

Our contemporary world in some ways represents a perfect storm for health informaticians. The convergence of technologies, the flood of information, and institutional changes in the health professions represent tremendous opportunities for informaticians who desire to more proactively shape the system. Figure 1.1 specifies the many possible relationships between information professionals, clinical practice, and the general public who may be patients or clients. Conditions b, d, and f represent in most cases our current state of affairs where these three parties are not collaborating with each other in their information searches, but rather are engaged in parallel activities. So, a patient searches the Internet with guidance from neither health professionals nor informaticians. The other states represent potentially collaborative relationships so path c represents the relationship between the public and health professionals. It is common for professionals to treat these relationships as one-way, top-down, but increasingly the citizen scientists' movement and websites such as Patients Like Me suggest both parties have something to offer the other.

The real issue is not the availability of information; in some ways this is the problem. The real issue is its uneven distribution. The single purpose of many health communication and drug marketing campaigns is to stimulate us to seek more information. So, every day we are asked to consult our doctor about the efficacy of a particular drug or to find out more about a particular disease that may affect our health or the health of our loved ones (path c). In the presence of all of this information we must confront the fact that our societal level of health literacy remains stubbornly low, and in the face of ever-increasing advances in knowledge, actually may be decreasing from the absolute levels needed to function in our increasingly complex world. Consultation with informaticians might be very helpful to designers of communication campaigns and health marketers who want to increase the information activity of the general public (path e).

Often exposure to information is only a tease, only whetting our appetites leading us to desire more. So, exposure to information on the Internet often leads us to want more contact with health professionals.[60] This desire for information can

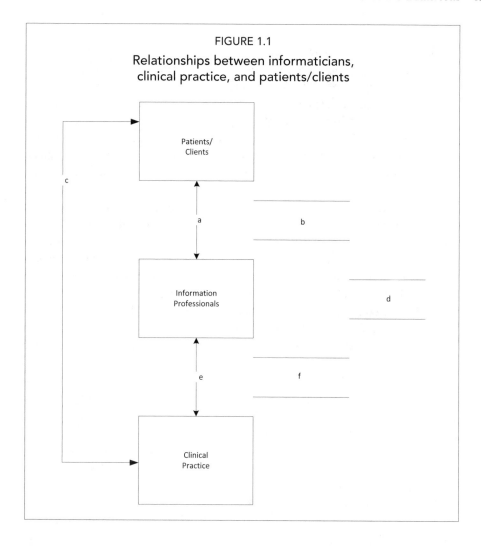

FIGURE 1.1

Relationships between informaticians,
clinical practice, and patients/clients

increasingly be met by turning to more engaging technology and/or health information science professionals (path a). As these examples illustrate, tremendous opportunities exist for collaboration with others in enhancing the efficiency of the public's searches, ensuring that they effectively uncover the most nutritious patches. In spite of often-voiced concerns of health professionals, a surprisingly small percentage of Internet users report harm, although surprisingly large percentages report no help (up to 50 percent),[61] highlighting their need for professional guidance in their searches (path a).

Gatekeeping in its various forms is seen as a key differentiating feature of the Internet: collective gatekeeping (e.g., bulletin boards, wiki), individual gatekeeping (e.g., blog, social networking sites), and unknown gatekeeping (e.g., Internet).[62] The possibilities for gatekeeping proliferate every day. Although it is well known that individuals often consult a variety of others before presenting themselves in clinical settings,[63] outside of HMO and organizational contexts, there have been few systematic attempts to shape the nature of these prior consultations. If these prior information searches happen in a relatively uncontrolled, random, parallel manner (conditions b, d, and f in figure 1.1), expectations (e.g., treatment options, diagnosis, drug regimens) may be established that will be unfulfilled in the clinical encounter.

There are a number of ways that these third parties, particularly knowledge brokers, can complement clinical practice. First, individuals who want to be fully prepared before they visit the doctor often consult the Internet.[64] In fact, Lowrey and Anderson suggest that prior information use may impact respondents' perception of physicians.[65] Second, there appears to be an interesting split among Internet users, with as many as 60 percent of users reporting that while they look for information, they only rely on it if their doctors tell them to.[66] While the Internet makes a wealth of information available for particular purposes, it is often difficult for the novitiate to weigh the credibility of the information, a critical service that a knowledge broker, such as a clinical professional or consumer health librarian, can provide. This suggests that a precursor to a better patient-doctor dialogue would be to increase the public's knowledge base and to provide alternative but complementary information sources, by shaping clients' information fields. Flay and his colleagues have found that to induce behavioral change regarding health promotion, a message must be repeated over a long period via multiple sources.[67–68]

By shaping and influencing the external sources a patient will consult both before and after visits (path c) clinical practices can at the same time reduce their own burden for explaining (or defending) their approach and increase the likelihood of patient compliance. Thus working within an interprofessional team, with reciprocal relationships in the collaborative paths in figure 1.1, with complementary information systems, would seem to offer some real benefits in this emerging information environment.

While there has been much concern over patient/client use of the Internet in their search for information given the often problematic quality of the information they find, until recently there have not been proactive efforts to guide their searches. There would seem to be a substantial advantage for health information services to operate in concert with physicians in this endeavor.[69] They could in effect arrange their services to provide more detailed information for those who would like it and to ensure that the information services that patients use are of high quality.

These concerns have been most recently expressed in systematic attempts to provide information prescriptions to patients as a regular part of their care, an attempt, in effect, to get paths a, c, and e all operating jointly. Just as patients get prescriptions for drugs, they would get written prescriptions for websites to consult related to their medical problems. This concept has been embraced by the National Library of Medicine in their MedlinePlus website. They have partnered with the American College of Physicians Foundation to assist physicians in this endeavor, developing an Information Rx Toolkit to assist clinicians in developing appropriate materials.

Research trials of this ACE idea have found that it increases use of authoritative sites such as MedlinePlus and that patients were more likely to find this information valuable if their physician prescribed it. The physicians involved in these trials found that there was greater patient compliance, reduced office time spent on education, and that they helped to explain difficult concepts.[70]

Physician's Unique Role

The most important gatekeeper in our traditional health-care system has been the physician. Increasingly the physician's most important role rests on his or her judgment and guidance on how a client should navigate an increasingly complicated health-care system where "the tacit boundary previous researchers have drawn around the patient-provider relationships seems outdated."[71] Physicians can provide critical guidance as to what specialist to turn to, and based on their prior experience, they can also offer critical advice on what the insurance company will cover and what institution will provide the best care.

The role of physicians in the emerging world of personalized medicine, and ready access to a variety of information sources, is constantly changing. Their role in imparting increasingly complex information is an important policy issue, especially since their time with patients is increasingly limited.[72] Their informatics skills, especially concerning the most trustworthy and accessible source, can provide critical guidance to patients. However, it is an unlikely role for physicians to adopt in part because their lack of training in the skills involved. But, as Slack long ago observed, any doctor who can be replaced by a computer deserves to be.[73] Ultimately, they could become more of an interpreter, an evaluator of information that a patient has acquired, serving as the ultimate arbiter of what actions patients should take as a result of their information seeking,[74] in this way fully realizing the collaborative roles specified in figure 1.1.

One thing that distinguishes our contemporary information age is a movement away from a focus on individual action to collaboration.[75] It would be nice if this information was from a trusted medical provider working in the context of an inter-professional team responsible for patient care, but the medical system often gives little thought, and more to the point perhaps, has little control over where people will go. Interest in collaborative information seeking where both parties seek information has grown, in part because the parties often have different perspectives and skills in pursuit of common information seeking goals.[76] Partly because of the decreasing time spent per patient in HMOs, physicians pursue only about 30 percent of the questions that arise during their practice.[77]

Because of the doctor's role as the key decision maker in hospitals, the benefits of advances in information technology have been slower to come in the health arena than in more commercial sectors of our society, lagging from seven to ten years behind other industries.[78] Physicians find information technology threatening on several levels: it removes their exclusive control over information; it increases the possibility that their behavior will be monitored (e.g., through assessment of medical records of their patients); and many physicians are loath to admit ignorance in any area, a key problem when they need to learn new technologies.[79] So, it is not only the patient who needs help in seeking information.

Countervailing pressures to drive down costs from insurers and government agencies are overcoming the traditional resistance of health professionals to information technologies.[80–81] The National Institutes of Health (NIH), for example, see significant synergies between health information technology and health communication, touting information technology's capacity to improve provider-patient interactions, improve self-maintenance of chronic diseases, enhance health promotion, enable more productive interactions among differing health professionals, and facilitate efficient information seeking.[82] These trends are only going to increase in the era of e-health and m-health and the exciting possibilities offered by remote sensing. These developments are going to be increasingly important in the management of chronic diseases and co-morbidities as baby-boomers continue their relentless march.

The effective use of information rests in part on the extent to which they truly are collaborative relationships. While physicians and informaticians interpret information for clients, clients are often immersed in more uncertainty than in the other roles that tend to absorb uncertainty for them. Understanding human information behavior becomes more critical to health outcomes and, ultimately, patient satisfaction depends on the collaborative informatics skills revealed in the relationships. When patients are actively involved in their own information seeking and they have a commensurate level of self-efficacy, they are more likely to comply with any information they uncover with the outcomes of information searches in effect becoming teachable moments.[83]

Conclusion

In answer to the question posed in the title of this chapter, health information seeking has changed, for the most part for the better, but there are still significant problems and issues. It is at times dangerous to rely on our perceptions of what should be done. Information seeking research suggests that rational, persistent approaches to channel selection are seldom used by individuals when they actually seek health information.[84] Are physicians keeping up with their changing roles? Are institutions meeting the challenge? Is everyone being overwhelmed? Health information seeking is a moving target; there is also a possibility for retrogression—people's level of ignorance has not really changed in spite of technological growth and increased access.[85] With the amount one needs to know increasing with every passing day, the gap between what individuals need to know and what they do know in relative terms actually may be growing.

As we have seen, the federal government has made considerable investments in health information technology, providing the national information structure that has supported the work of health information professionals. Like our basic physical infrastructure, there is a very real possibility that these investments will not continue. With fiscal cliffs and ever-expanding budget deficits there is even a very real possibility of considerable disinvestments in our health information infrastructure. A large part of the government's initial investment rested on the assumption that it would result in considerable cost savings in the delivery of health care. This has been realized for the outliers, cyberchondriacs who have been substantial users, and who might serve as very useful lobbyists for maintaining and enhancing our existing infrastructure if they are cultivated as true collaborators. However, little evidence supports that this infrastructure has improved the health literacy of the public at large. Health care reform and various changes in health funding, if we are not vigilant, may actually return us to a top-down system in which at least choices of treatment options are heavily constrained.

References

1. Jansen, B. J., and S. Y. Rieh. "The Seventeen Theoretical Constructs of Information Searching and Information Retrieval." *Journal of the American Society for Information Science and Technology* 61, no. 8 (2010): 1517–34. doi:10.1002/asi .21358.
2. Choi, B. C. "Understanding the Basic Principles of Knowledge Translation." *Journal of Epidemiology and Community Health* 59, no. 2 (2005).
3. Johnson, J. David, and Donald Owen Case. *Health Information Seeking*. New York: Peter Lang, 2012.

4. Borgman, Christine L. *From Gutenberg to the Global Information Infrastructure: Access to Information in the Networked World*. Cambridge, MA: MIT Press, 2000.
5. Ibid.
6. Johnson, Bonnie McDaniel, and Ronald E. Rice. *Managing Organizational Innovation: The Evolution from Word Processing to Office Information Systems*. New York: Columbia University Press, 1987.
7. Rogers, Everett M., and D. Lawrence Kincaid. *Communication Networks: Toward a New Paradigm for Research*. New York: Free Press, 1981.
8. Christensen, Clayton M. *The Innovator's Dilemma: When New Technologies Cause Great Firms to Fail*. Boston: Harvard Business School Press, 1997.
9. Pirolli, P., and S. Card. "Information Foraging." *Psychological Review NY* 106, no. 4 (1999): 643–75.
10. Jacoby, J. "Optimal Foraging." In *Theories of Information Behavior*, edited by Karen E. Fisher, Sanda Erdelez, and Lynne McKechnie, 259–64. Medford, NJ: Published for the American Society for Information Science and Technology by Information Today, 2005.
11. Walther, J. B., S. Pingree, R. P. Hawkins, and D. B. Buller. "Attributes of Interactive Online Health Information Systems." *Journal of Medical Internet Research* 7, no. 3 (2005).
12. Borgman, *Global Information Infrastructure*.
13. Ibid.
14. Smith Pfister, Damien, and Jordan Soliz. "(Re)Conceptualizing Intercultural Communication in a Networked Society." *Journal of International and Intercultural Communication* 4, no. 4 (2011): 246–51. doi:10.1080/17513057.2011.598043.
15. Lieberman, D. A. "Digital Games for Health Behavior Change: Research, Design, and Future Directions." In *eHealth Applications: Promising Strategies for Health Behavior Change*, edited by Seth M. Noar, Nancy Grant Harrington, and Kentucky Conference on Health Communication, 164–93. New York: Routledge, 2012.
16. Dockterman, E. "Playing for Keeps: Smart-Phone Games Could Make Health Care More Fun—and Effective." *TIME*, November 12, 2011.
17. Riley, W. T., D. E. Rivera, A. A. Atienza, W. Nilsen, S. M. Allison, and R. Mermelstein. "Health Behavior Models in the Age of Mobile Interventions: Are Our Theories Up to the Task?" *Translational Behavioral Medicine* 1, no. 1 (2011): 53–71.
18. Johnson, J. D. "Profiling the Likelihood of Success of Electronic Medical Records." In *The Culture of Efficiency: Technology in Everyday Life*, edited by Sharon Kleinman, 121–41. New York: Peter Lang, 2009.
19. Case, Donald Owen. *Looking for Information: A Survey of Research on Information Seeking, Needs and Behavior*. Bingley, UK: Emerald Group, 2012.
20. Johnson, J. David. *Cancer-Related Information Seeking*. Cresskill, NJ: Hampton Press, 1997.
21. Johnson and Case, *Health Information Seeking*.
22. Epstein, Ronald, and R. L. Street Jr. "Patient-Centered Communication in Cancer Care Promoting Healing and Reducing Suffering." NIH Publication No. 07-6225.

Bethesda, MD: National Cancer Institute, U.S. Department of Health and Human Services, National Institutes of Health, 2007.

23. Ibid.

24. Wright, Kevin B., Larry Frey, and Pradeep Sopory. "Willingness to Communicate about Health as an Underlying Trait of Patient Self-Advocacy: The Development of the Willingness to Communicate About Health (WTCH) Measure." *Communication Studies* 58, no. 1 (2007): 35–51.

25. Real, K., and R. L. Street Jr. "Doctor-Patient Communication from an Organizational Perspective." In *Communicating to Manage Health and Illness*, edited by Dale E. Brashers and Daena J. Goldsmith, 65–90. New York: Routledge/Taylor and Francis Group, 2009.

26. Epstein and Street, "Patient-Centered Communication."

27. Phillips, Gerald M., and J. Alfred Jones. "Medical Compliance: Patient or Physician Responsibility?" *The American Behavioral Scientist* 34, no. 6 (1991): 756–67.

28. Epstein and Street, "Patient-Centered Communication."

29. Lane, S. D. "Compliance, Satisfaction, and Physician-Patient Communication." In *Communication Yearbook 7*, edited by Robert N. Bostrom, Bruce H. Westley, and International Communication Association, 772–99. Beverly Hills, CA: Sage, 1983.

30. Thompson, T. L., B. B. Whaley, and A. M. Stone. "Explaining Illness: Issues Concerning the Co-construction of Explanations." In *The Routledge Handbook of Health Communication*, edited by Teresa L. Thompson, Roxanne Parrott, and Jon F. Nussbaum, 293–305. New York: Routledge, 2011.

31. Beisecker, A. E., and T. D. Beisecker. "Patient Information-Seeking Behaviors When Communicating with Doctors." *Medical Care* 28, no. 1 (1990): 19–28.

32. Mathews, J. J. "The Communication Process in Clinical Settings." *Social Science and Medicine (1982)* 17, no. 18 (1983): 1371–78.

33. Parrott, Roxanne. "Point of Practice: Keeping 'Health' in Health Communication Research and Practice." *Journal of Applied Communication Research* 39, no. 1 (2011): 92–102. doi:10.1080/00909882.2010.536848.

34. Cegala, D. J., and D. J. Broz. "Provider and Patient Communication Skills Training." In *Handbook of Health Communication*, edited by Teresa L. Thompson, 95–120. Mahwah, NJ: Lawrence Erlbaum Associates, 2003.

35. Post, Douglas M., Donald J. Cegala, and William F. Miser. "The Other Half of the Whole: Teaching Patients to Communicate with Physicians." *Family Medicine* 34, no. 5 (2002): 344–52.

36. Ibid.

37. Lichter, Ivan. *Communication in Cancer Care.* New York: Churchill Livingstone, 1987.

38. Shapiro, Andrew L. *The Control Revolution: How the Internet Is Putting Individuals in Charge and Changing the World We Know.* New York: PublicAffairs, 1999.

39. Lowrey, W., and W. B. Anderson. "The Impact of Internet Use on the Public Perception of Physicians: A Perspective from the Sociology of Professions Literature." *Health Communication* 19, no. 2 (2006): 125–31.

40. Shilling, Chris. "Culture, the 'Sick Role' and the Consumption of Health." *British Journal of Sociology* 53, no. 4 (2002): 621–38.

41. Macdonald, Keith M. *The Sociology of the Professions.* Thousand Oaks, CA: Sage, 1995.

42. Hew, K. F., and N. Hara. "Knowledge Sharing in Online Environments: A Qualitative Case Study." *Journal of the American Society for Information Science and Technology* 58, no. 14 (2007): 2310–24.

43. Sarasohn-Kahn, Jane. *The Wisdom of Patients: Health Care Meets Online Social Media.* San Francisco: California HealthCare Foundation, 2008.

44. Yifeng, Hu, and S. Shyam Sundar. "Effects of Online Health Sources on Credibility and Behavioral Intentions." *Communication Research* 37, no. 1 (2010): 105–32. doi:10.1177/0093650209351512.

45. Fox, Susannah, and Sydney Jones. *The Social Life of Health Information: Americans' Pursuit of Health Takes Place within a Widening Network of Both Online and Offline Sources.* Washington, DC: Pew Internet and American Life Project, 2009.

46. Chen, Ching-chih, and Peter Hernon. *Information Seeking: Assessing and Anticipating User Needs.* New York: Neal-Schuman, 1982.

47. Dervin, B. "Communication Gaps and Inequities: Moving toward a Reconceptualization." In *Progress in Communication Sciences*, vol. 2, edited by Brenda Dervin and Melvin J. Voigt, 74–112. Norwood, NJ: Ablex, 1980.

48. Doctor, R. D. "Social Equity and Information Technologies: Moving toward Information Democracy." In *Annual Review of Information Science and Technology*, vol. 27, edited by Martha E. Williams, 44–96. Melford, NJ: Learned Information, 1992.

49. Siefert, Marsha, George Gerbner, and Janice Fisher. *The Information Gap: How Computers and Other New Communication Technologies Affect the Social Distribution of Power.* New York: Oxford University Press, 1989.

50. Berkman, N. D., T. C. Davis, and L. McCormack. "Health Literacy: What Is It?" *Journal of Health Communication* 15 (2010): 9–19.

51. Cameron, K. S., M. S. Wolf, and D. W. Baker. "Integrating Health Literacy in Health Communication." In *The Routledge Handbook of Health Communication*, edited by Teresa L. Thompson, Roxanne Parrott, and Jon F. Nussbaum, 306–19. New York: Routledge, 2011.

52. Viswanath, K., J. R. Finnegan, P. J. Hannan, and R. V. Luepker. "Health and Knowledge Gaps: Some Lessons from the Minnesota Heart Health Program." *The American Behavioral Scientist* 34, no. 6 (1991): 712–26.

53. March, James G., and Chip Heath. *A Primer on Decision Making: How Decisions Happen.* New York: Free Press, 1994.

54. Johnson, M. O. "The Shifting Landscape of Health Care: Toward a Model of Health Care Empowerment." *American Journal of Public Health* 101, no. 2 (2011): 265–70.

55. Borgman, *Global Information Infrastructure.*

56. Walther et al., "Health Information Systems."

57. Pirolli and Card, "Information Foraging."

58. Mongalindan, J. P. "Quant Junkies." *Fortune* 49, October 8, 2012.

59. Mohammed, S. N. *The (Dis)information Age: The Persistence of Ignorance.* New York: Peter Lang, 2012.

60. Lee, Chul-Joo. "Does the Internet Displace Health Professionals?" *Journal of Health Communication* 13, no. 5 (2008): 450–64. doi:10.1080/10810730802198839.

61. Fox and Jones, *Social Life of Health Information.*

62. Sundar, S. S., R. E. Rice, H. Kim, and C. N. Sciamanna. "Online Health Information: Conceptual Challenges and Theoretical Opportunities." In *The Routledge Handbook of Health Communication*, edited by Teresa L. Thompson, Roxanne Parrott, and Jon F. Nussbaum, 181–202. New York: Routledge, 2011.

63. Ibid.

64. Fox, S., and L. Raine. "How Internet Users Decide What Information to Trust When They or Their Loved Ones Are Sick." Last modified May 22, 2002. http://www.pewin ternet.org/Reports/2002/Vital-Decisions-A-Pew-Internet-Health-Report/Summary -of-Findings.aspx.

65. Lowrey and Anderson, "Impact of Web Use."

66. Taylor, H., and R. Leitman. "Four-Nation Survey Shows Widespread but Different Levels of Internet Use for Health Purposes." *Health Care News.* Accessed July 22, 2013. http://www.harrisinteractive.com/newsletters_healthcare.asp.

67. Flay, B. R. "Mass Media and Smoking Cessation: A Critical Review." *American Journal of Public Health* 77, no. 2 (1987): 153–60.

68. Flay, B. R., D. DiTecco, and R. P. Schlegel. "Mass Media in Health Promotion: An Analysis Using an Extended Information-Processing Model." *Health Education Quarterly* 7, no. 2 (1980): 127–47.

69. Johnson, J. David. *Innovation and Knowledge Management: The Cancer Information Service Research Consortium.* Cheltenham, UK: Edward Elgar, 2005.

70. Coberly, E., S. A. Boren, J. W. Davis, A. L. McConnell, R. Chitima-Matsiga, B. Ge, R. A. Logan, R. H. Hodge, and W. C. Steinmann. "Linking Clinic Patients to Internet-Based, Condition-Specific Information Prescriptions." *Journal of the Medical Library Association* 98, no. 2 (2010): 160–64.

71. Lammers, J. C., and J. B. Barbour. "Exploring the Institutional Context of Physicians' Work: Professional and Organizational Differences in Physician Satisfaction." In *Managing Health and Illness: Communication, Relationships, and Identity*, edited by Dale Brashers and Daena Goldsmith, 91–112. Hoboken, NJ: Taylor and Francis, 2009.

72. Niederdeppe, J., D. L. Frosch, and R. C. Hornik. "Cancer News Coverage and Information Seeking." *Journal of Health Communication* 13, no. 2 (2008): 181–99. doi: 10.1080/108107307018554110.

73. Slack, Warner V. *Cybermedicine: How Computing Empowers Doctors and Patients for Better Health Care.* San Francisco: Jossey-Bass, 1997.

74. Lougo, D. R., S. L. Schubert, B. A. Wright, J. LeMaster, C. D. Williams, and J. N. Clore. "Health Information Seeking, Receipt, and Use in Diabetes Self-Management." *Annals of Family Medicine* 8, no. 4 (2010): 334–40.

75. Borgman, *Global Information Infrastructure.*

76. Hertzum, Morten. "Collaborative Information Seeking: The Combined Activity of Information Seeking and Collaborative Grounding." *Information Processing and Management* 44, no. 2 (2008): 957–62.

77. Dawes, Martin, and Uchechukwu Sampson. "Knowledge Management in Clinical Practice: A Systematic Review of Information Seeking Behavior in Physicians." *International Journal of Medical Informatics* 71, no. 1 (2003): 9–15. doi:10.1016/S1386-5056(03)00023-6.

78. Johnson, "Electronic Medical Records."

79. Schuman, T. M. "Hospital Computerization and the Politics of Medical Decision Making." *Research in the Sociology of Work* 4 (1988): 261–87.

80. Johnson, "Electronic Medical Records."

81. Edward, H. Shortliffe. "Strategic Action in Health Information Technology: Why the Obvious Has Taken So Long." *Health Affairs* 24 (2005): 1222. doi:10.1377/hltaff.24.5.1222.

82. Harris, L. M., C. Bauer, M. S. Donaldson, R. C. Lefebvre, E. Dugan, and S. Araya-sirikul. "Health Communication and Health Information Technology: Priority Issues, Policy Implications, and Research Opportunities for Healthy People 2020." In *The Routledge Handbook of Health Communication*, edited by Teresa L. Thompson, Roxanne Parrott, and Jon F. Nussbaum, 482–97. New York: Routledge, 2011.

83. Johnson and Case, *Health Information Seeking*.

84. Ibid.

85. Mohammed, *(Dis)information Age*.

PART II

The Reference Collection

CHAPTER 2

Organization and Management of the Reference Collection

ANNELIESE TAYLOR and JEAN BLACKWELL

The previous edition of *Introduction to Reference Sources in the Health Sciences* focused on the impact of e-resources on reference services and, by extension, reference collections. It noted that the rapid proliferation of electronic information resources had transformed how librarians do reference and observed that the ability to search full text turns every collection of electronic information resources into a potential reference collection. This chapter examines librarians' changing roles in health sciences libraries today and how these affect library services and the content and management of reference collections. It looks at issues related to the duplication of print and electronic formats and the presentation and management of online collections to enhance discovery and usability.

Given the emphasis on instant access to online resources, librarians continue to seek a solution for how best to balance collection development between print and online. Concerted efforts by some libraries to completely replace their print reference resources with online counterparts have revealed that print is the only option in many cases.[1] Users still express a preference for print for some types of resources and usage, as well as a willingness to use whichever format the library makes available.[2]

What Is Reference?

Reference as a place with a sign saying "Reference" is a nineteenth-century develop-ment, and the term "reference work" first appeared in the index to *Library Journal* in 1891.[3] Traditionally, libraries have had a reference desk staffed by reference librarians who made themselves available for giving directions, answering ques-tions, and assisting with literature searches and other information-finding needs of library users. Their work was supported by the reference collection, a conveniently located collection of the tools used most often to answer questions. Reference sources were typically consulted for specific and immediate information and usually included these categories of materials: dictionaries, manuals and guides, almanacs and statistical compilations, subject handbooks and data books, drug lists, directo-ries of organizations, biographical directories, geographic atlases, encyclopedias, library information, serials information, book catalogs, and lists of meetings and translations. These materials were not allowed to circulate, the idea being that the library should acquire, organize, and provide access to these resources just in case they were needed. In a time of rapid transition in library physical space, services, and information resources, however, the value of a traditional reference collection is increasingly under debate.

Collection Development Policy

Decisions about what materials to include in the reference collection should be guided by a reference collection development policy that is usually a part of the overall collection development policy (CDP) of the library. Some libraries may have a separate CDP just for the reference collection in order to provide supplemental cri-teria unique to reference. Liestman recommends this approach, noting that because reference needs change so rapidly, it helps to have a statement that can be frequently updated to reflect those changes.[4] A CDP defines the scope of a collection and pro-vides guidelines for the weeding and retention of materials. It can be used to jus-tify budget requests and to evaluate needs based on new curriculum and research demands and on new technology. It can also serve as a guide in defining areas of cooperative collection building with other libraries.

The parts of a collection development policy:

1. Purpose of the collection development policy
2. Responsibility for the collection development policy
3. Purpose of the reference collection
4. Target audience(s)
5. Budgeting and funding

6. Selection criteria
7. Selection aids and methods
8. Preferred format(s)
9. Duplicates
10. Preferred language(s)
11. Circulation
12. Treatment of specific resource groups
13. Resource sharing
14. Collection maintenance
15. Weeding and reviewing the collection
16. Policy revision[5]

Ideally, a collection development policy serves as a blueprint for adding and for getting rid of materials to ensure that a collection is current and responsive to the needs of library users. It can also be critical for informing new staff and maintaining institutional continuity. In reality, however, collection development policies are sometimes ignored because they do not take into account new publishing trends, a shifting information environment, the changing needs of users, and budget and space constraints.

When librarians at the University of Maryland Health Sciences and Human Services Library realized that their CDP, developed in 1999, was too dated to provide useful guidance for current challenges, they formed a task group to review the CDP and decide whether to revise it to reflect realities or to get rid of it altogether. After careful deliberation, they decided to revise the CDP to make it more flexible by avoiding specific collection procedures and encouraging the use of best practices. The result was a streamlined policy with useful guidelines for adapting the collection in a rapidly changing environment.[6] In contrast, when librarians at the University of Kentucky Ekstrom Library set out to revamp an unwieldy reference collection, it became clear that the existing reference CDP stood in the way of rethinking the collection. As a result, they abandoned it and wrote a new one that focused on meeting the needs of users, emphasized the importance of timeliness, and stressed a preference for electronic formats.[7]

A collection development policy should include guidelines for weeding and retention of materials. Weeding is the process of removing materials from the active collection. The disposition of outdated materials will depend to some extent on the type of library: a hospital library may choose to keep only the most recent edition of a work, while an academic health sciences library may need to retain earlier editions for historical and research purposes. When weeding reference collections, librarians can choose to move books to the circulating collection, replace them in electronic format, or get rid of them altogether.

A thorough weeding project requires significant time to plan and implement. In "Weeding the Reference Collection: A Case Study of Collection Management," Francis describes a reference collection weeding project, including the development of a reference collection development policy, a review of standing orders, the goals and outcomes of the review, and a discussion of the benefits of the project. At the conclusion of the project, librarians set up a schedule to review the collection every other year.[8]

Questions to consider before weeding:

1. Is it being used?
2. Is it available in another format?
3. Is it still current?
4. Is it valuable or rare or both?
5. What condition is it in?
6. Would it be more useful in the circulating collection?
7. Is it cited in standard abstracting or indexing tools?
8. Is it still on a standard list of recommended sources?
9. Does it have local relevance?
10. Does it fill a consortial agreement or regional need?
11. If available in electronic format, is continued access guaranteed?

It can be difficult to keep usage statistics on a print reference collection, but answering the question, "Is it being used?" is not usually a problem with electronic resources. Since e-books do not require shelf space and do not get worn out, the necessity of weeding is often overlooked. In "Weeding in a Digital Age," Moroni recommends that e-books be treated the same as physical collections, with guidelines based on use, accuracy of information, and relevance to library patrons.[9]

It has always been important for libraries to avoid bloated, outdated reference collections, but given users' preference for electronic access, the need has become even more pressing. In light of the trend toward re-purposing library space to accommodate shifting institutional priorities, libraries can no longer afford to dedicate valuable real estate and diminishing funds to a reference book collection that gathers dust due to lack of use. The experiences reported by Detmering and Douglas point out the benefits of reflecting on users' information needs and how best to meet them, as well as aligning the library's priorities with those of the institutions they serve.[10-11]

Selection Tools

A variety of selection tools assist librarians in making decisions about what to add to their collections. For almost forty years, health sciences and hospital librarians

depended heavily on the Brandon/Hill Selected Lists (http://library.mssm.edu/brandon
-hill/index.shtml) for guidance in choosing books and journals, with the "minimal
core" titles serving as a particularly helpful list from which to make reference selections. That all changed when Dorothy Hill retired in 2004, and the lists that she
and the late Alfred Brandon had created and offered as a free service were no longer being published. Doody Enterprises soon filled the vacuum with *Doody's Core
Titles in the Health Sciences* (*DCT*), produced annually and available for purchase.
DCT lists are also made available as a service to subscribers of online book vendors
such as YBP. *DCT* uses the expert opinion of health-care professionals and medical
librarians to identify books and software that constitute the core body of literature
for a health sciences library.[12]

Other selection aids available to health sciences librarians include reviews in
library journals, reviews in medical and allied health journals, publisher and vendor
notifications, approval plans, standing orders, and holdings lists of other libraries.
Librarians rely most heavily on publisher/vendor notifications and review sources
to identify new collection materials.[13] Doody's Review Service is the most comprehensive source of expert reviews in health sciences disciplines, written by experts in
more than 140 specialties and covering more than 130,000 books.[14] Reviews in journals such as *Medical Reference Services Quarterly*, *Journal of the Medical Library
Association*, and *JAMA,* as well as from online booksellers such as Amazon (http://
amazon.com), help round out the selection process. Many book vendors now integrate reviews from sources such as "Doody's Review Service," *Booklist*, and *New
York Times Book Review* so that selectors may easily find them at the point of purchase, alongside book descriptions.

The Collection Development Section of the Medical Library Association (http://
colldev.mlanet.org/index.html) provides a forum for communication and cooperation among health sciences librarians responsible for selection of library materials. MLA-CDS publishes an online newsletter and has an active e-mail discussion
list. Its open access webpage has a "Resources for Librarians" section which points
to vendors, subject-based resources, review sources, a methodology for comparing
approval plans, and other useful information.

Evaluation Criteria for New Material

Criteria for evaluating new materials include the following, which can also be used
for maintaining and weeding the reference collection:

1. Relevance and usefulness of the resource to the library's clientele
2. Intended audience: readership level, language

3. Scope and focus of the content
4. Amount of overlap with existing reference resources, and what gap the new material fills
5. Demand for resource by clientele
6. Authority and reputation of the author, publisher, or database producer
7. Favorable reviews in the professional literature
8. Inclusion of the resource in reference guides
9. Currency of the content and frequency of updates (if applicable)
10. Price, in particular related to:
    - Whether the information contained is available in another purchased resource, or freely available
    - Value and amount of anticipated use
    - Whether a one-time purchase or ongoing expense
11. Space required (print material)
12. Usability of the resource
13. Appropriate format (print vs. electronic)[15–16]

When looking at specific reference tools, librarians use a combination of measures for evaluation, with a definite focus on the materials' usefulness to *their* particular library's collection and clientele. Because budgets are frequently limited, librarians often look for new tools that will fill the gaps in their collection.[17]

Additional Evaluation Criteria for Online Resources

Most librarians would agree that selection criteria for e-resources are the same as for print, with regard to the authoritativeness, scope, and appropriateness of the resources for the audience. The U.S. National Library of Medicine's Collection Development Manual states, "When considering electronic resources for selection, the Library's intent is to apply the same criteria for scope, depth of coverage, and authoritativeness as for publications in other formats.[18] "Due to the nature of online resources and the enhanced functionality enabled by Web technology over print resources, evaluation of these resources presents several additional variables for consideration:

1. Search features and the ability to pull up results based on targeted field searches
2. Ability to save, download, print, and e-mail citations and content
3. Vendor's use of digital rights management (DRM) which may limit sharing and the long-term availability of downloaded content

4. Ability to export citations to bibliographic management tools such as EndNote, RefWorks, and Mendeley
5. Access method is via IP address or single sign-on (e.g., shibboleth) authentication
6. Mobile accessibility on devices such as smartphones and tablets via:
   - Mobile-optimized websites
   - Device-specific apps
7. Integration with technology standards such as OpenURL link resolvers
8. Accessibility considerations for sight-impaired users
9. Availability of usage statistics following the current COUNTER standard
10. Availability of vendor-supplied MARC records for resources with full-text titles
11. Terms of license agreement are acceptable and terms of use meet institutional needs
12. Availability of resources through a library consortium, for improved pricing and terms
13. Availability of archival access to full-text content for subscribers

Not all of these criteria will apply to every online resource considered for purchase. A librarian might decide that for an online statistical resource, for example, mobile optimization and archival access are not as important as search features; whereas for an aggregated database of online medical reference books, the mobile interface is very important but linking out is less important since the content is already full-text.

Doing a trial is a common method to help evaluate digital resources before committing to a purchase. The most common trial period is 30 days; however, trials of 60 days or longer may be arranged with some vendors. Because online resources represent recurring costs, getting feedback about the usefulness and quality of the resource after a trial can be crucial. A popular method is to target relevant and specific users for feedback. The library can also put up a brief online questionnaire to be filled out after the user logs out from the resource on trial, as well as advertising the trial on the library webpage.

Print or Electronic? Choosing the Format

Studies comparing usage measures of print versus online versions of the same resources reveal that measurable online usage typically far surpasses that of print.[19-21] The difference would seem to make a clear argument for buying online over print. However, the decision is not always so straightforward for a multitude of reasons. Despite the benefits of digital versions of reference resources compared to the print—more frequent updates, full-text search capabilities, more convenient access—there are additional aspects that need to be considered:

The cost for the online is often much higher than the print since publishers can charge prices that bear no relation to the print. For example, a popular reference such as *Harrison's Online* costs five to ten times as much as the print equivalent, *Harrison's Principles of Internal Medicine*. Publishers also bundle some titles into a collection, forcing libraries to subscribe to a more expensive product in order to have access to the premium content.

Online subscriptions typically require a yearly renewal and payment, even for content that has not been updated or has been only partially updated. This ongoing commitment eliminates the possibility for the library to extend its reference budget by purchasing a regularly updated resource only every couple of years or editions.

Online subscriptions are a form of leasing content rather than owning it. Most online reference resources are only accessible as long as the annual subscription is renewed, and the content remains with the provider rather than the subscriber.

Online content is ephemeral. When a new edition of a reference work such as *Nelson Textbook of Pediatrics* is available, the publisher removes the old edition and provides the new content online.

License agreements must be reviewed, negotiated, and signed for most online resources. These licenses can be time consuming for both the library and the vendor, and they can delay the beginning of the subscription until the wording meets both parties' licensing criteria.

Deciding between Formats

Librarians have plenty of anecdotal evidence that print reference resources are not used the way they were even as recently as five years ago. Our patrons rely heavily on online resources to answer their reference questions, and reference librarians do the same. The trends toward merged service desks combining circulation and reference assistance, and downsized reference collections, reflect the change in practice of how people get their information. However, a need still exists for selected resources in print and for others online, and librarians must consider each resource individually in order to make a format decision.

Print Selections

Factors that point a library to the print version of a reference resource include:

- Online cost is unaffordable. This scenario is the most common reason libraries do not convert a print resource to online.
- Library wants to keep all editions of the work for research and archival purposes. Some titles may be ordered in both print and online formats for this reason.
- Maintenance of a small core collection of print titles serves in the case of a power outage or network problems.
- Clientele prefers the print format. Some patrons still like to pick up a physical volume and flip through the pages, and certain types of resources such as dictionaries and statistical resources may be more convenient to have in print. Having a print companion of resources such as an anatomy book at the computer can also be helpful. Usability studies reveal that users in the medical environment prefer using print in some settings, and online or mobile in others.[22]
- No online version is available, or the access method is unacceptable (requiring a username and log-in, for example). Husted and Czechowski's examination of titles on the Doody's Essential Purchase list revealed that only 52 percent were available online.[23]

Online Selections

Factors that point the library to the online version of a reference resource include:

- Searchability is superior to that in the print format. Examples include online bibliographic indexes, encyclopedias, and voluminous clinical texts such as *Harrison's* or *Pharmacotherapy: Principles and Practice.*
- Clientele prefers online format.
- Title is available as a one-time purchase with perpetual access.
- Shelf space is limited.
- Users are dispersed amongst several hospitals and locations.

Print Reference Collections in the Electronic Environment

Though reference collections are being downsized, the majority of health sciences libraries have not done away with their print reference collections altogether. This is particularly true for libraries in small hospitals and nonprofit organizations which cannot afford many expensive online resources and still rely on print resources for reference. Surveys conducted for the past two editions of this book revealed that all respondents maintained a separate reference collection, though the trend was toward scaling back the size of print reference collections. Gone are the days when users had to come into the library to access library materials and relied on librarians to refer to a sizeable print collection to answer their reference questions. Many libraries have undertaken significant weeding projects to make their reference collections more current, relevant, and inviting.

In addition, some libraries have decided that they no longer need to maintain a separate "Ready Reference" section, and have integrated Ready Reference materials with the regular reference collection.[24-25] Factors other than space that contribute to this decision include: the elimination of a separate reference desk where librarians needed to have frequently used resources nearby, and the confusion for users (and library staff) of having reference materials in two locations.

One of the major trends in health sciences library buildings is to repurpose space formerly used for print collections. Reference collections have been particularly affected since they occupy prominent space near service desks and in highly trafficked areas. As our users' needs change, so must libraries adapt our collections, services, and space to accommodate the changes. Based on a 2009 survey of seventy-eight health sciences libraries, common trends for repurposed space include: creating a single service desk for circulation, information, and reference questions; putting cafes in libraries; adding group study rooms; and creating more collaborative work and social space.[26]

Print Reference Collection General Guidelines

The authors' own libraries have significantly reduced their print collections and have adapted their collection policies to reflect a "leaner and meaner" reference collection. The size of today's reference collection should be determined by the needs of each individual library; however, the following guidelines apply to any situation:

- Current resources encourage use and make a better impression of the collection.
- Having fewer, key resources that get used is more meaningful than a collection of indiscriminate scope and depth.
- The needs of the current library users should guide the selection of resources.
- Resources should truly be meant for reference, and not to be read cover to cover.

With respect to online resources, print resources should:

- Be supplementary or complementary to the online.
- Provide access to resources that work better in print than online.
- Provide a selection of resources to satisfy users still wedded to the print.
- Serve an archival function where the need exists.

While the number of reference transactions at health sciences libraries has dropped precipitously in the past decade, the nature of queries still demands the expertise of reference librarians. Health sciences librarians are providing more in-depth consultations, indicating that users have become more sophisticated information seekers.[27-28] Librarians strive to help users navigate the maze of information resources and to lead them to the best resources for their search. In her article tracing the evolution of reference collections, Margaret Landesman noted, "In the past, a reference simply pointed the way. Now users expect to be taken there."[29]

Discovery and Access

Subject Guides

Librarians have long struggled to make sure that the reference resources we purchase are found and used. This was true when reference collections were totally in print format and is equally true today.[30] In "Shelflessness as a Virtue," Ford observes that the traditional reference collection promotes serendipity by presenting key resources in a compact group. The organizational scheme of a print reference collection allows us to create a mental map of where to locate particular subjects. And because it is a microcosm of the larger collection, it is useful for training new library staff and educating library users on how to navigate the circulating collection. All of this is lost in an online environment.[31]

Some libraries have attempted to address this problem by creating online reference collections featuring key reference sources. The goal is not to link to every reference tool available but to provide a short list of the most important ones to meet users' needs and avoid information overload. An important advantage of these types of collections is the ability to customize to fit the needs of specific user groups. Other advantages are the capacity to include both print and electronic library holdings, to link to other relevant guides and websites, to insert a link to Ask-a-Librarian, and to feature selected resources and services. They allow librarians to make quick revisions to the collection and to solicit feedback from users. It is possible to gather usage statistics on individual sections of the collection and often on specific resources. Virtual collections can have clear branding: a library logo, photos of librarians, and other information about the library. The most important advantage is that they allow users to access the resources at any time from any location.

Disadvantages include difficulties with how best to organize and present the resources, maintaining the lists of links so they stay current, and what to call the collection. It is unclear whether "reference" holds any meaning for contemporary users, and there is no best practice for naming e-reference collections. Examples of names include Online Reference, Reference Shelf, Find, Quick Facts, Quick Reference, Virtual Reference, and Digital Reference. Another disadvantage is that findability is diminished if the e-collection is too many clicks away from the library's homepage. Moreover, browsability is limited because users need to know what they are looking for and must search individual categories of resources included in the guide.[32]

The advent of Web 2.0 technology has solved some of the problems inherent to locally produced subject guides; Web 2.0 tools make it easier for nonprogrammers to create and maintain dynamic and interactive subject guides with features like embedded video, RSS feeds, polls, and social networking features. In "From Pathfinders to Subject Guides: One Library's Experience with LibGuides," Glassman and Sorensen review tools such as wikis, blogs, and content management systems and describe their library's decision to go with LibGuides software from SpringShare for creating Web-based subject guides. They point to ease of use, customization, social networking, and content sharing as the main factors that influenced the decision. Further, they note that librarians feel empowered because they have control over their work, and the interactive nature of the guides forges stronger connections between librarians and patrons.[33]

Things to consider when creating an online collection:

- Is it accessed through a subject portal or guide?
- What is it called?
- How many clicks is it away from the library's homepage?
- Is it dynamically generated?
- Does it include Web 2.0 features such as tagging, browsing, and book covers?[34]

Federated Searching

Ever since libraries began collecting electronic resources in the 1990s, fragmentation has been a concern. Users are often unsure about where to look and are frustrated by having to duplicate their searches in individual silos of information—the library catalog, myriad databases on different platforms, and various collections of electronic books and journals. Libraries attempted to address these problems by using technologies such as Z39.50 to aggregate disparate sources and by educating users about the online information landscape. When Google came along, however, it drastically changed users' search habits and expectations, with enormous implications for libraries. The library marketplace responded with the federated search.[35]

The previous edition of *Introduction to Reference Sources in the Health Sciences* introduced meta-searching or *federated searching* as a recent development and noted that libraries were beginning to use these applications to ease the burden of users' having to select the best resource for their searches. It was a marked improvement over previous online search capabilities and greatly enhanced the discoverability of library resources across disciplines and formats. Despite this, federated search technology has several deficiencies. It is slow because live searches are broadcast out to individual databases; it is not feasible to federate all of a library's available resources due to performance and connectivity issues; each resource requires a connector and permission from the resource provider; and it is unfriendly in a mobile environment. The quest continued for a better solution that could search across multiple types of resources with the speed of an index search and the ability to move seamlessly from search results to full-text content. In other words, "a search experience that is both Google-like and library specific."[36]

Web Scale Discovery

Although there are various definitions of Web scale discovery, the core idea remains the same: a large vendor-supplied index of all kinds of materials coupled with a simple search interface, giving users the ability to search across a library's entire collection quickly and easily. At the heart of Web scale discovery systems is the index. In contrast to federated searches, users are searching a single comprehensive index of both library catalog materials and article-level content, and because the content is pre-indexed, relevance-ranked results are returned almost instantly. "Think of it as articles and books living side by side in harmony," says Wisniewski.[37] Users get quick, integrated results from a single search box, and search results are faceted so that users can home in on only books or articles or other types of media.

Advantages of Web scale discovery:

- Ease of use—one search box
- Breadth and depth of the indexes—covers a very wide range of databases and the library catalog; includes searchable full-text content
- Ability to index local content such as special collections and archives and digitized collections
- Increased use of library resources—increase in full-text downloads and link resolver clicks
- Increased return on investment for full-text resources—full-text resources are easier to find
- Accessible from mobile platforms

Disadvantages of Web scale discovery:

- Libraries are at the mercy of the discovery system provider in terms of the subscription content included
- Number of results and varied formats can be overwhelming—simple, nonspecific searches can produce a confusing jumble of results
- Lack of thesauri and other search features available in discipline-specific databases
- Search quality may be sacrificed for the convenience of "one-stop shopping"—users are unaware what content is being searched
- Costliness from a monetary and staff time perspective[38-40]

Hoy concludes that these tools are probably best suited for novice users in an undergraduate setting. More advanced users or those in a medical or other specialty may find it more effective to start in a discipline-specific database such as PubMed (MEDLINE), PsycINFO, or Web of Science. Key questions to consider when evaluating these products include: What content is indexed? What is the total cost of ownership? How intuitive is the interface, and how easily can it be integrated into existing systems? Selected Web scale discovery products and example installations are listed at the end of the Hoy article.[41]

Visibility and Accessibility

The explosion of biomedical information has led to an "information paradox," wherein the volume of available information has made it increasingly difficult to find relevant information effectively and efficiently.[42] Despite the advances in library-supplied electronic resources and the provision of new search technology, several studies show that a large percentage of health sciences students and practicing clinicians still begin their searches in a commercial search engine such as Google and on Web 2.0 information-sharing sites such as Wikipedia.[43-45] Librarians worry constantly about the quality of information users are finding in cyberspace. Meg White takes a different view, however. She states that librarians would be wise to adapt a "go where your users are" approach and work to ensure that library resources are discoverable whenever and wherever patrons search. Allowing commercial search engines to index one's library website is a good first step, she advises, and using effective indexing and keywords can help drive traffic to the library's collections.[46]

White also points out that the Web provides the opportunity for the library and its wealth of information to become part of the workflow of its patrons via course pages, learning management systems, and social networking outlets such as Facebook and Twitter. In a health sciences environment, library-subscribed clinical information resources can be embedded into the electronic medical record (EMR) to facilitate clinical decision making and evidence-based practice.[47] And numerous point-of-care (POC) resources can be accessed on mobile devices, literally providing "fingertip" answers to questions that come up during a clinical encounter. These resources synthesize and evaluate the most relevant evidence from the primary medical literature, potentially saving time for busy clinicians and improving the quality of patient care.

New Roles for Librarians

The changes brought upon information resources by Web technology have also introduced significant changes to the services provided by librarians. The emphasis has shifted from librarians helping users to navigate print collections within the library to librarians connecting with users in new ways both in and outside of the physical library building, including virtually. Some of these changes have come about as librarians make efforts to keep themselves aligned with the changing needs of their clientele. Others have been introduced proactively by library management, eager to stay ahead of the game and not be left behind as the institution outgrows the traditional library model.

As noted earlier in this chapter, a significant number of health sciences libraries have eliminated stand-alone reference desks and now have a single service desk offering a variety of circulation, information, reference, and occasionally computing services. The volume of in-depth reference questions at the service desk has decreased, justifying a transition to reference on-call during selected hours.[48-49] Relieving librarians from staffing service desks "just in case" frees them to expand their services outside the library and to schedule in-depth consultations "just in time." It also provides paraprofessional staff the opportunity to be trained to answer more involved questions at the service desk before referring patrons to a librarian.[50-51] Time that used to be spent at the reference desk can now be invested in establishing or strengthening liaison programs, thereby building connections between the library and members of the campus community. After moving to on-call reference, liaison librarians at the University of Florida Health Science Center Libraries developed a "house calls" service, traveling to campus offices, labs, classrooms, and clinics in order provide information services and instruction at the point of need.[52] The results of their experience echo that of other libraries that have developed similar services: increased visibility for the library and recognition of librarians for contributing a service where and when it is needed.

Going a step further, the idea of embedding librarians within the liaison community served is gaining momentum in health sciences libraries. Embedded librarians have a desk or office space in the college, hospital, or research unit corresponding to

their liaison area. Typically these arrangements are made between the library director and the dean or another high level administrative position within the unit. In
2007 and 2008, the Arizona Health Sciences Library placed librarians in three locations outside the library: the College of Public Health, the College of Pharmacy, and
the College of Nursing. The librarians spend between 50–95 percent of their time
in the college, and the remainder in a library office. The colleges have embraced
their liaison librarians and as a result the liaison librarians are "in great demand for
teaching, grants research, publications support, faculty and student consultation, and
work on college committees."[53]

Placing the librarian where the user population works, studies, and teaches creates more opportunities for the librarian to interact with the users, to have conversations and to remind users of the resources and services provided by the library. It
is one of the most effective methods to market the value of the library to its community. Libraries that have embraced point-of-care services have increased librarian
involvement in areas such as: attending grand rounds and supporting information
needs, inclusion in grant applications, serving on hospital or university committees,
participating in medical center groups related to evidence-based practice and patient
safety, and collaborating with research groups related to Clinical and Translational
Science Awards (CTSA).[54–55]

The role of informationist is also expanding in libraries. Researchers and clinicians are now expected to analyze large amounts of published research and all types
of biomedical data to detect patterns, support clinical decisions, and transform data
into knowledge, thereby affecting clinical practice. The informationist helps fill this
role as a member of a clinical health-care or research team. An informationist—
or information specialist in context—is trained in both information and clinical or
hard sciences. Their role is to gather, synthesize, and present biomedical information for the team.[56] The Medical Library Association and the National Library of
Medicine have both contributed to the advancement of the informationist concept
within libraries,[57–58] and a number of libraries have developed programs to support
clinical information and bioinformatics research at their institutions.[59–62]

Since "informationists are made, not born," the importance of investing in comprehensive and ongoing training is paramount. Though subject knowledge or background in clinical sciences or biosciences is not required, studies have suggested
that this knowledge is necessary to recognize the full potential of the informationist working with subject experts.[63–64] The Medical Library Association Educational
Clearinghouse includes a few bioinformatics classes,[65] and the National Center for
Biotechnology Information (NCBI) offers regular two-day Discovery Workshops
to orient users to the range of NCBI tools (NCBI discovery workshops). There are
a number of health informatics and medical informatics programs at the university level offering specialty certifications. Hospital libraries are also pushing to

transform themselves into knowledge managers, providing tools to address health-care system needs to achieve "meaningful use" requirements in electronic medical records and to help support evidence-based practice. The New England Region of the National Network of Libraries of Medicine developed a Healthcare Knowledge Services Center (HKSC) Template to help traditional hospital libraries transition to health-care knowledge service centers.[66]

The new roles for health sciences librarians discussed in the section are by no means comprehensive. Some of the changes highlighted will not apply to all libraries. Nevertheless, it is important for all health sciences libraries to be in tune with their institutional mission and to adapt to changing priorities at the local level. In order to take on new roles, we must be willing to let go of traditional services that no longer serve our community's needs. There has been much speculation in library literature about the future of health sciences libraries and the changes that librarians will see to their roles.[67-70] At the 2009 Symposium on Transformational Change in Health Sciences Libraries: Space, Collections, and Roles, keynote speaker Patricia Thibodeau highlighted librarian roles and skills and noted that librarians are in a key position to collaborate with multiple institutional groups. She encouraged librarians to participate in complex institution projects, to speak up at meetings, and to talk to academic vice deans, faculty, and information technologists.[71] When we align our services and resources with the priorities of our institution, we provide value.

Conclusion

Reference resources help searchers find context by answering the what, where, when, and who of their topic.[72] The traditional arrangement of a print-based reference collection is no longer relevant in the online environment, as resources categorized as "reference" in print are integrated with other information sources for enhanced search and retrieval. Online reference resources provide the same service of offering context, and when designed well, they can improve search experience and results. The quantity of digital information has increased to a level that requires ever more sophisticated tools to manage the volume. Librarians are increasingly stepping up to help integrate, manage, and search point-of-care tools, systematic literature reviews, and more. These tools do not change our mission; rather they enable us to apply our skills differently and perhaps even better. As Pat Thibodeau says, "Librarians are more than their collections. Librarians make libraries valuable."[73]

References

1. Husted, J. T., and L. J. Czechowski. "Rethinking the Reference Collection: Exploring Benchmarks and E-book Availability." *Medical Reference Services Quarterly* 31, no. 3 (2012): 267–79.

2. Folb, B. L., C. B. Wessel, and L. J. Czechowski. "Clinical and Academic Use of Electronic and Print Books: The Health Sciences Library System E-book Study at the University of Pittsburgh." *Journal of the Medical Library Association* 99, no. 3 (2011): 218–28.

3. Landesman, Margaret. "Getting It Right: The Evolution of Reference Collections." *The Reference Librarian* 44, no. 91–92 (2005): 5–22.

4. Liestman, Daniel. "Reference Collection Management Policies: Lessons from Kansas." *Educational Administration Abstracts* 38, no. 1 (2003): 3–139.

5. Singer, Carol A. *Fundamentals of Managing Reference Collections.* Chicago: American Library Association, 2012.

6. Douglas, C. Steven. "Revising a Collection Development Policy in a Rapidly Changing Environment." *Journal of Electronic Resources in Medical Libraries* 8, no. 1 (2011): 15–21.

7. Detmering, Robert, and Claudene Sproles. "Reference in Transition: A Case Study in Reference Collection Development." *Collection Building* 31, no. 1 (2012): 19–22.

8. Francis, Mary. "Weeding the Reference Collection: A Case Study of Collection Management." *The Reference Librarian* 53, no. 2 (2012): 219–34.

9. Moroni, A. E. "Weeding in a Digital Age: Physical and Digital Collections Are Very Different, but One Time-Honored Task—Weeding—Should Apply Equally to Both." *Library Journal—New York* 137, no. 15 (2012): 26–29.

10. Detmering and Sproles, "Reference in Transition."

11. Douglas, "Revising a Collection Development Policy."

12. Shedlock, J., and L. J. Walton. "Developing a Virtual Community for Health Sciences Library Book Selection: Doody's Core Titles." *Journal of the Medical Library Association* 94, no. 1 (2006): 61–66.

13. Blackwell, J. C., J. A. Boorkman, and A. Taylor. "Organization and Management of the Reference Collection." In *Introduction to Reference Sources in the Health Sciences*, 5th ed., edited by J. T. Huber, J. A. Boorkman, and J. C. Blackwell, 3–32. New York: Neal-Schuman, 2008.

14. "Doody's Review Service." Last modified 2013. http://www.doody.com/drs/.

15. Blackwell, Boorkman, and Taylor, "Management of the Reference Collection."

16. Singer, *Managing Reference Collections.*

17. Blackwell, Boorkman, and Taylor, "Management of the Reference Collection."

18. "NLM Individual Fellowship for Informationist Training." Program announcement number: PAR-06-509. National Library of Medicine. Last modified 2006; accessed February 11, 2013. http://grants.nih.gov/grants/guide/pa-files/PAR-06-509.html.

19. Grigg, Karen S., Bethany A. Koestner, Richard A. Peterson, and Patricia L. Thibodeau. "Data-Driven Collection Management: Through Crisis Emerge Opportunities." *Journal of Electronic Resources in Medical Libraries* 7, no. 1 (2010): 1–12.
20. Morgan, P. S. "The Impact of the Acquisition of Electronic Medical Texts on the Usage of Equivalent Print Books in an Academic Medical Library." *Evidence Based Library and Information Practice* 5, no. 3 (2010): 5–19.
21. Ugaz, Ana G., and Taryn Resnick. "Assessing Print and Electronic Use of Reference/Core Medical Textbooks." *Journal of the Medical Library Association* 96, no. 2 (2008): 145–47.
22. Hartel, L. J., and F. M. Cheek. "Preferred Book Formats in an Academic Medical Center." *Journal of the Medical Library Association* 99, no. 4 (2011): 313–17.
23. Husted and Czechowski, "Rethinking the Reference Collection."
24. Delwiche, F. A., and N. A. Bianchi. "Transformation of a Print Reference Collection." *Medical Reference Services Quarterly* 25, no. 2 (2006): 21–29.
25. Schulte, S. J. "Eliminating Traditional Reference Services in an Academic Health Sciences Library: A Case Study." *Journal of the Medical Library Association* 99, no. 4 (2011): 273–79.
26. Ludwig, L. "Health Sciences Libraries Building Survey, 1999–2009." *Journal of the Medical Library Association* 98, no. 2 (2010): 105–34.
27. Barrett, F. "An Analysis of Reference Services Usage at a Regional Academic Health Sciences Library." *Journal of the Medical Library Association* 98, no. 4 (2010): 308–11.
28. De Groote, S. I., K. Hitchcock, and R. McGowan. "Trends in Reference Usage Statistics in an Academic Health Sciences Library." *Journal of the Medical Library Association* 95, no. 1 (2007): 23–30.
29. Landesman, "Evolution of Reference Collections."
30. Singer, *Managing Reference Collections.*
31. Ford, Lyle, Lisa O'Hara, and Jared Hanson Whiklo. "Shelflessness as a Virtue: Preserving Serendipity in an Electronic Reference Collection." *Journal of Electronic Resources in Medical Libraries* 21, no. 3–4 (2009): 251–62.
32. Ibid.
33. Glassman, Nancy R., and Karen Sorensen. "From Pathfinders to Subject Guides: One Library's Experience with LibGuides." *Journal of Electronic Resources in Medical Libraries* 7, no. 4 (2010): 281–91.
34. Ford, O'Hara, and Whilko, "Shelflessness as a Virtue."
35. Wisniewski, J. "Web Scale Discovery: The Future's So Bright, I Gotta Wear Shades." *Online (Wilton, Conn.)* 34, no. 4 (2010): 55–57.
36. Boyer, G. M, and M. Besaw. "A Study of Librarians' Perceptions and Use of the Summon Discovery Tool." *Journal of Electronic Resources in Medical Libraries* 9, no. 3 (2012): 173–83.

37. Wisniewski, "Web Scale Discovery."

38. Boyer and Besaw, "Study of Librarians' Perceptions."

39. Hoy, M. B. "An Introduction to Web Scale Discovery Systems." *Medical Reference Services Quarterly* 31, no. 3 (2012): 323–29.

40. Wisniewski, "Web Scale Discovery."

41. Hoy, "Web Scale Discovery Systems."

42. Thiele, R. H., N. C. Poiro, D. C. Scalzo, and E. C. Nemergut. "Speed, Accuracy, and Confidence in Google, Ovid, PubMed, and UpToDate: Results of a Randomised Trial." *Postgraduate Medical Journal* 86, no. 1018 (2010): 459–65.

43. Haigh, Carol A. "Wikipedia as an Evidence Source for Nursing and Healthcare Students." *Nurse Education Today* 31, no. 2 (2011): 135–39.

44. Kingsley, K., G. M. Galbraith, M. Herring, E. Stowers, T. Stewart, and K. V. Kingsley. "Why Not Just Google It? An Assessment of Information Literacy Skills in a Biomedical Science Curriculum." *BMC Medical Education* 11, no. 1 (2011): 17.

45. Thiele et al., "Speed, Accuracy, and Confidence."

46. White, Meg. "Maximizing Use and Value of E-books in the Medical Library." *Journal of Electronic Resources in Medical Libraries* 8, no. 3 (2011): 280–85.

47. Ibid.

48. Lubker, I. M., M. E. Henderson, C. S. Canevari, and B. A. Wright. "Refocusing Reference Services Outside the Library Building: One Library's Experience." *Medical Reference Services Quarterly* 29, no. 3 (2010): 218–28.

49. Murphy, Beverly, Richard Peterson, Hattie Vines, Megan Isenburg, Elizabeth Berney, Robert James, Marcos Rodriguez, and Patricia Thibodeau. "Revolution at the Library Service Desk." *Medical Reference Services Quarterly* 27, no. 4 (2008): 379–93.

50. Ibid.

51. Schulte, "Eliminating Traditional Reference Services."

52. Tennant, M. R., B. Auten, C. E. Botero, L. C. Butson, M. E. Edwards, R. Garcia-Milian, J. A. Lyon, and H. F. Norton. "Changing the Face of Reference: Adapting Biomedical and Health Information Services for the Classroom, Clinic, and Beyond." *Medical Reference Services Quarterly* 31, no. 3 (2012): 280–301.

53. Freiburger, G., and S. Kramer. "Embedded Librarians: One Library's Model for Decentralized Service." *Journal of the Medical Library Association* 97, no. 2 (2009): 139–42.

54. Lubker et al., "Refocusing Reference Services."

55. Tennant et al., "Changing the Face of Reference."

56. Rankin, J. A., S. F. Grefsheim, and C. C. Canto. "The Emerging Informationist Specialty: A Systematic Review of the Literature." *Journal of the Medical Library Association* 96, no. 3 (2008): 194–206.

57. "NLM Individual Fellowship."

58. Shipman, J. P., D. J. Cunningham, R. Holst, and L. A. Watson. "The Informationist Conference: Report." *Journal of the Medical Library Association* 90, no. 4 (2002): 458–64.

59. Chattopadhyay, A., N. H. Tannery, D. A. Silverman, P. Bergen, and B. A. Epstein. "Design and Implementation of a Library-Based Information Service in Molecular Biology and Genetics at the University of Pittsburgh." *Journal of the Medical Library Association* 94, no. 3 (2006): 307–13.

60. Giuse, N. B., T. Y. Koonce, R. N. Jerome, M. Cahall, N. A. Sathe, and A. Williams. "Evolution of a Mature Clinical Informationist Model." *Journal of the American Medical Informatics Association* 12, no. 3 (2005): 249–55.

61. Minie, M., S. Bowers, P. Tarczy-Hornoch, E. Roberts, R. A. James, N. Rambo, and S. Fuller. "The University of Washington Health Sciences Library Biocommons: An Evolving Northwest Biomedical Research Information Support Infrastructure." *Journal of the Medical Library Association* 94, no. 3 (2006): 321–29.

62. Rein, D. C. "Developing Library Bioinformatics Services in Context: The Purdue University Libraries Bioinformationist Program." *Journal of the Medical Library Association* 94, no. 3 (2006): 314–20.

63. Cleveland, A. D., K. L. Holmes, and J. L. Philbrick. "'Genomics and Translational Medicine for Information Professionals': An Innovative Course to Educate the Next Generation of Librarians." *Journal of the Medical Library Association* 100, no. 4 (2012): 303–5.

64. Grefsheim, S. F., S. C. Whitmore, B. A. Rapp, J. A. Rankin, R. R. Robison, and C. C. Canto. "The Informationist: Building Evidence for an Emerging Health Profession." *Journal of the Medical Library Association* 98, no. 2 (2010): 147–56.

65. "Medical Library Association Educational Clearinghouse." Last modified 2007; accessed February 11, 2013, http://cech.mlanet.org/.

66. Goldstein, H. Mark, and Margaret H. Coletti. "Developing a Strategic Plan for Transitioning to Healthcare Knowledge Services Centers (HKSCs)." *Journal of Hospital Librarianship* 11, no. 4 (2011): 379–87.

67. Lynn, V. A., M. FitzSimmons, and C. K. Robinson. "Special Report: Symposium on Transformational Change in Health Sciences Libraries: Space, Collections, and Roles." *Journal of the Medical Library Association* 99, no. 1 (2011): 82–87.

68. McGowan, J. J. "Tomorrow's Academic Health Sciences Library Today." *Journal of the Medical Library Association* 100, no. 1 (2012): 43–46.

69. Lynn, FitzSimmons, and Robinson, "Special Report."

70. McGowan, J. J. "Evolution, Revolution, or Obsolescence: An Examination of Writings on the Future of Health Sciences Libraries." *Journal of the Medical Library Association* 100, no. 1 (2012): 5–9.

71. Lynn, FitzSimmons, and Robinson, "Special Report."

72. Buckland, Michael K. "The Digital Difference in Reference Collections." *Journal of Library Administration* 46, no. 2 (2007): 87–100.

73. Lynn, FitzSimmons, and Robinson, "Special Report."

PART III

Bibliographic Sources

CHAPTER 3

Bibliographic Sources for Monographs

JEFFREY T. HUBER

Historically, monographs have played a significant role in the dissemination of health sciences information. "The seventeenth century saw the culmination of medical bibliography predicated on the publication of medical works in monographic form and the first appearance of bibliographies taking into account publication of advances in medicine in periodicals."[1] While periodicals grew to become the preferred biomedical and scientific communication forum for current research and opinion, monographs continued to serve as an important means for conveying "gold standard" information. This trend remains true today, whether the monograph be in print or electronic format. Like the monograph itself, materials used for bibliographic control of monographs continue to serve as an integral component of a reference collection.

Over time, bibliographies have been developed to bring order out of chaos by providing information that identifies works within a particular discipline or group of disciplines.[2-3] These bibliographies serve as verification, location, and selection tools. *Verification* refers to standard information contained in bibliographical citations such as author, title, edition, and place of publication. It may be necessary to consult multiple sources in order to verify all of the needed information about a particular monograph, often moving from a general source to a particular one with a narrower subject area. *Location* indicates which library or other information agency owns a particular title or the vendor from which it may be purchased. Location also specifies where a title can be found in a particular library or information agency. Online bibliographic databases are the primary resources for identifying institutional holdings. Trade bibliographies, available in both print and electronic formats, are used to determine basic purchasing data. Since collection development is an essential function within a library or information setting, the *selection* function presupposes bibliographies that indicate the availability of titles within a particular subject domain, by a specific author, or in a given format.

Bibliographies in the health sciences often fulfill more than one of these three functions and typically contain entries for multiple types of materials (e.g., monographs, periodicals, government documents, etc.).

Current Sources

While print resources historically have been a mainstay for bibliographic data, the generic growth in electronic information resources is reflected in current sources for monograph information. Many print bibliographic resources for monograph titles have been replaced by electronic ones.

The National Library of Medicine (NLM) is the leading authority concerning current coverage of health science monographs.

3.1   LocatorPlus. Bethesda, MD: National Library of Medicine. Available: http://locatorplus.gov/.

3.2   NLM Catalog. Bethesda, MD: National Library of Medicine. Available: http://www.ncbi.nlm.nih.gov/nlmctalog.

LocatorPlus is the National Library of Medicine's (NLM) online catalog. In 1999, LocatorPlus replaced NLM's telnet-based online catalog, LOCATOR, and replaced the catalog databases CATLINE, SERLINE, and AVLINE. Prior to 1999, CATLINE was a primary bibliographic source for monograph records. LocatorPlus is updated continuously and includes more than 1.2 million catalog records for books, audiovisuals, journals, computer files, and other materials in NLM's collections. Records from the CATLINE, SERLINE, and AVLINE databases are available via LocatorPlus. LocatorPlus contains links from catalog records to Internet resources, including online journals, when available and appropriate. LocatorPlus includes circulation status information for materials, including those on-order or in-process at the Library. The LocatorPlus interface allows users to find unknown author or organization names if unsure about the exact name, view or use bibliographic records in MARC format, and view or use authority records for names and titles. Through its "Other Databases" menu, LocatorPlus provides direct access to additional free resources such as NLM databases (including PubMed/MEDLINE), consumer health information and MedlinePlus, history of medicine databases, NLM Catalog, PubMed

Central, TOXNET and toxicology databases, health services research and HSTAT, and catalogs of other U.S. medical and consumer health libraries. LocatorPlus contains only records that are available in machine readable format. Users may need to consult retrospective sources for early works covering the biomedical sciences. LocatorPlus is available free of charge.

The NLM Catalog is an alternative search interface to NLM bibliographic records for journals, books, audiovisuals, computer software, electronic resources, and other materials using the NCBI Entrez system. The NLM Catalog links to LocatorPlus for access to NLM holdings information. The NLM Catalog provides access to more than 10,000 citations. The interface allows users to explode on MeSH headings, identify or search primary subjects, find a known name of an author or organization, find a known item, and view or use bibliographic records in XML format. NLM's cataloging records are also available from other vendors, such as OCLC.

3.3   WorldCat. Dublin, OH: Online Computer Library Center (OCLC). Available: http://www.oclc.org/worldcat/.

OCLC provides shared cataloging records and bibliographic descriptions through its international network system. Cataloging records are included for a variety of materials, including monographs, in all subject domains. In addition to NLM, sources of cataloging information include the Library of Congress, National Agriculture Library, British Library, and member libraries. OCLC is a major source of bibliographic information for monographs. It also provides location information since cataloging records indicate the holding libraries for items included in its databases.

Founded in 1967, OCLC is a nonprofit, membership, computer library service and research organization serving more than 23,000 libraries, archives, and museums in 170 countries worldwide. The WorldCat database serves as the core for all OCLC services. WorldCat includes more than 82 million bibliographic records and 2 billion individual holdings contributed by libraries around the world.

3.4   *Doody's Book Reviews* [electronic resource]. Chicago: Doody Enterprises, 1993– . Continues *Doody's Health Sciences Book Review Journal.* Oak Park, IL: Doody Publishing, 1993–2002. Bimonthly. Cumulated with additional reviews in *Doody's Health Sciences Book Review Annual.* Oak Park, IL: Doody Publishing, 1993–1995/96. Annual.

3.5   *Doody's Health Sciences Book Review Journal* absorbed *Doody's Rating Service: A Buyer's Guide to the 250 Best Health Sciences Books.* Oak Park, IL: Doody Publishing, 1993–1997. Annual.

3.6   *Doody's Core Titles in the Health Sciences* [electronic resource]. Chicago: Doody Enterprises, 2004– . Annual. Available: http://www.doody.com/dct/.

Doody's earlier print resources, such as *Doody's Health Sciences Book Review Journal, Doody's Health Sciences Book Review Annual,* and *Doody's Rating Service: A Buyer's Guide to the 250 Best Health Sciences Books*, have been replaced with electronic counterparts (see http://www.doodyenterprises.com/). Doody's products and other general bibliographic sources, such as the National Union Catalog and American Book Publishing Record, are useful tools for verifying health science monograph information as well as identifying their location. However, these sources are not likely to be available in many health sciences libraries, particularly those outside of large academic settings.

Founded in 1993, Doody Enterprises, Inc. is a medical publishing company devoted to producing information products for health-care professionals. At the core of Doody's clinical information database are the *Doody's Book Reviews*, which evaluate books and electronic resources across a wide range of specialty areas including basic sciences, clinical medicine, nursing, and the allied health disciplines. Doody Enterprises maintains a database of health sciences titles with reviews. In addition, each review is accompanied by a Doody's Star Rating. The expert reviews and star ratings are available electronically as part of *Doody's Book Reviews* database and distributed via a weekly e-mail service and webpage. Doody commissions original expert reviews for approximately 3,000 books and electronic resources from over 250 publishers each year. About 2,000 of those titles are reviewed each year by a network of more than 5,000 academic-affiliated health-care professionals. Reviews feature the byline of the reviewer and consist of a general description of the book, intended audience, purpose, features, assessment, and a star rating. Doody's Star Rating is derived from a questionnaire completed by the expert reviewer during the course of completing a review. Bibliographic and descriptive information is contained in each entry for in-print and forthcoming books. Access to the database is available via the Web. Some jobbers such as YBP include an option to integrate Doody's reviews with their book ordering interface as an alternate method of access to this resource.

To serve as a replacement for the Brandon/Hill Selected Lists which were discontinued in mid-2004, Doody's began publishing *Doody's Core Titles in the Health Sciences*. This electronic resource is designed to serve as a collection development tool for health sciences libraries of all sizes. This resource rates core titles in more than 120 specialty areas in health sciences, basic sciences, clinical medicine, allied health, associated health sciences, and nursing.

Originally published in the *Journal of the Medical Library Association* (formerly titled *Bulletin of the Medical Library Association*), the Brandon/Hill Selected List of Print Books and Journals for the Small Medical Library, Brandon/Hill Selected List of Print Books and Journals in Allied Health, and Brandon/Hill Selected List of Print Books and Journals in Nursing are widely recognized collection development tools. The selected lists were the brainchild of Alfred N. Brandon who first published the *Selected List of Books and Journals for the Small Medical Library* in 1965. The selected list for nursing followed in 1979 and the selected list for allied health in 1984.

3.7   *National Union Catalog: Books.* Washington, DC: Library of Congress, 1983–2002. Monthly. Microfiche.

3.8   *American Book Publishing Record.* New York: R. R. Bowker, 1960– . Monthly; annual cumulation with quinquennial cumulations.

3.9   *The Publishers Weekly.* New York: F. Leypoldt, 1873– .

Published by the Library of Congress (LOC), the *National Union Catalog* (*NUC*) provides a cumulative record of materials cataloged by LOC and participating libraries for imprints published 1956 and later. The *NUC* is a vast bibliography that is frequently consulted since its holdings represent the broad scope of the world's output of monographs and other types of materials.

The microfiche *NUC: Books* was published in multiple sections using a register/index format. The five sections of *NUC: Books* include the register, name index, title index, LC series index, and LC subject index. Item records include all bibliographic elements traditionally found on LC printed cards. Since entries appear in *NUC* only if a participating library has acquired and cataloged a title, *NUC* serves as a location source as well as a verification tool.

The *American Book Publishing Record* cumulates the listings in *The Publishers Weekly*. This ongoing resource provides bibliographic information about English-language publications in all subject areas. The primary goal of this bibliographic resource is to list books that can be purchased from publishers and to provide enough information to order any given title. This resource is important to the health sciences librarian because the health science arena is impacted by disciplines outside of health and biomedicine. In addition, the *American Book Publishing Record* and *Publishers Weekly* provide a historical account of books published in the United States.

3.10   *Books in Print.* New Providence, NJ: R. R. Bowker, 1948– . Annual. Available: http://www.booksinprint.com/.

3.11   *Books in Print Supplement.* New Providence, NJ: R. R. Bowker, 1972/73– . Annual. Available: http://www.booksinprint.com/.

3.12   *Subject Guide to Books in Print.* New York: R. R. Bowker, 1957– . Annual. Available: http://www.booksinprint.com/.

3.13   *Medical and Health Care Books and Serials in Print.* New York: R. R. Bowker, 1985– , 2 vols. Annual. Continues *Medical Books and Serials in Print.* New York: R. R. Bowker, 1978–1984. Annual.

3.14   *Canadian Books in Print: Author and Title Index*. Toronto: University of
Toronto Press, 1975–2006. Annual. Continues *Canadian Books in Print*.
Toronto: University of Toronto Press, 1967–1975.

An ongoing task for a librarian is to determine the availability of a given title
for purchase. The librarian must first identify whether or not a title is still in print
and subsequently if it is for sale. The following resources are designed to assist with
this process.

Books in Print (*BIP*) is a broad resource that covers all subject areas. *Books in
Print* is indexed by *Subject Guide to Books in Print, 1957–1987/88* and *Books in
Print Subject Guide, 1988/89– . BIP* is kept updated by the annual publication of
Books in Print Supplement, 1972/73– . Each entry includes bibliographic elements,
cost information, and source(s) from which the book can be purchased. Although
the print version of *BIP* remains useful, Web access is becoming more common.
Bowker's *Books in Print* website provides the same resources as the print version
but with many enhanced features. For example, the website includes resource guides,
publisher spotlights, and new features. Whereas the print version supports author and
title access, the website allows for keyword, author, title, and ISBN/UPC access. The
website also allows the user to browse by subject area or by index whereas the print
version requires purchasing the annual *Subject Guide to Books in Print* to accommodate searching by subject headings. Booksinprint.com includes the full Books in
Print database of U.S. titles as well as Books Out-of-Print and Forthcoming Books.

Also produced by R. R. Bowker, *Medical and Health Care Books and Serials
in Print* continues *Medical Books and Serials in Print*. This title serves as an index
to literature in the health sciences and is of obvious interest to health sciences librarians. *Medical and Health Care Books and Serials in Print* lists more than 109,000
books under 6,000 health and medical subject areas, including some 3,500 new titles.
Ordering and publisher information is included in each entry to facilitate acquisitions.

Canadian Books in Print: Author and Title Index continues *Canadian Books in
Print*. This work serves as a companion resource to *Books in Print* and *Whitaker's
Books in Print* (formerly *British Books in Print*). *Canadian Books in Print: Author
and Title Index* includes entries for English-language titles produced by Canadian
publishers. It ceased publication in 2006.

3.15   Amazon.com. Seattle: Amazon.com. Available: http://www.amazon.com/.

3.16   Barnesandnoble.com. New York: Barnesandnoble.com. Available:
http://www.barnesandnoble.com/.

Commercial Internet vendors such as Amazon.com and Barnesandnoble.com
have become recognized bibliographic information sources. Their customer rating
and related purchases features are useful collection development tools.

Amazon.com is perhaps one of the most popular Internet vendors. Originally focusing on the book and music markets, Amazon.com has grown to include books, music videos, DVDs, magazine subscriptions, office products, apparel, electronics, toys, games, housewares, hardware, home and garden supplies, gift items, and registries among its retail offerings. To locate monograph titles, users may perform a keyword search or browse by subjects. Records may be sorted by featured title, bestsellers, customer ratings, price, publication date, or alphabetically. Monograph records include bibliographic elements, ordering information, and purchase availability. Records also include customer ratings and reviews as well as published editorial reviews when available. Links are provided to authors of similar works that were purchased by individuals who purchased a particular title. Amazon.com supplies new and used books.

Another popular Internet vendor of books, textbooks, music, videos, and DVDs, Barnesandnoble.com offers many of the same features as Amazon.com. Users may search for monograph titles by keyword or browse by subject. Titles may be sorted by bestsellers. Entries include ordering information and note title availability for purchase. Customer reviews with ratings are included, as are notes from the publisher. Records also indicate related titles purchased by individuals who purchased a particular book.

3.17   eBooks.com. Claremont, WA: eBooks.com. Available: http://www.ebooks.com/.

The greatest change where monographs are concerned since publication of the fifth edition of *Introduction to Reference Sources in the Health Sciences* is the ready availability of electronic books or e-books. An e-book is essentially an electronic copy of a book. Depending on publication platform, e-books may be read using a computer and Web browser, dedicated portable electronic device (i.e., e-book reader), or with an application for a smartphone (both iPhones and Androids). Information about e-books is available directly from publishers as well as from commercial Internet vendors. Typical means for library access to e-books is from aggregators such as eBrary, EBL, or EBSCOhost Books; publisher-hosted e-books; and various subscription models such as those that offer them annually or by semester. While some library options support downloads, download capacity is usually limited.

Sites such as eBooks.com sell books in multiple formats, in multiple platforms, and in various categories (e.g., academic and scholarly e-books, professional and technical e-books, popular consumer e-books). Users can download books to computers, e-book readers, or smartphones. Or users have the ability to read books directly online from any computer without downloading content or installing special software. In addition to sites like eBooks.com that are dedicated solely to providing access to e-books, more generic commercial vendors such as Amazon.com and Barnesandnoble.com provide access to e-books for their respective platforms. However, e-book services provided by sites such as eBooks.com, Amazon.com, and Barnesandnoble.com are typically limited to individual users and do not extend to libraries. (Some libraries do maintain a collection of Amazon Kindles or Barnes and Noble Nooks for checkout with books preloaded on them, but this is more the exception than the norm.)

3.18   Google Books. Mountainview, CA: Google. Available: http://books.google.com/.

3.19   Google Play. Mountainview, CA: Google. Available: http://play.google.com/store.

Google Books allows users to search the full text of books Google has scanned and stored in its digital repository. If a book is out of copyright, or the publisher has given Google permission, users may preview sections of a book or, in some cases, the entire text. Google Books includes bibliographic information for each book as well as book reviews when available. If a book is in the public domain, users can download a free PDF copy of the work. For books not in the public domain, Google allows users to buy a print copy via its Google Play page. Users can also purchase e-books from the Google Play site. In addition, Google Books provides links to publishers and booksellers for purchasing purposes.

Retrospective Sources

Using clay tablets, papyrus, parchment, and, ultimately, paper, man has sought to record information for future reference. Development of the printing press in the fifteenth century forever changed the communication process. Society moved farther away from oral tradition to the printed word. Subsequently, the printed book reigned as the primary source of information until the mid-nineteenth century. By that time, the periodical had grown in use and popularity as the preferred means for disseminating scientific information.

Prior to the mid-nineteenth century, bibliographies containing entries for medical works were published but were not all inclusive in subject coverage. In addition, these bibliographies were primarily concerned with medical works in monographic form. For a detailed account of early medical bibliography, the reader should consult *The Development of Medical Bibliography* by Estelle Brodman;[4] for a detailed account of medical bibliography since World War II, the reader should consult *Medical Bibliography in an Age of Discontinuity* by Scott Adams.[5]

3.20   *Index-Catalogue of the Library of the Surgeon-General's Office.* Ser. 1–5. Washington, DC: U.S. Government Printing Office, 1880–1961, 61 vols. IndexCat. Available: http://indexcat.nlm.nih.gov/.

3.21   *Index Medicus.* Ser. 1–3. Various publishers, 1879–1927, 45 vols.

John Shaw Billings, librarian of the Surgeon General's Library (forerunner of the National Library of Medicine) is considered the founding father of medical bibliography. Billings was responsible for the creation of the *Index-Catalogue of the Library of the Surgeon-General's Office* as well as the original *Index Medicus.* These two publications marked the beginning of a systematic attempt to provide bibliographic coverage of medical works worldwide.

First published in 1880, the *Index-Catalogue* contained a list of all monographic and periodical literature received by the Library of the Surgeon-General's Office (which became the Army Medical Library, the Armed Forces Medical Library, and, ultimately, the National Library of Medicine).

The *Index-Catalogue* was published in five series from 1880 to 1961, with a total of sixty-one volumes. Each series was intended to contain author and subject entries in dictionary form within a single alphabet. Monographic entries were listed under authors' names as well as under subject headings; entries for periodical articles were listed only under subject headings. Publication of the fourth series contained only alphabetical entries A through M, and series five did not include subject entries. Despite omissions, the *Index-Catalogue* was more comprehensive in coverage than any previous medical bibliography. Items were included as they were acquired by the library rather than by date of publication. Therefore, older items may be found in more recent series of the *Index-Catalogue.* Since the *Index-Catalogue* is comprised of only those items acquired by the library, it is not a comprehensive bibliography of medical works. However, the extent of the library's collection—a collection that eventually became the National Library of Medicine—makes the *Index-Catalogue* the most comprehensive listing of medical literature of the period. The *Index-Catalogue* continues to serve as a valuable retrospective bibliography and historical source. Digitizing of the *Index-Catalogue* was completed in 2004, resulting in the National Library Medicine's IndexCat.

IndexCat is the digitized version of the *Index-Catalogue of the Library of the Surgeon-General's Office.* The content of IndexCat reflects the bibliographic citations in the original publication of approximately 3.7 million references dated from the fifth century to the first half of the twentieth century. Some 616,000 references to monographs (books, pamphlets, and reports) are included as well as 470,000 dissertations and theses.

Given that the *Index-Catalogue* was published as a series over many years, Billings developed the *Index Medicus* (*IM*) as a bibliographic updating tool. The *Index Medicus* was published from 1879 to 1927, with publication suspended from May 1899 to 1902. *IM* was published monthly from 1879 to 1920 and then quarterly from 1921 to 1927. Entries for books and journal articles were arranged by subject with an author index. See chapter 4 for further discussion of *Index Medicus*.

Since the original *Index Medicus* ceased publication in 1927 and the *Index-Catalogue* contained entries for only those works purchased by the library, users should consult multiple resources in locating monograph titles published between 1927 and 1948 when the *Army Medical Library Catalog* began publication. These sources should not be limited to those specifically covering the health sciences, but should also include more general ones such as those compiled by the Library of Congress.

3.22   *Catalog.* Washington, DC: Library of Congress, 1956–1960/65. Issued annually with quinquennial cumulation (1955–1959) and a sexennial cumulation (1960–1965). *Catalog of the Army Medical Library*, 1952–1955. Continues *Army Medical Library (U.S.) Catalog*, 1948–1951.

From 1948 to 1965, these volumes were published as supplements to the printed catalogs published by the Library of Congress. They also serve as a bridge to *Index-Catalogue* series as well as the *National Library of Medicine Current Catalog* which began publication in 1966. Each volume contains bibliographic information for monographs cataloged during this period, regardless of date of publication.

3.23   *National Union Catalog, Pre-1956 Imprints.* Chicago: Mansell, 1968–1980, 685 vols. *Supplement*, 1980–1981, vols. 686–754.

National Union Catalog, Pre-1956 Imprints, compiled and edited with the cooperation of the Library of Congress and the National Union Catalog Subcommittee of the Resources and Technical Services Division of the American Library Association, is a centerpiece for verification of books and other materials prior to 1956. This work is also used to verify serials titles that closed prior to 1956. *Pre-1956 Imprints* consists of an alphabetical listing of materials published prior to January 1, 1956, which have been cataloged by the Library of Congress or by one of the *NUC* participating libraries.

3.24   *The American Book Publishing Record Cumulative, 1876–1949.* New York: R. R. Bowker, 1980, 15 vols.

3.25   *The American Book Publishing Record Cumulative, 1950–1977.* New York: R. R. Bowker, 1978, 15 vols.

3.26   *Health Science Books, 1876–1982.* New York: R. R. Bowker, 1982.

Essentially, the two *American Book Publishing Record Cumulative* works contain bibliographic data for every book published and distributed in the United States between 1876 and 1977. More than 1.5 million titles, with full bibliographic and cataloging information, are included in these resources.

Health Science Books, 1876–1982 contains bibliographic and cataloging information from the Library of Congress for more than 133,000 titles published and distributed in the United States between 1876 and 1982. All areas of the health sciences are represented in this work.

References

1. Brodman, Estelle. *The Development of Medical Bibliography*. Washington, DC: Medical Library Association, 1954.
2. Katz, William A. *Introduction to Reference Work*. New York: McGraw-Hill, 1997.
3. Gaskell, Philip. *A New Introduction to Bibliography*. New York: Oxford University Press, 1972.
4. Brodman, *Development of Medical Bibliography*.
5. Adams, Scott. *Medical Bibliography in an Age of Discontinuity*. Chicago: Medical Library Association, 1981.

CHAPTER 4

Bibliographic Sources for Periodicals

FEILI TU-KEEFNER

The creation of scientific journals began in the seventeenth century. The first scientific journal, *Philosophical Transactions*, was created in 1665 under the editorship of Henry Oldenburg by the Royal Society of London for Improving Natural Knowledge, founded in 1662.[1-3] In the same year, *Journal des Sçavans* (later *Journal des Savants*), was produced in France by Denis de Sallo.[4] Periodicals are often the most frequently consulted library resources, with journals having a narrower proportion of the user population.[5] However, these publications are often the first sources to disseminate information about a new subject or development,[6] so currency of the information distributed is a prime feature. In 2004, Tenopir, King, and Bush surveyed medical faculty's use of print and electronic journals; the results show that currency of content is related to the usefulness of the information.[7] Many research findings report that health professionals prefer to read journal articles within the first three years of publication.[8-9]

Definition of Journals

According to the *ODLIS: Online Dictionary of Library and Information Science*, a periodical is "a serial publication with its own distinctive title, containing a mix of articles, editorials, reviews, columns, or other short works written by more than one contributor issued more than once, generally at regular stated intervals of less than a year."[10] The *ALA Glossary of Library and Information Science* defines journal as "a periodical, especially one containing scholarly articles and/or disseminating current information on research and development in a particular subject field."[11] In the 2010 eighth edition of the *Introduction to Technical Services*, Evans, Intner, and Weihs provide detailed descriptions of the categories of journals. The following are the types important to health professional communities: (1) learned journals for specialists (for example, research journal publications), and (2) practical professional journals in applied fields, including medicine.[12] The words *periodical, journal,* and *serial* are commonly used interchangeably to describe these types of publications.

Health Sciences Information Environments and User Communities

Today, health sciences (HS) libraries are in complex environments; they may serve hospitals, medical schools, academic medical centers, or entire health systems.[13–16] Periodicals, in both printed and electronic formats, are one of the major components of the collections in HS information settings. Overall, they are the most used resources in many HS libraries.[17] Butter et al. state that academic health communities consume vast amounts of information, primarily in the form of electronic scholarly articles.[18] Many research findings show that health-related professionals use scholarly journals as the preferred sources for cutting-edge information.[19–21] In 1980, Stinson and Mueller surveyed 402 health professionals and identified their health information usage; the findings show that a typical health professional spent approximately five hours per month using medical journals, the most popular sources of information.[22] Health-related professionals may also publish the findings of their research and results of their work in scholarly journal publications and that eventually contributes to scholarly communication.[23]

Medical journals play a significant role in support of health care, education, research, and translational medicine. These resources may affect how physicians provide patient care, as well as how public health professionals develop policies and take action.[24] Currently, many health-care providers (including physicians, nurses, and allied health professionals) are required to integrate evidence-based medicine (EBM) models into their practices. Physicians and clinicians must have immediate access to relevant evidence (usually journal articles) when critical clinical decisions are to be made.[25] De Groote and Dorsch report that print journal usage decreased significantly following the introduction of online journals, regardless of whether a journal was available only in print, online, or both at an academic health sciences library.[26] Due to the increasing use of full-text journals in electronic format, many HS information settings are currently maintaining, but decreasing, subscriptions to printed journals and acquiring substantial collections of full-text journals in electronic format.[27] However, the health information user communities expect and demand easy access to current journal resources anywhere, anytime, regardless of their locations.[28] Therefore, most HS libraries have chosen to greatly reduce or even eliminate print journals.[29–31]

Quality of Health Sciences Journals: Peer-Review Process and Journal Impact Factors

Many HS periodicals are scholarly journals; therefore, they are peer-reviewed publications. The publishers of the periodicals include, but are not limited to, scholarly societies, university presses, professional associations, trade organizations, commercial publishers, and nonprofit organizations.[32] The peer-review process means that an article is chosen to be published based on evaluations by the journal editor and a panel of experts on the subject. These experts, known as referees, "are responsible for determining if the subject of the article falls within the scope of the publication and for evaluating originality, quality of research, clarity of presentation, etc."[33]

Miguel, Chinchilla-Rodríguez, and de Moya-Anegón state that "journal quality depends largely upon compliance with editorial standards for the presentation and organization of contents to ensure the scientific rigor of all articles published and thereby fortify the journal's standing."[34] The peer-review process has become an unavoidable assessment used in scholarly publishing "as a gatekeeper for error correction and selection of quality work."[35] Therefore, it is important for HS information professionals to understand the peer-review process and its purposes and why this process is seen as "a mark of credibility and worthiness" of a scholarly journal's content.[36] A journal's impact factor is another of the most commonly used mechanisms to measure the perceived influence of a scientific research journal.[37–38] It is essential for HS librarians to be aware of impact factor calculations and their importance in selecting journals.

Peer-Review Process and Editorial Policies

The current format of the peer-review process was introduced by the Royal Society of London for Improving Natural Knowledge 100 years after the establishment of *Philosophical Transactions*.[39–40] The manuscripts submitted were inspected by a select group of the Society's members and then recommended to the editor.[41–42] Birukou et al. identify key themes of peer-review practices as:

... a concern for ensuring the correctness of work and not allowing demon-
strably false claims to distort the literature; the need for authors to have
their work certified as valid; the reputation of the society, publisher, or
editorial board responsible for the work; and at the same time, concern to
not inhibit the introduction of valuable new ideas.[43]

In an editorial published in 2012, Thistlethwaite describes the confidential, double-blind anonymous peer-review system, including the process, procedures, and
evaluation criteria used by *The Clinical Teacher* journal.[44] Six steps are taken after
a manuscript is submitted online: (1) making initial assessment; (2) selecting and
inviting three appropriate reviewers to appraise the manuscript; (3) conducting the
external review process; (4) collecting recommendations and then sending them to
the editor; (5) considering all the feedback by the editor and making final decisions;
(6) returning reviews to the author(s) of the manuscript and distributing final decisions to the reviewers.[45] The length of a review can be as long as necessary.[46] The
Journal of the American Medical Association's acceptance rate is approximately
9 percent of the more than 3000 manuscripts received annually.[47] Regarding the
rejection rates, Rockman reports that approximately two-thirds of the manuscripts
submitted to *The Journal of Clinical Investigation* are rejected.[48] The rejection rate
is about 95 percent for biomedical papers in *Nature*.[49] Undoubtedly, the peer-review
process is a necessary procedure to critically assess the contents of manuscripts and
to select legitimate papers for publication.

However, the peer-review process is not flawless. Thistlethwaite states that
peer-reviewing is relatively unstudied; no research results prove that "peer-review
improves the quality of published articles."[50] In addition, subjectivity is an unavoidable bias in external reviewers' ratings.[51] Even though alternative approaches of
the peer-review process have been explored, a double-blind, confidential, anonymous peer-review system remains the common practice in HS scholarly journal
publishing. Usually journal publishers clearly describe the review process and its
procedures in the editorial policies, sometimes including the numbers of external
reviewers invited to appraise each manuscript and the length of turnaround time.
For example, the *New England Journal of Medicine* invites two outside reviewers to appraise each manuscript.[52] *JAMA* (the *Journal of the American Medical
Association*) provides the following instructions to potential authors:

> Median turnaround times from submission to acceptance are 42 days
> (including review and author revision) for all manuscripts and 17 days for
> articles published Online First; for acceptance to publication: 33 days for
> all manuscripts; 18 days for articles published Online First; and 6 days for
> manuscript submission to rejection.[53]

HS librarians need to constantly review the scholarly journals' editorial policies,
especially of the heavily used journals. This is an effective approach for monitoring

the quality of journal collections. Indeed, journal quality is a primary consideration when researchers seek to publish their research findings.[54] Familiarity with the editorial policies of the journal titles with high impact factors can eventually help potential authors choose the appropriate titles and prepare manuscripts for submission.

Journal Impact Factors

The origin of the development of journal impact factor measurements can be traced to the early 1960s. Eugene Garfield and Irving H. Sher created the journal impact factor to help select journals for the new *Science Citation Index* (*SCI*) published by the Institute for Scientific Information (now by Thomson Reuters), which began in 1961.[55-57] As is commonly known, the *SCI* covers major journals related to the fields of clinical science and life sciences.[58] At present, consulting the journal impact factor (IF) information is the de facto approach for determining the importance of a journal.

The method of calculating a journal's IF is based on two elements: "the numerator, which is the number of citations in the current year to items published in the previous 2 years, and the denominator, which is the number of substantive articles and reviews published in the same 2 years."[59] In this case, it's the number of citations in a year to all articles published by a journal in the two preceding years divided by the number of articles published in the same two years.[60-61] For example, according to the *2011 Journal Citation Report Science Edition*, the *New England Journal of Medicine* has an impact factor of 53.298 [citations (total = 37,149) / number of items (total = 697)]; the interpretation of the result is that each article published in this journal between 2009–2010 was cited on average 53.298 times in 2011.[62] If the journal IF value is higher, the scientific prestige of the journal is also higher.[63] Users can use the Web of Knowledge's *Journal Citation Reports* to search for the IF information of specific journals and to run the ranking report of a list of journals by subject areas.

There has been a lot of criticism on the use of journal IF to measure the influence of journals. In a report published by the International Mathematical Union of the Joint Committee on Quantitative Assessment of Research, the authors argue:

> For journals, the impact factor is most often used for ranking. This is a simple average derived from the distribution of citations for a collection of articles in the journal. The average captures only a small amount of information about that distribution, and it is a rather crude statistic. In addition, there are many confounding factors when judging journals by citations, and any comparison of journals requires caution when using impact factors. Using the impact factor alone to judge a journal is like using weight alone to judge a person's health.[64]

However, this practice has become a widely accepted tool for assessing the perceived influence of scientific scholarly journals.[65-67] Many authors use the IF information and the journal's rank to help determine where to submit their manuscripts. On the other hand, some researchers think that the journal IF report was originally created as a tool to help librarians identify which journals to purchase, not as a measure of the scientific quality of an article's research.[68]

HS librarians are responsible for various types of scholarly communication activities, including helping users to identify potential journal sources for manuscript submissions. To users in HS communities, publishing in reputable and influential peer-reviewed journals that have high impact factors and being cited by peers help validate their professional contributions. According to Garfield and Sher (1961), the sociological applications of citation indexes for "personnel evaluation, faculty promotions, and awards, etc." are also legitimate.[69] In a 2013 editorial published in *Science*, Alberts says that the journal IF "was never intended to be used to evaluate individual scientists, but rather as a measure of journal quality."[70] Goodman, Altman, and George state that journals with high IFs tend to have lower rates of manuscript acceptance;[71] Alberts further points out that authors have a tendency to overload highly cited journals with inappropriate submissions.[72] Based on Opthof's research findings, the IF is a valid tool for the quality assessment of scientific journals, but not of individual papers and of individual researchers.[73] In the "Sources for Periodical Selection and Development" section, there are discussions of several almetrics, such as Journal Citation Reports, Eigenfactor scores, and the SCImago Journal and Country Rank.

In response to various kinds of flaws and overuses of journal IF in scientific manuscript submission and journal publishing, the American Society for Cell Biology (ASCB) sponsored a meeting during its 2012 annual meeting in San Francisco and developed a set of recommendations by the attendees, referred to as the *San Francisco Declaration on Research Assessment* (DORA).[74–75] The Declaration states that the IF must not be used as "a surrogate measure of the quality of individual research articles, to assess an individual scientist's contributions, or in hiring, promotion, or funding decisions."[76–77] Issues related to scholarly journal publications and their influence on the development of professional knowledge will continue to be the central points of discussion. Nonetheless, for the time being, the journal IF remains the current standard for evaluating the quality of scientific journals.

Scholarly Communication and Open Access: Trends and Issues

According to a white paper published by the American Library Association in 2013, "scholarly communication refers to the systems by which the results of scholarship are created, registered, evaluated, disseminated, preserved, and reshaped into new scholarship."[78] In general, the process proceeds from the creation, review, and dissemination of scholarly works to preservation for future access.[79] There has been a growing interest in recent years, especially in higher education, in promoting international collaborations for scholarly activities.[80] Butter et al. point out that in HS communities, many health professionals and students travel globally for educational, research, and health-care experience.[81] Therefore, users prefer to access scholarly resources in electronic format, which can be used without geographic barriers. Moreover, they desire a scholarly publishing infrastructure that is able to meet their needs to reach out to a broader audience with a greater impact.[82]

Each year, serial costs use up an increasing amount of the total library resource budget.[83] Many professional publications refer to this problem as a "serials crisis," the "results of declining library budgets and rising journal subscription costs."[84] Scholarly journals are subject to rapid price escalations, but no direct connections have been found between price and journal quality.[85] Regardless of steadily increasing costs, e-journal collections allow HS libraries to better serve their user communities.[86] A lot of recent developments related to scholarly communication first grew out of concerns about increasing costs of information access,[87] but the emergent Internet technology is available and mature enough to explore new publishing models and venues. HS libraries and librarians must continue to experiment with more cost-effective and user-friendly alternatives to the traditional scholarly publishing formats for the provision of greater access and contribution to new knowledge.[88]

Open-Access Literature: Definitions

Suber provides a concise definition of open-access literature:

> Open-access (OA) literature is digital, online, free of charge, and free of most copyright and licensing restrictions. What makes it possible is the internet and the consent of the author or copyright-holder.[89]

OA publications have been established on the Internet for a long time, but the term "open access" was coined as a result of the formal launch of the Budapest Open Access Initiative (BOAI) in 2002.[90–91] In the BOAI statement, two complementary strategies are recommended to achieve the goals of providing "free availability on the public internet, permitting any users to read, download, copy, distribute, print, search, or link to the full texts of these articles, crawl them for indexing, pass them as data to software, or use them for any other lawful purpose, without financial, legal, or technical barriers other than those inseparable from gaining access to the internet itself. . . .":

"Self-Archiving: First, scholars need the tools and assistance to deposit their refereed journal articles in open electronic archives, a practice commonly called, self-archiving. When these archives conform to standards created by the Open Archives Initiative, then search engines and other tools can treat the separate archives as one. Users then need not know which archives exist or where they are located in order to find and make use of their contents."

"Open-access Journals: Second, scholars need the means to launch a new generation of journals committed to open access, and to help existing journals that elect to make the transition to open access. Because journal articles should be disseminated as widely as possible, these new journals will no longer invoke copyright to restrict access to and use of the material they publish. Instead they will use copyright and other tools to ensure permanent open access to all the articles they publish. Because price is a barrier to access, these new journals will not charge subscription or access fees, and will turn to other methods for covering their expenses. There are many alternative sources of funds for this purpose, including the foundations and governments that fund research, the universities and laboratories that employ researchers, endowments set up by discipline or institution, friends of the cause of open access, profits from the sale of add-ons to the basic texts, funds freed up by the demise or cancellation of journals charging traditional subscription or access fees, or even contributions from the researchers themselves. There is no need to favor one of these solutions over the others for all disciplines or nations, and no need to stop looking for other, creative alternatives."[92]

It has been argued that the only reason for copyright should be to give "authors control over the integrity of their work and the right to be properly acknowledged and cited."[93] In 2012, ten years after the BOAI, a new statement was released to provide more recommendations for the development of OA in the next ten years, including the use of "CC-BY [created by Creative Commons][94] or an equivalent license as the optimal license for the publication, distribution, use, and reuse of scholarly work."[95] Creative Commons (CC) is a nonprofit organization established in 2001; it provides free copyright licensing tools for authors and media creators who want fewer restrictions on the "sharing and use of creativity and knowledge."[96] CC licenses provide flexibility for authors in protecting and sharing their works with readers, as well as using and reusing their own creations.[97] The CC-BY license allows for "unrestricted reuse of content, subject only to the requirement that the source work is appropriately attributed," and the only rights reserved are: "No Commercial use (NC), No Derivatives (ND) and Share-Alike (SA)."[98] In order to better understand the status quo of OA publishing, it is necessary to discuss the current business models for publishing, information dissemination and use, and resource preservation.

OA's Business Models:
Gold OA, Green OA, and the Hybrid Model

There are two primary OA journal publishing routes: gold OA and green OA. Following are basic descriptions of these two styles of publication.

GOLD OA JOURNALS

The gold OA scholarly journals are peer-reviewed serial publications that offer unrestricted free access to full-text articles. They are funded through article processing fees charged to authors, advertisements, grants, and other sources.[99–100] These periodicals provide immediate open access on the Internet when the articles are published. Examples follow:

> *PLOS Medicine* (http://www.plosmedicine.org/): published by the Public Library of Science (PLOS) since 2004. It is a research journal with a high impact factor (16.269) and is fully indexed in PubMed, MEDLINE, Embase, Scopus, and other indexes according to information found in the *Ulrich's International Periodicals Directory*.[101–103] Since August 2009, the standard publication fee charged to authors has been U.S. $2,900, with discounts offered to authors who are PLOS institutional members. There are different fee scales for authors from low and lower-middle income countries.[104–105] The Creative Commons Attribution License (CCAL) is applied to all works the journal publishes.[106]

> *PeerJ* (https://peerj.com/): published by PeerJ, which began accepting submissions in 2012. Since it is relatively a new peer-reviewed publication, no impact factor is available. It is fully indexed in PubMed according to the record found in the *Ulrich's International Periodicals Directory*.[107–108] The publisher charges a one-time membership fee for article processing, and there are different fee scales.[109] This journal applies public user content licensed CC-BY 3.0 to all works published.[110]

Because of the fee structure, the gold OA model is not free from criticism, even though the users are able to enjoy immediate free access to journal articles without restrictions. The article processing fees charged to authors vary, and some fees are high. For example, the fee for *Cell Reports* is $5,000, and BioMed Central, an OA publisher, charges over $2,000 to authors for most of their journals.[111–112] Some researchers choose to write a publication fee into their grant proposals;[113] however, it is not a feasible approach for those independent researchers who have no funding support for their projects. Many academic institutions and their libraries have established OA policies and also provide author funding to publish in OA journals. The

Scholarly Publishing and Academic Resources Coalition (SPARC) website provides a listing of available open access author funding.[114]

GREEN OA JOURNALS

The green OA route (also called post-print archiving or author self-archiving) begins when authors publish their work in traditional subscription-based journals, with the articles eventually being offered for permanent public access via OA repositories.[115–117] The authors may deposit OA editions of the approved final manuscripts or the publisher's versions, if allowed.[118] The authors can choose to post their articles on their own homepages, make deposits to their institutional repositories, or archive their OA publications in subject-specific repositories available on the Internet (e.g., PubMed Central, http://www.ncbi.nlm.nih.gov/pmc/).[119–120] According to Harnad et al., the self-archiving method has the greatest potential for providing unrestricted public access, and the venues should be the authors' OA-compliant institutional repositories.[121] Issues related to the green route revolve mostly around access to the authors' published articles.[122] A number of journal publishers allow authors to post personal versions in public depositories with the requirement of a delay time.[123] The SHERPA/RoMEO website provides a list of publishers' copyright conditions for authors archiving their works online in repositories.[124]

THE HYBRID OA MODEL

Some subscription journals provide authors with the option of paying a publication fee to make their articles open access. This model is the hybrid OA.[125–126] Several major journal publishers, such as Elsevier, Springer, and Wiley, have implemented this model.[127–128] For example, Elsevier offers an open access option in over 1,500 peer-reviewed subscription journals, with publication fees ranging from $500–$5,000.[129] In addition, Elsevier has agreements with several funding bodies to reimburse article fees to authors who have received research grants from several government agencies and research institutions worldwide, for example, NIH (United States), the Wellcome Trust (United Kingdom), and the World Health Organization.[130] These agreements help the authors "comply with funding body open access policies."[131] On the SHERPA/RoMEO website, there is a list of publishers with paid options for open access and their fee information.[132]

Institutional Repositories (IRs) and Subject-Based Repositories

Institutional repositories, as defined by the SPARC, are "collections capturing and preserving the intellectual output of a single university or a multiple institution community of colleges and universities."[133] Lynch refers to them as "a set of services that a university offers to the members of its community for the management and dissemination of digital materials created by the institution and its community members."[134] These repositories are centralized sources that preserve and make accessible the intellectual capital of individual institutions or a group of institutions, as well as providing broader dissemination of scholarly publications.[135] Lynch states:

> At the most basic and fundamental level, an institutional repository is a recognition that the intellectual life and scholarship of our universities will increasingly be represented, documented, and shared in digital form, and that a primary responsibility of our universities is to exercise stewardship over these riches: both to make them available and to preserve them. An institutional repository is the means by which our universities will address this responsibility both to the members of their communities and to the public. It is a new channel for structuring the university's contribution to the broader world, and as such invites policy and cultural reassessment of this relationship.[136]

IR resources have become local sources in which authors may deposit their publications. They are also channels to promote the adoption of the green OA model. For example, in 2009, Harvard University's Countway Library developed a repository to assist National Institutes of Health grant recipients with their manuscript submissions, in addition to offering the authors the opportunity to deposit their manuscripts in the repository.[137] The ROARMAP website, a registry of mandatory OA archiving policies, has a list of institutional mandate resources online.[138–139]

Subject repositories are "repositories that collect and provide access to the literature of a single subject or a set of related subjects."[140] PubMed Central (PMC) is a good example of a subject-based repository.[141] PMC was launched in 2000 and was developed by the NLM's National Center for Biotechnology Information (NCBI).[142] It is a free archive of biomedical and life sciences journal literature at the NIH/NLM, which provides permanent access to all the content deposited in it.[143] Since 2005, PMC has also been the designated repository for researchers who are NIH grant recipients.[144–145] In addition, PMC is also a repository for participating journal publishers; the Medical Library Association has made the past issues of its publication, *Journal of the Medical Library Association* (JMLS), available on PMC.[146–147] On the PMC website, users can find a downloadable list of the journal titles deposited in the PMC archive.[148] Currently, the PMC has two international extensions, Europe PMC and PMC Canada, both of which are supported by the NLM.[149] The Directory of Open Access Repositories (OpenDOAR) is an authoritative source for identifying academic open-access repositories; the site offers searchable functions by repository contents.[150]

The NIH Public Access Policy

The NIH Public Access Policy is the legal mandate from the NIH, voted into law by Congress in January 2008, and is a significant facilitator of the OA movement.[151] The law states:

> *The Director of the National Institutes of Health shall require that all investigators funded by the NIH submit or have submitted for them to the National Library of Medicine's PubMed Central an electronic version of their final, peer-reviewed manuscripts upon acceptance for publication, to be made publicly available no later than 12 months after the official date of publication: Provided, That the NIH shall implement the public access policy in a manner consistent with copyright law* [italics in original].[152]

Since April 7, 2008, the NIH Public Access Policy has applied "to all peer-reviewed articles that arise, in whole or in part, from direct costs funded by NIH, or from NIH staff, that are accepted for publication," and the PMC is the "NIH digital archive of the full-text, peer-reviewed journal articles."[153] However, according to the NIH Public Access Policy's copyright statement, "all of the material available from the PMC site is provided by the respective publishers or authors"[154]; this leaves the copyright with the author of the work.[155] Butter et al. explain these copyright issues and say that not all NIH Policy articles are made freely accessible because the license the article is published under still applies; about 20 percent of articles have OA licenses.[156]

■ ■ ■

In summary, HS librarians face serious challenges in handling scholarly communication and managing their serials collections. Due to the current development of the OA movement, an increasing number of high-quality, peer-reviewed scholarly journals are free for use. Subscription-based journals alone no longer meet user demands. Librarians can consult the PMC journal list to identify qualified titles for their library collections.[157] Today, new information is available quickly, and there is a growing interest among authors who wish to see their scholarly output reach out to a wider audience, create a broader impact, and be more open for use and reuse.[158] The following section provides several useful sources for finding information on current HS periodical titles, including subscription-based and OA journals.

Sources for Periodical Selection and Development

HS information professionals use a variety of aids for the selection of periodical titles. Some librarians look at what other libraries have in their collections to help them decide what to include in their own journal collections. The information regarding electronic journal aggregators provided by vendors is also a useful tool for deciding what information systems should be included in a library's print and e-collections.

Catalog and Directory

4.1   LocatorPlus. Bethesda, MD: National Library of Medicine. Available: http://locatorplus.gov/.

The National Library of Medicine (NLM) is a well-known guiding force for health sciences libraries worldwide. Currently, the NLM acquires, licenses, and processes more than 22,000 print, nonprint, and electronic serial titles.[159] According to the NLM's collection development policy, the Library's priority is to collect "scientific or scholarly journals containing signed papers that report original research from all countries and in any language; clinical and other practice journals emphasizing those of interest to U.S. health professionals; review journals summarizing and sometimes analyzing recent research in a field; current awareness periodicals providing cursory summaries that are of particular interest to U.S. health professionals."[160] LocatorPlus is the NLM online catalog and a comprehensive source to search for information on periodical publications. It can be accessed for free on the Internet. LocatorPlus is continuously updated and includes:

- over 1.2 million catalog records for books, audiovisuals, journals, computer files, and other materials in the Library's collections
- holdings information for journals and other materials
- links from catalog records to Internet resources, including online journals
- circulation status information for materials, including those on-order or in-process at the Library[161]

LocatorPlus provides direct access through its "Other Databases" menu to additional free resources:

- NLM databases, including MEDLINE®/PubMed®
- Consumer health information and MedlinePlus®
- History of Medicine databases
- NLM Catalog
- PubMed Central®
- TOXNET® and toxicology databases

- Health services research and HSTAT

- Catalogs of other U.S. medical and consumer health libraries[162]

4.2   NLM Catalog. Bethesda, MD: National Library of Medicine. Available: http://www.ncbi.nlm.nih.gov/nlmcatalog/.

"The NLM catalog is an alternative search interface to NLM bibliographic records for journals, books, audiovisuals, computer software, electronic resources, and other materials using the NCBI Entrez system. The NLM Catalog links to LocatorPlus for access to NLM holdings information."[163]

4.3   *Ulrich's Periodicals Directory.* New Providence, NJ: Bowker (an affiliated business of ProQuest). 1932– . Ulrichsweb.com. Ann Arbor, MI: ProQuest. Available: http://www.ulrichsweb.com/ulrichsweb/.

For more than 80 years, *Ulrich's Periodicals Directory* has been the preferred source of information about periodical publications worldwide. The 2013 edition, a four-volume set, was published in November 2012 with more than 220,000 regularly and irregularly issued serials classified under 903 subject headings.[164] *Ulrich's Periodicals Directory* was first published in 1932 by R. R. Bowker under the title "*Periodicals Directory: A Classified Guide to a Selected List of Current Periodicals Foreign and Domestic.*" This title continued through the third edition, published in 1938. A title change to *Ulrich's Periodicals Directory: A Selected Guide to Current Periodicals, Inter-American Edition* occurred in the fourth edition in 1943. The next change, to *International Periodicals Directory*, was in the eleventh edition, published in 1965. The current title has been the same since 2000, with the publication of the thirty-ninth edition.[165] *Ulrich's Periodicals Directory* is available in both printed and online formats. The electronic edition, Ulrichsweb, is available at Ulrichsweb.com, and the publisher is ProQuest LLC. This electronic resource also includes information on open-access journals, e.g., titles in the Directory of Open Access Journals (DOAJ).[166]

Electronic Databases' Periodical Lists

Health professionals rely on evidence-based resources (especially journal publications) for their practices. Given the huge number of publications, users must access more than a few key journals to stay current.[167–168] Usually, the contents of the health-related subject databases cover mostly journal citations, for example, PubMed/MEDLINE and Embase; therefore they are utilized to retrieve evidence-based journal articles and systematic reviews.[169–170] Following are descriptions of several authoritative subject databases that can be used as sources for scholarly journal titles.

4.4   PubMed/MEDLINE Resources Guide: List of Journals Indexed for MEDLINE. Bethesda, MD: National Library of Medicine. Available: http://www.nlm.nih .gov/tsd/serials/lsiou.html.

This list provides bibliographic information for all journals ever indexed for MEDLINE. Currently, 5,623 titles can be accessed through the NLM catalog. It includes titles that have ceased publication, changed titles, or were deselected. The entire list can be downloaded through ftp (http://www.ncbi.nlm.nih.gov/books/ NBK3827/table/pubmedhelp.pubmedhelptable45/).[171] This downloadable list covers not only currently indexed journals, but MEDLINE's whole range of publications.[172] As of March 2013, 5,064 out of the total (5,623) are journals indexed as *Index Medicus*; a breakdown of information regarding the number of titles in other subsets in PubMed is also available (http://www.nlm.nih.gov/bsd/num_titles.html).[173] The NLM uses a comprehensive journal selection policy to determine whether to include and index a journal in the MEDLINE database. It is recommended that HS librarians review and adopt similar criteria for practice.[174]

4.5   *Abridged Index Medicus* (*AIM* or "core clinical") journal titles. Bethesda, MD: National Library of Medicine. Available: http://www.nlm.nih.gov/bsd/ aim.html.

The *Abridged Index Medicus* (*AIM*) list is a set of core medical journals.[175] The first edition of the *AIM*, a monthly, was published in 1969 and indexed 100 English language journals of clinical interest.[176] It was designed to provide access to literature in English that would be of immediate interest to physicians and libraries in small hospitals and clinics.[177] The hardcopy publication ceased at the end of 1997.[178] Currently, 119 titles are covered, and the *AIM* is available in PubMed as a search subset limit called "Core clinical journals."[179]

4.6   "About Embase." Philadelphia: Elsevier B.V. Available: http://www.elsevier .com/online-tools/embase/about.

Embase is an international database, concentrating on the drug and biomedical literature. This journal database contains more than 25 million indexed records at present and covers 7,600 journal titles (including 2,000 journals not covered by MEDLINE).[180] The title list is available to subscribers only.

4.7   "BIOSIS Previews—Journal List." Philadelphia: Thomson Reuter. Available: http://ip-science.thomsonreuters.com/cgi-bin/jrnlst/jlresults.cgi?PC=BP.

BIOSIS Previews is a comprehensive reference source for life sciences and biomedical research.[181] This database covers 4,817 international serials from biological abstracts. The full list of serials is available online.

4.8   "CINAHL Plus with Full Text: Database Coverage List." Ipswich, MA: EBSCO. Available: http://www.ebscohost.com/biomedical-libraries/cinahl-plus-with-full-text.

CINAHL provides an extensive index for issues related to nursing and allied health. It covers 4,900 journals, including complete coverage of English-language nursing journals.[182] The publisher provides the journal coverage list in HTML, Excel, and PDF format. Users are able to download the PDF file and Excel file on this website. Selection criteria for journal articles are also available.[183]

4.9   Science Citation Index Expanded—Subject Categories. Philadelphia: Thomson Reuter. Available: http://science.thomsonreuters.com/cgi-bin/jrnlst/jlsubcatg.cgi?PC=D.

Science Citation Index is a multidisciplinary index for the science, technology, and biomedicine literature.[184] This source covers more than 8,300 major journals across 150 disciplines.[185] It is easiest to use the subject category search engine to retrieve journal titles related to the target subject areas. However, because each journal may be assigned to multiple subject areas, it is important to remove duplicate records from the search results.

4.10   Scopus Title List. Amsterdam: Elsevier B.V. Available: http://www.info .sciverse .com/documents/files/scopus-training/resourcelibrary/xls/title_list.xls.

Scopus is a very large multidisciplinary citation index covering 19,500 peer-reviewed journals, of which 1,900 are open-access journals. Its subject coverage includes the scientific, technical, and medical fields, as well as the social sciences, arts, and humanities.[186] The title list contains all the resource titles, including journals. It is a downloadable spreadsheet file, so users are able to save the file to a local source and then sort the records by both subject area and source type. The publisher of Scopus has a content selection policy. The publisher lists the percentage of titles by subject area as follows:

- Health sciences: 33 percent
- Physical sciences: 30 percent
- Social sciences: 22 percent
- Life sciences: 15 percent[187]

4.11   PsycINFO Journal Coverage List. Washington, DC: American Psychological Association. Available: http://www.apa.org/pubs/databases/psycinfo/coverage.aspx.

PsycINFO is a subject-specific index covering peer-reviewed literature in psychology, the behavioral sciences, and mental health, of which 80 percent of the entries are journal records.[188] Approximately 2,500 journals are indexed in this database.[189] The publisher provides the journal coverage list in HTML, Excel, and PDF format. Users are able to download the PDF file and Excel file on this website. Selection criteria for journal articles are also available.[190]

4.12   CAplus Core Journal Coverage List. Columbus, OH: American Chemical Society. Available: http://www.cas.org/content/references/corejournals.

According to the website, CAplus covers "international journals, patents, patent families, technical reports, books, conference proceedings, and dissertations from all areas of chemistry, biochemistry, chemical engineering, and related sciences."[191] Use the SciFinder system to access this source. This system also includes the MEDLINE database.[192] A list of all the journal titles indexed is available on this website.

Journal Publishers' Periodical Lists

HS libraries are able to provide online access to all the subscription-based journals published by a specific publisher through a database. Following are descriptions of several publishers' periodical lists included in HS library collections.

4.13   "ScienceDirect Journals: Browse by Subject." Amsterdam: Elsevier B.V. Available: http://www.sciencedirect.com/science/journals/sub/selected/a.

ScienceDirect covers more than 2,500 peer-reviewed journals and more than 11,000 books in full-text format published by Elsevier.[193] The resources cover a wide range of subject areas. Users are able to browse the journal list by subject to view specific groups of journal titles.

4.14   "Wiley Online Library: Browse by Subject." Malden, MA: John Wiley and Sons. Available: http://onlinelibrary.wiley.com/browse/subjects#.

The Wiley online library contains 1,500 journals, more than 13,000 books, and other types of resources in full-text format.[194] The material covers a wide range of subject areas. Users can access each subject area to browse the titles of journals, books, and other types of materials available, and then identify the journal sources included.

4.15   "SpringerLink: Browse by Discipline." Dordrecht, Netherlands: Springer Science+Business Media B.V. Available: http://link.springer.com/.

The SpringerLink provides online access to journals, books, book series, protocols, and reference works.[195] HS libraries are able to access subscription-based journals in full-text format online through this portal.

Journal Impact Factor Report Databases

4.16   Journal Citation Reports. Philadelphia: Thomson Reuters.

The Journal Citation Reports, published by Thomson Reuters, can be accessed through libraries with an online subscription to the Web of Science database portal. This resource provides quantitative tools for ranking, evaluating, categorizing, and comparing journals. The impact factor is a measure of the frequency with which the average article in a particular journal has been cited in a specific year or time.[196]

4.17   Eigenfactor. Seattle: University of Washington. Available:
        http://www.eigenfactor.org/index.php.

Eigenfactor is a free resource on the Internet, with the original citation data coming from the Journal Citation Reports.[197] Eigenfactor ranks journals in a way similar to Google's ranking of websites. Google's PageRank algorithm is designed to bring the best-known, most popular pages to the top of the results page, according to the number of times those pages are linked by other pages in the Google database, regardless of the relevancy of the sites' contents to the search topics.[198] If the number is higher, the probability of being placed at the top of the results is higher.[199] The Eigenfactor score is a "measure of the journal's total importance to the scientific community."[200] Eigenfactor metrics consist of the Eigenfactor score and the Article Influence score.[201] The Article Influence score is a measure of the average influence of each of a journal's articles over the first five years after publication, based on citations received over five years.[202] It rates the journal's IF by measuring the average influence of an article. For example, a score above or below 1.0 indicates that papers published in the specific journal have an influence above or below average.[203]

4.18   SCImago Journal and Country Rank. Granada, Spain: Scimago Lab.
        Available: http://www.scimagojr.com/index.php.

SCImago Journal and Country Rank (SJR) is a free source on the Internet. The original data are from the information in the Scopus database published by Elsevier.[204-205] The indicator was developed based on the use of the Google PageRank algorithm.[206] The calculations attempt to determine the prestige per article of a journal in the analyzed year. Self-citations are excluded from the analysis because a journal can receive prestige only from other journals, not from itself.[207] In addition, the SJR indicator includes only citable articles (primarily original articles and reviews) in measuring IF.[208]

Selected Journal Lists Developed by Librarians

Shearer, Klatt, and Nagy suggest that core lists and selection tools for HS libraries can be used for selection and evaluation purposes for the development of journal collections.[209] Following are several selection tools and core lists developed by HS information professionals.

4.19   "Recommended Core List of Books and Journals for Alabama Public Libraries." Smith, K. H., for Health InfoNet. Available: http://www .healthinfonet.org/Documents/HealthInfoNetCoreListrev2012.pdf.

A list of suggested consumer health journal, magazine, and newsletter titles is included in this resource.

4.20   "Recommended Dental Texts." Medical Library Association Dental Section. Available: http://wdl.usc.edu/services/recommended-dental-texts/.

This is a core list of book and journal titles recommended for acquisition by the Dental Section of the Medical Library Association in support of clinical dentistry.

4.21   "History of the Health Sciences World Wide Web Links." Gallagher, P. E., and S. J. Greenberg for the Health Sciences Section of the Medical Library Association. Available: http://www.mla-hhss.org/histlink.htm.

This is a suggested list of Web resources on the Internet. Users must scroll down to the end of the document to locate a list of journal titles.

4.22   *Essential Nursing Resources for the Interagency Council on Information Resources in Nursing (ICIRN)*. Schnall, J. G., and S. Fowler. Available: http:// www.icirn.org/Homepage/Essential-Nursing-Resources/Essential-Nursing -Resources-PDF.pdf.

Published in 2012, this is the twenty-sixth edition of the ICIRN *Essential Nursing Resources* (*ENR*) list presented as a resource for locating nursing information and for collection development. The list includes print, electronic, and Web sources to support nursing practice, education, administration, and research activities.

4.23   *AACP Core List of Journals for Libraries That Serve Schools and Colleges of Pharmacy: Libraries and Educational Resources Section*. 4th ed. Brown, C., N. Ragland, K. Shields, and B. Yff. Available: http://www.aacp.org/ governance/SECTIONS/libraryinformationscience/Documents/2010% 20Core%20Journals%20List.pdf.

The fourth edition of the *Core Journals List* (published in 2010) is a companion list to *AACP Basic Resources for Pharmaceutical Education* and is an updated version of the 2009 *Core Journals List*. Committees of the Libraries/Educational Resources Section of American Association of Colleges of Pharmacy (AACP) prepare both the Journals List and the Resources List.

4.24   Core Public Health Journals—Version 2.0. Public Health/Health Administration Section, Medical Library Association. Available: http://info.med.yale.edu/eph/phlibrary/phjournals/v2/.

This is a core list of public health journals. Users can browse the key journal list, the titles list, and the subject specific resource lists. Several subject specific lists have been updated:

"Biostatistics"
(http://bit.ly/rFpG8w; PDF, http://bit.ly/tclpIs)—September 2011

"Epidemiology"
(http://bit.ly/v4z9EO; PDF, http://bit.ly/tUkfp3)—November 2011

"Health Education/Behavioral Science"
(http://bit.ly/zHtUbg; PDF, http://bit.ly/AqqyiV)—January 2012

"Health Services Administration"
(http://bit.ly/zXaPmg; PDF, http://bit.ly/GJZwTw)—March 2012

OA Journal Sources

4.25 PMC Journals. Bethesda, MD: National Library of Medicine. Available: http://www.ncbi.nlm.nih.gov/pmc/journals/.

Since 2000, PubMed Central (PMC) has been a free archive of biomedical and life sciences journal literature at the NIH/NLM. A full listing of all the journal titles is on this website, and a downloadable file of the list is also available.[210]

4.26 HighWire Press: Free Online Full-Text Articles. Palo Alto, CA: Board of Trustees of Leland Stanford Junior University. Available: http://highwire.stanford.edu/lists/freeart.dtl.

HighWire Press, a division of Stanford University Libraries, has been partnering with "independent scholarly publishers, societies, associations, and university presses to facilitate the digital dissemination of 1,779 journals, reference works, books, and proceedings."[211] It develops and maintains the Web versions of important journals, including OA titles, in biomedicine and other disciplines. On this Web host, a large number of journals published by learned societies are available for free access after a delay period ranging from 6 to 24 months.[212] A list of journals with free full-text articles online is available on this website.

4.27 Directory of Open Access Journals (DOAJ), "Browse by Subject." SemperTool. Available: http://www.doaj.org/doaj?func=subject&uiLanguage=en.

This free online directory provides comprehensive listings of all open-access scientific and scholarly journals on the Internet. Currently, by June 2013, 9,642 journal titles published worldwide are available, but no journal reviews are available. Users can browse the journal information by title or by subject. Since there are so many titles in this database, an effective way is to browse titles by subject. In addition, users can use the advanced search mode to search articles by author, title, ISSN, journal title, abstract, publisher, or key words fields. "The aim of the Directory of Open Access Journals is to increase the visibility and ease of use of open access scientific and scholarly journals, thereby promoting their increased usage and impact."[213]

Conclusion

Developing a core periodical collection is an important task for HS information professionals and requires a thorough understanding of the user community and the environment. Since every environment is different, the selection of periodical titles varies, based on the user communities, needs and purposes, health-related specialties, services provided, setting sizes, missions of the parent organizations, consortial agreements, and other factors.[214] Periodical publications change frequently as new titles appear, old ones disappear, and names are changed.

Because of the changing environments of scholarly publishing, the provision of access to library-owned or subscription-based scholarly journal publications only is no longer a sufficient determinant of both quality and adequacy of information services.[215] Today, there is a growing number of high-quality, peer-reviewed scholarly journals that are free for use. These OA journals will eventually become major resources in HS library journal collections. HS librarians must sufficiently understand "copyright and fair use, authors' rights, open access, citation metrics, publishing options, digital preservation, and institutional repository development and management."[216] Information professionals must be aware of the most current information regarding periodical publications. In addition, careful bibliographic control must be done to ensure that the periodical information recorded in the library resource databases is current and accurate. That is the only way to guarantee that library OPACs will provide their users with the information they need and expect.

References

1. "*Philosophical Transactions*—The World's First Science Journal." The Royal Society. Last modified 2013; accessed April 15, 2013. http://rstl.royalsocietypublishing.org/.
2. Priem, J. "Scholarship: Beyond the Paper." *Nature* 495, no. 7442 (2013): 437–40.
3. Board on Chemical Sciences and Technology. *Are Chemical Journals Too Expensive and Inaccessible? A Workshop Summary to the Chemical Sciences Roundtable.* Washington, DC: National Academy of Sciences, 2005, p. 4.

4. "History of Publishing." *Encyclopædia Britannica Online*. Accessed April 15, 2013. http://www.britannica.com/EBchecked/topic/482597/publishing.

5. Evans, G. Edward, Sheila S. Intner, and Jean Riddle Weihs. "Serials—Print and Electronic." In *Introduction to Technical Services*, 159–82. Santa Barbara, CA: Libraries Unlimited, 2011.

6. Ibid.

7. Tenopir, C., D. W. King, and A. Bush. "Medical Faculty's Use of Print and Electronic Journals: Changes over Time and in Comparison with Scientists." *Journal of the Medical Library Association* 92, no. 2 (2004): 233–41.

8. Ibid.

9. De Groote, S. L. "Citation Patterns of Online and Print Journals in the Digital Age." *Journal of the Medical Library Association* 96, no. 4 (2008): 362–69.

10. Reitz, J. M. *Online Dictionary for Library and Information Science*. Westport, CT: Libraries Unlimited, 2004–2013. Accessed March 30, 2012. http://lu.com/odlis/odlis_p.cfm.

11. "Collection Development Manual: Journals." National Library of Medicine. Accessed November 15, 2012. http://www.nlm.nih.gov/tsd/acquisitions/cdm/formats29.html.

12. Evans, Intner, and Weihs, "Serials—Print and Electronic."

13. Butter, Karen, Anneliese Taylor, Emma Cryer, and Patricia Thibodeau. "The Growing Crisis: Scholarly Publishing Pressures Facing Health Sciences Libraries." *Journal of Library Administration* 52, no. 8 (2012): 672–98.

14. Aaron, Henry J. *The Future of Academic Medical Centers*. Washington, DC: Brookings Institution, 2001.

15. Kohn, Linda T., ed., and Institute of Medicine Committee on the Roles of Academic Health Centers in the 21st Century. *Academic Health Centers: Leading Change in the 21st Century*. Washington, DC: National Academies Press, 2004.

16. Mallon, William T., and Association of American Medical Colleges. *The Handbook of Academic Medicine: How Medical Schools and Teaching Hospitals Work*. Washington, DC: Association of American Medical Colleges, 2004.

17. Shaw-Kokot, J., and C. de la Varre. "Using a Journal Availability Study to Improve Access." *Bulletin of the Medical Library Association* 89, no. 1 (2001): 21–28.

18. Butter et al., "The Growing Crisis."

19. Ibid.

20. Meadows, Arthur J. *Communication in Science*. London: Butterworths, 1974.

21. Tenopir, King, and Bush, "Use of Print and Electronic Journals."

22. Stinson, E. R., and D. A. Mueller. "Survey of Health Professionals' Information Habits and Needs: Conducted through Personal Interviews." *JAMA* 243, no. 2 (1980): 140–43.

23. Mallon and AAMC, *Handbook of Academic Medicine*.

24. Smith, Richard. *The Trouble with Medical Journals*. London: Royal Society of Medicine, 2006.

25. Alper, B. S., J. A. Hand, S. G. Elliott, S. Kinkade, M. J. Hauan, D. K. Onion, and B. M. Sklar. "How Much Effort Is Needed to Keep Up with the Literature Relevant

for Primary Care?" *Journal of the Medical Library Association* 92, no. 4 (2004): 429–37.

26. De Groote, S. I., and J. L. Dorsch. "Online Journals: Impact on Print Journal Usage." *Bulletin of the Medical Library Association* 89, no. 4 (2001): 372–78.

27. De Groote, S. I., and J. L. Dorsch. "Measuring Use Patterns of Online Journals and Databases." *Journal of the Medical Library Association* 91, no. 2 (2003): 231–40.

28. Butter et al., "The Growing Crisis."

29. Tenopir, King, and Bush, "Use of Print and Electronic Journals."

30. Rupp-Serrano, Karen, Sarah Robbins, and Danielle Cain. "Canceling Print Serials in Favor of Electronic: Criteria for Decision Making." *Library Collections, Acquisitions, and Technical Services* 26, no. 4 (2002): 369–78.

31. Spencer, John, and Christopher Millson-Martula. "Serials Cancellations in College and Small University Libraries: The National Scene." *The Serials Librarian* 49, no. 4 (2005): 135–55.

32. Reitz, *Online Dictionary.*

33. Ibid.

34. Miguel, S., Z. Chinchilla-Rodríguez, and F. de Moya-Anegón. "Open Access and Scopus: A New Approach to Scientific Visibility from the Standpoint of Access." *Journal of the American Society for Information Science and Technology* 62, no. 6 (2011): 1130–45.

35. Birukou, A., J. R. Wakeling, C. Bartolini, F. Casati, M. Marchese, K. Mirylenka, N. Osman, et al. "Alternatives to Peer Review: Novel Approaches for Research Evaluation." *Frontiers in Computational Neuroscience* 5 (2011): 56.

36. Thistlethwaite, J. "Peer Review: Purpose, Process and Publication." *The Clinical Teacher* 9, no. 4 (2012): 201–4.

37. Evangelou, E., K. C. Siontis, T. Pfeiffer, and J. P. Ioannidis. "Perceived Information Gain from Randomized Trials Correlates with Publication in High–Impact Factor Journals." *Journal of Clinical Epidemiology* 65, no. 12 (2012): 1274–81.

38. Garfield, E. "The History and Meaning of the Journal Impact Factor." *JAMA* 295, no. 1 (2006): 90–93.

39. Spier, Ray. "The History of the Peer-Review Process." *Trends in Biotechnology* 20, no. 8 (2002): 357–58.

40. Rockman, H. A. "Great Expectations." *Journal of Clinical Investigation* 122, no. 4 (2012): 1133.

41. Spier, "Peer-Review Process."

42. Rockman, "Great Expectations."

43. Birukou et al., "Alternatives to Peer Review."

44. Thistlethwaite, "Peer Review."

45. Ibid.

46. Ibid.

47. "JAMA Instructions for Authors." American Medical Association. Last modified 2013; accessed June 10, 2013. http://jama.jamanetwork.com/public/instructionsForAuthors.aspx.

48. Rockman, "Great Expectations."

49. Lawrence, P. A. "The Politics of Publication." *Nature* 422, no. 6929 (2003): 259–61.

50. Thistlethwaite, "Peer Review."

51. Ibid.

52. Campion, E. W., G. D. Curfman, and J. M. Drazen. "Tracking the Peer-Review Process." *New England Journal of Medicine* 343, no. 20 (2000): 1485–86.

53. "JAMA Instructions for Authors."

54. Miguel, Chinchilla-Rodriguez, and de Moya-Anegón, "Open Access and Scopus."

55. Garfield, "Journal Impact Factor."

56. Garfield, E., and I. E. Sher. "Genetics Citation Index: Experimental Citation Indexes to Genetics with Special Emphasis on Human Genetics." Philadelphia: Institute for Scientific Information. Created 1961; accessed June 10, 2013. http://www.garfield .library.upenn.edu/essays/v7p515y1984.pdf.

57. Garfield, E. "The Agony and the Ecstasy: The History and the Meaning of the Journal Impact Factor." International Congress on Peer Review and Biomedical Publication. Last modified 2005; accessed June 10, 2013. http://garfield.library .upenn.edu/papers/jifchicago2005.pdf.

58. Opthof, T. "Sense and Nonsense about the Impact Factor." *Cardiovascular Research* 33, no. 1 (1997): 1–7.

59. Garfield, "Journal Impact Factor."

60. The PLOS Medicine Editors. "The Impact Factor Game." *Public Library of Science Medicine* 3, no. 6 (2006): e291.

61. "Glossary—Impact Factors: Understanding the Journal Impact Factor and the Author Impact Factor." Health Sciences Library, University of Washington. Last modified 2013; accessed June 10, 2013. http://libguides.hsl.washington.edu/con tent.php?pid=229635&sid=1985555.

62. "2011 Journal Citation Report Science Edition—Journal: *New England Journal of Medicine*." Thomson Reuters. Last modified 2013; accessed June 10, 2013. http:// admin-apps.webofknowledge.com/JCR/JCR?RQ=RECORD&journal=NEW+ ENGL+J+MED&rank=1#impact.

63. Opthof, "Sense and Nonsense."

64. Adler, R., J. Ewing, and P. Taylor. "Citation Statistics: A Report from the International Mathematical Union." The International Mathematical Union, Joint Committee on Quantitative Assessment of Research. Last modified 2008; accessed June 10, 2013. http://www.mathunionorg/publications/report/citationstatistics0.

65. Opthof, "Sense and Nonsense."

66. Garfield, "Journal Impact Factor."

67. Solomon, D. J., and B. C. Bjork. "Publication Fees in Open Access Publishing: Sources of Funding and Factors Influencing Choice of Journal." *Journal of the American Society for Information Science and Technology* 63, no. 1 (2012): 98–107.

68. "San Francisco Declaration on Research Assessment (DORA)." American Society for Cell Biology. Last modified 2013; accessed June 10, 2013. http://am.ascb.org/dora/.

69. Garfield and Sher, "Genetics Citation Index."

70. Alberts, B. "Impact Factor Distortions." *Science (New York, N.Y.)* 340, no. 6134 (2013): 787.

71. Goodman, S. N., D. G. Altman, and S. L. George. "Statistical Reviewing Policies of Medical Journals: Caveat Lector?" *Journal of General Internal Medicine* 13, no. 11 (1998): 753–56.
72. Alberts, "Impact Factor Distortions."
73. Opthof, "Sense and Nonsense."
74. Alberts, "Impact Factor Distortions."
75. "San Francisco Declaration on Research Assessment (DORA)."
76. "San Francisco Declaration on Research Assessment: Putting Science into the Assessment of Research." American Society for Cell Biology. Last modified 2013; accessed June 10, 2013. http://am.ascb.org/dora/files/SFDeclarationFINAL.pdf.
77. Alberts, "Impact Factor Distortions."
78. "Intersections of Scholarly Communication and Information Literacy: Creating Strategic Collaborations for a Changing Academic Environment.." Association of College and Research Libraries. Last modified 2013. http://acrl.ala.org/intersections.
79. Reitz, *Online Dictionary*.
80. "Intersections of Scholarly Communication."
81. Butter et al., "The Growing Crisis."
82. "Intersections of Scholarly Communication."
83. Evans, Intner, and Weihs, "Serials—Print and Electronic."
84. "Intersections of Scholarly Communication."
85. International Federation of Library Associations and Institutions. "IFLA Statements on Open Access." *Italian Journal of Library and Information Science* 3, no. 2 (2012): 1–5.
86. Butter et al., "The Growing Crisis."
87. "Intersections of Scholarly Communication."
88. Butter et al., "The Growing Crisis."
89. Suber, P. "A Very Brief Introduction to Open Access." Last modified 2004; accessed June 10, 2013. http://legacy.earlham.edu/~peters/fos/brief.htm.
90. Butter et al., "The Growing Crisis."
91. Bjork, B. C., and P. Paetau. "Open Access to the Scientific Journal Literature—Status and Challenges for the Information Systems Community." *Bulletin of the American Society for Information Science* 38, no. 5 (2012): 39–44.
92. "Budapest Open Access Initiative." Last modified 2002; accessed June 10, 2013, http://www.budapestopenaccessinitiative.org/read.
93. Ibid.
94. "Attribution 2.0 Generic (CC BY 2.0)." Creative Commons. Accessed June 10, 2013. http://creativecommons.org/licenses/by/2.0/.
95. "Ten Years on from the Budapest Open Access Initiative: Setting the Default to Open." Last modified 2012; accessed June 10. 2013. http://www.budapestopenaccessinitiative.org/boai-10-recommendations.
96. "About." Creative Commons. Accessed June 28, 2013. http://creativecommons.org/about.
97. "Attribution 2.0 Generic."
98. Redhead, C. "Why CC-BY?" Open Access Scholarly Publisher Association. Last modified 2012; accessed June 10, 2013. http://oaspa.org/why-cc-by/.

99. Butter et al., "The Growing Crisis."

100. Bjork and Paetau, "Scientific Journal Literature."

101. "Publications: Journals." PLOS. Accessed June 11, 2013. http://www.plos.org/pub
lications/journals/.

102. "2011 Journal Citation Report Science Edition—Journal: PLOS Medicine." Thomson Reuters. Last modified 2013; accessed June 10, 2013. http://admin-apps
.webofknowledge.com.pallas2.tcl.sc.edu/JCR/JCR?RQ=RECORD&rank=1&journ
al=PLOS+MED.

103. "Ulrich's International Periodicals Directory: PLOS Medicine (Print)." ProQuest.
Last modified 2013; accessed June 10, 2013. http://www.ulrichsweb.serialssolu
tions.com.pallas2.tcl.sc.edu/title/1371579601631/458679.

104. "Publication Fees." PLOS. Accessed June 11, 2013. http://www.plos.org/publish/
pricing-policy/publication-fees/.

105. "About PLOS Medicine." PLOS. Accessed June 11, 2013. http://www.plosmedicine
.org/static/information;jsessionid=CB71CE243FB671DBDAE4160A35322657.

106. Ibid.

107. Butter et al., "The Growing Crisis."

108. "Ulrich's International Periodicals Directory: PeerJ." ProQuest. Last modified
2013; accessed June 10, 2013. http://www.ulrichsweb.serialssolutions.com.pallas2
.tcl.sc.edu/title/1371582513046/746632.

109. "Pay Once, Publish for Life." *PeerJ.* Last modified 2013; accessed June 11, 2013.
https://peerj.com/pricing/.

110. Ibid.

111. "Cells Reports: Frequently Asked Questions." Elsevier. Last modified 2013;
accessed June 11, 2013. http://www.cell.com/cell-reports/faq.

112. "3. How Much Is BioMed Central Charging?" BioMed Central. Last modified 2013;
accessed June 11, 2013. http://www.biomedcentral.com/about/apcfaq/howmuch.

113. Butter et al., "The Growing Crisis."

114. "Campus-Based Open-Access Publishing Funds: Open-Access Funds in Action."
Scholarly Publishing and Academic Resources Coalition: 2007–2013. Accessed
June 11, 2013. http://www.sparc.arl.org/bm~doc/oa-funds-in-action-attachment-31
913.pdf.

115. Butter et al., "The Growing Crisis."

116. Bjork and Paetau, "Scientific Journal Literature."

117. Harnad, S., T. Brody, F. Vallieres, L. Carr, S. Hitchcock, Y. Gingras, C. Oppenheim,
H. Stamerjohanns, and E. Hilf. "The Access/Impact Problem and the Green and
Gold Roads to Open Access." *Serials Review* 30, no. 4 (2004): 310–14.

118. Butter et al., "The Growing Crisis."

119. Bjork and Paetau, "Scientific Journal Literature."

120. Ibid.

121. Harnad et al., "Access/Impact Problem."

122. "NIH Public Access and PMC." National Library of Medicine. Accessed June 12,
2013. http://www.ncbi.nlm.nih.gov/pmc/about/public-access-info/.

123. Bjork and Paetau, "Scientific Journal Literature."

124. "Publisher Copyright Policies and Self-Archiving." University of Nottingham, SHERPA/RoMEO. Last modified 2006; accessed June 11, 2013. http://www.sherpa .ac.uk/projects/sherparomeo.html.
125. Butter et al., "The Growing Crisis."
126. Bjork and Paetau, "Scientific Journal Literature."
127. Butter et al., "The Growing Crisis."
128. Bjork and Paetau, "Scientific Journal Literature."
129. "Open Access Articles: Elsevier Provides Authors with Open Access Options." Elsevier. Last modified 2013; accessed June 11, 2013. http://www.elsevier.com/ about/open-access/sponsored-articles#publication-fee.
130. "Funding Body Agreements." Elsevier. Last modified 2013; accessed June 11, 2013. http://www.elsevier.com/about/publishing-guidelines/policies/funding-body -agreements.
131. Ibid.
132. "Publishers with Paid Options for Open Access." University of Nottingham, SHERPA/RoMEO: 2008–2013. Accessed June 11, 2013. http://www.sherpa.ac.uk/ romeo/PaidOA.html.
133. "SPARC Institutional Repository Checklist and Resource Guide." Scholarly Publishing and Academic Resources Coalition. Last modified 2002; accessed June 12, 2013. http://www.sparc.arl.org/sparc/bm~doc/IR_Guide_&_Checklist_v1.pdf.
134. Lynch, C. "Institutional Repositories: Essential Infrastructure for Scholarship in the Digital Age. *ARL: A Bimonthly Report* 226 (2003): 1–7, 2.
135. Ibid.
136. Ibid.
137. "SPARC Institutional Repository Checklist."
138. Butter et al., "The Growing Crisis."
139. "ROARMAP: Registry of Open Access Repositories Mandatory Archiving Policies." University of Southampton. Last modified 2012; accessed June 13, 2013. http://roarmap.eprints.org/.
140. Adamick, J., and R. Rezni-Zellen. "Representation and Recognition of Subject Repositories." D-Lib. Last modified September 10, 2010; accessed June 13, 2013. http://www.dlib.org/dlib/september10/adamick/09adamick.html.
141. Armbruster, C., and L. Romary. "Comparing Repository Types: Challenges and Barriers for Subject-Based Repositories, Research Repositories, National Repository Systems and Institutional Repositories in Serving Scholarly Communication." SSRN: Social Science Research Network. Last modified 2009; accessed June 12, 2013. http://papers.ssrn.com/sol3/papers.cfm?abstract_id=1506905.
142. "PMC Overview." National Center for Biotechnology Information, National Library of Medicine. Accessed June 13, 2013. http://www.ncbi.nlm.nih.gov/pmc/ about/intro/.
143. Ibid.
144. "NIH Public Access and PMC." National Center for Biotechnology Information, National Library of Medicine. Accessed June 13, 2013. http://www.ncbi.nlm.nih .gov/pmc/about/public-access-info/.

145. Butter et al., "The Growing Crisis."
146. "PMC Overview."
147. "JMLA: Journal of the Medical Library Association." Medical Library Association. Accessed June 13, 2013. http://www.mlanet.org/publications/jmla/index.html.
148. "PMC Journals." National Center for Biotechnology Information, National Library of Medicine. Accessed June 13, 2013. http://www.ncbi.nlm.nih.gov/pmc/journals/.
149. "PMC International." National Center for Biotechnology Information, National Library of Medicine. Accessed June 13, 2013. http://www.ncbi.nlm.nih.gov/pmc/about/pmci/.
150. "The Directory of Open Access Repositories—OpenDOAR." University of Nottingham, UK: 2006–2011. Accessed June 13, 2013. http://www.opendoar.org/.
151. Collins, M. "Open Access Literature Review 2008–9: A Serials Perspective." *Library Resources and Technical Services* 55, no. 3 (2011): 138–47.
152. "Revised Policy on Enhancing Public Access to Archived Publications Resulting from NIH-Funded Research." National Institutes of Health. Last modified 2008; accessed June 13, 2013. http://grants.nih.gov/grants/guide/notice-files/NOT-OD-08-033.html.
153. Ibid.
154. "PMC Copyright Notice." National Center for Biotechnology Information, National Library of Medicine. Accessed June 13, 2013. http://www.ncbi.nlm.nih.gov/pmc/about/copyright/.
155. Collins, "Open Access Literature Review."
156. Butter et al., "The Growing Crisis."
157. "PMC Journals."
158. "Intersections of Scholarly Communication."
159. "Collection Development and Acquisitions." National Library of Medicine. Last modified 2012; accessed June 13, 2013. http://www.nlm.nih.gov/tsd/acquisitions/mainpage.html.
160. "Collection Development Manual: Journals." National Library of Medicine. Last modified 2012; accessed June 13, 2013. http://www.nlm.nih.gov/tsd/acquisitions/cdm/formats29.html#1027134.
161. "LocatorPlus Fact Sheet." National Library of Medicine. Last modified 2012; accessed June 13, 2013. http://www.nlm.nih.gov/pubs/factsheets/locatorplus.html.
162. Ibid.
163. Ibid.
164. "Ulrich's Periodicals Directory." R. R. Bowker. Last modified 2013; accessed June 13, 2013. http://www.bowker.com/en-US/products/printed_directories/servprintdir_dir_upd.shtml.
165. "Ulrichsweb.com: Frequently Asked Questions (FAQs)." ProQuest. Last modified 2013; accessed June 13, 2013. http://www.ulrichsweb.com/ulrichsweb/faqs.asp.
166. Ibid.
167. Shariff, S. Z., J. M. Sontrop, R. B. Haynes, A. V. Iansavichus, K. A. McKibbon, N. L. Wilczynski, M. A. Weir, et al. "Impact of PubMed Search Filters on the Retrieval of Evidence by Physicians." *Canadian Medical Association Journal* 184, no. 3 (2012): 303.

168. Hildebrand, A. M, A. V. Iansavichus, C. W. Lee, W. F. Clark, A. X. Garg, R. B. Haynes, N. L. Wilczynski, et al. "Glomerular Disease Search Filters for PubMed, Ovid MEDLINE, and Embase: A Development and Validation Study." *BMC Medical Informatics and Decision Making* 12, no. 1 (2012): 49.

169. Lee, C. W., A. V. Iansavichus, R. B. Haynes, S. Z. Shariff, N. Wilczynski, A. McKibbon, F. Rehman, and A. X. Garg. "Kidney Transplantation Search Filters for PubMed, Ovid, MEDLINE, and Embase." *Transplantation* 93, no. 5 (2012): 460–66.

170. "Journal Lists." National Center for Biotechnology Information, National Library of Medicine. Accessed June 13, 2013. http://www.ncbi.nlm.nih.gov/books/NBK3827/table/pubmedhelp.pubmedhelptable45/.

171. "List of All Journals Cited in PubMed." National Library of Medicine. Last modified 2012; accessed June 13, 2013. http://www.nlm.nih.gov/bsd/serfile_addedinfo.html.

172. "Number of Titles Currently Indexed for *Index Medicus* and MEDLINE on PubMed." National Library of Medicine. Last modified 2013; accessed June 13, 2013. http://www.nlm.nih.gov/bsd/num_titles.html.

173. "MEDLINE Journal Selection." National Library of Medicine. Last modified 2012; accessed June 13, 2013. http://www.nlm.nih.gov/pubs/factsheets/jsel.html.

174. De Groote and Dorsch, "Measuring Use Patterns."

175. "Editorials: *Abridged Index Medicus*." *Bulletin of the Medical Library Association* 58, no. 1 (1970): 70.

176. "Editorials: *Abridged Index Medicus*." *JAMA* 210, no. 12 (1969): 2272–73.

177. "Abridged Index Medicus (AIM or "Core Clinical") Journal Titles." National Library of Medicine. Last modified 2012; accessed June 13, 2013. http://www.nlm.nih.gov/bsd/aim.html.

178. Ibid.

179. Ibid.

180. "About Embase." Elsevier B.V. Last modified 2013; accessed June 13, 2013. http://www.elsevier.com/online-tools/embase/about.

181. "BIOSIS Previews: Fact Sheet." Thomson Reuters. Last modified 2011; accessed June 13, 2013. http://thomsonreuters.com/products/ip-science/04_045/biosis-factsheet.pdf.

182. "CINAHL Plus with Full Text: Database Coverage List." EBSCOhost. Last modified 2012; accessed June 13, 2013. http://www.ebscohost.com/biomedical-libraries/cinahl-plus-with-full-text.

183. Ibid.

184. "SCISEARCH—A Cited Reference Science Database." Dialog. Last modified 2013; accessed June 13, 2013. http://library.dialog.com/bluesheets/html/bl0034.html.

185. "Web of Science: Fact Sheet." Thomson Reuters. Last modified 2011; accessed June 13, 2013. http://thomsonreuters.com/products/ip-science/04_059/web-of-science-factsheet.pdf.

186. "What Does Scopus Cover?" Elsevier B.V. Last modified 2013; accessed June 13, 2013. http://www.info.sciverse.com/scopus/scopus-in-detail/facts.

187. "Scopus: Content Coverage Guide." Elsevier B.V. Last modified 2012; accessed June 13, 2013. http://files.sciverse.com/documents/pdf/ContentCoverageGuide -jan-2013.pdf.
188. "PsycINFO: Quick Facts." American Psychological Association. Last modified 2013; accessed June 13, 2013. http://www.apa.org/pubs/databases/psycinfo/index .aspx?tab=2.
189. Ibid.
190. "PsycINFO Journal Article Selection Criteria." American Psychological Association. Last modified 2013; accessed June 13, 2013. http://www.apa.org/pubs/databases/ psycinfo/publishers/journal-article.aspx.
191. "References—CAplus—Worldwide Coverage of Many Scientific Disciplines All in One Source." American Chemical Society. Last modified 2013; accessed June 13, 2013. http://www.cas.org/content/references.
192. "SciFinder Content." American Chemical Society. Last modified 2013; accessed June 13, 2013. http://www.cas.org/products/scifinder/content.
193. "About ScienceDirect." Elsevier B.V. Last modified 2013; accessed June 13, 2013. http://www.info.sciverse.com/sciencedirect/about.
194. "Wiley Online Library: Product." John Wiley and Sons. Last modified 2013; accessed June 13, 2013. http://olabout.wiley.com/WileyCDA/Section/id-404508.html.
195. "SpringerLink: Browse by Discipline." Springer Science+Business Media B.V. Last modified 2013; accessed June 13, 2013. http://link.springer.com/.
196. Garfield, "The Agony and the Ecstasy."
197. "Eigenfactor.org: Frequently Asked Questions." University of Washington. Last modified 2012; accessed June 13, 2013. http://www.eigenfactor.org/faq.php.
198. Vine, Rita. "Going Beyond Google for Faster and Smarter Web Searching." *Teacher Librarian* 32, no. 1 (2004): 19.
199. Ibid.
200. Bergstrom, C. T., J. D. West, and M. A. Wiseman. "The Eigenfactor Metrics." *Journal of Neuroscience* 28, no. 45 (2008): 11433–34.
201. "Eigenfactor.org."
202. "Glossary—Impact Factors."
203. Bergstrom, West, and Wiseman, "Eigenfactor Metrics."
204. Spreckelsen, C., T. M. Deserno, and K. Spitzer. "Visibility of Medical Informatics Regarding Bibliometric Indices and Databases." *BMC Medical Informatics and Decision Making* 11 (2011): 24.
205. "Glossary—Impact Factors."
206. "The SCImago Journal and Country Rank: About Us." SCImago Lab, Granada, Spain: 2007–2013. Accessed June 13, 2013. http://www.scimagojr.com/index.php.
207. Siebelt, M., T. Siebelt, P. Pilot, R. M. Bloem, M. Bhandari, and R. W. Poolman. "Citation Analysis of Orthopaedic Literature: 18 Major Orthopaedic Journals Compared for Impact Factor and SCImago." *BMC Musculoskeletal Disorders* 11 (2010): 4.

208. Falagas, M. E., V. D. Kouranos, R. Arencibia-Jorge, and D. E. Karageorgopoulos. "Comparison of SCImago Journal Rank Indicator with Journal Impact Factor." *FASEB Journal* 22, no. 8 (2008): 2623–28.

209. Shearer, B. S., C. Klatt, and S. P. Nagy. "Development of a New Academic Digital Library: A Study of Usage Data of a Core Medical Electronic Journal Collection." *Journal of the Medical Library Association* 97, no. 2 (2009): 93–101.

210. "PMC Journals."

211. "About HighWire." Board of Trustees of Leland Stanford Junior University. Palo Alto, CA: 1995–2013. Accessed June 13, 2013. http://highwire.stanford.edu/about/.

212. Glover, S. W., A. Webb, and C. Gleghorn. "Open Access Publishing in the Biomedical Sciences: Could Funding Agencies Accelerate the Inevitable Changes?" *Health Information and Libraries Journal* 23, no. 3 (2006): 197–202.

213. "SemperTool: Directory of Open Access Journals: FAQ." Directory of Open Access Journals. Accessed June 13, 2013. http://www.doaj.org/doaj?func=subject&uiLanguage=en.

214. Thompson, L. I., L. J. Toedter, and F. J. D'Agostino. "Zero-Based Print Journal Collection Development in a Community Teaching Hospital Library: Planning for the Future." *Journal of the Medical Library Association* 93, no. 4 (2005): 427–30.

215. "Intersections of Scholarly Communication."

216. Ibid.

CHAPTER 5

Indexing, Abstracting, and Digital Database Resources

LAURA ABATE

As information resources on the Web continue to expand, evolve, and interconnect, health sciences indexes and databases follow suit. MEDLINE, a key dataset of research articles in the health sciences, expanded its coverage by making more of its historical backfiles available online, while PubMed, a popular and freely accessible access point for MEDLINE data, grew in scope to include some additional item types including prepublication records, out-of-scope citations, and articles from the freely accessible archive PubMed Central.[1] CRISP, previously useful for identifying research that had been funded but not necessarily completed, evolved into NIH RePORT and NIH RePORTER, which provide access to NIH-funded research projects and the resulting publications and patents along with a suite of tools designed to analyze NIH research activities.[2-3] PDQ, once a self-contained repository of cancer research and treatment information, transformed into a dynamic and more accessible resource by publishing its information summaries on National Cancer Institute webpages and by integrating and enhancing clinical trials information obtained from ClinicalTrials.gov with additional information useful to cancer researchers and patients.[4]

Health sciences indexes and databases reflect the range of information needed by health-care professionals, researchers, and students, as well as health-care consumers. Consumer health resources (see chapter 11) provide accessible information at a range of reading levels and in a variety of languages to support patient education on health and disease topics. Online textbooks (e.g., AccessMedicine, STAT!Ref) provide health sciences students and health-care professionals with background information, allowing searchers to explore the scope of information available and documenting health sciences knowledge at the time of publication. Where textbooks provide foundational and background information, point-of-care information tools (see chapter 16) are concise, condensed information tools designed to allow health-care professionals to quickly locate, assess, and apply information for patient care. Research databases (e.g., PubMed, Scopus, etc.) provide access to the continuously expanding record of scientific knowledge by documenting and describing individual studies and experiments to support both knowledge acquisition and further scientific inquiry.

While health sciences indexes and databases reflect the range of information needs, they can also be used as a prism for viewing the research process. New information is first available via journal articles that are indexed and abstracted in research databases. The new information may be confirmed or refuted by additional research (and journal articles), and subsequently included in a compendium of information available on a topic and published in a textbook. If the information is strengthened by additional studies and relevant to clinical care, it will be incorporated into a point-of-care information tool. Using health sciences indexes and databases, it is possible to follow information from its first appearance in the scientific literature to its current application. As scientific publications follow the long-standing practice of citing information sources, health sciences databases and indexes can trace the use of information both forward and backward in time via resource citations.

In addition to using health sciences indexes and databases to trace the evolution and aggregation of scientific knowledge over the past sixty years, specialized health sciences databases can go beyond what is published. Using online tools, searchers can identify ongoing research projects as well as those that haven't yet resulted in publication. Searchers can also identify historical materials including both published documents and items from the grey literature and can increasingly access these materials online as digital repositories increase their holdings and new repositories are established. Health sciences indexes and databases are also being deployed in new ways to contribute to the research process by supporting researchers in the identification of potential collaborators, selection of publications for their research, and creation of novel paths for research via translational research or expansion into new disciplines.

This chapter describes the research databases and foundational resources that are most important to health sciences students, researchers, and practitioners. Resources will be described both in terms of their unique contribution to health sciences research and how they interconnect and relate to additional information tools and knowledge sources. This chapter complements information available and the online resources described in chapter 16, "Point-of-Care and Clinical Decision Support Resources," and chapter 11, "Consumer Health Sources."

Contemporary Practice

As indexes have evolved from print to electronic tools and database searching has changed from librarian-mediated to being accomplished by the individual, user expectations have shifted. Many of today's users cannot fathom an information world where only an "expert" conducts searches. Most users and librarians have grown accustomed to or only known an environment in which searches are conducted by the individual. Users may still rely on librarians for assistance in getting started on a project; for advice on locating materials which are proving difficult to identify; and for systematic and comprehensive searches, but few will request searches primarily through a librarian. In 2007, De Groote, Hitchcock, and McGowan published data showing that mediated searches declined from 2,157 searches in 1990–1991 to 18 searches in 2004–2005.[5]

As part of their experience as information consumers, today's users have high expectations for the information tools at their disposal. Both users who have accessed the Web from their earliest years and those who began using it later in their educational or professional careers may have a faulty understanding regarding information availability and the information resources landscape. The seamless delivery of full text via open-linking systems, whether a user is searching PubMed or Google Scholar, may lead users to believe that all information is free and freely accessible. This perception may leave users ill-informed regarding the scope and breadth of information available and of the value of the resources available from health sciences libraries. The rapid retrieval provided by typing keywords into a Web search tool may make it difficult for users to understand the use, impact, and possible advantages of indexing schemes versus full-text searching. Finally, users' ability to harness the breadth of the Web to find *some* information on virtually *any* topic may leave users poorly prepared to identify the best information resource for their needs and to evaluate information retrieved for quality and application.

As the onus of searching has shifted from the librarian to the individual user, the role of the librarian has changed. While librarians remain expert searchers due to their knowledge of information tools and their highly honed skills with individual resources, librarians must now redouble their efforts as instructors to enable users to locate information effectively and efficiently. In their role as instructors, librarians should educate users on the content and prospective uses of information, the structure and design of the data resources, and the search strategies that work best for each resource. This education will occur in a variety of settings according to the library environment, availability of professional staff, and needs of the users. Educational sessions will vary from informal to formal settings (e.g., from Reference Desk inquiries to prepared remarks at Grand Rounds), from general topics to specific resources (e.g., from locating background information to searching Health and Psychosocial Instruments), and one-on-one interactions to classes ranging from a dozen to several hundred students.

While users expect immediate and direct access to electronic information resources, librarians must remain knowledgeable and skilled in locating information in print resources. Some indexes remain accessible only in print format; the information available in print indexes may not be accessible through online search tools. From 1996–2010, the National Library of Medicine completed a project to add older material from Index Medicus and Cumulative Index Medicus to MEDLINE, thereby extending coverage back to 1946.[6] While this change added twenty years of data to the MEDLINE database, indexing data from MEDLINE's various precursors extends even further back, into the nineteenth century. Users who rely exclusively on searching MEDLINE online may miss relevant information that is available in print indexes.

As database coverage changes and electronic resources evolve, librarians need to maintain their knowledge of both print and electronic indexes in order to select the most appropriate research tools. Librarians should monitor coverage dates for relevant databases as the coverage years continue to change, and be able to identify corresponding print indexes that can be used when searches need to be extended to earlier years. Librarians are also advised that comprehensive literature searches will likely require the use of print indexes. In the fourth edition of this book, Perry, Howse, and Schlimgen produced an extensive table describing key print abstracts and indexes, which serves as a valuable reference tool for identifying relevant print indexes.[7] In the third edition of this book, Boorkman provided additional detail on the history of medical indexes, including the titles and coverage years of MEDLINE's predecessors.[8] For detailed information on print indexes and their coverage, readers should refer to these editions.

In addition to monitoring the coverage in terms of year spans, librarians should also monitor the content coverage of online indexes. The specific titles and content indexed by databases change over time, and new resources may offer subject-oriented portals to publications. Librarians should be cognizant of the breadth of the indexes and databases which they select, including the journal titles included and whether those journal titles are indexed comprehensively, selectively, or in some combination of those approaches. Comprehensive searches, such as those conducted for systematic reviews, may require careful searching of multiple databases.

Over the past several years, federated search systems and Web scale discovery systems have been launched by health sciences libraries. These search systems frequently provide a single box search interface similar to popular general Web search engines (e.g., Google, Bing) with the goal of providing a straightforward interface for searching across the library's print and online collections. Federated search systems (e.g., 360 Search, ExLibris's MetaLib, etc.) function by searching multiple disparate resources (e.g., the library's OPAC plus licensed and freely accessible databases) in real time. Web scale discovery systems (e.g., EBSCO Discovery System [EDS], SerialsSolutions's Summon) access a master index composed of data previously harvested from internal sources (e.g., the library's OPAC and/or local repositories), existing databases (e.g., PubMed, CINAHL, etc.), and external scholarly publishing platforms (e.g., Science Direct, HighWire, etc.). Both types of systems are highly customizable so the specific content and coverage of a particular system will likely vary from library to library. As with other indexes and databases, librarians should be aware of the breadth and depth of the available search system and be ready to select an alternative resource depending on the needs of the user and the scope of the search.

From Indexing and Abstracting to Full Text

As the electronic environment has evolved, users' perceptions about databases have shifted. Initially, literature databases mirrored their previously published print counterparts and described articles by author, title, and topic. Early online users were grateful for the convenience and speed with which a literature search could be conducted to identify all articles by a particular author or to identify all articles on one or more topics. However, while early users appreciated the newfound convenience of online searching, users and librarian expectations changed rapidly. Users were no longer satisfied with a printout of citations and abstracts, but began to seek and expect immediate online access to full-text articles.

In contrast to previous decades when print indexes provided the key to locating pertinent full-text articles, contemporary databases offer a range of full-text content. Indexing and abstracting resources such as MEDLINE still echo their print counterparts by recording who/what/where data about journal articles. However, these indexing sources are now frequently integrated with linking systems, which allow users to jump from indexing information describing who wrote an article, what it is about, and where it can be found, to a full-text copy of the original article. Link resolvers such as 360 Link and SFX maintain databases of information about a library's electronic journal titles and their coverage dates, and serve as an intermediary, connecting an article's record in an online index to the appropriate electronic full-text copy of the article. Link resolvers are also commonly used in full-text databases to connect users from a reference list citation to a full-text copy of the document.

In contrast to the previous example where users continue to search an indexing and abstracting source and link from that database to a full-text document, some databases provide all or part of their content in full-text format. For example, Clinical Key provides access to a range of document types including journal articles, books, practice guidelines, and synoptic clinical care information. Much of the information in ClinicalKey is available in full-text format, while indexing and abstracting information alone persists in other areas. ClinicalKey users will find that the search system pulls results from the ClinicalKey's extensive full-text holdings as well as from MEDLINE data for which the full-text availability will vary depending on the collections of the particular library. For some articles in ClinicalKey, indexing and abstracting data alone is available and searched, while for other articles ClinicalKey may retrieve a match based on more extensive indexing of the full-text document as well as the indexing and abstracting data.

Continuing on the spectrum of full-text availability are databases that are full text in their entirety. Databases in this category include resources with the online equivalent of traditional textbooks such as AccessMedicine or STAT!Ref, collections of full-text topic reviews such as the Cochrane Database of Systematic Reviews, and full-text point-of-care databases such as DynaMed and UpToDate (see chapter 16). While items from these databases may be indexed in traditional indexing and abstracting sources (as is the Cochrane Database), more frequently, these databases stand on their own as individual knowledge sources.

Core Research Databases

Core research databases form the backbone of medical research. These databases index and abstract original research articles as they are published in scholarly journals. As such, core research databases contain the latest information available by publishing research reports (e.g., clinical trials results), recommendations (e.g., practice guidelines), and opinion pieces (e.g., letters, editorials), and news articles. The core research databases described in this chapter are integral to comprehensive information searches as they provide an ongoing record of scientific information as it is made available to the public.

Core research databases are generally citation and abstract databases, though they nearly always provide some mechanism for linking to full-text documents. Indexing systems and standards vary by database, but some generalizations can be made. Indexing usually contains some subject classification system which can range from an informal collection of author-provided keywords to a highly structured, consistently applied thesaurus of terms. Core research databases also frequently provide additional information about the article, including type of publication (e.g.,

Meta Analysis, Peer-Reviewed Journal Article), language, and date, as well as information about the research subjects (e.g., human, rabbit), patient characteristics (e.g., gender, age, ethnicity), and research locale (e.g., Taiwan, California).

> 5.1   MEDLINE. Bethesda, MD: U.S. National Library of Medicine. Available:
> http://www.nlm.nih.gov/pubs/factsheets/medline.html.

MEDLINE is the premier biomedical research database in the world. It is produced by the U.S. National Library of Medicine, which provides free access to MEDLINE via the PubMed Web interface. The National Library of Medicine also leases MEDLINE data to commercial database vendors and websites who may provide free access to MEDLINE, or who may sell access to MEDLINE via proprietary search interfaces. Even as the availability of information on the Web and the number of databases has proliferated, MEDLINE has maintained its position as likely the most important research tool in the health sciences and serves as a baseline for health sciences research against which other literature databases are measured.

MEDLINE is highly valued as a research resource for a number of reasons: breadth of medicine and health sciences topics covered; quality standards applied to journals selected for indexing; expanded year coverage; variety of languages and geographic span of journals indexed; a consistent and evolving indexing scheme; and wide accessibility. MEDLINE indexes about 5,600 publications, primarily scholarly journals.[9] MEDLINE covers medicine and health sciences broadly including "life sciences, behavioral sciences, chemical sciences, and bioengineering needed by health professionals and others engaged in basic research and clinical care, public health, health policy development, or related educational activities."[10]

Journals selected for MEDLINE indexing undergo a stringent review process through which they are evaluated for scope and coverage, quality of content, quality of editorial work, production quality, audience, and types of content, and geographic coverage.[11] In 2010, MEDLINE coverage expanded to go back to 1946 by digitizing and incorporating data that was previously available in print: Index Medicus and Cumulative Index Medicus.[12] Although MEDLINE is produced by the United States National Library of Medicine, it covers journals published worldwide. Currently, MEDLINE includes journal articles written in thirty-nine languages, and historically has included articles in sixty languages.[13]

Journal articles are indexed for MEDLINE using a controlled vocabulary called MeSH (Medical Subject Headings). The power of MeSH indexing lies in its consistent application and ongoing adaptation to new concepts and terminology in health sciences. MEDLINE's consistent and detailed indexing can be used to retrieve and sort items to answer specific research questions. Indexers assign MeSH terms to describe the topics of each article, the publication type (e.g., controlled clinical trial, editorial), and geographics (e.g., continent, region, country, state, etc.).[14] MeSH terms can also contain qualifiers or subheadings to further specify the type of information contained in an article (e.g., Economics, Epidemiology, Enzymology, etc.).[15] Multiple MeSH terms may be applied to describe different aspects of an article. For example, an article on assessing a chickenpox vaccination program in Brazil might contain the following MeSH terms:

- Brazil
- Chickenpox/Prevention and Control
- Chickenpox Vaccine/Administration and Dosage
- Child
- Humans
- Immunization Programs/Organization and Administration
- Journal Article
- Review

Part of MEDLINE's influence as a research tool undoubtedly lies in its broad accessibility. Free access to MEDLINE is provided via PubMed (http://www.pubmed.gov/), and numerous additional free and fee-based sources of MEDLINE are available.

5.2   PubMed. Bethesda, MD: U.S. National Library of Medicine. Available: http://www.pubmed.gov/.

PubMed is a popular tool for searching MEDLINE as it is freely accessible and offers a flexible and powerful search environment. The terms PubMed and MEDLINE are frequently used synonymously, although more strictly speaking MEDLINE refers to the dataset, which is available via numerous free and fee-based search interfaces, while PubMed refers to the search interface offered by the National Library of Medicine to search primarily MEDLINE data. PubMed is easily navigable by novice searches, and can also be harnessed by experienced users for complex searches. PubMed can be customized by individual users via "My NCBI" personal accounts, and by libraries or other institutions to reflect local search and display preferences. PubMed customizations include the ability to reflect preferences for full-text linking and local holdings, preferred search filters, and default display formats.[16] Via "My NCBI" accounts, users can store searches and citations. PubMed also offers additional search tools including Clinical Queries and other search filters, a single citation matcher, and the ability to make connections with information in other NLM databases (e.g., MedlinePlus, TOXNET).

In addition to MEDLINE data, PubMed contains records for "In Process" citations, which are generally waiting for the addition of MeSH terms. PubMed also contains several other types of articles, which are not in MEDLINE, including citations from MEDLINE journals that precede that journal's indexing for MEDLINE;

additional citations from journals where only selected articles are indexed for MEDLINE; citations to journals that submit full-text articles to PubMed Central; citations to manuscripts of articles written by NIH-funded researches; and citations to book chapters and books available on NCBI Bookshelf.[17]

    5.3   CINAHL. Ipswich, MA: EBSCO. Available: http://www.ebscohost.com/ biomedical-libraries/the-cinahl-database.

CINAHL, the Cumulative Index to Nursing and Allied Health, is a bibliographic database that provides access to the nursing and allied health literature going back to 1981.[18] While MEDLINE covers health sciences broadly, CINAHL focuses specifically on the numerous and varied disciplines of nursing (e.g., Anesthesia Nursing, Gerontologic Nursing, Private Duty Nursing, etc.), as well as allied health-care fields, including athletic training, physical therapy, physician assistants, nutrition and dietetics, and respiratory therapy, among others.[19-20] Presently, CINAHL indexes approximately 3,000 journals,[21] a significant proportion of which are not picked up in MEDLINE or Scopus.[22]

CINAHL's primary focus is journal articles, but unlike MEDLINE, CINAHL also indexes other sources of information. In CINAHL, users can find references to books, audiovisuals, pamphlets, software, dissertations, and research instruments. In CINAHL, the "Publication Types" field describes the format of the original item (i.e., book, journal article, pamphlet, etc.), as well as aspects of information within that document. For example, research results may be indexed to multiple entries under publication type to reflect that the publication was a journal article, and also that it included tables or charts and included a questionnaire or scale. CINAHL also uses several unique publication types that are useful to nursing and allied health personnel including Clinical Innovations, Care Plan, Accreditation, Legal Cases, and Research Instrument.[23]

CINAHL is indexed using CINAHL subject headings, which are modeled after MeSH.[24] CINAHL's indexing terms include a subject heading to which a subheading can be added in order to specify the type of information presented on a specific topic (e.g., Emergency Nursing/Legislation and Jurisprudence). While many of CINAHL's subject headings reflect its focus on nursing and allied health literature and so echo the terminology used in these professions, other portions of the CINAHL thesaurus are drawn directly from MeSH, including disease and drug topics.[25]

While CINAHL is primarily a bibliographic database, some full-text publications are incorporated. The selected full text in CINAHL includes research instruments, critical paths, standards of practice, government publications, and patient education materials, among others. EBSCO Publishing also provides additional versions of CINAHL with varying levels of full-text and access and indexing of additional titles: CINAHL with Full-Text, CINAHL Plus with Full-Text, and CINAHL Plus.[26]

5.4   International Pharmaceutical Abstracts. Philadelphia: Thomson Reuters. Available: http://thomsonreuters.com/products_services/science/science_products/a-z/ipa/.

International Pharmaceutical Abstracts (IPA) provides in-depth coverage of pharmacy and pharmacology literature. Whereas MEDLINE covers health sciences literature broadly and CINAHL focuses on information relevant to a subset of health sciences professions, IPA provides deep coverage of a specific discipline within the health sciences. In addition to its exhaustive topical coverage of pharmacy and pharmacology, IPA's coverage is geographically extensive and indexes journals published worldwide.

IPA is a bibliographic database that began its life as a print index in 1964.[27] IPA became an electronic index in 1970 and the database generally covers from 1970 through the present.[28] From its inception until 2005, IPA was produced by the American Society of Health Systems Pharmacists.[29] IPA was acquired from this group in 2005 by Thomson Scientific (now Thomson Reuters), a company that now makes IPA commercially available through several database vendors.

To complement the authority of its exhaustive coverage of pharmacology literature, IPA is indexed using seven indexes to provide detailed information on the topics of each article including pharmacy and pharmacology topics and specific drugs or compounds discussed. In 2002, Wolfe described IPA's indexing scheme, which incorporates the IPA thesaurus of pharmacy-related principles; MeSH terms; AHFS Therapeutic Classification System to provide the drug class name, a code number for the specific drug, and the drug's generic name; Drug Trade Names; USAN to supply generic names for drugs; CAS Registry Numbers to link the specific chemical compound(s) in a drug; and IPA's Natural Products Index to document plants and other naturally occurring agents.[30]

While IPA is a valuable research tool for pharmacy-related research, it does not entirely supplant MEDLINE as a research tool in this area. In 1996, Fishman, Stone, and DiPaula showed that both research tools are valuable for pharmacy information searches, and that there is very little overlap between the two databases.[31]

5.5   PsycINFO. Washington, DC: American Psychological Association. Available: http://www.apa.org/pubs/databases/psycinfo/.

PsycINFO differs from MEDLINE, CINAHL, and IPA in both its content coverage of the behavioral sciences and mental health, and also in its broader coverage of item types. While journal records account for 80 percent of the database content, PsycINFO also indexes entire books, book chapters, and dissertations.[32] This diversity in item types and the flexibility of the indexing lends to the depth of PsycINFO, as it permits users to identify items not only by subject but by publication type (e.g., Peer-Reviewed Journal, Edited Book, etc.), document type (e.g., Chapter, Journal

Article, Dissertation, etc.), and methodology (e.g., Clinical Case Study, Literature Review, Treatment Outcome/Clinical Trial). For example, users in need of an introduction to a particular topic might limit a search in PsycINFO to a chapter or literature review, while users seeking the latest scholarly research might limit their search to peer-reviewed journals and specific methodologies, as appropriate.

In terms of subject, PsycINFO covers the breadth of topics related to psychology including the behavioral sciences and mental health. PsycINFO's subject coverage tends to be inclusive, pulling relevant materials from other disciplines as their topics intersect with psychology. For example, PsycINFO is useful for health sciences users when researching the behavioral causes and effects of disease and the behavioral treatment of disease, among other topics. While PsycINFO has considerable overlap with MEDLINE, its specific focus on psychology-related research and its coverage of additional item types support its importance as a health sciences database.

PsycINFO indexes articles from nearly 2,500 journals. Within that group of titles, PsycINFO selectively indexes articles based primarily on their relevance to psychology, and secondarily based on the type of article.[33] Among article types, PsycINFO generally indexes original research reports, literature reviews, meta analyses, surveys, case studies, theoretical reviews, bibliographies, substantive commentary pieces, and errata and usually does not select editorials, news, letters, conference papers, or obituaries.[34–39]

5.6   Scopus. Amsterdam: Elsevier B.V. Available:
       http://www.info.sciverse.com/scopus/.

Unlike the research databases described previously in this chapter, Scopus is not solely a health sciences research resource but is an interdisciplinary research-oriented database. Broadly, Scopus covers the life sciences, health sciences, physical sciences, and social sciences, and indexes the same journal titles as are covered in MEDLINE. Scopus also indexes journal articles from the broader pool of publications in scientific, technical, social sciences, and arts and humanities fields.[40] Scopus's particular strengths derive from its broad topical coverage and its ability to link articles by cited and citing information, both of which permit users to draw upon a deeper pool of research and find connections between research studies which may not have been otherwise apparent.

While Scopus is primarily a citation and abstract database, Scopus records contain additional information on citing and cited research. For the majority of articles published from 1996 through the present, Scopus provides a list of the documents which are cited in the original article's bibliography.[41] This allows users to work backward in time to locate the research findings upon which the articles' author or authors relied. Scopus also provides information on citing articles. Drawing on the same data regarding articles cited, Scopus links individual articles to subsequently published items which cite them. This function also allows users to work forward in time to locate research which drew on and cited a particular article.

In addition to its broad and interdisciplinary topical coverage, Scopus has a more international focus than MEDLINE or CINAHL. Produced by Elsevier B.V., which is based in Amsterdam, Scopus indexes over 20,500 journals from more than 5,000 international publishers.[42] Scopus's primary coverage, including cited and cited by references for most citations, is from 1996 through the present.[43] Scopus also provides significant historical coverage with citations and abstracts, where available, for articles from 1823 through 1995.[44] Unlike MEDLINE, CINAHL, International Pharmaceutical Abstracts or PsycINFO, Scopus does not adhere to a single system for subject classification and organization. Rather, whereas 85 percent of records contain professional indexing terms as well as author-provided keywords, the professional indexing derives from a combination of indexing systems including EMTREE and MeSH.[45]

Additional Research Databases

While the primary research databases can be differentiated by important differences in scope and indexing, these databases are similar in that they are primarily citation and abstract databases and they cover overlapping segments of the original health sciences research. In contrast, the secondary research databases vary widely in format, scope, and representation of original research.

Many of the secondary research databases contain records similar to those of the primary research databases. These databases contain citation and abstract information describing original publications, and may link to or contain selected full-text documents. However, certain secondary research databases demonstrate the ability of databases to provide access to information in other formats. Entrez provides a search interface for retrieving textual information in the form of journal articles and books, as well as for retrieving graphical information on genetic sequencing and chemical compounds. As databases continue to evolve, librarians should remain open to databases that provide information in nontextual formats and innovations in the representation of information.

The secondary research databases tend to be more specialized in scope and to provide more in-depth information for specific health sciences disciplines. While the primary research databases cover a wide range of topics, the secondary research databases cover narrow fields of research in even greater depth than is available in the primary databases. The secondary research databases may focus on a particular population; for example, AgeLine focuses on the geriatric population, and the Native Health Database covers health-related information on Native Americans. Secondary research databases may focus on information relevant to specific health professional fields; for example, AMED provides information relevant to a spectrum of allied health professions. And certainly, secondary health databases can focus on a specific discipline; for example, TOXNET provides toxicology information via a number of different databases, and SPORTDiscus focuses on the field of sports medicine.

While some of the secondary research databases mimic the primary research databases in that they also contain citations and abstracts to original research, other databases provide information on diverse phases of the research process. Citations and abstracts in MEDLINE and other primary research databases generally described completed research. The projects described have usually been designed, funded, executed, and analyzed before entering the databases. Some secondary research databases can be used to identify research at earlier phases in this process, as well as to find commentary on previously published research. NIH RePORTER can be searched to identify research that has been funded but not necessarily completed, and ClinicalTrials.gov and PDQ can be used to identify clinical studies which may be ongoing and still accruing patients. HaPI can be used to identify research instruments in relationship to the studies in which they were deployed.

The following list of secondary research databases is not meant to be exhaustive, but rather representative of the types of databases currently available. Indeed, as database development has accelerated in recent years, it would be nearly impossible to accurately maintain a comprehensive list of health sciences databases. Librarians can use this list both as a guide to the most valuable current resources, and as a reminder to investigate additional databases which may contain information relevant to a specific research question.

Several subsets of databases have been intentionally omitted from this list. Drug information databases are described in chapter 10, "Drug Information Sources"; consumer health resources are detailed in chapter 11, "Consumer Health Sources"; online directories are discussed in chapter 14, "Directories and Biographical Sources"; and point-of-care information tools are featured in chapter 16, "Point-of-Care and Clinical Decision Support Resources."

5.7   AgeLine. Washington, DC: AARP. Available: http://www.csa.com/factsheets/ageline-set-c.php.

- Scope: Professional and selected consumer information related to aging and social gerontology.
- Record type: Indexing and abstract
- Coverage: 1978–Present
- Availability: Vendor

5.8   Allied and Complementary Medicine (AMED). London: British Library. Available: http://www.ovid.com/site/catalog/DataBase/12.jsp.

- Scope: Complementary medicine, palliative medicine, and information for allied health professions including physiotherapy, occupational therapy, rehabilitation, podiatry, palliative care, and speech and language therapy.
- Record type: Indexing and abstract
- Coverage: 1985–Present
- Availability: Vendor

5.9 Biological Abstracts. Philadelphia: Thomson Reuters. Available: http://www.ebscohost.com/academic/biological-abstracts.

- Scope: International coverage of life sciences including biochemistry, biotechnology, microbiology, neurology, pharmacology, public health, and toxicology.
- Record type: Indexing and abstract
- Coverage: 1969–Present
- Availability: Vendor

5.10 ClinicalTrials.gov. Bethesda, MD: U.S. National Library of Medicine. Available: http://clinicaltrials.gov/.

- Scope: Registry and results of clinical trials sponsored by the U.S. federal government and by private industry, occurring in the United States and worldwide.
- Record type: Full-text information on purpose, eligibility, location(s), and contact information on recruiting and closed clinical trials
- Coverage: Open and closed clinical trials
- Availability: Free

5.11 Cochrane Central Register of Controlled Trials (CENTRAL). Oxford, UK: Cochrane Collaboration. Available: http://www.thecochranelibrary.com/.

- Scope: Published controlled trials identified in published databases and from additional published and unpublished sources.
- Record type: Indexing and abstract
- Coverage: No dates specified
- Availability: Vendor

5.12 Database of Abstracts of Reviews of Effects (DARE). York, UK: Centre for Reviews and Dissemination. Available: http://www.crd.york.ac.uk/crdweb/AboutDare.asp.

- Scope: Summaries of systematic reviews that evaluate health-care interventions and the delivery and organization of health services.
- Record type: Indexing and critical abstract of original article

- Coverage: 1994–Present
- Availability: Free

5.13   Embase. Amsterdam: Elsevier B.V. Available: http://www.embase.com/.

- Scope: Broad bibliographic database covering biomedical literature with emphasis on drug-related information; includes MEDLINE records as well as significant proportion of unique records.
- Record type: Indexing and abstract
- Coverage: 1947–Present
- Availability: Vendor

5.14   Entrez. Bethesda, MD: National Center for Biotechnology Information. Available: http://www.ncbi.nlm.nih.gov/gquery.

- Scope: Search interface for forty databases including PubMed (MEDLINE), PubMed Central, Books, and OMIM (Online Mendelian Inheritance in Man); search interface and database structure integrates literature databases with molecular databases including DNA and protein sequence, structure, gene, genome, genetic variation, and gene expression.
- Record type: Varies by database
- Coverage: Varies by database
- Availability: Free

5.15   Global Health. Wallingford, UK: CABI Publishing. Available: http://www.cabi.org/default.aspx?site=170&page=1016&pid=328.

- Scope: International coverage of public health documents including journal articles, books, reports, and conferences.
- Record type: Indexing and abstract
- Coverage: 1973–Present
- Availability: Vendor

5.16   Google Scholar. Mountain View, CA: Google. Available: http://scholar.google.com/.

- Scope: Search tool for scholarly information including journal articles, conference papers, books, theses and dissertations, technical reports, court opinions, and patents.
- Record type: Brief summary
- Coverage: Varies by data source
- Availability: Free

5.17   Grey Literature Report. New York: New York Academy of Medicine Library. Available: http://www.greylit.org/.

- Scope: Grey literature on health services and public health topics including health policy, healthy aging, prevention, health disparities, community engagement, and global health.
- Record type: Indexing and full-text link or document
- Coverage: 1999–Present
- Availability: Free

5.18   Health and Psychosocial Instruments (HaPI). Pittsburgh, PA: Behavioral Measurement Database Services (BMDS). Available: http://www.bmdshapi.com/.

- Scope: Index to research instruments including questionnaires, interview schedules, tests, checklists, rating and other scales, coding schemes, and projective techniques.
- Record type: Indexing and abstract
- Coverage: 1985–Present
- Availability: Vendor

5.19   Health Policy Reference Center. Ipswich, MA: EBSCO. Available: http://www.ebscohost.com/biomedical-libraries/health-policy-reference-center.

- Scope: Broad coverage of health policy including journal articles, books, magazines, and trade publications.
- Record type: Indexing and abstract plus full-text
- Coverage: 1921–Present
- Availability: Vendor

5.20   IndexCat. Bethesda, MD: U.S. National Library of Medicine. Available: http://www.nlm.nih.gov/hmd/indexcat/ichome.html.

- Scope: Historical medical database provides access to online version of the *Index-Catalogue of the Library of the Surgeon-General's Office* which indexed monographs and periodical literature from 1880 through 1961 and several catalogs of historical books, pamphlets, and reports.
- Record type: Indexing
- Coverage: Antiquity–1961
- Availability: Free

5.21   Mosby's Index. Bethesda, MD: U.S. National Library of Medicine. Available: http://www.nlm.nih.gov/hmd/indexcat/ichome.html.

- Scope: International nursing literature including peer-reviewed journals, trade publications, and electronic-only titles.
- Record type: Indexing and abstract
- Coverage: 1974–Present
- Availability: Vendor

5.22   Native Health Database. Albuquerque, NM: University of New Mexico
Health Sciences Library and Informatics Center. Available: http://hsc.unm
.edu/community/cnah/nhd.shtml.

- Scope: Health-related information including journals, articles, reports, and
surveys on American Indians, Alaska Natives, and Canadian First Nations.
- Record type: Indexing and abstract
- Coverage: 1672–Present
- Availability: Free

5.23   NIH RePORTER. Bethesda, MD: National Institutes of Health. Available:
http://projectreporter.nih.gov/reporter.cfm.

- Scope: Information on NIH-funded research projects and publications and
patents resulting from NIH funding.
- Record type: Indexing and abstract
- Coverage: 1987–Present
- Availability: Free

5.24   PDQ. Bethesda, MD: National Cancer Institute. Available:
http://www.cancer.gov/cancertopics/pdq/cancerdatabase.

- Scope: Cancer information summaries for health professionals and patients; Dictionary of Cancer Terms; NCI Drug Dictionary cancer clinical trials
registry, directory of health professionals and organizations involved with
cancer.
- Record type: Full-text articles; full-text clinical trials information; directory
- Coverage: Current
- Availability: Free

5.25   POPLINE. Baltimore, MD: Knowledge for Health (K4Health) Project.
Available: http://www.popline.org/.

- Scope: Index to scholarly articles, reports, books, and grey literature on
population and family planning.
- Record type: Indexing and abstract
- Coverage: 1970–Present
- Availability: Free

5.26   Rare Disease Database. Danbury, CT: National Organization for Rare
Disorders. Available: http://www.rarediseases.org/rare-disease-information/
rare-diseases.

- Scope: Consumer-oriented information on symptoms, causes, standard
and investigational therapies, and related organizations for rare diseases.
- Record type: Full-text articles

- Coverage: Current
- Availability: Vendor

5.27   REHABDATA. Landover, MD: National Rehabilitation Information Center. Available: http://www.naric.com/?q=en/REHABDATA.

- Scope: Articles, reports, and books on disability and rehabilitation topics.
- Record type: Indexing and abstract plus select full-text articles
- Coverage: 1956–Present
- Availability: Free

5.28   SPORTDiscus with Full-Text. Ottawa: Sport Information Resource Centre (SIRC). Available: http://www.sportdiscus.com/.

- Scope: Scholarly information on sport and exercise science including journal articles, books and book chapters, theses and dissertations, conference proceedings, and magazine articles.
- Record type: Indexing and abstract plus full-text
- Coverage: 1800–Present
- Availability: Vendor

5.29   TOXNET. Bethesda, MD: U.S. National Library of Medicine. Available: http://toxnet.nlm.nih.gov/.

- Scope: Collection of fourteen databases on toxicology, hazardous chemicals, environmental health, and toxic releases; databases may be searched individually or via an integrated search interface.
- Record type: Varies by database
- Coverage: Varies by database
- Availability: Free

5.30   Web of Science. Philadelphia: Thomson Reuters. Available: http://thomson reuters.com/products_services/science/science_products/a-z/web_of _science/.

- Scope: Multidisciplinary scholarly database with extensive coverage of science disciplines as well as additional scholarly fields. Tracks "cited by" information at article level to permit users to find related articles as well as analyze citation patterns by article, journal, author, etc.
- Record type: Indexing and abstract
- Coverage: 1900–Present
- Availability: Vendor

Background Information Sources

As health sciences literature databases have evolved from strictly indexing and abstracting tools to repositories providing access to full-text and linkages to related articles and documents, textbooks have also evolved. Long a mainstay of library resources, textbooks now exist as both in the classic model of discrete static volumes issued periodically as well as in the form of dynamic interconnected information resources. In both print and online formats, textbooks continue to serve as essential sources of background information for health-care students and professionals.

In addition to using standard methods of evaluating textbooks, librarians evaluating online textbook resources should consider quality criteria that are specific to the online environment including additional content available on the platform, update and/or edition availability, and available digital formats. In terms of content available on a platform, some online textbook publishers provide essentially a digital bookshelf that the individual library can populate with desired titles and editions (e.g., Books@Ovid, R2 Library, etc.), while other textbook publishers offer integrated access to a preestablished roster of titles along with supplementary content and tools (e.g., AccessMedicine, ClinicalKey). Librarians may need to weigh the ability to customize the selection of content against the value of more integrated access to information, which may drive higher usage.

To date, the majority of online textbook publishers offer numbered editions of e-texts, although at least one online textbook, Harrison's Online, is updated online as new information is available and in advance of the release of the next numbered edition. Publishers and platforms vary in their sales and licensing terms and librarians may need to select the option that best meets their library's needs, be it access via an annual subscription or perpetual access purchase. Annual subscriptions offer the advantage of continuously updated editions with the disadvantage of paying yearly for that content. Perpetual access subscriptions offer more options for customization of a collection, but require vigilance to maintain a current collection and may also pose additional questions regarding how to manage outdated purchased online editions.

Most online textbooks are available online in some combination of HTML and/or PDF formats although the availability of health sciences books via e-readers and on mobile platforms is increasing. Librarians need to maintain awareness of their users' needs to make appropriate platform and format selections, especially as a single text may be available from multiple vendors.

5.31   AccessMedicine. Columbus, OH: The McGraw-Hill Companies. Available: http://www.accessmedicine.com/.

- Scope: Full-text access to more than sixty basic sciences and clinical medicine texts including Harrison's Principles of Internal Medicine; access to additional content and tools including multimedia files, self-assessment tools, drug information, diagnostic test information, clinical guidelines, case files, and patient education. Related resources providing access to specialty resource libraries include AccessAnesthesiology, AccessEmergencyMedicine, AccessPharmacy, and AccessSurgery.

- Coverage: Current

- Availability: Vendor

5.32   Bookshelf. Bethesda, MD: National Center for Biotechnology Information. Available: http://www.ncbi.nlm.nih.gov/books.

- Scope: Full-text life-sciences, health-care, and public health books.

- Coverage: Current and prior editions

- Availability: Free

5.33   Books@Ovid. New York: Ovid Technologies. Available: http://www.ovid.com/site/products/books_landing.jsp.

- Scope: Full-text access to current and prior editions of books in medicine, nursing and health professions, behavioral sciences, and basic sciences primarily from the publisher Lippincott Williams and Wilkins. Titles may be acquired by edition purchase or annual subscription; titles can be selected individually or in packages.

- Coverage: Current and prior editions

- Availability: Vendor

5.34   ClinicalKey. Philadelphia: Elsevier, Inc. Available: http://www.clinicalkey.com/.

- Scope: Full-text access to collection of textbooks, journals, clinics, and practice guidelines as well as drug information and patient education handouts. Standard collection includes current editions of more than 1,000 books and access to more than 500 journal and Clinics of North America titles. Additional book and journal content may be licensed by package via specialty collections (e.g., Advanced Basic Sciences, Critical Care Medicine, etc.).

- Coverage: Current editions, most recent five years rolling coverage

- Availability: Vendor

5.35   EBSCOhost E-Books. Ipswich, MA: EBSCO. Available: http://www.ebscohost.com/ebooks.

- Scope: Full-text access to current and prior editions of books in medicine, nursing and health professions, and public health. Titles may be acquired by edition purchase or annual subscription; titles can be selected individually, in packages, or via patron-driven acquisition.

- Coverage: Current and prior editions
- Availability: Vendor

5.36   JAMAevidence. Columbus, OH: McGraw-Hill. Available: http://jamaevidence.com/.

- Scope: Full-text access to information on evaluating the medical literature. This resource provides the complete contents of three highly regarded books designed to support education on medical literature evaluation and assessment skills: *Users' Guides to the Medical Literature: A Manual for Evidence-Based Clinical Practice, The Rational Clinical Examination: Evidence-Based Clinical Diagnosis,* and *Care at the Close of Life: Evidence and Experience.* Supplementary educational materials are also available including educational guides, a glossary, and worksheets.
- Coverage: Current editions
- Availability: Vendor

5.37   Mosby's Nursing Consult. Philadelphia: Elsevier. Available: http://info.mdconsult.com/.

- Scope: Full-text clinical nursing resource provides access to more than forty books, evidence-based nursing monographs, forty journals, practice guidelines, clinical updates, and Mosby's Index.
- Coverage: Current editions
- Availability: Vendor

5.38   Pediatric Care Online. Elk Grove Village, IL: American Academy of Pediatrics. Available: http://www.pediatriccareonline.org/.

- Scope: Primary care pediatrics information including full-text textbook and point-of-care information tool.
- Coverage: Current
- Availability: Vendor

5.39   PsychiatryOnline. Arlington, VA: American Psychiatric Publishing. Available: http://psychiatryonline.org/.

- Scope: Psychiatry resource provides full-text access to the DSM (current and prior editions), nine textbooks, four journals, APA practice guidelines, continuing education and self-assessment resources, and patient education.
- Coverage: Current
- Availability: Vendor

5.40   R2 Library. King of Prussia, PA: Rittenhouse Book Distributors. Available: http://www.r2library.com/.

- Scope: Full-text access to current and prior editions of books in medicine, allied health, nursing, pharmacy, public health, and consumer health. Titles selected individually and acquired by edition.
- Coverage: Current and prior editions
- Availability: Vendor

5.41   STAT!Ref. Jackson, WY: Teton Data Systems. Available: http://www.statref.com/.

- Scope: Full-text access to current and prior editions of books in medicine, dentistry, nursing, and pharmacy. Titles available by annual subscription; titles can be selected individually or in packages.
- Coverage: Current editions
- Availability: Vendor

5.42   Unbound Medicine. Charlottesville, VA: Unbound Medicine. Available: http://www.unboundmedicine.com/.

- Scope: Mobile and desktop access to clinical reference texts.
- Coverage: Current editions
- Availability: Vendor

Education Support Sources

As health sciences information resources have evolved and grown, new resources have emerged to support education. These resources frequently integrate text and audiovisual components, and also provide mechanisms for instructors and/or students to track progress or identify areas for further study. This type of resource includes platforms that integrate background and/or descriptive information with complementary audiovisual content; skills portals where users can read about, watch, and assess their knowledge of specific clinical skills; and question banks designed to support study for educational and licensing exams.

5.43   Exam Master. Newark, DE: Exam Master Corporation. Available: http://www.exammaster.com/.

- Scope: Question banks designed to support study for and simulate experience of USMLE, medical board certification, PANCE/PANRE, NBDE, NAPLEX, and NCLEX exams. Includes questions and answer explanations.
- Resource type: Exam questions and answers
- Availability: Vendor

5.44   Imaging Reference Center. Salt Lake City, UT: Amirsys. Available:
        http://www.amirsysrc.com/.

   • Scope: Database of x-ray, CT, MR, ultrasound, and illustrated images with
     detailed clinical annotations written by imaging experts and supported by
     medical literature citations. This resource is designed to support students
     and clinicians in the interpretation of imaging tests.

   • Resource type: Annotated images

   • Availability: Vendor

5.45   Introduction to Physical Examination. Athens, OH: Fitne. Available:
        http://www.fitne.net/.

   • Scope: Online videos providing instruction in physical exam techniques.
     Additional resources from this vendor include additional video content
     (e.g., nurse theorists) as well as interactive instructional programs (e.g.,
     surgical instruments, vital signs, etc.).

   • Resource type: Videos

   • Availability: Vendor

5.46   Lippincott's Nursing Procedures and Skills. Philadelphia: Wolters Kluwer
        Health. Available: http://lippincottsolutions.com/solutions/lnps.

   • Scope: Detailed written instructions plus images for clinical nursing pro-
     cedures and skills including skills checklists and quick lists.

   • Resource type: Written instructions and images

   • Availability: Vendor

5.47   Mosby's Nursing Skills. St. Louis, MO: Elsevier. Available:
        http://confidenceconnected.com/products/mosbys_skills/overview/.

   • Scope: Instructional tool for learning nursing skills. Information on each
     skill includes a quick sheet, extended text description, supply list, video
     demonstration, images, skill assessment, and checklist.

   • Resource type: Written instructions and videos

   • Availability: Vendor

5.48   Nursing Education in Video. Alexandria, VA: Alexander Street Press.
        Available: http://mcom.alexanderstreet.com/.

   • Scope: Videos designed and created to provide instruction to nurses
     and nursing assistants on clinical (e.g., airway management), professional
     (ethical issues in nursing), and management topics (quality assurance).

   • Resource type: Videos

   • Availability: Vendor

5.49   Primal Interactive Human. London: Primal Pictures. Available:
        http://www.primalpictures.com.

•   Scope: 3D anatomy viewer and image library includes annotations and
    labels and permits the user to study anatomy from three-dimensional
    models. Related resources provide access to additional information (e.g.,
    Anatomy and Physiology Online) and specific anatomical regions (e.g., 3D
    Anatomy for Otolaryngology and Head and Neck Surgery).

•   Resource type: 3D images

•   Availability: Vendor

5.50   USMLEasy. Columbus, OH: McGraw-Hill. Available:
        http://www.usmleasy.com/.

•   Scope: Question banks designed to support study for and simulate
    experience of USMLE exam steps one through three. Includes questions
    and answer explanations.

•   Resource type: Exam questions and answers

•   Availability: Vendor

References

1. "Fact Sheet: What's the Difference between MEDLINE and PubMed?" National Library of Medicine. Last modified 2010. http://www.nlm.nih.gov/pubs/factsheets/dif_med_pub.html.
2. Ibid.
3. "RePORT Frequently Asked Questions (FAQs)." National Institutes of Health. Last modified 2012. http://report.nih.gov/faq.aspx.
4. "PDQ—NCI's Comprehensive Cancer Database." National Cancer Institute. Last modified 2011. http://www.cancer.gov/cancertopics/pdq/cancerdatabase.
5. De Groote, S. I., K. Hitchcock, and R. McGowan. "Trends in Reference Usage Statistics in an Academic Health Sciences Library." *Journal of the Medical Library Association* 95, no. 1 (2007): 23–30.
6. "OLDMEDLINE Data." National Library of Medicine. Last modified 2012. http://www.nlm.nih.gov/databases/databases_oldmedline.html.
7. Perry, J., D. K. Howse, and J. Schlimgen. "Indexing, Abstracting, and Digital Database Resources." In *Introduction to Reference Sources in the Health Sciences*, 5th ed., edited by Jeffrey T. Huber, Jo Ann Boorkman, and Jean C. Blackwell, 53–98. New York: Neal-Schuman, 2008.
8. Boorkman, Jo Ann. "Electronic Bibliographic Databases." In *Introduction to Reference Sources in the Health Sciences*, 3rd ed., edited by Fred W. Roper and Jo Ann Boorkman, 75–95. Chicago: Scarecrow Press, 1994.
9. "Fact Sheet MEDLINE." National Library of Medicine. Last modified 2011. http://www.nlm.nih.gov/pubs/factsheets/medline.html.

10. Ibid.
11. "Fact Sheet MEDLINE Journal Selection." National Library of Medicine. Last modified 2012. http://www.nlm.nih.gov/pubs/factsheets/jsel.html.
12. "OLDMEDLINE Data."
13. "Fact Sheet MEDLINE."
14. "MeSH Record Types." National Library of Medicine. Last modified 2012. http://www.nlm.nih.gov/mesh/intro_record_types.html.
15. Ibid.
16. "Fact Sheet: What's the Difference between MEDLINE and PubMed?"
17. Ibid.
18. "The CINAHL Database." EBSCOhost. Accessed July 16, 2013. http://www.ebsco host.com/biomedical-libraries/the-cinahl-database.
19. Ibid.
20. "Subject Headings and Subject Coverage." EBSCOhost. Accessed July 16, 2013. http://www.ebscohost.com/resources/cinahl-plus-with-full-text/lma/subject-head ings.htm.
21. "The CINAHL Database."
22. Hill, B. "Comparison of Journal Title Coverage between Cinahl and Scopus." *Journal of the Medical Library Association* 97, no. 4 (2009): 313–14.
23. "Document Types." EBSCOhost. Accessed July 16, 2013. http://www.ebscohost .com/resources/cinahl-plus-with-full-text/lma/document-types.htm.
24. "Subject Headings and Subject Coverage."
25. "CINAHL Subject Headings." Last modified 2002. http://library.med.utah.edu/ed/ eduservices/handouts/CINAHL_Web/cinahl_headings.pdf.
26. "CINAHL via EBSCOhost." EBSCOhost. Last modified 2012. http://www.ebsco host.com/uploads/general/CINAHL_CHART_0512.pdf.
27. "International Pharmaceutical Abstracts (IPA)." Thomson Reuters. Accessed July 16, 2013. http://thomsonreuters.com/products_services/science/science_products/ a-z/ipa/.
28. Ibid.
29. Ibid.
30. Wolfe, C. "International Pharmaceutical Abstracts: What's New and What Can IPA Do for You?" *American Journal of Health-System Pharmacy* 59, no. 23 (2002): 2360–61.
31. Fishman, D. L., V. L. Stone, and B. A. DiPaula. "Where Should the Pharmacy Researcher Look First? Comparing International Pharmaceutical Abstracts and MEDLINE." *Bulletin of the Medical Library Association* 84, no. 3 (1996): 402–8.
32. "PsycINFO." American Psychological Association. Last modified 2012. http:// www.apa.org/pubs/databases/psycinfo/index.aspx.
33. "Journal Article Selection Criteria." American Psychological Association. Last modified 2012. http://www.apa.org/pubs/databases/psycinfo/publishers/journal -article.aspx.
34. "PsycARTICLES." American Psychological Association. Last modified 2012. http://www.apa.org/pubs/databases/psycarticles/index.aspx.

35. "PsycBOOKS." American Psychological Association. Last modified 2012. http://www.apa.org/pubs/databases/psycbooks/index.aspx.
36. "PsycEXTRA." American Psychological Association. Last modified 2012. http://www.apa.org/pubs/databases/psycextra/index.aspx.
37. "PsycCRITIQUES." American Psychological Association. Last modified 2012. http://www.apa.org/pubs/databases/psyccritiques/index.aspx.
38. "PsycTESTS." American Psychological Association. Last modified 2012. http://www.apa.org/pubs/databases/psyctests/index.aspx.
39. "PsycTHERAPY." American Psychological Association. Last modified 2012. http://www.apa.org/pubs/databases/psyctherapy/index.aspx.
40. "What Does Scopus Cover?" Elsevier B.V. Accessed July 16, 2013. http://www.info.sciverse.com/scopus/scopus-in-detail/facts.
41. Ibid.
42. Ibid.
43. Ibid.
44. Ibid.
45. "FAQs." Elsevier B.V. Accessed July 16, 2013. http://www.info.sciverse.com/scopus/scopus-training/faqs.

CHAPTER 6

U.S. Government Documents and Technical Reports

MELODY ALLISON

In recent decades electronic formats and the Internet have created vast changes in the way government information is accessed. The federal government has been an early and proliferative adopter of using the Internet to provide access to the information it generates through public monies on behalf of the public. This change from print- to electronic-centric access has in turn greatly changed the way government information is found. Discerning reference sources from nonreference ones in this digital landscape requires adaptation of the traditional reference source definition to one useful for the electronic environment, especially necessary concerning government information. For this chapter in the sixth edition of *Introduction to Reference Sources in the Health Sciences*, the scope of reference resource is broadened to encompass any source that points to or provides access to desired information. It includes traditional reference sources such as reference books as well as digital versions of print reference works. Most important, it also includes websites that provide access to literature and other databases, publications, reports, histories, timelines, regulations, legislation, briefings, fact sheets, tools and toolkits, data and statistics, blogs, RSS feeds, audio and video files, images galleries, news communications and updates, social networking (including Facebook, Twitter, YouTube, and mobile), live chat and other personal communication opportunities, and much, much more.

This chapter begins with an overview of government information as it relates to health care. Sections follow on sources for a number of major government health-care focus areas (open access, translational sciences, patient rights and empowerment, initiatives and gateways). Finally, various selected federal government agencies that produce and provide access to information about health care are presented *in relation to their affiliated units*. This is an attempt to bring perspective about where agencies fall in the complex federal hierarchy. The Department of Health and Human Services and i ts affiliated units are not the only government units that produce and provide access to information about health care. The U.S. Department of Agriculture (USDA), U.S. Environmental Protection Agency (EPA), U.S. Department of Labor (DOL), National Aeronautics and Space Administration (NASA), U.S. Department of Veterans Affairs (VA), and the White House also do, and information generated from them is included in this chapter as well. Government statistics will be more extensively covered in "Medical and Health Statistics," chapter 12 of this book.

Introduction

Typically government information is seen as synonymous with lawmaking, and indeed this is a major function of our government. In addition to creating laws and regulations, the three branches of federal government—executive, legislative, and judicial branches—each have their own operations with documents that relate to their activities. The federal government is an immensely rich source of information related to activities that are funded by its branches, offices, institutes, agencies, and other entities. It invests billions of dollars into research and development in the sciences, making it an important if not essential source of information for a variety of scientific areas. There are no better examples than those that relate to health care.

Each year the U.S. Department of Health and Human Services (HHS) is the largest federal grant-awarding agency,[1] funding "almost a quarter of all federal outlays . . . more than all other federal agencies combined."[2] A great deal of health-care information can be located from the websites of those governmental entities that supported the research. Examples of the types of health information resources that can be accessed from these sites are government-funded research summaries, technical reports (see Technical Reports in Dissemination of Government Health Research), health topic fact sheets, topic summaries, histories, timelines, regulations, legislation, briefings, tools and toolkits, data and statistics, newsletters, list-servs, blogs, RSS feeds, audio and video files, image galleries, social networking (including Facebook, Twitter, YouTube, and mobile), and live chat and other personal communication opportunities. Also, the government has a number of health initiatives, such as HHS's Health Communication, Health Literacy and e-Health; Healthy People; Dietary Guidelines; Physical Activity Guidelines initiatives; and

the HHS Secretary's FLU.gov, FoodSafety.gov, HealthCare.gov, InsureKidsNow
.gov, LetsMove.gov, OrganDonor.gov, StopBullying.gov, and StopMedicareFraud
.gov initiatives; and the USDA's ChooseMyPlate.gov initiative, with website portals
to related information.

But this does not entail all the information output produced by public monies. Currently much of the publicly funded research is disseminated through scholarly journal publication. Private publishers take the submitted work of researchers/
authors, including ownership (copyright), and distribute through a fee-based publication system. A large constituency of library, academic, and consumer organizations have joined forces to advocate for free access to publicly taxpayer-funded
research, through such proposed legislation as the Federal Research Public Access
Act.[3] Public access advocacy groups feel that free public access is a right of taxpay-
ers who fund research and that it will promote wider dissemination, and use, of the
latest research by anyone, not just those who can afford the price of publications.
There are a number of issues concerning the viability of this "open-access" model of
research dissemination, and it remains to be seen if this will become the standard in
the future, though currently there is a growing body of new and established publishers that are committing to whole or hybrid open-access publications.

Government information is a challenge to find for several reasons. For instance,
standards and methods for information organization and location vary considerably from entity to entity. One cannot extrapolate the content organization from one
entity website to another, making it necessary to learn how to find similar kinds of
content type from site to site. Websites such as Search.USA.gov allow a federated
search of multiple government sites. USA Search is a strategic resource that allows
the public to search for government information across websites from all levels of
government. The ability to search across the government space is critical to creating
an open, transparent, and accessible government.

Additionally, the names of federal government entities can be very confusing, sometimes seem redundant, and even have the same name abbreviation. For
instance, there is the Office on Women's Health (OWH), the Office of Research
on Women's Health (ORWH), and Office of Women's Health (OWH). If the sponsoring agent is not provided, it can take considerable finesse to find out who it
is. In this example they are respectively the Department of Health and Human
Services (HHS); the National Institutes of Health (NIH); and the Food and Drug
Administration (FDA), Health Resources and Services Administration (HRSA), and
the Centers of Disease Control and Prevention (CDC)/Agency for Toxic Substances
and Disease Registry (ATSDR) (all with the same latter name!). Not knowing the
exact wording, including preposition, can make a significant difference in accessing
information from each source.[4-6] And there is the Office of Special Health Affairs
in the U.S. Health Resources and Services Administration (HRSA) as well as the

Occupational Safety and Health Administration in the U.S. Department of Labor (DOL) that both use the same abbreviation, OSHA.[7-8]

There are also agencies that on the surface seem related but are affiliated with entirely different main units. For example, the U.S. Food and Drug Administration (FDA) has an Office of Foods and a Center for Food Safety and Applied Nutrition.[9-10] The U.S. Department of Agriculture (USDA) has the Center for Nutrition Policy and Promotion, the Food and Nutrition Service (FNS), and the Food Safety and Inspection Service (FSIS).[11-13] And the Centers for Disease Control and Prevention has a Food Safety Office.[14] Again it is important to know that these agencies exist and how they relate, interrelate, or don't relate, when pursuing information queries.

The terms used for government information types can be no less confusing. In one place a title may be called a *document* and a similar title elsewhere may be called a *publication*. Many times they are used interchangeably in the same publication or from the same source. Spellings of terms can also create a barrier to finding information that is available. For example *health care* and *healthcare* are stylistic variations of the same term which may be based on agency editorial preferences (or the writer's) and consistently applied throughout a website or publication (or not). Sometimes both ways of spelling may be found throughout a single piece. The term used may even differ between the agency name and content published by that same agency (e.g., see reference 91). Finding the information depends on searching for the term as it is spelled, or it is not found. Note: the formatting style for this book used the term *health care* versus *healthcare*, though the term *healthcare* is used as quoted from source (e.g., Agency for Healthcare Research and Quality).

Knowledge about how our government is organized and what information products are produced will bring considerable order to what may seem to be overwhelming chaos. In addition to a growing amount of full-text government information directly available online, there are many bibliographic resources to bring order and control over the vast amount of government information that is created. On those occasions when success is limited, or remains elusive or overwhelming, assistance is as close as contact with a federal depository librarian.

Resources about Government Information Fundamentals

6.1   Forte, Eric J., Cassandra J. Hartnett, and Andrea L. Sevetson. *Fundamentals of Government Information: Mining, Finding, Evaluating, and Using Government Resources*. New York: Neal-Schuman, 2011.

6.2   Forte, E., and M. Mallory. "Government Information and Statistics Sources." In *Reference and Information Services: An Introduction*, edited by Richard

Rainer Bopp and Linda C. Smith, 637–714. Santa Barbara, CA: Libraries Unlimited, 2011.

6.3   Hernon, Peter, Harold C. Relyea, Robert E. Dugan, and Joan F. Cheverie. *United States Government Information: Policies and Sources.* Westport, CT: Libraries Unlimited, 2002.

Fundamentals of Government Information: Mining, Finding, Evaluating, and Using Government Resources gives a basic overview of history of government information, legislative and regulatory process, judicial and other law, presidential documents, and the executive branch agencies. Government information is addressed in several areas—executive, statistical, education, environment and energy, business and economic, consumer, scientific and technical, and health. In the "Health Information" chapter, an overview and history of the U.S. Department of Health and Human Services, National Library of Medicine, *Index Medicus*, MEDLINE, PubMed, and MeSH (Medical Subject Headings) are given. Finding older medical journal articles not in PubMed is clearly outlined. Sources of health information are discussed, such as vital statistics, survey data, and research/clinical trials. An introduction to federal, state, local, tribal, and international health resources and organizations are broached. The book also describes distribution methods for scientific and technical information and subject search strategies to locate them.

Forte and Mallory present a comprehensive overview of government information in their chapter "Government Information and Statistics Sources" found in the fourth edition of *Reference and Information Services: An Introduction.*[15] They address the transition of government information from print to electronic resources. Major government reference sources are covered (e.g., guides, fact sheets, directories, catalogs, bibliographies, catalogs, indexes, legislative, and statistical information) along with related search strategies. Though health information per se is not covered, health information may be found in these categories, such as legislative and statistical information reference sources, and related search strategies may be most helpful when using these resources to locate it, nonetheless.

In addition to identifying basic federal government information sources, the book *United States Government Information: Policies and Sources* examines government information policies, all within a historical framework. Coverage includes information about all three branches of government, agencies, information-finding aids, privacy protection, the Freedom of Information Act, government publishing, depository library programs, paperwork reduction, and electronic government. Although very limited coverage of health-related topics is provided (e.g., Health Insurance Portability and Accountability Act [HIPAA] and health statistics), this important work is extremely valuable in understanding how the federal government is organized and works, past and present. It was created as a tool to help make the vast wealth of government information (which has publications on most every topic), more accessible and thus more easily utilized by the public and professionals. A CD-ROM is also included that contains reprints of key documents cited in print volume, digital copies of select historical out-of-print documents, tutorials, examples of concepts from print volume, exercises, and questions and answers about government information.

Resources to Find Government Publications

6.4   *Catalog of U.S. Government Publications* (*CGP*). Washington, DC: U.S. Government Printing Office, 1976– . Available: http://catalog.gpo.gov/F. [Note: Electronic counterpart of the *Monthly Catalog of the United States Government Publications*. Washington, DC: U.S. Government Printing Office, 1895–2004. (Print format) Monthly; annual cumulative indexes.]

6.5   Federal Depository Library Program (FDLP) Desktop. Washington, DC: Federal Depository Library Program. Available: http://www.fdlp.gov/.

6.6   MetaLib. Washington, DC: Government Printing Office. Available: http://metalib.gpo.gov/.

6.7   U.S. Government Bookstore. Washington, DC: U.S. Government Printing Office, 2007. Available: http://bookstore.gpo.gov/.

6.8   U.S. Government Accountability Office. "Reports and Testimony." Washington, DC: U.S. General Accountability Office, 1971– . Available: http://www.gao.gov/.

6.9   THOMAS. Washington, DC: Library of Congress. Available: http://www.thomas.gov/. [Note: Congress.gov (currently in Beta version) will replace THOMAS by the end of 2014.]

6.10   U.S. Government Printing Office (GPO). Washington, DC: U.S. Government Printing Office. Available: http://www.gpo.gov/.

The *Catalog of U.S. Government Publications* (*CGP*), online counterpart of the *Monthly Catalog of the United States Government Publications*, is "the finding tool for electronic and print publications from the legislative, executive, and judicial branches of the U.S. government."[16] The *CGP* contains more than 500,000 records dating from July 1976. Updates are provided daily. For records from original issue in 1895 to 1976, the print version titled *Monthly Catalog of United States Government Publications* must be used.[17] Links to online versions of documents are provided when available. As of 2004, the *Monthly Catalog of United States*

Government Publications was discontinued and the *CGP* became the only version.[18] National bibliographic standards such as *Anglo-American Cataloguing Rules*, 2nd ed.; Library of Congress Rule Interpretations; MARC21; CONSER; OCLC's second edition of *Bibliographic Formats and Standards*; and GPO Cataloging Guidelines are used to create *CGP* records. Catalog records include title, publisher information, SuDoc number, item number, variation in title, edition, description, abstract, system details, subject, subject—LC, holdings, OCLC number, and system number.[19]

The *CGP* can be searched using a Basic or Advanced Search. The Basic Search allows keyword, title, author, and subject searches. The Advanced Search provides three concept boxes, each of which can be limited to one of many record fields. This search can be limited by year(s), format, and language. It can also be limited by one or more of the following subset catalogs: Congressional Serial Set Catalog (July 1976–), Congressional Publications Catalog (July 1976–), GPO Historic Shelflist (1870s–1992), Internet Publications Catalog (July 1976–), Periodicals catalog (1976–), and Serials catalog (1976–). Links to electronic versions are provided when available. Also a "Locate in a Library" feature can be used to find a Federal depository library with a hard copy of the title or to locate assistance.[20]

A principal component of the *CGP* is the National Bibliography of U.S. Government Publications.[21] Due to a number of access concerns, including multiple records for the same resource and inability to limit just to federal government information, and in keeping with its statutory requirements, the GPO made the decision to create the National Bibliography of U.S. Government Publications, a comprehensive catalog of unclassified U.S. government information.[22] The National Bibliography of U.S. Government Publications is comprised of publications from the *CGP*, and includes "any information product, regardless of form or format, that any U.S. Government agency discloses, publishes, disseminates, or makes available to the public, as well as information produced for administrative or operational purposes that is of public interest or educational value."[23] Between 1976 and 2004, more than 337,000 records for federal publications were contributed to OCLC WorldCat, "resulting in a de facto national bibliography for U.S. Government publications."[24]

The Federal Depository Library Program (FDLP) Desktop "serves as a centralized resource for the Federal Depository Library Program (FDLP), which disseminates U.S. Government information to the American public through libraries across the nation."[25] This site provides information for FDLP libraries to support their role in providing this access.

MetaLib is a federated library portal that can search information in a variety of federal government electronic resources, such as catalogs, reference and other databases, digital repositories, and Web gateways simultaneously for articles, reports, citations, and other information. Basic, Advanced, and Expert searches provide flexible search keyword, field, topic, and resource selection or browsing search capabilities.[26]

The U.S. Government Bookstore is the "official online bookstore for U.S. Government publications for purchase from the U.S. Government Printing Office."[27] Items from the *Catalog of U.S. Government Publications* (*CGP*) that are not available electronically, or when a personal copy is desired, can be purchased here. The Bookstore can be searched by subject, keyword, stock number, or title; or browsed by subject. Health-related subjects include aging, cancer, diseases, health care, mental health, nutrition, physical fitness, physically challenged, safety, and substance abuse. Orders can be done online, or by fax, phone, or mail.

The U.S. Government Accountability Office (GAO; formerly General Accounting Office) is an independent, nonpartisan agency that evaluates audits, investigates, and provides legal decisions and opinions regarding government policies and procedures, operations, and other activities for Congress to use in their oversight role. This includes research about health topics and issues. Reports and congressional testimony of these endeavors can be searched by keyword or report number in a search box on the upper right corner of any GAO webpage. Once this is done, Advanced Searches becomes an option. There are two search boxes with the title, keyword, summary, full text, and report number field options as well as limits for date(s). Reports and testimonies can be browsed by date, topic (e.g., Health), collection, or agency (e.g., Department of Health and Human Services). Results can be narrowed by source, date, topic, and agency.

GAO Reports from 1995 to present can also be searched using the Government Printing Office's Federal Digital System (FDsys) (http://www.gpo.gov/fdsys/). The Advanced Search allows limits to Available Collections, e.g., GAO Reports and Comptroller General Decisions, by Publication Date and keyword. Search can be narrowed by Date, Government Author, Organization, Person, Location, Keyword, and Document Category. GAO Reports and Comptroller General Decisions can also be browsed by collection using FDsys Browse Government Publications option.

THOMAS is a free Library of Congress service that provides federal legislative information to the public, such as bills/resolutions, congressional activity, access to the Congressional Record, schedules/calendars, and committee information. Bill texts and Public Laws can be searched by Congress (101–present) or browsed by sponsor. Appropriations Bills can be browsed by year (1998–present). Links to information about current legislative activities are accessible from the homepage. On September 19, 2012, the Library of Congress launched a new Web resource, Congress.gov (currently in Beta version), which will replace THOMAS.gov by end of 2014. The beta version of Congress.gov contains legislation from 2001-present, and member profiles from 1973–present with some from 1947–1972.[28] The *Congressional Record, Congressional Record Index*, congressional calendars, committee reports (1995–present), nominations (1987–present), treaties (1975–present), and Senate Executive communications (1979–present) will be incorporated from

THOMAS soon.[29-30] Congress.gov includes enhanced searching features such as ability to search all available content at once and refine results by Congress, legislative source, chamber of Congress, legislation type, subject of legislation, status of current legislation, committee, sponsor, cosponsor, and political party. Search results include bill and congressional number, latest bill title, sponsor, cosponsors, status of legislation, and latest action. Complete record includes bill summary, text, major actions, titles, amendments, cosponsors, committees, and related bills in tabular format. Support resources are available about the legislative process and current legislative activities, and Congressional profiles with biography, home state, district, party, time served, member website, and contact information. The clean design and search platform present access to a massive amount of information without overwhelming the user, providing much to look forward to here.

Another important source of government information is the U.S. Government Printing Office (GPO), which is "the Federal Government's primary centralized resource for gathering, cataloging, producing, providing and preserving published information in all its forms."[31] Official information from all three branches of government, such as the *Congressional Record*, *House Journal*, *U.S. Code*, *Congressional Serial Set*, and *Code of Federal Regulations*, is distributed by the GPO, which provides electronic access to a growing number of these information products via its online Federal Digital System (FDsys) service.[32-33] Official government records can be an important source of health-care information. For instance, access to information about legislation, such as the Medicare prescription drug benefit program or the inclusion of women in biomedical research and drug analysis by the U.S. Food and Drug Administration, can be important for both health-care consumers and professionals. In partnership with the GPO, the Federal Depository Library Program (FDLP), a program of the GPO Office of Information Dissemination (SuDocs), provides free access to our government's information through disseminating "information products from all three branches of the government to over 1,250 [federal depository] libraries nationwide."[34]

Dissemination of Government Health Research

Clinical Trials

A clinical trial is "a research study in human volunteers to answer specific health questions . . . conducted according to a plan called a protocol" that defines who, what, and how the study is being done and then evaluated for outcomes.[35] Information about clinical trials can be used to learn about current research endeavors on particular health conditions, and can be a cutting-edge resource for locating research information. Literature reviews on publications from researchers with clinical trials of interest may identify useful, current information related to condition that has already been published. Caution: Although outcomes of studies may be interesting, only when these outcomes are published in a peer-reviewed medical journal should they be considered, and then with due diligence. Patients with some conditions may be interested in volunteering for consideration as participants in specific clinical trials. One place to investigate for information about clinical trials is ClinicalTrials.gov.

6.11   ClinicalTrials.gov. Bethesda, MD: U.S. Department of Health and Human Services, National Institutes of Health. Available: http://clinicaltrials.gov/.

ClinicalTrials.gov is a registry of government and non-government-supported clinical trials conducted in the United States plus more than 170 countries that can be searched by medical condition or other variables. Guidelines for registration of clinical trials by investigator are provided. Each trial record includes information about participant flow, baseline characteristics, outcome measures and statistical analyses, adverse events, administrative information, and results, when available. There are guidelines about who can participate with contact information for the clinical trial. Information is available about what clinical trials are, benefits and risks, informed consent, etc., to assist those who are considering participation in a clinical trial to become knowledgeable about them.

Guidelines

Guidelines and standards for health care are important mechanisms to disseminate and promote incorporation of best practices based on evidence-based research. The standard definition for "clinical practice guidelines" comes from the Institute of Medicine: "Clinical practice guidelines are systematically developed statements to assist practitioner and patient decisions about appropriate health care for specific clinical circumstances."[36] Accepted clinical practice guidelines are by experts in the focus area and sponsored by recognized entities, such as medical specialty associations, professional societies, and health-care government agencies. The process to create them is complex and includes a thorough, comprehensive literature review for prevailing and latest research evidence. This information is used to create recommendations with potential benefits, risks, contraindications, and caveats, which are then peer-reviewed and published and/or disseminated in appropriate venues.

6.12   National Guideline Clearinghouse. Washington, DC: U.S. Department of Health and Human Services, Agency for Healthcare Research and Quality. Available: http://guideline.gov/.

The U.S. Department of Health and Human Services's (HHS) Agency for Healthcare Research and Quality (AHRQ), in collaboration with the American Medical Association (AMA) and the America's Health Insurance Plans (AHIP), created the National Guideline Clearinghouse (NGC) to provide "an accessible mechanism for obtaining objective, detailed information on clinical practice guidelines and to further their dissemination, implementation, and use."[37]

Content is identified by audits of established guideline makers and literature searches in major biomedical databases as well as submissions that satisfy NGC Inclusion Criteria. The NCG content can be searched, compared, or browsed. Expert commentaries, guideline syntheses, annotated bibliographies, and other resources are available including a free My NGC account. The My NCG account, when created, has a number of features, such as a display of the three most recent searched and the five most recent viewed summaries and ability to save "favorite" guidelines and organizations. Free topic, favorite information, and expert commentary alerts can be subscribed to.

Open Access

A vast amount of government-funded research has been done with results traditionally disseminated in scholarly journal publications. But due in large part to the "serials crisis" of the 1980s, 1990s, and early 2000s where serial price inflation rose considerably higher than the Consumer Price Index, new models for delivery of scholarly output were explored by academic and research libraries that would contain costs.[38] One such model was the "Open Access (OA)" model where the scholarly work "is digital, online, free of charge, and free of most copyright and licensing restrictions."[39]

In 2008 the National Institutes of Health (NIH) created the NIH Public Access Policy that boosted support for the Open Access model. This policy was implemented to advance science and improve public health through public access to published NIH-funded research results.[40] The NIH policy requires that electronic versions of final, peer-reviewed manuscripts emanating from NIH-funded research and accepted for publication must be submitted to the National Library of Medicine's (NLM) PubMed Central (PMC), the NLM's free archive repository of biomedical and life sciences journal literature, and available for public access within twelve months of publication.[41] Currently PMC archives more than 2.4 million articles from more than 3,000 journal titles. Some journal titles are archived completely back to their first issues; some journal titles are archived completely from a later point on; and some journals provide only articles that were funded by NIH. More information about the NIH Public Access and the NIH Manuscript Submission System can be found at the PMC website.

Federal Research Public Access Act (FRPAA) was originally introduced in the Senate in 2006 but not in the House of Representatives. In 2009 the Federal Research Public Access Act (FRPAA) was introduced as S. 1373 in the Senate and in 2010 it was introduced as HR 5037 in the House. In 2012 it was again introduced into the U.S. Senate as Senate 2096 and H.R. 4004 into the House of Representatives.[42–46] This legislation would essentially expand the NIH policy to all federal agencies with a budget of more than 100 million dollars and have a shorter time frame for open access to related published works. It would make the final manuscripts accepted for publication in peer-reviewed journals emanating in whole or part from federally funded research from any federal agency freely available online in a stable repository maintained by the federal agency within six months of publication.

In December 2011, opposing factions arose with the introduction of the Research Works Act (RWA) (H.B. 3699) "to ensure the continued publication and integrity of peer-reviewed research works by the private sector," including overturning the NIH Public Access Policy.[47] The Research Works Act, supported by the Association of American Publishers and the Copyright Alliance, would prohibit open-access mandates for federally funded research, including the NIH's Public Access Policy. Numerous scholarly societies and academic entities, including the Medical Library Association, opposed this Act.[48] Considerable debate and lobbying ensued, including a boycott by thousands of scholars who stated they would not edit, review, and/or contribute to journal publications that do not support this policy, effectively killing this legislation.[49] Those who opposed still oppose, and other renditions of the RWA to foil FRPAA enactment are likely.

Additionally, the open-access movement has expanded to data created by federally funded research. The HHS believes that government data creates important benefits for its citizens and that sharing this data is fundamental to advancing our citizens' health.[50] Since January 18, 2011, the National Science Foundation (NSF) has required a "data management plan" with all funding proposals. The NSF policy mandates that investigators

> are expected to share with other researchers, at no more than incremental cost and within a reasonable time, the primary data, samples, physical collections and other supporting materials created or gathered in the course of work under NSF grants. Grantees are expected to encourage and facilitate such sharing.[51]

Proposals must include how the investigator(s) will carry out this policy. The data management plan must include a description of the types of data and other research output, the standards and metadata to be used, policies for access and sharing with privacy and other protections as well as for reuse, and archival and access preservation plans.[52] There are two guides to policy implementation for biomedical areas–the Biological Sciences Dictorate (BIO) and the Social, Behavioral, and Economic Sciences Dictorate (SBE).[53–54] Specific guidance will likely evolve over time as standards and metadata are created and refined. There may also be political lobbying from various entities about federal government data mandates as conflicts of interest are identified by these entities.

6.13   *HHS Open Government Plan.* Washington, DC: U.S. Department of Health and Human Services, 2012. Available: http://www.hhs.gov/.

6.14   "Dissemination and Sharing of Research Results." In *Award and Administration Guide.* Arlington, VA: National Science Foundation, 2011. Available: http://www.nsf.gov/pubs/policydocs/pappguide/nsf11001/ aag_6.jsp#VID4.

6.15   "Overview." In NIH Public Access Policy. Bethesda, MD: U.S. Department of Health and Human Services, National Institutes of Health. Available: http:// publicaccess.nih.gov/.

6.16   PubMed Central (PMC). Bethesda, MD: U.S. National Library of Medicine, 2011. Available: http://www.ncbi.nlm.nih.gov/pmc/.

Technical Reports

The federal government sponsors a vast amount of research and development (R&D) through universities, corporations, and other organizations. Outlays for the conduct of nondefense research and development total more than 60 billion dollars, including more than 30 billion expended by the National Institutes of Health; over 500 million dollars of the total nondefense outlays goes to grants.[55] Reports that include technical details are generated to document progress and results of this research, as well as to account for these expenditures of public monies. The National Technical Information Service (NTIS), an agency of the U.S. Department of Commerce, manages a fee-based clearinghouse of approximately 3 million scientific and technical information reports in over 350 subject areas.[56–57] In recognition of the public's need, and right, to have access to unclassified information that it financially supports, the federal government through the *U.S. Code* (15 USC 3704b-2: Transfer of federal scientific and technical information) mandates that executive departments and agencies provide R&D results to the National Technical Information Service for dissemination to the public.[58–59] Although this code mandates that information about research supported by executive branch agencies is to be provided to NTIS, a GAO report found that this is not always done.[60] At the time of the report GAO found 19 percent of NTIS technical reports could also be acquired from the issuing agency, Google.com, FirstGov.gov, or the GPO, with 37 percent of these available for free from the organization's website.[61] This likelihood increased exponentially since 1988, particularly for availability of technical reports from their issuing organization.[62] These actualities have raised questions about whether a central, self-sustaining repository is the suitable way for dissemination of technical reports to the public, which has implications for the relevance and future of NTIS.[63] The National Commission on Libraries and Information Science (NCLIS) concluded in a study that the NTIS should be retained for "fail-safe" permanent access and proper bibliographic control of research results.[64] They additionally recommended that rather than be self-sustaining, the NTIS should be funded by Congress to acquire, maintain, and provide free access to the full text of these reports.[65-66]

Technical reports may be comprehensive in coverage about the research or brief summaries; they may cover preliminary, progress, or final results. Locating technical reports is still not a "one-stop shopping" venture. Publications may not be easily recognized as technical reports; contract/grant number and accession/report series codes can be bibliographic indicators. As part of a comprehensive search strategy, it is important to "consider the source," and it may well take a number of search tools to do a complete search. There are several to consider.

The National Technical Information Services (NTIS) is "the largest central resource for government-funded scientific, technical, engineering, and business information available today" and *the* clearinghouse for related technical reports, so this is the first place to begin searches.[67] Government agencies may also provide access to technical reports for research that they have sponsored, sometimes without charge. Other stops along the journey include portals and databases such as the Information Bridge: DOE Scientific and Technical Information, NASA Technical Reports Server (NTRS), National Service Center for Environmental Publications (NSCEP), PubMed, Research Portfolio Online Reporting Tools (RePORT) Expenditures and Results (RePORTER) System, and Research Portfolio Online Reporting Tools (RePORT) Report Catalog. Although it is not a major source of technical reports, the Government Printing Office (GPO) may have selected technical reports from federal agencies and thus be indexed in the *Catalog of U.S. Government Publications* (*CGP*) and available through the federal depository libraries system.[68]

Depository librarians are important resources to assist in locating technical reports using their expertise and knowledge about government resources as well as their access to *NTIS Database* subscription via commercial vendors. Current advocacy for public access to results from publicly financed research, such as the National Institutes of Health's (NIH) *Policy on Enhancing Public Access to Archived Publications Resulting from NIH-Funded Research* (Public Access Policy), along with technological advancements, holds great anticipation for increasingly improved access to technical reports and other government information.[69]

6.17   "DTIC Online: Public Technical Reports." Ft. Belvoir, VA: U.S. Department
of Defense, Defense Technical Information Center. Available:
http://www.dtic.mil/dtic/.

Defense Technical Information Center's (DTIC) Public Technical Reports from
the U.S. Department of Defense (DoD) provides access to unclassified technical
report citations and full-text reports from the DoD via its Public Technical Reports
database. DoD research interests encompass a number of areas outside military science including biological and medical sciences. Quick, guided, or advanced searches
can be performed. Limited or classified information requires registration by eligible
entities, as does ordering printed documents. Unregistered public users can order
DTIC unclassified, unlimited documents from the National Technical Information
Service (NTIS) (see NTIS "Customer Service at a Glance" at http://www.ntis.gov/
help/cs_ov.asp). Minimal fees are charged for DTIC technical reports. Note: DTIC
Public Technical Reports are also searchable using Science.gov's "Deep Web"
Advanced Search.

6.18   Energy Citations Database. Oak Ridge, TN: U.S. Department of
Energy, Office of Scientific and Technical Information, 2012. Available:
http://www.osto.gov/energycitations.

This database includes bibliographic citations from literature, including technical
reports, in areas of interest to DOE, including biomedical sciences, such as anatomy,
physiology, molecular biology, genetics, pharmacology/toxicology, medicine, surgery,
and public health (see thesaurus via Fielded Search > Subject Select). Searches can be
limited to technical reports in "Fielded Search." Citation dates cover 1943–present.

6.19   Information Bridge: DOE Scientific and Technical Information. Oak
Ridge, TN: U.S. Department of Energy, Office of Scientific and Technical
Information; Washington, DC: U.S. Government Printing Office, 2012.
Available: http://www.osti.gov/bridge/.

Information Bridge, via the Office of Scientific and Technical Information
(OSTI) Science Accelerator gateway, provides access to research report citations
and full-text Department of Energy (DOE) documents from 1991 to the present in
areas such as biology, biology and medicine (basic and applied), radiobiology, radio-
therapy, human radiation studies, health physics, industrial health, health monitoring
systems, and other health topics. Content is updated two times each week. Note:
Information Bridge is also searchable using Science.gov's "Deep Web" Advanced
Search (see Science.gov in this section). Through a recent collaboration with the
DOE, full-text OSTI technical reports are also now available through Elsevier's free
SciVerse Hub (http://www.hub.sciverse.com/action/home) and Scirus (http://www
.scirus.com/) search tools.[70]

6.20   NASA Technical Reports Server (NTRS): "Search NTRS." Washington, DC:
        National Aeronautics and Space Administration, 2012. Available: http://ntrs
        .nasa.gov/search.jsp.

The National Aeronautics and Space Administration (NASA) Technical Reports
Server (NTRS) is a database of NASA's technical literature. NTRS includes the
National Advisory Committee for Aeronautics (NACA) (1916–1958), NASA (1958–
present), and NASA Image eXchange (NIX) (1900–present) collections. Searches
can be limited to technical reports in Advanced Search by clicking on "Document
Type," selecting "Technical Report," and then using the search options to enter
search terms. Links are included to full-text PDFs when available. Those not available online may be ordered. In addition to technical reports, many different types
of materials are indexed including images/photos, NASA reports, preprints, theses,
dissertations, conference papers, NASA Reports, and movies. Note: NASA Technical
Reports Server is also searchable using Science.gov's "Deep Web" Advanced
Search.

6.21   National Technical Information Service (NTIS). Springfield, VA: U.S.
        Department of Commerce, Technology Administration, National Technical
        Information Service, 2012. Available: http://www.ntis.gov/.

A bureau of the U.S. Department of Commerce, the NTIS with its 3 million+
products (publications, technical reports, computer products, databases, and other
product types) is the "largest central resource for government-funded scientific, technical, engineering, and business related information."[71] Health-related subject areas
that are covered include Biomedical Technology and Human Factors Engineering,
Health Care, and Medicine and Biology, and comprise nearly 30 percent of content.[72]
The Department of Health and Human Services is one of more than 600 federal agencies from which NTIS collects information. NTIS responsibilities include collecting
and distributing unclassified government-sponsored research as well as ensuring its
archival via a permanent repository.[73]

NTIS is a self-sustaining agency and recoups its costs through fees for its products and services. Information for more than 600,000 publication products since
1990 can be searched via the tab "Technical Search" and, when an item is available,
purchased from the NTIS website. Many purchased publication products may be
downloaded via a link from the online item record. Formats vary from paper, CD,
microfiche, multimedia, downloadable products (1997–present, with some from the
early 1970s on), and other format types. When an item requires a phone order, a
contact phone order number is provided. More ordering, payment, and other related
information is provided on the website. Links to free full-text publication from the
source agency's website may be found on selected records.

With more than 2 million bibliographic records, the NTIS Database is *the* resource for identifying U.S.-sponsored research from 1964 to the present. The NTIS Database receives federally funded scientific, technical, engineering, and business information within fifteen days of public availability. It also contains titles from state and local governments, academic institutions, private sector organizations, foreign governments, and international organizations. NTIS leases the NTIS Database through several commercial services. Update frequency of this database depends on the commercial vendor although NTIS provides updates weekly to the vendors. NTIS also provides access to more than 2 million titles and more than 600,000 full-text PDFs with daily updates, through their own subscription product, the National Technical Reports Library (NTRL).[74] NTIS Database document requests can be made by phone, fax, e-mail, or website (see NTIS website). Help Desk assistance and free NTIS Database Search Guide can be accessed via the NTIS website. Note: NTIS is also searchable using Science.gov's "Deep Web" Advanced Search (see in this section).

6.22   National Service Center for Environmental Publications (NSCEP). Washington, DC: U.S. Environmental Protection Agency, 2012. Available: http://www.epa.gov/nscep/.

Through its many research programs, the EPA is an important source of health information related to the effects of pollution on health. Free Environmental Protection Agency (EPA) electronic and paper titles, including technical reports, are available from the EPA's National Environmental Publications Internet Site (NEPIS) database. Though there is no specific "Field Search" option for technical reports, one can put the topic keyword(s) of interest (e.g., health AND pesticides) in the "Field Search" subject option with other selected "Search Field" options and then "Search." [Notes: Be sure to select "subject" option box or search won't work. Apostrophes for phrases do not work. And keyword topics must be separated by "AND.") A browse of the results is necessary to determine if the item is a report versus other types of publications. Technical reports published from 1991 on can generally be ascertained by "R" (equals "Report, Symposium Report, Proceedings") or "S" (equals "Summary, Research Brief, Conference Summary, Issue Paper") "Alpha Descriptor" in the EPA document numbers on the item. For more EPA document codes, see the *EPA Publication Numbering System* (http://www.epa.gov/nscep/nscep-codes.html).[75]

When electronic full-text publications are not available, they can be ordered from the National Service Center for Environmental Publications (NSCEP) online, by phone, by fax, or by mail. Information about regional and state EPAs, including their publications, can be found directly from state environmental agencies (see http://www.epa.gov/aboutepa/states/). Note: NSCEP is also searchable using Science.gov's "Deep Web" Advanced Search.

6.23   PubMed. Bethesda, MD: National Library of Medicine. Available: http://www.ncbi.nlm.nih.gov/pubmed/.

PubMed provides access to technical report citations for a wide range of bio-medical topics using its "Publication Type/Type of Article" Limit, then selecting "Technical Report." Topics, both keyword and Medical Subject Headings (MeSH), are used with Boolean search techniques to define types of technical reports that are being sought. As with periodical titles of all publication types indexed in PubMed, there may be access via the record to full text of technical reports available from the free digital biomedical literature archive PubMed Central (PMC) or via the local institution's e-journal subscriptions, when available, which may be linked to PubMed citations. Additional "Publication Type/Type of Article" limits that may be of use to locate technical report types of information are "Research Support, U.S. Gov't" and "Evaluation Studies." Note: PubMed is also searchable using Science.gov's "Deep Web" Advanced Search.

6.24   Research Portfolio Online Reporting Tools (RePORT) Expenditures and Results (RePORTER) System. Bethesda, MD: U.S. Department of Health and Human Services, National Institutes of Health, Office of Extramural Research, 2012. Available: http://projectreporter.nih.gov/reporter.cfm.

Replacing the former CRISP (Computer Retrieval of Information on Scientific Projects) database in 2009, the RePORTER (part of the Research Portfolio Online Reporting Tools, or RePORT) enhances and expands upon CRISP functionality. RePORTER searches a repository of intra- and extramural research projects (1985–present) for biomedical R&D support to universities, hospitals, and other research institutions by government agencies within the Department of Health and Human Services (HHS), *and* related access publications (from PubMed or PubMed Central) and patents. The RePORTER search engine allows a great deal of flexibility with multiple field and limits options. Considerable information is available about project description, details, results, history, and subprojects with links to associated and similar publications, similar projects, NIH Topic Maps, PI Profile Links, news, and more. Although complete full text of technical reports may not be available, the project details can be used for further investigation and inquiries.

6.25   Research Portfolio Online Reporting Tools (RePORT) Report Catalog. Bethesda, MD: U.S. Department of Health and Human Services, National Institutes of Health, Office of Extramural Research, 2012. Available: http://report.nih.gov/catalog.aspx.

The Report Catalog (part of the Research Portfolio Online Reporting Tools, or RePORT), is a repository of hundreds of reports, data, analyses, and Report Catalog search tools. The Catalog can be searched using various filters—NIH institute or center (IC), activities, program, topic (e.g., Outputs/Outcomes), mechanism, and variable. Information includes topic, NIH institute or center, funding sources, and budget activities.

6.26   Science Inventory. Washington, DC: U.S. Environmental Protection Agency, 2012. Available: http://cfpub.epa.gov/si/.

The Science Inventory is "a database of EPA science activities and scientific and technical products conducted by the EPA or funded by EPA." As environmental pollution is a major influence on health and contributor to disease, this database is relevant to identify related technical reports. NTIS records can be located by NTIS number using Advanced Search > Record ID. Keyword search length is limited in "Advanced Search." Document (Report) is found in the "Record Type" field, though there is no specific field to search it in the "Advanced Search." Suggest keyword search utilizing Boolean phrase "[keyword concept] AND report" (without quotes but use caps for Boolean operative).

6.27   Science.gov. Oak Ridge, TN: Department of Energy, Office of Scientific and Technical Information, 2012. Available: http://www.science.gov/.

Replacing OSTI's Federal R&D Project Summaries and GrayLit Network, the Science.gov gateway allows "Deep Web" searching of more than 200 million web-pages and nearly fifty scientific databases from twelve federal agencies including the Department of Energy, the Department of Health and Human Services (NIH, NLM, FDA), the National Science Foundation, the Environmental Protection Agency, the Department of Agriculture, and the Library of Congress. Agency databases can be searched individually or in any combination. Records contain research project information such as grant number, primary investigator details, report/patent number, publication information, meeting information, document source, research site, abstract, thesaurus terms, project dates, and agency sponsor. Although complete full text of technical reports may not be available through these databases, the project details can be used for further investigation and inquiries.

Translational Science

Basic biomedical research is the foundation of clinical therapeutics. A great deal of basic research is done. But the results of these studies can take up to twenty years or more to filter to clinical application under conventional dissemination methods.[76-77] The reason for doing basic biomedical research is to form an evidence-based basis for treatments and health promoters that improve the lives of patients using the best, most current research findings. Translational research, "the process of translating the basic biology of a disease into real-world therapeutics in the lives of patients," is an attempt to bridge this gap between knowledge and practice in a *timely* way.[78] The federal government is keenly interested in getting the results of research to the point of care as quickly as possible. Utilizing the most current findings for clinical care greatly increases the chances for positive health outcomes for patients. They use a multipronged approach—through dissemination of research findings and clinical practice knowledge to researchers, health-care practitioners, information specialists, and the general public via their websites and various scholarly communication vehicles; open-access initiatives for sharing of raw biomedical research data of government-funded research to use for academic purposes; and promotion of the tools and resources to support and encourage patients and their families to take the lead role in their health-care decisions.

In 2004 after consultation with researchers, health-care providers, and the public, the NIH Roadmap for Medical Research was created to address and overcome research impediments and hurdles "through harmonization efforts of regulatory policies, multidisciplinary training, development of new networking and diagnostic tools, and facilitating the establishment of academic homes for clinical and translational research."[79-80] Created in 2006, the NIH Common Fund supports The Roadmap and other trans-NIH programs, and is coordinated by the Office of Strategic Coordination (OSC) within the NIH Director's Division of Program Coordination, Planning, and Strategic Initiatives (DPCPSI). The ultimate goal is to "to increase effectiveness and efficiency in advancing science, ultimately resulting in the acceleration of basic research discoveries and speed translation of those discoveries into applications that improve the health of the American people."[81]

To encourage and fund translational research, the NIH created the Clinical and Translational Science Awards (CTSA) program which "funds a national consortium of medical research institutions dedicated to improving clinical and translational research."[82] The consortium provides opportunities for its 60 institutional members to collaborate on training, resource sharing, and other research activities to advance translational research and clinical application. The CTSA program and grants were formerly administered by the NIH National Center for Research Resources (NCRR). In 2011 the NCRR was dissolved by the federal government and in 2012 a new NIH National Center for Advancing Translational Sciences (NCTS) was established in its place to "focus on addressing scientific and technical challenges to reduce, remove or bypass bottlenecks in the development of new treatments and tests that will ultimately improve human health."[83-84] The CTSA was assigned selected functions of the former NCRR, including administration of the CTSA programs, which it does though its Division of Clinical Innovation.[85] The NCATS unifies three program areas—Clinical and Translational Activities, Rare Diseases Research and Therapeutics, and Re-engineering Translational Sciences—to improve the development of diagnostics and therapeutics that make "make translational science more efficient, less expensive and less risky."[86] The NCATS is the latest of federal initiatives to streamline and transform the process of making basic research available for application at the bedside, and promises not to be the last.

6.28   Clinical and Translational Science Awards. Bethesda, MD: U.S. Department of Health and Human Services, Division of Clinical Innovation, National Center for Advancing Translational Sciences, National Institutes of Health. Available: https://www.ctsacentral.org/.

6.29   National Center for Advancing Translational Sciences. Bethesda, MD: U.S. Department of Health and Human Services, National Institutes of Health. Available: http://www.ncats.nih.gov/.

6.30   *Fact Sheet: NIH Roadmap for Medical Research.* Bethesda, MD: U.S. Department of Health and Human Services, National Institutes of Health, Office of the Director, Division of Program Coordination, Planning, and Strategic Initiatives, Office of Strategic Coordination, NIH Common Fund, 2006. Available: http://opasi.nih.gov/documents/NIHRoadmap_FactSheet _Aug06.pdf.

Patient Rights and Empowerment

Patients as Health-Care Consumers, Partners, Decision Makers

Serious inadequacies in health-care delivery lead to an alarming number of medical errors and patient suffering and death each year despite an explosion of information and knowledge creation. What can be done to help fill this gap between knowledge and practice? Enter "the patient" as "health-care consumer." The inclusion of patients as active participants in medical decisions about their health care has been growing since the early 1990s. The term *health-care consumer* provides recognition that the patient is buying a service and that, like the purchase of any service, this health-care consumer should be able to assess what services are available, decide what services work for the need, and select who provides that service. Numerous government resources are available to support health-care consumers in becoming educated not only about health topics, but also about how to be active participants on their health-care team, including participation as decision makers.

In the National Academies of Sciences (NAS) Institute of Medicine (IOM) *Crossing the Quality Chasm* report, patient-centered care is a guiding principle.[87] The report states that twenty-first-century health-care systems "must be designed to serve the needs of patients, and to ensure that they are fully informed, retain control and participate in care delivery whenever possible, and receive care that is respectful of their values and preferences,"[88] with the following rules:

1. Care based on continuous healing relationships
2. Customization based on patient needs and values
3. The patient as the source of control
4. Shared knowledge and the free flow of information
5. Evidence-based decision making
6. Safety as a system property
7. The need for transparency
8. Anticipation of needs
9. Continuous decrease in waste
10. Cooperation among clinicians[89]

The inclusion of patients as decision makers is seen as an essential piece of improving quality of care throughout all health-care systems.

6.31   Effectiveness Health Care Program: Helping You Make Better Treatment Choices. Rockville, MD: U.S. Department of Health and Human Services, Agency for Healthcare Research and Quality, 2011. Available: http://www.effectivehealthcare.ahrq.gov/index.cfm.

6.32   *Expanding Patient-Centered Care to Empower Patients and Assist Providers.* Rockville, MD: U.S. Department of Health and Human Services, Agency for Healthcare Research and Quality, 2002. Available: http://www.ahrq.gov/qual/ptcareria.htm.

6.33   "Patients and Consumers." Rockville, MD: U.S. Department of Health and Human Services, Agency for Healthcare Research and Quality. Available: http://www.ahrq.gov/consumer/.

6.34   Consumer Assessment of Healthcare Providers and Systems. Rockville, MD: U.S. Department of Health and Human Services, Agency for Healthcare Research and Quality, 2011. Available: https://cahps.ahrq.gov/.

6.35   "Patient Rights: MedlinePlus." Bethesda, MD: U.S. Department of Health and Human Services, National Institutes of Health, National Library of Medicine, 2012. Available: http://www.nlm.nih.gov/medlineplus/patientrights.html.

6.36   "Shared Decision-Making." Rockville, MD: U.S. Department of Health and Human Services, Agency for Healthcare Research and Quality, Consumer Assessment of Healthcare Providers and Systems, 2011. *Available: https://cahps.ahrq.gov/Quality-Improvement/Improvement-Guide/Browse-Interventions/Communication/Shared-Decision-Making/index.html.*

6.37   *Shared Decision-Making in Mental Health Care: Practice, Research, and Future Directions.* Publication SMA09-4371. Rockville, MD: U.S. Department of Health and Human Services, Substance Abuse and Mental Health Services Administration. Available: http://store.samhsa.gov/product/Shared

-Decision-Making-in-Mental-Health-Care/SMA09-4371. [Both print (order) and electronic (PDF) versions are free.]

6.38   "Shared Decision Making." Rockville, MD: U.S. Department of Health and Human Services, Substance Abuse and Mental Health Services Administration. Available: http://www.integration.samhsa.gov/clinical -practice/shared-decision-making [good tools for any health-care consumer].

Patient Safety

The Agency for Healthcare Research and Quality (AHRQ) is "the lead Federal agency charged with improving the quality, safety, efficiency, and effectiveness of health care for all Americans."[90] It sponsors, conducts, and provides "information that helps people make better decisions about health care."[91] The AHRQ was charged by the IOM to identify priority conditions and develop, with input from consumers and other stakeholders, plans to attain significant progress in care quality in these areas as well as other approaches to health care (best practices, information technologies, care coordination, and assessment).[92]

The Agency for Healthcare Research and Quality (AHRQ) recognizes that our health-care system is not as safe as desired despite ongoing efforts to improve it.[93] In fact, according to the AHRQ, patients get accurate care at doctors' offices only about half the time and medical mistakes cause 100,000 patients to die each year.[94] The ARHQ advocates that the health-care consumer "can play an important role in pushing the health-care system to improve by being more involved in your own care."[95] Participation of patients in their own care is a key component of a strategy to improve patient safety. A wealth of information resources is available through the AHRQ, as well as various agencies of the federal government, for health-care consumers to get educated about wellness, diseases, and health conditions, to assist them in making informed decisions that will ultimately improve the safety and outcomes of their health care.[96]

6.39   *20 Tips to Help Prevent Medical Errors: Patient Fact Sheet.* Rockville, MD: U.S. Department of Health and Human Services, Agency for Healthcare Research and Quality, 2011. Available: http://www.ahrq.gov/ consumer/20tips.htm.

6.40   AHRQ Patient Safety Network. Rockville, MD: U.S. Department of Health and Human Services, Agency for Healthcare Research and Quality, 2012. Available: http://psnet.ahrq.gov/.

6.41   "CDC Features—Patient Safety: Ten Things You Can Do to Be a Safe Patient." Atlanta: U.S. Department of Health and Human Services, Centers for Disease Control and Prevention, 2011. Available: http://www.cdc.gov/ features/Patientsafety/.

6.42   Patient Safety and Clinical Pharmacy Services Collaborative (PSPC). Rockville, MD: U.S. Department of Health and Human Services, Health Resources and Services Administration, 2012. Available: http://www.hrsa. gov/publichealth/clinical/patientsafety/index.html.

6.43   "Patient Safety: MedlinePlus." Bethesda, MD: U.S. Department of Health and Human Services, National Institutes of Health, National Library of Medicine, 2012. Available: http://www.nlm.nih.gov/medlineplus/ patientsafety.html.

6.44   VA National Center for Patient Safety. Washington, DC: U.S. Department of Veterans Affairs, 2012. Available: http://www.patientsafety.gov/.

Health Literacy

Health literacy is "the capacity to obtain, process, and understand basic health information and services needed to make appropriate health decisions"[97] that improve health and promote patient safety. A variety of federal government offices and agencies promote and provide health literacy resources for both the health-care consumer and professional, such as the following:

6.45   AHRQ Pharmacy Health Literacy Center. Rockville, MD: U.S. Department of Health and Human Services. Available: http://www.ahrq.gov/ pharmhealthlit/.

6.46   "Clear Communication: An NIH Health Literacy Initiative." Rockville, MD: U.S. Department of Health and Human Services, National Institutes of Health, 2011. Available: http://www.nih.gov/clearcommunication/.

6.47   "Culture, Language and Health Literacy." U.S. Department of Health and Human Services, Health Resources and Services Administration. Available: http://www.hrsa.gov/culturalcompetence/.

6.48   "Health Communication and Health Information Technology." Washington, DC: HealthyPeople.gov, U.S. Department of Health and Human Services, 2012. Available: http://healthypeople.gov/2020/topicsobjectives2020/ overview.aspx?topicid=18.

6.49   "Health Literacy." Bethesda, MD: U.S. Department of Health and Human Services, National Institutes of Health, National Library of Medicine, National Network of Libraries of Medicine, 2011. Available: http://nnlm.gov/ outreach/consumer/hlthlit.html.

6.50   "Health Literacy." Rockville, MD: U.S. Department of Health and Human Services, Health Resources and Services Administration. Available: http:// www.hrsa.gov/publichealth/healthliteracy/index.html.

6.51   "Health Literacy." Rockville, MD: U.S. Department of Health and Human Services, Office of the Secretary, Office of the Assistant Secretary for Health, Office of Disease Prevention and Health Promotion, 2012. Available: http://www.health.gov/communication/literacy/.

6.52   Health Literacy: Accurate, Accessible and Actionable Health Information for All. Atlanta: U.S. Department of Health and Human Services, Centers for Disease Control and Prevention, 2011. Available: http://www.cdc.gov/healthliteracy/.

6.53   "Health Literacy and Cultural Competency." Rockville, MD: U.S. Department of Health and Human Services, Agency for Healthcare Research and Quality. Available: http://www.ahrq.gov/browse/hlitix.htm.

6.54   "How to Read Health News." London: England's National Health Service. Available: http://www.ncbi.nlm.nih.gov/pubmedhealth/behindtheheadlines/how-to-read/.

6.55   "MEDLINE/PubMed Search and Health Literacy Information Resources: Health Literacy Search." Bethesda, MD: U.S. Department of Health and Human Services, National Institutes of Health, National Library of Medicine, 2011. Available: http://www.nlm.nih.gov/services/health_literacy.html.

6.56   "Health Literacy: MedlinePlus." Bethesda, MD: U.S. Department of Health and Human Services, National Institutes of Health, National Library of Medicine, 2012. Available: http://www.nlm.nih.gov/medlineplus/healthliteracy.html.

6.57   "Content Quality Guidelines" [used by HealthFinder.gov]. Washington, DC: U.S. Department of Health and Human Services, 2012. Available: http://www.healthfinder.gov/aboutus/content_guidelines.aspx.

6.58   "Quality Guidelines for Health Information in Multiple Languages" [used by MedlinePlus]. Rockville, MD: U.S. Department of Health and Human Services, National Institutes of Health; National Library of Medicine, 2012. Available: http://www.nlm.nih.gov/medlineplus/languages/criteria.html.

6.59   Plain Language.gov. "Popular Topics: Improving Health Literacy." Plain English Network [federal employees group]. Available: http://www.plainlanguage.gov/populartopics/health_literacy/index.cfm.

6.60   Proceedings of the Surgeon General's Workshop on Improving Health Literacy. Rockville, MD: U.S. Department of Health and Human Services, Office of the Surgeon General, 2006. Available: http://www.surgeongeneral.gov/topics/healthliteracy/pdf/proceedings120607.pdf.

Major Resources for Patients and Professionals

The health-care consumer and professional not only need information but also need tools to identify and locate this information. The following finding tools support patient empowerment and decision making.

Finding Tools

6.61   HealthFinder.gov. Washington, DC: U.S. Department of Health and Human Services, 2012. Available: http://www.healthfinder.gov/.

6.62   MedlinePlus. Rockville, MD: U.S. Department of Health and Human Services, National Institutes of Health, National Library of Medicine, 2012. Available: http://www.nlm.nih.gov/medlineplus/.

6.63   PubMed (MEDLINE). Bethesda, MD: U.S. Department of Health and Human Services, National Institutes of Health, National Library of Medicine, National Center for Biotechnology Information, 2012. Available: http://www .ncbi.nlm.nih.gov/pubmed/.

6.64   PubMed Central. Bethesda, MD: U.S. Department of Health and Human Services, National Institutes of Health, National Library of Medicine, National Center for Biotechnology Information, 2012. Available: http://www .ncbi.nlm.nih.gov/pmc/.

6.65   PubMed Health. Bethesda, MD: U.S. Department of Health and Human Services, National Institutes of Health, National Library of Medicine, National Center for Biotechnology Information, 2012. Available: http://www .ncbi.nlm.nih.gov/pubmedhealth/.

6.66   Quality Care Finder. Baltimore, MD: U.S. Department of Health and Human Services, Centers for Medicare and Medicaid. Available: http://www .medicare.gov/quality-care-finder/index.html.

HealthFinder.gov is a resource for health-care consumers provided by the U.S. Department of Health and Human Services (HHS). It contains evidence-based information gleaned from over 1,600 government and nonprofit organizations utilizing quality guidelines, ones that can be used by anyone to help make informed decisions.[98–99] Its "Quick Guide to Healthy Living" provides consumers information on a wide variety of health topics, such as wellness, nutrition and fitness, heart health, cancer, pregnancy, and screening tests. It connects health-care consumers with a variety of personal health tools including planners, health calculators, health widgets, podcasts, videos, and slideshows. Search for topics in its online encyclopedia. Users can find services and information for doctors and other health-care providers, health centers or home health care, health organizations, and libraries. Drug interactions can be searched through HHS access to DrugDigest drug interaction checker (Popular Requests). Get current news through weekly newsletters, e-News, RSS, and e-mail updates. Live chat is available on Tuesdays and Thursdays from 1:00–5:00 pm EST. General health advice can be obtained by entering basic demographic information (e.g., age, sex) into the myhealthfinder widget. Results include general recommendations for all in the demographic category and federal agency source of recommendations.

MedlinePlus, an award-winning service of the National Library of Medicine and the National Institutes of Health, is a portal to current, reliable information about health, diseases, and medical treatments for more than 900 topics. Medical directories, an encyclopedia, a dictionary, and tutorials are just some of the tools that cover information about conditions, tests, treatments, drugs, organizations, and clinical trials. Topics can be browsed or searched. Searches can be refined by source/type and keyword. Content for MedlinePlus is chosen using quality guidelines. Keep up-to-date with e-mail alerts, RSS feeds, and Twitter. MedlinePlus Connect is a free service that connects patient portals and electronic health records of U.S. health organizations and providers to context-sensitive MedlinePlus content on health topics, medications, symptoms, treatments, clinical trials, and recent health news.[100]

PubMed is the free premier biomedical database produced by the National Center for Biotechnology Information (NCBI) at the National Library of Medicine (NLM). It provides access to over 21 million citations in its MEDLINE bibliographic database, other life sciences journals, and online books. MEDLINE coverage begins with 1946 with daily updates. MEDLINE citations in PubMed are indexed with Medical Subject Headings (MeSH), a hierarchical-based controlled vocabulary thesaurus. MeSH can also be searched and searches can be created with them using the MeSH database. A number of PubMed citations link to free full text of articles from the PubMed Central archive repository or publisher when available; some citations link to publishers who provide fee-based access. Many libraries use PubMed Linkout to connect content from their electronic journal subscriptions directly to related citations, so using their link to PubMed will provide expanded access to free full text for their affiliates. MyNCBI is a free account in PubMed where searches can be saved, alerts and citation collections can be created, and preferences can be customized. There are many tools available in PubMed including Help, tutorials, and guides. News Feed and PubMed Mobile are also available. PubMed is one of several NCBI databases accessible through the Entrez search platform, which can all be searched simultaneously. PubMed is a resource for all—researchers, professionals, and healthcare consumers and their families.

PubMed Central (PMC) was created in 2000 by the National Library of Medicine's (NLM) National Center for Biotechnology Information (NCBI) as a free full-text digital archive of biomedical and life sciences journals. As a result of the

NIH Public Access Policy in 2005, papers accepted for publication that were funded by NIH funds have to be submitted to PMC within six months of publication. Basic and advanced searches can be done in PMC. PMC journals can be browsed by title. Keep current with PMC News, PMC News Mail List, and PMC News RSS.

A recent new resource in PubMed is PubMed Health, a service provided by the National Center for Biotechnology Information at the National Library of Medicine. PubMed Health is a resource that health-care consumers and clinicians use to locate effectiveness studies and see what treatments and clinical practices have been proven to work to help them make informed medical decisions. Systematic reviews of clinical trials, technical reports, clinical, and other guides, such as *Understanding the Basics of Systematic Reviews* are available here.[101] Behind the News takes selected news headlines and analyzes their coverage in the news, such as what the news is about, what were its findings, how treatment or a drug works, how it compares to current treatments, and other information. It links to support materials such as How to Read Health News.[102–103] Keep current with PubMed Health news via Google+, Twitter, and RSS feeds for Featured Reviews and Behind the Headlines.

In the spirit of supporting the health-care consumer in making informed health-care decisions, the HHS has created the portal Quality Care Finder, gateway to a suite of tools to find and compare quality of care and services for doctors, hospitals, plans, and suppliers. The following tools are available: Hospital Compare, Nursing Home Compare, Home Health Compare, Dialysis Facility Compare, Physician Compare, and Medicare Plan Finder, along with related guides about steps for choosing a facility or service, contact information, plan finder, questions to ask, patient rights, how to file complaints, and other related information.[104–109]

Other Resources

6.67   DrugDigest, "Check Interactions." Express Scripts, 2011. Available: http://www.drugdigest.org/wps/portal/ddigest.

6.68   Find a Health Center. Washington, DC: U.S. Health and Human Services, 2012. Available: http://findahealthcenter.hrsa.gov/.

6.69   "Health Privacy: Health Insurance Portability and Accountability Act (HIPAA)." Washington, DC: U.S. Department of Health and Human Services, 2012. Available: http://www.hhs.gov/ocr/privacy/index.html.

6.70   National Library of Medicine. Bethesda, MD: U.S. Department of Health and Human Services, National Institutes of Health, National Library of Medicine, 2012. Available: http://www.nlm.nih.gov/.

6.71   "Recalls, Market Withdrawals, and Safety Alerts." Silver Spring, MD: U.S. Department of Health and Human Services, U.S. Food and Drug

Administration, 2012. Available: http://www.fda.gov/safety/recalls/
default.htm.

Drug Interaction Checker via *DrugDigest* is a free resource accessible through
healthfinder.gov where health-care consumers can find *lots* of different kinds of
information about drugs. Searchable databases are available for more reviews about
drugs, vitamins, herbs, supplements, and other remedies. Drugs can be selected and
potential interactions identified. Drug and side effects can be compared. Pill images
can be found by drug name. Administration guidelines are provided for using ear-
drops, eye ointments, eyedrops, inhalers, insulin (injecting, mixing, preparing), nose
drops, and rectal suppositories, as well as safety tips. Overviews of health conditions
and treatment options are provided. Glossary, eBulletin, and more can be found here.

Federally funded health centers provide fee-based care based on income, insurance not necessary. Use Find a Health Center to locate centers close to a particular
address, county, or state.

Health-care consumers have a number of privacy rights afforded them by the
Health Insurance Portability and Accountability Act (HIPAA). Learn what they are
at this site, such as the right to see and get a copy of one's health records, the right
to get corrections added to one's record, and the right to give permission on how
one's information is used or shared in some areas. These rights are described here for
the health-care consumer, the medical professional, health plans, and other entities.
Complaints about privacy compromise can be submitted by anyone from this website. HIPAA privacy protections as it relates to public health, research, emergency
preparedness, health information technology, and genetic information are covered,
as well as certain agencies such as the Substance Abuse and Mental Health Services
Administration and the Centers for Medicare and Medicaid Services. Information
about the broader HIPAA statute and rules is available as well.

The National Library of Medicine is the world's largest biomedical library. Not
only does it have an immense print collection with more than 12 million titles, it also
has numerous electronic information services, such as MEDLINE/PubMed (more
than 19 million biomedical journal article citations, some linking to free full-text articles), PubMed Central (biomedical journal literature repository), MedlinePlus (consumer health information portal), ClinicalTrials.gov (public and privately funded
clinical trials) and environmental health and toxicology databases (e.g., TOXNET,
Household Products Database, Dietary Supplement Labels Database, ChemID*plus*,
Drug Information Portal, Haz-Map, LactMed, Pillbox) that are freely searchable
by researchers, health professionals, and health-care consumers. In addition to disseminating the biomedical research results of others, it does its own bioinformatics
and communications research. Additionally, it coordinates the National Network of
Libraries of Medicine (NN/LM), a consortium of eight regional libraries with over
600 members with the mission to foster access to biomedical information. The NLM

provides a wealth of information and services that only an investigation of their website can do justice.

The U.S. FDA Recalls, Market Withdrawals, and Safety Alerts website provides information about recalls for food, drugs, animal health, biologics, medical devices, and cosmetics issued in the past sixty days. Twitter recall feed also available.

Conclusion

The federal government supports and is an extremely important source of healthcare information and research. It recognizes the importance of open access of this information to researchers, professionals, and patients to promote dissemination of research findings into clinical practice. It also recognizes that patients play immense—-even essential—roles in positive health outcomes, and as such, it provides a wealth of information to assist them in making informed decisions.

Finding health information from the complex federal labyrinth can be quite overwhelming. There are numerous resources and tools for laypeople and professionals, this chapter being one of them. A growing number of federal websites have interactive communication such as live chat or e-mail support. And for more personal support, a biomedical librarian is an essential resource.

References

1. "Division of Grants: Grant Information for Current and Prospective HHS Grantees." Washington DC: U.S. Department of Health and Human Services. Office of Grants and Acquisition Policy. Last modified July 7, 2011; accessed July 16, 2012. http://dhhs.gov/asfr/ogapa/aboutog/grantsnet.html.
2. "About HHS." Washington, DC: U.S. Department of Health and Human Services. Accessed July 16, 2012. http://www.hhs.gov/about/.
3. "Federal Research Public Access Act." Washington, DC: The Alliance for Taxpayer Access. Last modified May 21, 2012; accessed July 16, 2012. http://www.taxpayer access.org/issues/frpaa/.
4. "About Us." Washington, DC: U.S. Department of Health and Human Services, Office on Women's Health. Last modified July 16, 2012; accessed July 16, 2012. http://womenshealth.gov/about-us/.
5. "About ORWH." Bethesda, MD: U.S. Department of Health and Human Services, National Institutes of Health, Office of Research on Women's Health. Accessed July 16, 2012. http://orwh.od.nih.gov/about.html.
6. "Office of Women's Health." Rockville, MD: U.S. Department of Health and Human Services, U.S. Food and Drug Administration, Office of Women's Health.

Accessed July 16, 2012. http://www.fda.gov/AboutFDA/CentersOffices/OC/Office ofWomensHealth/.

7. "Office of Special Health Affairs." Rockville, MD: U.S. Department of Health and Human Services, Health Resources and Services Administration. Accessed July 16, 2012. http://www.hrsa.gov/about/organization/bureaus/osha/index.html.

8. "Occupational Safety and Health Administration." Washington, DC: U.S. Department of Labor, Occupational Safety and Health Administration. Accessed July 16, 2012. http://www.osha.gov/.

9. "Office of Foods." Silver Spring, MD: U.S. Department of Health and Human Services, U.S. Food and Drug Administration. Last modified April 19, 2012; accessed July 16, 2012. http://www.fda.gov/AboutFDA/CentersOffices/Officeof Foods/default.htm.

10. "Center for Food Safety and Applied Nutrition." College Park, MD: U.S. Department of Health and Human Services, U.S. Food and Drug Administration. Last modified April 11, 2012; accessed July 16, 2012. http://www.fda.gov/aboutfda/cen tersoffices/officeoffoods/cfsan/default.htm.

11. "Center for Nutrition Policy and Promotion." Alexandria, VA: U.S. Department of Agriculture, Center for Nutrition Policy and Promotion. Last modified July 11, 2012; accessed July 16, 2012. http://www.cnpp.usda.gov/.

12. "About FNS." Alexandria, VA: U.S. Department of Agriculture, Food and Nutrition Service. Last modified February 9, 2012; accessed July 16, 2012. http://www.fns .usda.gov/fns/about.htm.

13. "Food Safety and Inspection Service (FSIS)." Washington, DC: U.S. Department of Agriculture, Food Safety and Inspection Service. Last modified July 13, 2012; accessed July 16, 2012. http://www.fsis.usda.gov/.

14. "CDC Food Safety Office." Atlanta: U.S. Department of Health and Human Services, Centers for Disease Control and Prevention. Last modified May 24, 2012; accessed July 16, 2012. http://www.cdc.gov/foodsafety/food-safety-office.html.

15. Forte, E., and M. Mallory. "Government Information and Statistics Sources." In *Reference and Information Services: An Introduction*, 4th ed., edited by Richard Rainer Bopp and Linda C. Smith, 637–714. Santa Barbara, CA: Libraries Unlimited, 2011.

16. "About the Catalog of U.S. Government Publications (CGP)." Washington, DC: U.S. Government Printing Office, Office of the Superintendent of Documents. Accessed July 16, 2012. http://catalog.gpo.gov/F/YPD84IY3UVI6AN4D85CXJPAC5EA77 E8MNUHV3P3NMRL5RJH6EY-19463?func=file&file_name=about-gpo01.

17. "Catalog of U.S. Government Publications (CGP) Search Tips/Help." Washington, DC: U.S. Government Printing Office, Office of the Superintendent of Documents. Accessed July 16, 2012. http://catalog.gpo.gov/F/YPD84IY3UVI6AN4D85CXJPA C5EA77E8MNUHV3P3NMRL5RJH6EY19791?func=file&file_name=help-1.

18. "About the Catalog."
19. "Catalog Search Tips/Help."
20. Ibid.

21. "The National Bibliography of U.S. Government Publications: Initial Planning Statement." Washington, DC: U.S. Government Printing Office, 2004: 3. Accessed July 16, 2012. http://www.fdlp.gov/home/repository/doc_view/1909-the-national -bibliography-of-us-government-publications-initial-planning-statement.

22. Ibid.

23. Ibid.

24. Ibid.

25. "Federal Depository Library Program (FDLP) Desktop." Washington, DC: U.S. Government Printing Office. Accessed July 16, 2012. http://www.fdlp.gov/.

26. "MetaLib." Washington, DC: U.S. Government Printing Office. Accessed July 16, 2012. http://metalib.gpo.gov/.

27. "U.S. Government Bookstore." Washington, DC: U.S. Government Printing Office. Last modified June 28, 2012; accessed July 16, 2012. http://bookstore.gpo.gov/.

28. "About Congress.gov." Washington, DC: Library of Congress, 2012. Accessed October 12, 2012. http://beta.congress.gov/about.

29. Ibid.

30. "Coverage Dates for Legislative Information." Washington, DC: Library of Congress, 2012. Accessed October 12, 2012. http://beta.congress.gov/help/coverage -dates/.

31. "About GPO: Frequently Asked Questions." Washington, DC: U.S. Government Printing Office. Accessed July 16, 2012. http://www.gpo.gov/about/faq.htm.

32. Ibid.

33. "About FDsys." Washington, DC: U.S. Government Printing Office, 2007. Accessed July 16, 2012. http://www.gpo.gov/fdsysinfo/aboutfdsys.htm.

34. "Federal Depository Library Program." Washington, DC: U.S. Government Printing Office. Accessed July 16, 2012. http://www.gpo.gov/help/federal_depository_li brary_program.htm.

35. "Basic Questions and Answers about Clinical Trials." Silver Spring, MD: U.S. Department of Health and Human Services, Food and Drug Administration. Last modified July 16, 2009; accessed October 31, 2012. http://tinyurl.com/c54sw9r.

36. Institute of Medicine, Committee to Advise the Public Health Service on Clinical Practice Guidelines. *Clinical Practice Guidelines: Directions for a New Program*, edited by Marilyn J. Field and Kathleen N. Lohr. The National Academies Press, 1990. Accessed October 31, 2012. http://www.nap.edu/openbook.php?record_id= 1626&page=38.

37. "About." Rockville, MD: U.S. Department of Health and Human Services, Agency for Healthcare Research and Quality. Accessed October 31, 2012. http://guideline .gov/about/index.aspx.

38. Panitch, Judith M., and Sarah Michalak. "The Serials Crisis: A White Paper for the UNC–Chapel Hill Scholarly Communications Convocation." Chapel Hill, NC: University of North Carolina, Chapel Hill, 2005. Accessed July 23, 2012. http://www .unc.edu/scholcomdig/whitepapers/panitch-michalak.html.

39. Suber, Peter. "Open Access Overview. Harvard Open Access Project." Last modified June 18, 2012; accessed July 23, 2012. http://www.earlham.edu/~peters/fos/overview.htm.

40. "NIH Public Access." Bethesda, MD: U.S. Department of Health and Human Services, National Institutes of Health, Office of Extramural Research, 2005. Accessed May 17, 2007. http://publicaccess.nih.gov/.

41. "PMC Overview." Bethesda, MD: U.S. Department of Health and Human Services, National Institutes of Health, National Library of Medicine. Last modified November 14, 2012; accessed July 23, 2012. http://www.ncbi.nlm.nih.gov/pmc/about/intro/.

42. THOMAS. "Federal Research Public Access Act of 2006: Bill Summary and Status, 106th Congress (2005–2006), S. 2695." Washington, DC: The Library of Congress. Accessed July 23, 2012. http://thomas.loc.gov/cgi-bin/bdquery/D?d106:2695:./list/bss/d106SN.lst::.

43. THOMAS. "Federal Research Public Access Act of 2009: Bill Summary and Status, 111th Congress (2009–2010), S. 1373." Washington, DC: The Library of Congress. Accessed July 23, 2012. http://thomas.loc.gov/cgi-bin/bdquery/z?d111:S1373:.

44. THOMAS. "Federal Research Public Access Act of 2009: Bill Summary and Status, 111th Congress (2009–2010), H.R. 5037." Washington, DC: The Library of Congress. Accessed July 23, 2012. http://thomas.loc.gov/cgi-bin/bdquery/z?d111:HR5037:.

45. THOMAS. "Federal Research Public Access Act of 2012: Bill Summary and Status, 112th Congress (2011–2012), H.R. 4004." Washington, DC: The Library of Congress. Accessed July 23, 2012. http://thomas.loc.gov/cgi-bin/bdquery/z?d112:h.r.04004:.

46. THOMAS. "Federal Research Public Access Act of 2012: Bill Summary and Status, 112th Congress (2011–2012), S. 2096." Washington, DC: The Library of Congress. Accessed July 23, 2012. http://thomas.loc.gov/cgi-bin/bdquery/z?d112:s.02096:.

47. THOMAS. "Research Works Act (RWA): Bill Summary and Status, 112th Congress (2011–2012), H.R. 3699, All Information." Washington, DC: The Library of Congress. Accessed July 23, 2012. http://thomas.loc.gov/cgi-bin/bdquery/z?d112:HR03699:@@@L&summ2=m&.

48. "Letter to Honorable Darrell E. Issa and Honorable Elijah Cummings Opposing H.R. 3699 the Research Works Act." Chicago: Medical Library Association and Association of Academic Health Sciences Libraries. Last modified January 30, 2012; accessed July 23, 2012. http://www.mlanet.org/government/gov_pdf/2012_jan%2030_researchworksact_lttr_final.pdf.

49. Howard, Jennifer. "Legislation to Bar Public-Access Requirement on Federal Research Is Dead." *Chronicle of Higher Education*, February 27, 2012. Accessed July 23, 2012. http://chronicle.com/article/Legislation-to-Bar/130949/.

50. "HHS Open Government Plan." Washington, DC: U.S. Department of Health and Human Services. Last modified April 7, 2010; accessed July 23, 2012. http://www.hhs.gov/open/plan/opengovernmentplan/ourplan_openhhs.pdf.

51. "Award and Administration Guide (AAG): Chapter VI.D.4, Dissemination and Sharing of Research Results." Arlington, VA: National Science Foundation, January 2011. Accessed July 23, 2012. http://www.nsf.gov/pubs/policydocs/pappguide/nsf11001/aag_6.jsp#VID4.

52. "Grant Proposal Guide (GPG): Chapter II.C.2.j (2nd bullet), Dissemination and Sharing of Research Results." Arlington, VA: National Science Foundation, January 2011. Accessed July 23, 2012. http://www.nsf.gov/pubs/policydocs/pappguide/nsf11001/gpg_2.jsp#dmp.

53. "Data Management for NSF SBE Directorate Proposals and Awards." Arlington, VA: National Science Foundation, June 2011. Accessed July 23, 2012. http://www.nsf.gov/sbe/SBE_DataMgmtPlanPolicy.pdf.

54. "Directorate for Biological Sciences, Information about the Data Management Plan Required for All Proposals." Arlington, VA: National Science Foundation, June 2011. Accessed July 23, 2012. http://www.nsf.gov/bio/pubs/BIODMP061511.pdf.

55. "Table 9.8—Composition of Outlays for the Conduct of Research and Development: 1949–2017 (in Millions of Dollars)." In *Fiscal Year 2013: Historical Tables: Budget of the United States Government*." Washington, DC: The White House, the Administration, Office of Management and Budget, 2011. Accessed July 23, 2012. http://www.whitehouse.gov/sites/default/files/omb/budget/fy2013/assets/hist.pdf.

56. "About NTIS." Alexandria, VA: U.S. Department of Commerce, National Technical Information Service. Accessed July 23, 2012. http://www.ntis.gov/about/index.aspx.

57. "United States Code, 2006 Edition, Supplement 4, Title 15—Commerce and Trade, Chapter 23—Dissemination of Technical, Scientific and Engineering Information, Sections 1151-1157." Washington, DC: U.S. Government Printing Office. Accessed July 23, 2012. http://tinyurl.com/75pjybe.

58. "United States Code, 2006 Edition, Supplement 4, Title 15—Commerce and Trade, Chapter 63—Technology Innovation, Sec. 3704b—National Technical Information Service. 15 USC Sec. 3704b-2. (Source: Pub. L. 100-519, title II, §212, Oct. 24, 1988, 102 Stat. 2594; Pub. L. 102-140, title II, Oct. 28, 1991, 105 Stat. 804; Pub. L. 102-245, title V, §506(c), Feb. 14, 1992, 106 Stat. 27; Pub. L. 110-161, div. B, title I, §109, Dec. 26, 2007, 121 Stat. 1893)." Washington, DC: U.S. Government Printing Office. Accessed July 23, 2012. http://tinyurl.com/7oxhtt8.

59. "American Technology Preeminence Act: Responsibilities of Federal Agencies for the Transfer of Scientific, Technical, and Engineering Information to the National Technical Information Service (NTIS) under the American Technology Preeminence Act (ATPA). Public Law 102-245, Section 108, American Technology Preeminence Act of 1991 (15 U.S.C. 3704b-2)." Springfield, VA: U.S. Department of Commerce, Technology Administration, National Technical Information Service. Accessed July 23, 2012. https://www.ntis.gov/pdf/ATPA.pdf.

60. "Report to Congressional Requesters: Information Management: Dissemination of Technical Reports." GAO-01-490. Washington, DC: U.S. General Accounting Office. Last modified May, 2001; accessed March 19, 2012. http://www.gao.gov/new.items/d01490.pdf.

61. Ibid.
62. Ibid.
63. Ibid.
64. Ibid.
65. Ibid.
66. "A Comprehensive Assessment of Public Information Dissemination Final Report: Executive Summary." Washington, DC: U.S. National Commission on Libraries and Information Science. Last modified January, 2001; accessed October 30, 2012. http://catalog.hathitrust.org/Record/003616677.
67. "About NTIS." Alexandria, VA: U.S. Department of Commerce, National Technical Information Service. Accessed October 29, 2012. http://www.ntis.gov/about/index .aspx.
68. Morehead, Joe. *Introduction to United States Government Information Sources.* Englewood, CO: Libraries Unlimited, 1999.
69. "NIH Public Access."
70. Reller, Tom. "Elsevier Collaborates with the Office of Scientific and Technical Information (OSTI) at the U.S. Department of Energy (DOE) to Increase Access to and Visibility of Research." Philadelphia: Elsevier, 2012. Last modified October 29, 2012; accessed October 31, 2012. http://tinyurl.com/cdqdnj3.
71. "About NTIS."
72. "Subject Coverage of the NTIS Collection." Alexandria, VA: U.S. Department of Commerce, National Technical Information Service. Accessed October 29, 2012. http://www.ntis.gov/about/coverage.aspx.
73. "NTIS Database Search Guide." Alexandria, VA: U.S. Department of Commerce, National Technical Information Service. Accessed October 29, 2012. http://www .ntis.gov/pdf/dbguid.pdf.
74. "National Technical Reports Library." Alexandria, VA: U.S. Department of Commerce, National Technical Information Service. Accessed October 29, 2012. http://www.ntis.gov/products/ntrl.aspx.
75. Melody Allison, "Wright, H. NSCEP Web Comments" [e-mail message]. October 31, 2012, 8:21 a.m. EST.
76. Bala, E. A., and S. A. Boren. "Review Paper: Managing Clinical Knowledge for Health Care Improvement." In *Yearbook of Medical Informatics 2000: Patient-Centered Systems*, edited by Jan H. van Bemmel and Alexa T. McCray, 65–70. New York: IMIA, 2000.
77. "Translating Research into Practice (TRIP)—II (AHRQ Pub. No. 01-P017)." Washington, DC: The U.S. Department of Health and Human Services, Office on Women's Health, Agency for Healthcare Research and Quality, 2001. Accessed July 23, 2012. http://www.ahrq.gov/research/trip2fac.pdf.
78. Hanson, Sarah, Lori Nadig, Bruce Altevogt, Forum on Neuroscience and Nervous System Disorders, and Institute of Medicine. *Venture Philanthropy Strategies to Support Translational Research: Workshop Summary.* Washington, DC: The National Academies Press, 2009. Accessed July 23, 2012. http://books.nap.edu/cat alog.php?record_id=12558.

79. "About the NIH Roadmap." Washington, DC: U.S. Department of Health and Human Services, National Institutes of Health, Division of Program Coordination, Planning and Strategic Initiatives. Last modified December 28, 2011; accessed July 23, 2012. http://commonfund.nih.gov/aboutroadmap.aspx.

80. "NIH Roadmap for Medical Research: Fact Sheet." Bethesda, MD: U.S. Department of Health and Human Services, National Institutes of Health, 2006. Accessed July 23, 2012. http://opasi.nih.gov/documents/NIHRoadmap_FactSheet_Aug06.pdf.

81. Ibid.

82. "Clinical and Translational Science." Bethesda, MD: U.S. Department of Health and Human Services, National Institutes of Health, National Center for Advancing Translational Sciences. Accessed July 23, 2012. http://www.ncats.nih.gov/research/cts/cts.html.

83. THOMAS. "Consolidated Appropriations Act, 2012: Bill Summary and Status, 112th Congress (2011–2012), H.R. 2055, Sec. 461, 479. 287, 301–304." Washington, DC: Library of Congress. Accessed July 23, 2012. http://thomas.loc.govcgi-bin/bdquery/D?d112:2055:./list/bss/d112HR.lst::.

84. "Research." Bethesda, MD: U.S. Department of Health and Human Services, National Institutes of Health, National Center for Advancing Translational Sciences. Accessed July 23, 2012. http://www.ncats.nih.gov/research/research.html.

85. "Clinical and Translational Science."

86. "Catalyzing Innovation Fact Sheet." Bethesda, MD: U.S. Department of Health and Human Services, National Institutes of Health, National Center for Advancing Translational Sciences, 2012. Accessed July 23, 2012. http://www.ncats.nih.gov/files/factsheet.pdf.pdf.

87. Institute of Medicine, Committee on Quality of Health Care in America. *Crossing the Quality Chasm: A New Health System for the 21st Century*. Washington, DC: National Academy Press, 2001. Accessed July 23, 2012. http://www.nap.edu/catalog.php?record_id=10027.

88. Ibid.

89. Ibid.

90. "The Effective Health Care Program Stakeholder Guide." Rockville, MD: U.S. Department of Health and Human Services, Agency for Healthcare Research and Quality, 2011. Accessed July 23, 2012. http://www.ahrq.gov/clinic/epcpartner/stakeholderguide/.

91. "The Effective Health Care Program Stakeholder Guide: Chapter 1." Rockville, MD: U.S. Department of Health and Human Services, Agency for Healthcare Research and Quality, 2011. Last modified March, 2012; accessed July 27, 2012. http://www.ahrq.gov/clinic/epcpartner/stakeholderguide/stakehold1.htm.

92. Institute of Medicine, *Crossing the Quality Chasm*.

93. Clancy, C. "Navigating the Health Care System: Becoming an Involved Health Care Consumer." Rockville, MD: U.S. Department of Health and Human Services,

Agency for Healthcare Research and Quality, 2007. Accessed July 23, 2012. http://www.ahrq.gov/consumer/cc/cc103007.htm.

94. Ibid.

95. Ibid.

96. "Health.gov: Health Literacy." Rockville, MD: U.S. Department of Health and Human Services, Office of Disease Prevention and Health Promotion. Last modified July 27, 2012; accessed July 27, 2012. http://www.health.gov/communication/literacy/.

97. Nielsen-Bohlman, L., A. M. Panzer, and D. A. Kindig (eds.) and Institute of Medicine, Board on Neuroscience and Behavioral Health, Committee on Health Literacy. "Health Literacy: A Prescription to End Confusion." Washington, DC: National Academies Press, 2004. Accessed August 7, 2012. http://www.iom.edu/Reports/2004/Health-Literacy-A-Prescription-to-End-Confusion.aspx.

98. "About HealthFinder.gov." Washington, DC: U.S. Department of Health and Human Services. Last modified July 27, 2012; accessed July 27, 2012. http://www.http://www.healthfinder.gov/aboutus/.

99. "Quality Guidelines." Washington, DC: U.S. Department of Health and Human Services. Last modified July 27, 2012; accessed July 27, 2012. http://www.healthfinder.gov/aboutus/content_guidelines.aspx.

100. "Quality Guidelines for Health Information [used by MedlinePlus.gov]." Rockville, MD: U.S. Department of Health and Human Services, National Institutes of Health, National Library of Medicine. Last modified April 19, 2012; accessed July 30, 2012. http://www.nlm.nih.gov/medlineplus/languages/criteria.html.

101. "The Basic Principles of Evidence-Based Medicine." Bethesda, MD: U.S. Department of Health and Human Services, National Institutes of Health, National Library of Medicine, National Center for Biotechnology Information. Last modified February 12, 2012; accessed July 30, 2012. http://www.ncbi.nlm.nih.gov/pubmed health/PMH0005078/.

102. Ibid.

103. White, Alicia. "Behind the Headlines: How to Read Health News." London: England's National Health Service, 2012. Last modified July 30, 2012. http://www.ncbi.nlm.nih.gov/pubmedhealth/behindtheheadlines/how-to-read/.

104. "Hospital Compare." Baltimore, MD: U.S. Department of Health and Human Services, Centers for Medicare and Medicaid. Accessed July 30, 2012. http://www.hospitalcompare.hhs.gov/.

105. "Nursing Home Compare." Baltimore, MD: U.S. Department of Health and Human Services, Centers for Medicare and Medicaid. Accessed July 30, 2012. http://www.medicare.gov/NursingHomeCompare/search.aspx.

106. "Home Health Compare." Baltimore, MD: U.S. Department of Health and Human Services, Centers for Medicare and Medicaid. Accessed July 30, 2012. http://www.medicare.gov/quality-care-finder/index.html#home-health-compare.

107. "Dialysis Facility Finder Compare." Baltimore, MD: U.S. Department of Health and Human Services, Centers for Medicare and Medicaid. Accessed July 30, 2012. http://www.medicare.gov/quality-care-finder/index.html#dialysis-facility-compare.

108. "Physician Compare." Baltimore, MD: U.S. Department of Health and Human Services, Centers for Medicare and Medicaid. Accessed July 30, 2012. http://www .medicare.gov/quality-care-finder/index.html#physician-compare.

109. "Medicare Plan Finder." Baltimore, MD: U.S. Department of Health and Human Services, Centers for Medicare and Medicaid. Accessed July 30, 2012. http://www .medicare.gov/quality-care-finder/index.html#medicare-plan-finder.

Conferences, Reviews, and Translations

BEATRIZ VARMAN

Conferences

Professional development activities such as conferences and seminars continue to serve as venues for health science professionals and researchers to increase their career connections and skills. The Internet has made it easier to disseminate logistical information—such as conference venues, dates, and sponsors—to a wider audience in a timely manner. Consequently, printed resources such as indexes listing annual health-related conferences have become less relevant for those seeking up-to-date information. Many websites from professional organizations are dedicated to providing only conference information to attendees. Some of these websites provide past and future conference information; others provide only future conference information.

With the advent of the Internet, an increasing number of conferences are available in the virtual world. Virtual conferences such as webinars or webcasts have grown increasingly popular, sometimes eliminating the need for professional travel. Social media websites like Facebook, Twitter, and blogs allow instant sharing of information where conference attendees can acquire knowledge without physically attending. Conference presentations and seminars can be viewed almost in real time. Though virtual meetings began in the business world and grew out of a need to reduce overall costs of conference travel, this business model—which takes advantage of technological advances in communication to lower travel expenses—has also been embraced by the medical and health science communities. A large number of health-related professional development opportunities are becoming increasingly available online. More conference organizers are publishing conference programs in virtual environments ranging from live satellite telecasts with two-way communication capabilities to downloadable files for Apple, Blackberry, and Android mobile products.

In the world of Internet websites, mobile resources, and social media, it has become easier for librarians to identify these virtual offerings and make them available to interested health professionals. Regardless of the system of delivery, the librarian's role in identifying these offerings requires effective online search strategies and careful evaluation of retrieved content. Though the search may yield some unfamiliar sponsors, the results can be used to compile a working list of blogs, discussion lists, and special-interest forums, all of which are beneficial sources of conference information.

Despite the accessibility of virtual conferences, many critics question their value. Viewing webcasts or webinars from the privacy of one's own computer is limiting, they say, and eliminates a core benefit of conference attendance: the opportunity to network with colleagues.

This section of the chapter intends to provide a brief introduction to some of the popular free online websites that include conference information. These sites are continuously updated so it is worthwhile to visit them to find relevant up-to-date conference information.

Calendars

In the past, calendars were available in print format and were a valuable resource for locating conferences. The *Journal of the American Medical Association* (*JAMA*), for example, was a good point of reference for physicians and researchers seeking information about upcoming health science meetings. Other major health professional and research-oriented periodicals could also be consulted for listings of meetings and conferences in their specific interest areas. Print directories are now either obsolete or no longer in publication. Conference calendars are now available online, so the information is typically more comprehensive and up-to-date. It is common to obtain an entire program of events, abstracts of presentations, and even presenters' bios online. Content is also easily updated and links to important peripheral information—such as lodging, maps, and conference center floor plans—are usually just a click away.

Medical Conferences' Websites

The medical conferences' websites listed below are just a few that have been identified by searching major medical associations, sponsoring organizations, and medical specialties websites. The list is intended to give an overview of where to find medical conferences and is by no means fully comprehensive.

7.1   JN: The JAMA Network, "Medical Meetings." Chicago: American Medical Association. Available: http://jamanetwork.com/public/MedicalMeetings. aspx.

JAMA Network Medical Meetings provides U.S. and international coverage with links to conference organizers, websites, and venues. The website displays only current and upcoming events, including conferences, seminars, workshops, and continuing education courses. The calendar of events is searchable by journal (*JAMA, Archives of Internal Medicine*, etc.), type of event (conference, course, meeting, symposium), topic, location, and date.

Content is submitted online to The JAMA Network and is regularly updated. Conference organizers can also submit events for website consideration. Updates are available from the JAMA Network Medical Meetings by subscribing to e-mail, RSS feeds, Atom feed, or iCalendar Feed, or by downloading an iCalendar file.

7.2   AllConferences.com. Stafford, TX: Castles of the World, doing business as AllConferences.com. Available: http://www.allconferences.com/Health/ Medicine.

AllConferences.com is a commercial Beta test site that includes a global directory of international and domestic conferences and conference planned events. Medical and health events include those pertaining to various specific medical disciplines as well as other health-related specialties such as public health, nursing, and nutrition. Selecting the link to search on medical conferences retrieved more than 4,000 records that included links to more than forty different medical disciplines. Conference information is searchable by category, organizer, date, keywords, and venue. The website includes current and past conference information and even allows users to register for conferences online. To receive updated information via e-mail, one must complete the free registration.

7.3   TheConferencewebsite.com. Durham, UK: RF (Medical). Available: http:// www.medical.theconferencewebsite.com/.

Produced by RF (Medical) Limited, the website includes only medical conference information. Registration is required to access the complete listing of medical conferences and to receive e-mail conference alerts. Filling out the online registration form allows users to select their interest in medical specialties. Visitors can access ten conference links for information—such as conference website, title, venue, date, and location—before they are required to register.

Users can search for current and future domestic and international conferences by title, keywords, specialty, dates, and location by using basic and advanced search features. The navigation bar on the left of the page includes links to the registration page, current medical conferences, organizers directory, venue directory, and FAQs. One can also register a conference for website inclusion. The free iPhone, iPad, and iPod Touch applications for this website are available from the Apple application store.

7.4   Frontiers. Lausanne, Switzerland. Available:
       http://www.frontiersin.org/events/Medicine.

Frontiers is an expanding open-access collection of scientific and medical titles. Developed in 2007 by scientists from the Swiss Federal Institute of Technology in Lausanne, Frontiers is primarily an academic publishing website. However, the link titled Frontiers Events takes visitors to a calendar of academic events listing conference information such as speakers, organizers, and links to the conference website and Frontiers event blog.

The Frontiers website also features a keyword search for international conference and events, and the results can be displayed by most recent or most popular events. Users are required to register in order to participate fully and to contribute postings of any kind. However, visitors can log in to this website by using their Facebook, Twitter, Google, or LinkedIn usernames and passwords.

7.5   Health On the Net Foundation (HON). Geneva. Available:
       http://www.hon.ch/cgi-bin/confevent.

HON is a Swiss foundation portal offering medical information to worldwide medical meetings in English, French, and German. It's also a portal to reliable sources of health-care information for patients and medical professionals. It was developed after experts from eleven countries met at the Use of the Internet and World-Wide Web for Telematics in Healthcare conference in Geneva in 1995. HON was created in 1996 to "promote the effective and reliable use of the new technologies for telemedicine in healthcare around the world."[1]

The section on medical meetings lists conference titles, descriptions, dates, topics, venues and—if relevant—available CME credits. The most current events are displayed on the first page, but information on past conferences is also included. Users can search for conferences by year, theme, location, keywords, subject, and language. Users can also receive conference news via e-mail or RSS feeds. Visitors can submit a conference to be listed on the website as well.

7.6   Virtual Medical Centre (VMC). Australia: Virtual Medical Center
         Headquarters. Available: http://www.virtualmedicalcentre.com/
         conferences/.

VMC is an Australian website that delivers information on medical videos, drug supplements, diagnoses, disease treatment, and other medical news. VMC's website has a listing of future conferences organized by event date as well as a section on conferences where users can search by medical specialty. At the bottom of the page, there are links to medical conferences in twenty-two medical specialties. By selecting the conference title link, one can find more complete information, such as dates, descriptions, locations, organizations, websites, and contact information.

To receive this information, one can register to receive VMC's free electronic newsletter, subscribe to RSS feeds or join a discussion forum. VMC also allows users to share the conference information via LinkedIn, Facebook, Twitter, Google, Blogger, and other such services.

7.7   Medical Education Resources. Littleton, CO: Medical Education Resources.
         Available: http://www.mer.org/.

Medical Education Resources, or MER, is a nonprofit company in Colorado. Accredited by the Accreditation Council for Continuing Education, MER is considered one of the leaders in providing high-quality continuing medical education for physicians. Its website includes more than sixty CME-accredited programs in the United States, Caribbean, Mexico, and Canada. The website includes links to seminars and other specialty conferences under the tabs named "Conference by Title," "Conference by Location," and "Conference by Date." These links display an overview of the conference, including location, registration prices, accommodations, and program information.

7.8   Doctor's Review. Montreal, Quebec, Canada: Parkhurst Publishing.
         Available: http://www.doctorsreview.com/meetings/.

Canadian publishing company Parkhurst Publishing has developed this comprehensive website to complement the print version of their *Doctor's Review* magazine. Updated weekly, Doctor's Review includes information on more than 2,000 medical meetings and allows visitors to search for upcoming medical conferences by keyword, specialty, date, and travel destination. The website also offers links on tips for traveling, places to visit, and food choices during one's travel. Organizations and other conference organizers can submit a conference to be listed on the website. The website also includes a link to submit corrections to a listing.

7.9   *New England Journal of Medicine*, "Medical Meetings." Boston:
         Massachusetts Medical Society. Available: http://www.nejm.org/medical-
         conference.

The *New England Journal of Medicine* has a brief section on medical meetings on their website, which lists more than twenty past and forthcoming domestic and international conferences that can be searched by specialty, location, and date. Listings include conference organizers, important information for authors, a link to the conference website, and contact information.

7.10   Physicians Travel and Meeting Guide (PTMG). Parsipanny, NJ: Frontline Medical Communications. Available: http://ptmg.com/.

PTMG is a comprehensive database of domestic, international, and online CME information. It includes more than 2,000 future medical meetings that can be searched by specialty, location, date, and keyword. The website is updated daily with comprehensive information such as sponsoring organization as well as conference topic or title. The website also lists CME credits available, registration fee, recreational activities, and special events for attendees.

One can search conferences by date, city, country, medical specialty, and keyword. Physicians Travel and Meeting Guide also provides users with a variety of timely travel information, including travel news and city guides as well as dining and lodging options where medical meetings take place. Registration is required to access the full website and receive a free e-newsletter. One can also subscribe to the RSS feeds from forty-two different medical specialties to receive updates.

7.11   MD Conference Finder. Cambridge Technologies. Available: http://www.mdconferencefinder.com/.

This website is produced by Cambridge Technologies. Developed by physicians, the website includes information on more than 3,000 past and present U.S. medical conferences, reviews of past conferences from physicians who attended, board review courses for every ABMS specialty and on-demand webinars to help users find online CME events. Users can search for conferences by state, specialty, specialty societies, location, presenter, organizer, and date. The website also includes a list of the top medical conferences and a link to CME requirements by state. Conference organizers can add a conference to the website.

7.12   Medscape Today. New York: WebMD. Available: http://www.medscape.com/medscapetoday/conferences.

The Medscape website includes information on drugs, diseases, and medical procedures as well as daily medical news and highlights from recent conferences. The website includes information from upcoming national and international conferences as well. Past conferences have provided video commentaries and reviews from expert scientists in the subject field. The site also includes links to conference organizations, dates, locations, and specialty. Users can share this information with colleagues via e-mail, Facebook, or Twitter. To access this information, one must complete a free registration. Once registered, one can subscribe to breaking conference news. Medscape is accessible via iPad, iPhone, Android, Blackberry, and Kindle Fire.

Mobile Applications

The proliferation of medical mobile applications has provided an array of conference information that can be downloaded to a mobile device to keep one up-to-date on where conferences are scheduled in a particular medical specialty. Most of these applications are from individual medical societies or conference organizers promoting their specific conference venue rather than from a full website where one can find all available medical conferences. Conferencewebsite.com and Medscape are the only full websites that have an application for mobile Apple devices at the time of publication.

Papers Presented at Meetings— Conference Proceedings and Meeting Abstracts

Locating papers presented at meetings, conferences, symposia, or workshops often poses a challenge for the health sciences librarian. It is becoming popular for presented papers to be self-published on the Web or exist in a digital commons at an associated academic institution. Traditionally, papers presented at meetings are published as conference proceedings. These proceedings can be published as books or individual papers and are sometimes submitted to journals as a separate publication. Conferences sometimes publish abstracts of papers to be presented at an upcoming conference or distribute proceedings on site in CD-ROM or USB flash memory format.

Following are different methods for how proceedings of meetings can be identified:

1. A multivolume work encompassing the total proceedings of a conference or meeting.
2. A monograph or report with a specific title and editor.
3. A supplement, special number, or entire issue of an established journal (from either an official publication of the sponsoring society or agency or an unaffiliated publication that the society elects because of the subject content of the symposium or conference).
4. Selected papers or abstracts published in a journal because it is the official organ or because of subject content.
5. Reports of a meeting or conference in a journal that has a special section devoted to "congress or conference proceedings."

6. Dual publication as both an issue or part of a journal and as a monograph or report.[2]

Papers presented at conferences usually represent the current trends and hot topics in the field, and are thus often sought after by health professionals and researchers. Presentations at conferences may be cited in later literature even if there is no corresponding publication.

Some papers will be included by indexing and abstracting services that index journals. Revised papers published under a different title are also somewhat difficult to track. Expert database searches using controlled vocabulary, authors' names, and unique keywords such as convention, colloquia, congress, forum, etc., can help in the location of these resources.

When looking for conference publications, one needs to make the distinction between conference papers and meeting abstracts. A final full-text version of a research paper (i.e., a journal article) is a conference paper; they are usually included in the conference proceedings. Meeting abstracts are usually short summaries of an ongoing research project that are frequently published in advance of a conference; conference papers are made available after the conference as part of a proceedings volume. The following is a short list of databases, websites, and search engines that index conference materials and are helpful in locating conference proceedings, posters, and meeting abstracts presented at conferences.

7.13   Conference Papers Index (CPI). Ann Arbor, MI: ProQuest. Available by subscription from ProQuest: http://www.csa.com/factsheets/cpi-set-c.php.

Conference Papers Index (CPI) provides citations to papers and poster sessions and papers presented at major scientific meetings around the world. This source includes scientific meetings in its list of citations, and is prepared from final programs or abstract publications, published proceedings, and questionnaire responses from conferences.

Though CPI has been published since 1973, its emphasis on the life sciences, environmental sciences, and aquatic sciences began in 1995. The database contains more than 3 million records and includes citations from 1982 to the present. Records include title and author information needed to track specific papers presented at the conference, as well as complete ordering information to obtain preprints, abstracts, proceedings, and other publications derived from the conference.

7.14   PapersFirst. Dublin, OH: OCLC. Available by subscription from OCLC: http://www.oclc.org/en-US/home.html.

PapersFirst, an OCLC product, indexes papers presented at conferences worldwide. PapersFirst contains more than 6.9 million records in a wide variety of subjects and is updated semimonthly. Each of the papers contained in the database from 1993 forward are available through the British Library Document Supply Centre.

Coverage includes every published congress, symposium, conference, exposition, workshop, and meeting received by the British Library Document Supply Centre. Searchable fields are by keyword, author, conference location, conference name, dates, and subject.

7.15   ProceedingsFirst. Dublin, OH: OCLC. Available by subscription from OCLC: http://www.oclc.org/en-US/home.html.

ProceedingsFirst, also an OCLC product, indexes every published congress, symposium, conference, exposition, workshop, and meeting received by the British Library Document Supply Centre. It differs from PapersFirst in that a list of the authors and papers presented at each conference is included in each record. Available from 1993–present, it includes more than 192,000 records and is updated twice a week.

7.16   F1000 Posters. London: F1000 Research. Available: http://f1000.com/posters.

F1000 Posters is an open-access repository of conference posters and oral presentation slides in the field of biology and medicine. This website provides access to posters and slides after the work has been presented at a conference, giving the possibility to access the information without delays to a wider array of scientists. F1000 Posters includes 4,000 posters and slides.

Users can browse by poster, slide, biology and medicine disciplines, conference, institution, society, and faculty or perform a keyword search in the search box. Information on upcoming meetings and how to deposit one's posters or slides is also available. Registration is required to download one's poster or slides. This repository is available by individual or institutional subscription.

7.17   Google Scholar. Mountain View, CA: Google. Available: http://scholar.google.com/.

Created by Google in 2004, Google Scholar specifically retrieves scholarly publications from academic publishers, scientific professional societies, online repositories, and university websites. Users can retrieve information across different disciplines from books, journal articles, theses, abstracts, and conference papers. The search can be limited by year, and the capability to include patents as well as citations is also available.

7.18   Microsoft Academic Search. Seattle: Microsoft. Available: http://academic.research.microsoft.com/.

Microsoft Academic Search is an extensive website, the Microsoft answer to Google Scholar. Both search engines provide information on authors, publications, journals, and citation metrics. Microsoft Academic Search also lists and ranks the top twenty past conferences based on the cumulative number of citations from presentations at these conferences. The information is displayed in a graphic where one can easily visualize the trends of cumulative or annual citations. Google Scholar and Microsoft Academic Search could be a convenient place to look for conference papers to complement a search from other databases.

7.19   Web of Science. Philadelphia: Thomson Reuters. Available: http:// thomsonreuters.com/.

Web of Science indexes original research articles, reviews, editorials, chronologies, and abstracts covering biological sciences, medical and life sciences, physical and chemical sciences, agriculture, social sciences, arts, and humanities. The database includes a multidisciplinary content of more than 12,000 journals, including open-access journals and more than 150,000 conference proceedings.

7.20   Scopus. Philadelphia: Elsevier B.V. Available: http://www.info.sciverse.com/scopus.

Scopus is an extensive database that includes more than 10,000 life and health sciences publications (including all journals in MEDLINE and Embase). Scopus also indexes more than 20,000 journal titles from other disciplines in sciences and humanities and indexes more than 700 conference proceedings. Scopus has an extensive coverage of approximately 5.3 million records of conference papers from proceedings and journals.

From the Scopus website: "Scopus only indexes serial publications: journals, trade journals, book series and conference materials that have an ISSN (International Standard Serial Number) assigned to them. The only exception concerns conference papers, which can be captured via different routes than by being published in a serial publication with an ISSN."[3] Please note that meeting abstracts are not covered by Scopus.

7.21   CAB Abstracts. Oxfordshire, UK: CABI. Available: http://www.cabdirect.org/.

Produced by CABI, a nonprofit science-based development and information organization, CAB Abstracts includes information in the life sciences, agriculture, environment, veterinary sciences, applied economics, and food and science nutrition. The international coverage includes more than 100 publications in 50 languages. The database is available from 1973–present, and includes 7.1 million records from 10,000 serials, books, general reports, theses, and conference proceedings.

7.22   Embase. Philadelphia: Elsevier B.V. Available:
        http://www.elsevier.com/online-tools/embase.

Embase is a biomedical and pharmacological database available from 1974–present. The database contains approximately 27 million records and indexes more than 8,000 peer-reviewed journals. The database also indexes more than 3,000 conferences and more than 900,000 conference abstracts that have been published in journals and journal supplements.

Over 300,000 conference abstracts from 1,000 conferences are indexed every year in Embase, providing a unique and extensive coverage of conference abstracts in the biomedical and pharmacology fields.

7.23   Biological Abstracts/RRM (Reports, Reviews, Meetings). Philadelphia:
        Thomson Reuters. Available: http://thomsonreuters.com/.

With well over 2.5 million records, Biological Abstracts/RRM provides the most comprehensive coverage of worldwide meeting literature, conferences, literature reviews, patents, and books in the life sciences with particular attention to reports, reviews, and meetings. Biological Abstracts/RRM complements Biological Abstracts by supplying unique coverage of these increasingly important sources of information. Serving as the essential nonjournal literature resource, the database includes citations to biological and biochemical meeting papers presented at more than 1,500 meetings, symposia, and workshops. Available by subscription from Thomson Reuters from 1989–present, the database adds more than 165,000 records to its collections each year.

7.24   IEEE Explore Digital Library. Institute of Electrical and Electronics Engineers
        (IEEE). Available: http://ieeexplore.ieee.org/xpl/conferences.jsp.

IEEE Explore Digital Library provides full-text access to technical literature in electrical engineering, computer science, and electronics. IEEE Xplore contains full-text documents from IEEE journals, transactions, magazines, letters, conference proceedings, standards, and IEE publications from 1988, with select content back to 1952. It allows users to browse conference publications by title or by topic. One can also search by keyword or unique phrases to find out conference proceedings titles.

7.25   Conference Proceedings Citation Index (CPCI). Philadelphia: Thomson
        Reuters. Available: http://thomsonreuters.com/products_services/science/
        science_products/a-/conf_proceedings_citation_index/.

Conference Proceedings Citation Index (CPCI) includes published literature from books and journals that have been presented at conferences, symposia, seminars, colloquia, workshops, and conventions worldwide. The database is updated weekly, and approximately 400,000 records from 12,000 conferences are added each year. CPCI can be searched in Web of Science.

7.26   Conference Proceedings. London: The British Library Document Supply
        Center. Available: http://www.bl.uk/reshelp/findhelprestype/confproc/
        index.html.

Conference Proceedings are available from the British Library Document Supply Services, which owns one of the most comprehensive collections of unrestricted reports available for public use in the world. The collection of reports, conferences, and theses numbers 4.9 million. Conference papers alone number more than 400,000, with approximately 16,000 added each year. The British Library Document Supply Centre supports a fee-based online delivery service.

Other sources for finding conference proceedings could be using WorldCat and LocatorPlus for papers or proceedings treated like monographs. For conference papers that get published as journal articles, PubMed, Scopus, or Embase are good sources. Another excellent source for locating conference proceedings is a Digital Commons. Most libraries have this open-access digital library that contains pre-prints, conference proceedings, working papers, and dissertations when full text is not immediately available.

Other suggestions to consider consulting when looking for conference proceedings follow:

- Search the conference name as an author or as keywords in the Library Catalog.
- Search in WorldCat, using words from the full name of the conference as a conference name query.
- Search the paper's author(s) in an index database such as Chemical Abstracts. While an unpublished conference paper will not be indexed, one might find a later journal article based on it. Work-in-progress is often presented at conferences and then later submitted to journals.
- Search in Google Scholar or Microsoft Academic Search. An author might have posted a copy of the paper or a slide presentation in an open repository or website.
- Proceedings.com (http://www.proceedings.com/bookstore.html) from Curran Associates is a vendor service that prints and sells hardcopy conference proceedings (not single papers) from many professional organizations that are otherwise available only in electronic formats or to members.
- Try contacting the paper's author.

Reviews

Reviews are secondary documents designed to provide an overview of a detailed concept. In the health sciences, reviews are written by experts in the field to provide a synopsis, evaluation, or analysis of a documented research topic. Reviews are also written to cover health science information resources. Reviews range in complexity from fact sheets prepared for lay audiences to evidence-based systematic reviews for health-related intervention decisions.

For example, MedlinePlus is the database of choice for consumer health information. At a minimum, reviews (fact sheets) can contain a brief definition of a diagnosis, causes, symptoms, and treatment options. Specifically created for the lay audience by the National Library of Medicine, MedlinePlus provides links to reputable organizations' prepared data as well. MedlinePlus is discussed in more detail in chapter 11, "Consumer Health Sources."

Health sciences professionals' interest in reviews may be to become acquainted with a health-related topic, update their existing knowledge base, or gather key information to aid in patient care decisions or research plans.

Monographs

Review articles published in monographic series are generally used by healthcare professionals to update their knowledge base. Titles such as *Annual Reviews*, *Reviews in Biochemical Toxicology*, *Concepts in Biochemistry*, *Clinical Reviews in Allergy and Immunology*, and *State-of-the-Art Reviews* publish reviews in a series of monographs. These resources provide high-level content and include extensive bibliographies for additional support information. The reviews are widely used in teaching and research, and serve the purposes both of current awareness and introduction to a new subject.

The reviews are written in a compact narrative style, with a minimum of descriptive text for each article covered. Many authors provide lists of summary points and future issues. The length of each review and the number of articles covered vary widely depending on both the topic and the preferences of the author. The articles are written by authors who are accepted authorities on the material covered.

Articles

Review articles published in journals exist primarily in the form of literature reviews, systematic reviews, meta-analysis, and overviews (sometimes referred to as tutorials). In addition to these most popular forms, several different types of review articles can be identified in indexes and databases.

Literature review articles analyze and discuss research previously published by others, rather than reporting new experimental results. Review articles are published materials that provide an examination of recent or current literature in a wide range of subject matter at various levels of completeness findings. They come in the form of systematic reviews and literature reviews and are a form of secondary literature. Systematic reviews determine an objective list of criteria, and find all previously published original experimental papers that meet the criteria. They then compare the results presented in these papers. Literature reviews, by contrast, provide a summary of what the authors believe are the best and most relevant prior publications.

Some academic journals specialize in publishing review articles; they are known as review journals. A review article is separate from the concept of peer-reviewed literature. It is possible for a review to be peer-reviewed, and it is possible for a review to be non-peer-reviewed.

Literature reviews are built with the intent to provide the reader with a brief overview of a topic supported by an extensive bibliography of reputable articles in a specific area of health research. Composed of findings from currently published articles, literature reviews are excellent sources as they consider and report findings based on all items listed in the bibliography. These reviews will also typically contain the titles of the databases or indexes used to identify the sources, dates searched, and the search strategies used.

Systematic reviews are a synopsis of several clinical trials that have been compared and contrasted by experts in the field. The framework by which this document rests is usually consistent so that the information seeker can rely on this arrangement to locate specific areas within the systematic review. Lengthy in many cases, a systematic review can be considered a living document. It is updated periodically to include additional clinical trials of "like" subject matter as they are completed. As additional data is integrated into a systematic review, the conclusions and results may change over time. Evidence-based content is used to develop systematic reviews so they are considered to contain the best evidence regarding interventions for direct patient care or research. Systematic reviews are often used as a primary support piece for practice guidelines in medicine.

Meta-analysis is a quantitative method for analyzing data included in independent experimental and clinical studies collectively. In the interest of validating data and providing another resource for evidence-based information, articles summarizing these findings are published as reviews known as meta-analyses.

Review articles published as overviews or tutorials have been an excellent source of information in a compressed manner. Depending upon the primary source of information, review articles can provide the reader with a synopsis of a detailed research or experimental study, an overview of a case study, or an overview of a health-related concept.

Point-of-care resources such as UpToDate, MD Consult, the Cochrane Library or Dynamed contain reviews subdivided into small bits of quality information for bedside patient care for physicians. Some of these electronic resources can be accessed using a mobile device.

It is quite common in the health science field to find databases and indexes that provide bibliographic control of reviews. Many databases have provided value-added limits to aid the end user in specifying the type of review sought. The following list of databases or subsets of databases are dedicated to providing an avenue for identifying reviews in the health sciences.

7.27   Web of Science (see 7.19).

7.28   PubMed Clinical Queries. Bethesda, MD: National Library of Medicine. Available: http://www.ncbi.nlm.nih.gov/pubmed/clinical.

PubMed is the primary database interface for citations from the biomedical literature. It incorporates bibliographic information from MEDLINE and covers the journal literature of medicine, nursing, dentistry, veterinary medicine, and the preclinical biological sciences. PubMed contains bibliographic citations and author abstracts from more than 4,800 biomedical journals published in the United States and seventy other countries. The database contains more than 22 million citations dating back to the mid-1940s. Articles in many languages are indexed, but all abstracts are in English.

7.29   Cochrane Reviews. Boston: The Cochrane Collaboration. Available: http://www.cochrane.org/.

The Cochrane Library is a collection of six databases that contain different types of independent evidence to inform health-care decision making, and a seventh database that provides information about groups in the Cochrane Collaboration. Cochrane Reviews are a collection of systematic reviews of research in health care and health policy; these reviews are internationally recognized as the highest standard in evidence-based medicine.

The reviews investigate the effects of interventions for prevention, treatment, and rehabilitation; they also assess the accuracy of a diagnostic test for a given condition in a specific patient group and setting. The reviews assess the accuracy of specific conditions and diagnostic tests. The reviews are very comprehensive and updated regularly. The records tend to be very large and they are published online in the Cochrane Library (http://www.cochrane.org/cochrane-reviews/about-cochrane-library).

7.30   Embase (see 7.22).

7.31   Biological Abstracts/RRM (Reports/Reviews/Meetings) (see 7.23).

A Review of Online Products for Language Translation

This section of the chapter provides an update of some of the most popular free online machine-translation tools available via the Web and an overview of search engines that provide translation texts. The products were identified by literature review of two databases: Library Literature and Information Full Text and Library Information Science and Technology Abstracts. The demand for high-quality reliable language translation services keeps growing steadily. In addition to traditional human-centered translation centers, there has been a rapid growth in translation software products, search engines, and online machine translation tools available via the Web.

Translating arbitrary documents from one language to another is not an easy task. In addition to requiring proficiency in the source and destination languages, accurate translation requires domain knowledge of the subject of the original document, and sensitivity to cultural nuances of the languages. Machine translation (MT)—the use of computers to translate from one language to another—is cheaper and faster than professional translation by a trained human specialist and provides a tremendous advantage in situations such as online Web browsing, where webpages that were created in one language must be translated and displayed in the reader's language in real time.

There are several general-purpose search engines and specialized websites that provide machine language translations. None of these, however, can claim 100 percent translation accuracy since a "machine" is never 100 percent accurate to do the work. For simpler translation needs such as words, phrases, nontechnical text, and even complete webpages, these resources may be adequate. In more discipline-specific contexts these resources are a helpful starting point, providing an easy and cost-effective method to filter content for relevance. However, to have a reliable translated document in a specific discipline, human translation is currently the right choice.

Computer programs for language translation have been around for more than forty years. One of the earliest applications of machine translation still used today is to convert high-level human-oriented programming languages to more primitive languages understood by the computer hardware. Translation of natural languages, however, is considerably more difficult due to their richness, complexity, and underlying ambiguities in meaning. Over the years, machine translation programs have become increasingly sophisticated, providing both greater accuracy and a larger repertoire of languages. The typical quality of translation from English to languages like Japanese, Russian, or Chinese has improved considerably, and the numbers of pairs of languages that can be mutually translated has increased greatly. Historically most of the translation software programs and search engines have been for applications in business; however, there has been a growing increase in applications in other disciplines.

Online language translation products come in two main categories: dictionaries and translators. Dictionaries provide translation of single words or short phrases. Translators provide two different functions: translation of websites or general text translation. The former enables a webpage created in one language, say in English, to be translated and displayed in the browser in a different language just by typing in its URL in the provided search box. Individuals can then surf the Web in their own language by using the Web translators to convert foreign-language webpages.

Text translators can be used to translate arbitrary user text between different languages. Here too, two kinds of usage can be found. The most common mode is to provide a text box on a website into which the user can type or cut and paste the text to be translated. The translated text will usually be displayed in a separate textbox on the webpage as well. Free Web translators usually limit the number of characters or words allowed in a single transaction. In some cases they may also limit the total number of transactions allowed, thereby limiting the maximum size of the text that can be translated without registration and payment. The average size tends to be approximately 800 words. Some sites allow more sophisticated and flexible machine translations for a fee, and offer instant human translation at somewhat higher rates as well.

The second mode of text translation is to download software from the website into the client computer. The downloaded software provides greater flexibility and ease of use. For instance the source text can be chosen from a preexisting document by merely highlighting the desired sections in an editor like Microsoft Word or other Microsoft Office application. Products differ in the number of languages supported and the combinations of language pairs that can be mutually translated.

Some sites provide additional tools to supplement the translation process. For instance, multilingual spell-checkers and virtual keyboards with non-English or accented characters greatly facilitate the input of text for translation, while automatic simultaneous retranslation of the translated text back into the original source language provides quick feedback on the accuracy of the translation. In addition, some websites provide a facility to directly e-mail or print the translated text merely by selecting the appropriate command on the page. Some websites are powered by their own translation engines while others are merely consolidators with links to the free services provided by the primary translation service website.

Free Online Translation Tools

Several online language translation products are discussed as follows. The author of this section is a native Spanish speaker and chose to translate text from English to Spanish using some of the free online tools to assess their accuracy.

7.32   Bing Microsoft Translator. Redmond, WA: Microsoft. Available:
        http://www.bing.com/translator/.

Powered by Microsoft Translator, this search engine currently supports thirty-nine languages including Simplified and Traditional Chinese, Haitian Creole, Hindi, and Hebrew. Bing Translator allows text and webpage translations and is fairly straightforward to use. For text translations, enter the text to be translated in the search box: the translator recognizes the original language using the default Auto-Detect, but one can also select the original translation language from a drop-down menu. Type or paste the text to be translated and then click the Translate button. Text translations of images in PDF or in Flash graphics formats are not supported.

For webpage translations, select the original and translation language from the "Languages" drop-down menu and then type or paste the webpage URL in the indicated box. Click the "Translate" button. Once the page is translated, the user is directed to the Bilingual Viewer mode page, where he or she can choose from several viewing modes, including side-by-side and top and bottom displays of the original and translated webpages. Other options allow users to view the original or translated text with hover translation capabilities, in which moving the mouse over the text will show the translated and original versions, respectively.

Bing Translator allows users to listen to the audio version of the translated text, search the translated text in Bing, or e-mail the translated text to another user. Bing also allows users to rate the translation. One can download the Bing Translator widget to Microsoft Office versions 2003 and higher to translate text inside those programs. Please note that Bing Translator doesn't support secure webpages (https) or pages using a meta tag in the HTML.

7.33   Google Translate. Mountain View, CA: Google. Available:
        http://translate.google.com/.

This search engine can translate text and webpages between any combinations of sixty-four supported languages. If one downloads the free Website Translator plugin, he or she can translate websites into more than sixty languages. The plugin provides an HTML code that can be pasted into every page one wants to translate, but one must be signed into Google for the Translator to work.

To use Google Translator, either enter the text to be translated in the search box of the Google Translator page or use the virtual keyboard icon located in the search box. Google automatically detects the language of the original text. Select the language one wants to translate the text into and click the Translate button. An accurate translated version of the text is automatically displayed in a window to the right of the original text. Pointing the mouse to specific words in the translated text highlights the text on both sides of the Google Translator window, allowing users to edit and replace the translated word. Google translator also allows users to click and drag the words in the translated text and reorder them within that text. Another feature of Google Translator is the audio feature, which allows users to listen to the original and the translated texts by clicking on the audio button. It also displays examples of usage of words and the option to rate the translation.

Another option to translate a website is to enter the URL in the search box and click on Translate. The Translator will display the translated webpage. Under "View" mode, one has the option of displaying either the translated or the original page but not both.

7.34   El Mundo Traductor. Madrid, Spain; Mundinteractivos, SA. Available: http://www.elmundo.es/traductor/.

This site can be used to translate short text, phrases, idioms, expressions, and webpages between English and either Spanish, French, or German. Special characters are available below the translation box. This website is powered by Reverso owned by Softissimo (see description of Reverso in 7.36).

7.35   FreeTranslations.com. England: SDL International, 2000. Available: http://www.freetranslation.com/.

FreeTranslation.com translates both text and webpages using Enterprise Translation Server, an automatic translation engine. It translates to and from twenty-nine different languages and includes the auto detect feature. Some of the unique languages available in this software are Hausa, Hindi, and Somali. Their website offers the option to use either free machine translation limited to 750 words at a time, or a fee-based human translation service. If one is not satisfied with the results of the free translation, one can click on the button labeled "Human Translation"; another screen will pop up with the cost of translating the text. More accurate translations by using advanced translation options (up to 10,000 words each time) and specialized dictionaries are available for a fee. Specialized software such as SDLDesktop Translator, SDL Chat Translator, and SDLClipboard Translator are also available for a fee.

The help section and FAQs on the website contain very good information. They also offer helpful information on how to enter accented characters used in other languages. FreeTranslation.com is owned by SDL International, with headquarters in the United Kingdom and offices in North America, Asia, Europe, and the Middle East. One can also subscribe to the RSS feeds and blog or follow it using Twitter and Facebook. Users can also translate from within Facebook or post translations to their walls. Advanced translation software and professional translation services are available for a fee. A free mobile application is available from the Apple Application store. FreeTranslation is compatible with iPhone or iPod Touch.

7.36   Reverso. Paris, France: Softissimo, 2004. Available: http://www.reverso.net/text_translation.asp?lang=EN.

This site provides software powered by Softissimo, for online translation between English and Arabic, Chinese, French, German, Hebrew, Italian, Japanese, Portuguese, Spanish, and Russian, as well as between these languages.

In addition to the translation software, Reverso includes a dictionary, a conjugation tool, and grammar and spell-check links. Conjugations are offered in English, French, German, and Spanish only. Grammar and spell-check links are offered for English and French languages. Reverso also includes a virtual keyboard as well as additional characters unique to each language that can be added to the search box just by clicking on them. A tool bar that includes all the Reverso features to be used with just one click can be downloaded for free. Other features include links to dictionaries in eleven languages, French grammar online lessons, and additional dictionaries in 104 different languages with links to Google and Bing translators.

Software Language Translation

7.37   Babylon. Tel Aviv, Israel: Babylon, 1997. Available: http://babylon.com/.

Babylon translates terms, paragraphs, websites, and documents and includes dictionary results in Excel, Word, and PowerPoint formats. This feature is supported in fifteen different languages. To use Babylon 10 on a PC or Mac, one must download the software for a free trial period. The trial version of Babylon 10 contains limited features compared to the full version of the software. Once the software is downloaded, users can access a basic translating mode. The trial version only allows fifteen free translations before expiring and requiring users to purchase the software from the Babylon website. The cost depends on the selected subscription type and added features. Once downloaded, Babylon Translator add-ins are loaded in Microsoft Word, Excel, and Power Point. For a fee, one can add the sound feature, where a computer-generated voice will read the original and translated text.

To start using Babylon, simply enter the text or term to be translated: the software recognizes the original language of the text. Then, select the desired language and click the Translate button. Babylon supports both translation and dictionary software. The free version of Babylon text translator translates up to 320 characters (including spaces and punctuation marks) from English to twenty-seven other languages ranging from French, German, and Spanish to Farsi, Korean, and Ukrainian. Babylon also exists as a free mobile application, iBabylon. It provides translations and dictionary results from Babylon's servers for the iPhone, Android, Blackberry, and Windows Phone.

7.38   ImTranslator.net. Irvine, CA: Smart Link Corporation, 2003. Available: http://imtranslator.net/translation/.

ImTranslator is a comparison translator tool: once one enters the text to be translated, one can select a specific translator software by clicking on the Translator tab. PROMT, Babylon, Google Translate, and Microsoft Translator are listed. Use the Compare tab to compare the translated text between PROMT, Babylon Translator, Google Translate, and Microsoft Translator. Translated text results are displayed into four different columns. By clicking on the *I Like This* icon, the translator used will be displayed, and one can then choose the best translation results for one's needs.

One also has the option of listening to the translated text by clicking on the *Text to Speech* icon located above the search box or by clicking on the TTS Voice icon link. Please note that only eight languages are supported by the voice portal. The website, which offers free translations between thirty-three languages, includes a translator and a dictionary as well as a suite of tools such as an eight-language spell-checker, a virtual keyboard, and a decoder. The translator software can translate up to 500 characters at a time. If a user wants to use ImTranslator in his or her own language, the translator search box can be displayed in twenty-three different languages.

The software is easy to use. From the translator window, one can choose from the icons displayed for editing functions (copy, cut, paste, and delete) and various tools (virtual keyboard, dictionary, spelling, decode, print, e-mail, or text and speech). There are three different window frames in the middle of the webpage. The top window displays the original text, whose translation can be found in the middle window. This translated text can be re-translated back to the original language in the bottom window (aptly labeled "back translation"). However, don't expect the twice-translated text to exactly match the original!

Another feature is a spell-checker server called Spellink, which checks the spelling of words in English, French, German, Italian, Portuguese, Russian, Ukrainian, and Spanish. It can proof passages of up to 500 characters at once, flag misspelled words in red, and provide a list of suggested spellings. The virtual keyboard allows users to enter accent marks, making it easy to deal with special characters in thirty-three different languages like Russian, Turkish, German, or French. Decoder helps with incorrect display of Russian characters in e-mails, webpages, or applications. Decoder identifies the encoding of a Russian text, and converts it, if needed, into the Windows standard encoding (Cyrillic Windows) using a sophisticated algorithm.

7.39   PROMT Online Translator. St. Petersburg, Russia: PROMT, 2003. Available: http://www.online-translator.com/text.asp#tr_form.

This free online software supports translations from text and websites in seven different languages: English, French, German, Italian, Portuguese, Russian, and Spanish. Unregistered users can submit text up to 3,000 characters (including spaces and paragraph breaks) long. Registration is free. Registered users can translate text up to 10,000 characters long, send translated text via e-mail, print text and website translations, and subscribe to Online-Translator.com news to receive information on PROMT software products. An online virtual keyboard is available in the search box with different characters used by the seven supported languages. Downloadable Translator software is available for a limited time on a free trial basis, but needs to be purchased once the trial ends. PROMT also offers professional human translation services for a fee.

A mobile translator application is available for phones with WAP (Wireless Application Protocol) support, communicators, or Pocket PCs. Text, messages, or terms can be translated anywhere cellular service is available. Text translation, a virtual keyboard, and an electronic dictionary are available in the mobile version, which is free (http://m.online-translator.com).

7.40   SYSTRAN. Paris, France: SYSTRAN, 2007. Available:
       http://www.systransoft.com/.

SYSTRAN provides language translation software products for desktops and servers. The desktop products can translate text or webpages from the user's desktop and Microsoft office applications. The server products are offered to larger companies and are accessed from their Intranet or LAN. Subscribers to the online service product can have real-time multilingual information on-demand delivered directly to their personal computers without having to download the software. The software translates webpages and text from English to any of fourteen languages including Arabic, both traditional and simplified Chinese, German, Dutch, Italian, Japanese, Korean, Portuguese, Russian, and Swedish. SYSTRAN allows five free uses of the text translation service before requiring users to purchase the software.

7.41   WorldLingo. Las Vegas, NV: World Lingo Translations, 2007. Available:
       http://www2.worldlingo.com/en/products_services/worldlingo
       _translator.html.

This website offers free text, e-mail, and website translation services in thirty-three different languages. There are some restrictions on the free services: the free and the e-mail translators will only translate the first 500 words of the input text. One can, however, use it repeatedly to copy and translate successive batches of 500 words of text. The website translator also has a limit of 500 words. Special characters boxes are displayed at the bottom of the displayed window to enter accents and other foreign symbols.

The site claims their automated translations are approximately 70–75 percent accurate. If the text requires a higher accuracy rate, professional translators, also known as human translations, are available for a fee. The company offers professional translations in more than 141 languages.

CHAPTER 7: CONFERENCES, REVIEWS, AND TRANSLATIONS 179

When sending or receiving a translated e-mail message via WorldLingo e-mail translator, the website will automatically register the user and provide access to a secured page that offers a summary of WorldLingo translation products. For people shopping online, an interesting feature offered is the eBay Listing Translator that WorldLingo states "gives you the ability to tap into potential clients who may not speak your language." According to their website, one can buy the listing translator application for $2.00.

Dictionaries and Specialized Translation Sites

A vast variety of translation dictionaries are available on the Internet. The following list is only a small sample of the available resources.

7.42   Dictionary.com Translator. Long Beach, CA: Lexico Publishing Group, 2007. Available: http://dictionary.reference.com/translate/.

Powered by SYSTRAN, this site can translate phrases and long sentences from English and ten other languages including Japanese, Korean, and Chinese.

7.43   Globalgate. Tokyo, Japan: Amikai Enterprise, 2006. Available: http://tool.nifty.com/globalgate/.

Globalgate provides English-Japanese translations of text and websites.

7.44   *Multilingual lemmas: dizionario medico multilingue* (*Glossary of Medical Terms*). Italy: UniPlan Software, 2007. Available: http://www.salus.it/voca4/language.html.

This site includes alphabetical lists of medical terms and glossaries in English, Spanish, German, Danish, Dutch, Italian, French, and Portuguese. Begin at the URL listed above and select the preferred language to be directed to the appropriate medical glossary.

7.45   Word2Word.com. San Jose, CA: Bigben, 1995. Available: http://www.word2word.com//dictionary.html.

This website includes links to a vast array of dictionaries in almost 200 languages as well as links to other free translators. It also offers links to language courses, alphabets of the world, language learning podcasts, and forums for translators. This is a good site to visit for a comprehensive list of translation resources.

7.46   WordReference.com. Vienna, VA: Michael Kellogg, 1999. Available from: http://www.wordreference.com/.

WordReference.com translates words in Spanish, French, Italian, and twelve other foreign languages. The site provides links to other dictionaries in these languages, as well as links to language forums where native speakers can answer questions about language usage.

Mobile Translation Applications

This section lists just a few mobile medical translation applications that were found while searching iMedicalApps[4] and the Apple Application Store.

7.47   MediBabble Translator. NiteFlota. Version 2.0 available from iTunes. Compatible with iPhone, iPod Touch, and iPad. Available: http://itunes .apple.com/us/app/medibabble-translator/id355398880?mt=8.

The application includes thousands of translated questions and instructions that can be played as audio recordings. It includes helpful phrases that physicians can use to communicate with patients during physical examinations. All content is written and reviewed by physicians. This resource is also available in Cantonese, Haitian Creole, Mandarin, and Russian. The application is available for free from Apple's App Store and is compatible with the iPhone, iPod Touch, and iPad.

7.48   Polyglot Med Spanish. Duke AHEC Program. Version 1.1. Available: http://itunes.apple.com/us/app/polyglot-med-spanish/id421199869?mt=8.

This application offers immediate audio translation of more than 3,000 common words and phrases from English to Spanish and vice versa, making it easier for the physician to communicate with Spanish-speaking patients. This interface allows for continuous playing of conversations in English and Spanish. Content is written and reviewed by physicians and includes key phrases available to health-care personnel. The application is available for free from Apple's App Store and is compatible with the iPhone, iPod Touch, and iPad.

7.49   Medical Spanish 1.2. Mavro. Available: http://mavroinc.com/medical.html.

As the name implies, this application helps users communicate with Spanish-speaking patients. The application includes thousands of key medical terms as well as a pharmacy section with detailed instructions on how to take medications. Reviewers claim the website is easy to use even if one doesn't have knowledge of the Spanish language. Other applications from the same company—such as Dental Spanish Guide and Physical and Occupational Therapy Spanish Guide—are available for purchase.

Notes on Translation Tools

This section of the chapter is intended to provide a brief introduction to some of the free online translation resources available. There are certainly many other free search engines and online dictionaries available on the Web. These sites are continually evolving, so it is worthwhile to visit them to see the latest services being offered. Among the freely available translation search engines, Bing and Google are excellent sources for translating text, websites, and phrases.

These resources are also available via phone. Since translation software companies have gained the ability to offer mobile access to their software, translation mobile applications have proliferated.

However, machine translation software has its flaws. Most machine translations lack the ability to infer higher-level semantics or contextual information; instead, they simply recognize characters and words and translate the text literally. When using machine translation it is worthwhile to follow the tips suggested on individual websites to achieve the best results. To achieve high accuracy in translating documents, whether scientific or in some other discipline, human translation should be considered.

References

1. "About HON." Health On the Net Foundation. Accessed January 20, 2013. http://www.hon.ch/Global/index.html.
2. Cruzat, G. S. "Keeping Up with Biomedical Meetings." *Bulletin of the Medical Library Association* 56, no. 2 (1968): 132–37.
3. "Scopus in Detail: What Does Scopus Cover?" Elsevier B.V. Accessed April 27, 2013. http://www.info.sciverse.com/scopus-in-detail/facts.
4. "iMedicalApps.com." iMedicalApps. Accessed April 20, 2013. http://www.imedical apps.com/.

PART IV

Information Sources

CHAPTER 8

Terminology

MICHELLE L. ZAFRON

Understanding medical terminology is crucial to gaining competency with the literature of the health sciences. Reference tools that define terms or that provide insight into how such terms are formed are essential to learning medical terminology. Fortunately, there are a number of reference sources extant to assist with just this goal. These have been organized in the following categories: general medical dictionaries; specialized dictionaries, which can be used to locate etymologies or abbreviations; subject dictionaries; foreign-language dictionaries; and compilations of syndromes, eponyms, and quotations.

General Dictionaries

General medical dictionaries may be divided into two categories: unabridged and abridged. A good medical dictionary should be updated to keep up with the discoveries, treatments, procedures, techniques, and advances that occur in the field of medicine and the health sciences with each passing day. Unabridged medical dictionaries are necessary because they are comprehensive in nature. There are two major unabridged medical dictionaries used in the United States.

8.1   *Dorland's Illustrated Medical Dictionary.* 32nd ed. Philadelphia: W. B. Saunders. Available: http://www.dorlands.com/.

8.2   *Stedman's Medical Dictionary.* 28th ed. Philadelphia: Lippincott Williams and Wilkins. Available: http://www.stedmansonline.com/.

Considered by many to be the premier medical dictionary in the United States, *Dorland's Illustrated Medical Dictionary* has been in existence for more than 100 years. The thirty-second edition offers definitions on more than 122,000 terms, 1,500 illustrations, and a very helpful section on medical etymology. *Dorland's* is thumb-indexed, a useful feature in a book that weighs nearly nine pounds. There is a very practical guide on using the source printed on the inside of the front cover.

Entries have pronunciations, etymologies, synonyms, and subentries. MeSH headings are provided for some terms. Terms that are considered subentries are grouped under their larger headword. Definitions of the subentries are included within the body of the main entry. In cases of synonyms, they are cross-referenced to the preferred terms. Thus, Alzheimer's disease leads to cross-references under *dementia* as well as *disease*. A CD-ROM is included with purchase of the print edition. It is also available as an e-book in several formats. Purchase also includes access to the website (http://www.dorlands.com/).

Now in its twenty-eighth edition, *Stedman's Medical Dictionary* boasts over 107,000 entries. Its organization is not unlike *Dorland's*; alphabetization is letter by letter. Subentries are defined within the framework of the main entry. Synonyms are also cross-referenced with "see" references, printed in blue, to preferred terms.

There are extensive illustrations and photographs. This edition features three large sections of color plates dispersed evenly throughout the dictionary. An effort was made to update the design in order to increase ease-of-use. The print edition of *Stedman's* is thumb-indexed so that the reader can more quickly locate a term. Another feature is the addition of usage notes that are used extensively "to enhance the usefulness of the dictionary by alerting users to common errors of sense, spelling, and pronunciation, including confusion between words of similar form or meaning" (from the preface).

The expanded appendixes provide information on units of measure, abbreviations and symbols, medical etymology, physical terminology, reference values, coding and classification systems, body mass and surface calculations, tests, botanicals, and infection control.

Stedman's Medical Dictionary Online (http://www.stedmansonline.com/) offers the same content as its print counterpart. Audio pronunciations are available for 60,000 of the more than 107,000 terms. The terms can be searched by keyword and browsed. There are approximately fifty videos of anatomy in motion. Users have the ability to create and save customizable entries through the use of the "My Stedman's" feature.

Dorland's Illustrated Medical Dictionary and *Stedman's Medical Dictionary* enjoy comparable coverage, authority, depth, and breadth. There are, however, differences between the two. Some terms are present in one, but not the other. W. B. Saunders, the publisher for *Dorland's*, continues to issue new editions. Lippincott Williams and Wilkins has not issued a new print edition of *Stedman's* since 2006 and it may be preferable to opt for their online product. Although some databases and clinical tools have one or the other integrated into their products, they are not adequate substitutions for the dictionaries themselves. It can be difficult or impossible to access the dictionary directly from the database. Users may need to make many mouse clicks to get to the definition of the term they need. As there is no one current source with total comprehensiveness, it is recommended that all medical libraries make every effort to have both of these dictionaries, whether in traditional print, e-book, or online formats.

8.3   *Taber's Cyclopedic Medical Dictionary*. 21st ed. Philadelphia: F. A. Davis, 2009.

8.4   Marcovitch Harvey, ed. *Black's Medical Dictionary*. 42nd ed. London: A&C Black, 2010.

8.5   *The Bantam Medical Dictionary*. 6th ed. New York: Bantam Books, 2009.

8.6   *Merriam-Webster's Medical Dictionary Online*. Springfield, MA: Merriam-Webster. Available: http://www.merriam-webster.com/browse/medical/a.htm.

8.7   Dox, I., B. J. Melloni, J. L. Melloni, and G. Eisner, eds. *Melloni's Illustrated Medical Dictionary*. 4th ed. Boca Raton, FL: CRC Press, 2001.

An abridged dictionary, *Taber's Cyclopedic Medical Dictionary* contains nearly 60,000 definitions. It is suitable for clinicians, students, allied health professionals, and nurses. Written in encyclopedic format, many entries have subheadings on etiology, symptoms, treatment, prognosis, and patient care. Cross-references and patient care sections are highlighted in red. The majority of the 1,000 illustrations are in color.

The latest edition includes increased coverage of alternative and complementary medicine, bioethics, evidence-based care, informatics, nutrition, and patient safety. There are also a number of very useful appendixes on topics such as medical emergencies, integrative therapies, laboratory values, nomenclature, phobias, immunization schedules, and health professions. One appendix of note is called "The Interpreter in Three Languages," which provides questions and answers that could be used during an examination. It is available in e-book as well as traditional print format. *Taber's Online* is the Web option for the same content and is available with a one-year subscription model. *Taber's Medical Dictionary for Mobile and Web*, which has the same subscription model, also allows access to the content on a variety of mobile devices.

Black's Medical Dictionary is meant not so much for the medical professional as it is for someone who wishes to have informed communication with the physician.

Both the headings and language are broad, making the source more accessible to the layman. Over 5,000 terms and 100 diagrams and drawings are provided in this source. Entries are encyclopedic in nature; where appropriate, these contain cross-references. The format is clear and readable. It is also available as an e-book.

Providing definitions for over 11,000 medical terms, *The Bantam Medical Dictionary* is meant to be accessible to laymen as well as those in the health professions. In order to allow space for more current terminology, older and obsolete terms were removed from this edition. One particular feature worth noting is the inclusion of subentries, that is, definitions within definitions. The source is cross-referenced and has 150 illustrations. The layout is clear and readable, making this useful as a quick reference tool.

Merriam-Webster's Medical Dictionary Online is free to search. It is the dictionary that MedlinePlus incorporates into its site. It is written with a lay audience in mind and contains more than 59,000 entries. It can be searched by keyword or browsed. Most entries have audio files to aid in pronunciation. Entries are brief, but are cross-referenced. This is a source best suited to libraries serving consumers. Merriam-Webster also offers a free API that allows for the incorporation of their content onto the sites of noncommercial organizations.

Melloni's Illustrated Medical Dictionary offers definitions for nearly 30,000 medical terms. The extensive illustrations, of which there are more than 3,000, play an enormous part in the usefulness of this source. Entries and illustrations are color coded in order to make the information more comprehensible. Where applicable, entries contain phonetic pronunciations, synonyms, cross-references, and abbreviations. Using easily understood language, *Melloni's* is accessible to both the layman and the health sciences student. Despite its age, this source still has usefulness.

Medical Etymology

Etymological sources are critical to anyone attempting to comprehend medical terminology. Medical terms generally have their basis in Latin and Greek prefixes, suffixes, and roots. By understanding how medical words and phrases are formed, one can arrive at a reasonable definition of a word. While there are many ways to look up medical etymologies online, at this time, no truly authoritative single site replaces extant written sources. The following sources focus exclusively on etymology.

8.8   Skinner, Henry Allen. *Origin of Medical Terms.* 2nd ed. Baltimore, MD: Williams and Wilkins, 1961.

8.9   Haubrich, William S. *Medical Meanings: A Glossary of Word Origins.* 2nd ed. Philadelphia: American College of Physicians, 2003.

8.10   Casselman, Bill. *A Dictionary of Medical Derivations: The Real Meaning of Medical Terms.* New York: Parthenon Publishing Group, 1998.

8.11   Jaeger, Edmund C. *A Source-Book of Biological Names and Terms*, 3rd ed. Revised 2nd printing. Springfield, IL: Charles C Thomas, 1959.

Origin of Medical Terms covers both medicine and the basic sciences. The book is illustrated. Some eponyms are included, although others are cross-referenced to the official medical term. Biographical information is provided for the eponymous individual. Some sources are cited and there is an extensive bibliography. Although the source has considerable breadth and scope, it is out of print.

According to its author, *Medical Meanings: A Glossary of Word Origins* was to fill the gap left since the last edition of *Origin of Medical Terms* was published. This source contains more than 3,000 words and phrases. Since the first edition, almost one-third have been revised and updated. Entries are cross-referenced. *Medical Meanings* is accessible to the layman. Both the format and the engaging narrative make for a very readable reference source.

A Dictionary of Medical Derivations: The Real Meaning of Medical Terms contains etymologies for 50,000 Latin and Greek words. It is meant to be accessible to anyone in the health sciences. The very readable section explaining how words are formed breaks down words into understandable parts. There is also a review listing of frequently used Latin and Greek roots used in medical words. Both terms and roots are indexed.

A Source-Book of Biological Names and Terms is somewhat different from the other books in this section. Although medical terms are included, the scope of the source is considerably larger; it encompasses biology as well as medicine. Over 13,000 words and phrases are listed and there are some illustrations. In general, an entry includes the language of origin, the etymologic meaning, and an example of its use in scientific nomenclature. With a few exceptions, geographic and biographical names are limited and confined to an appendix. There is a section on the formation of words.

Medical Abbreviations

The use of abbreviations and acronyms is pervasive in every field of health care and the health sciences. Their popularity is unsurprising given the length and complexity of some medical terms and phrases, and the general need for medical shorthand. However, as any given abbreviation can have multiple meanings, it becomes necessary not only for care but also for accurate reference tools. Given that some of these sources have listings that the others do not, more than one source is needed.

8.12   Jablonski, Stanley, ed. *Jablonski's Dictionary of Medical Acronyms and Abbreviations*. 6th ed. Philadelphia: Saunders/Elsevier, 2009.

8.13   *Stedman's Abbreviations, Acronyms, and Symbols*. 5th ed. Baltimore, MD: Wolters Kluwer Health/Lippincott Williams and Wilkins, 2012.

8.14   Davis, Neil M. *Medical Abbreviations: 32,000 Conveniences at the Expense of Communication and Safety*. 15th ed. Warminster, PA: Neil M. Davis Associates, 2011. Available: http://www.medabbrev.com/.

8.15   Tsur, Samuel A. *Elsevier's Dictionary of Abbreviations, Acronyms, Synonyms, and Symbols Used in Medicine*. 2nd ed. Amsterdam: Elsevier, 2004.

Jablonski's Dictionary of Medical Acronyms and Abbreviations is a simply organized source of a small, convenient size. Acronyms and abbreviations are listed alphabetically in bold typeface, with possible expanded terms listed beneath them. There are no definitions, which might be considered a disadvantage. Some of the new terms reflect the advances of the latest virus nomenclature, computer technology, medical informatics, and molecular biology. There is an expanded section on symbols in the latest edition. The sixth edition is accompanied by a searchable CD-ROM. The book is also available in e-book format.

Stedman's Abbreviations, Acronyms, and Symbols has more than 75,000 entries. As with *Jablonski's Dictionary*, there are no definitions. Slang terms are also included and are printed in red ink. All of these terms are alphabetized by letter. The book is cross-referenced. Eleven useful appendixes cover angles, triangles, and circles; arrows; genetic symbols; numbers; pluses, minuses, and equivalencies; primes, checks, dots, roots; statistical symbols; professions, titles, and degrees; professional associations and organizations; chemotherapy and other drug regimens; and clinical trials. Three months' access to the online component comes with purchase of the fifth edition. A yearly subscription model to the online component is also available. Terms can be searched by keyword or browsed. Customization through the "My Stedman's" feature is also available.

The easy-to-use *Medical Abbreviations: 32,000 Conveniences at the Expense of Communication and Safety* contains as its title suggests, 32,000 of medical abbreviations' possible meanings and a list of nearly 3,500 cross-referenced commonly prescribed brand and generic drug names. Neil Davis makes a convincing case on the need for standardization in the form of a controlled vocabulary. There are several chapters including one on dangerous, contradictory, and ambiguous abbreviations. Multi-user licenses are available. It is also possible to purchase website access only. The website provides searches for abbreviations, drugs, symbols and numbers, and more.

Elsevier's Dictionary of Abbreviations, Acronyms, Synonyms and Symbols Used in Medicine contains more than 30,000 abbreviations. The coverage extends to related medical fields such as anatomy, pathology, pharmacology, and bacteriology. It also includes biology, chemistry, and veterinary medicine. Regardless of type, terms are organized alphabetically, making this a straightforward source to use.

Word Finders and Concept Dictionaries

Conventional dictionaries are traditionally used when one knows a term, but not its meaning. If, however, one does not know the proper term, one can look up the concept or definition and locate the word. These are a selection of word finders or inverted concept dictionaries that can assist in filling this need.

8.16   Lorenzini, Jean A., and Laura Lorenzini-Ley. *Medical Phrase Index:*
        A Comprehensive Reference to the Terminology of Medicine. 5th ed.
        Los Angeles: Practice Management Corporation, 2006.

8.17   Stanaszek, Mary J., et al. *The Inverted Medical Dictionary.* 2nd ed.
        Lancaster, PA: Technomic, 1991.

8.18   Willeford, George, Jr., comp. *Webster's New World Medical Word Finder.*
        4th ed. New York: Prentice-Hall, 1987.

Of the sources listed in this section, *Medical Phrase Index* is the most comprehensive. Compiled by two medical transcriptionists, it contains more than 280,000 formal and informal medical phrases. In addition, common abbreviations and "sound alike" words and phrases are included. If the terms have multiple spellings, all are presented, with the most commonly used spelling indicated. All entries are cross-referenced. For ease of use the book is thumb-indexed.

The Inverted Medical Dictionary consists of alphabetical lists of terms and of definitions or concepts. As described previously, this is ideal when one is unsure of the proper word or phrase for a known concept. For example, if one were trying to find the word that describes a fear of open spaces, one would look up "fear of open spaces" and discover that the proper term was "agoraphobia." *The Inverted Medical Dictionary* also contains several useful sections on abbreviations, terms used for writing prescriptions, chemical abbreviations, as well as eponyms. This last segment presents the eponymic term, the proper medical term, and then a short description.

Webster's New World Medical Word Finder is meant to help health professionals quickly spell, syllabicate, divide, and accentuate medical terms. The source is divided into ten sections. Of these, two focus on phonetic spellings and one offers a list of troublesome or difficult words. These should be of especial help to medical transcriptionists. Due to the age of the book, certain sections such as the drug names lists may be outdated.

Subject Dictionaries

Subject dictionaries are many in number and varied in topics. Although their breadth is limited, the depth of their coverage is not.

8.19   *Mosby's Dental Dictionary.* 2nd ed. St. Louis, MO: Mosby, 2008.

8.20   Jablonski, Stanley. *Jablonski's Dictionary of Dentistry.* Reprint ed. of *Illustrated Dictionary of Dentistry.* Malabar, FL: Krieger, 1992.

8.21   Miller, Benjamin F. *Miller-Keane Encyclopedia and Dictionary of Medicine, Nursing, and Allied Health.* 7th ed. Philadelphia: Saunders, 2005.

8.22   Anderson, Douglass M. *Mosby's Medical, Nursing, and Allied Health Dictionary.* 6th ed. rev. St. Louis, MO: Mosby, 2005.

8.23   King, Robert C., Pamela Khipple Mulligan, and William D. Stansfield. *A Dictionary of Genetics.* 8th ed. New York: Oxford University Press, 2012.

8.24   Campbell, Robert Jean. *Campbell's Psychiatric Dictionary.* 9th ed. New York: Oxford University Press, 2009.

8.25   Blauvelt, Carolyn Taliaferro, and Frank R. T. Nelson. *A Manual of Orthopaedic Terminology.* 7th ed. St. Louis, MO: Mosby, 2007.

Mosby's Dental Dictionary offers definitions for more than 10,000 terms from all fields of dentistry. Its appendixes cover such topics as symbols and abbreviations; American Dental Association Dental Codes; clinical oral structures; HIPAA; how dental terms are made and read; and pharmacology. Terms are listed alphabetically and are cross-referenced. It is accompanied by a CD-ROM with a searchable database and audio pronunciations. It is also available in e-book format.

Jablonski's Dictionary of Dentistry presents a compilation of dental terms from all dental and dental-related specialties. Older and more obscure terms are also included. The source is illustrated. Standard entries have the preferred name of the term, the pronunciation, the etymology, a definition, and, if applicable, synonyms, trademarks, and cross-references.

The Miller-Keane Encyclopedia and Dictionary of Medicine, Nursing, and Allied Health is exceptionally well organized. The book's "How to Use Miller-Keane" section is a model of clarity. In addition to the briefer dictionary definitions, there are encyclopedic entries. These are lengthier and much more detailed. Many of the shorter entries are cross-referenced. *Miller-Keane* is illustrated. All entries are given phonetic respellings. The useful appendixes include anatomical plates; assessment charts; nutrition; weights and measures; immunization schedules; symbols; reference intervals for laboratory tests; nursing vocabularies; and a great deal more.

Mosby's Medical, Nursing, and Allied Health Dictionary is targeted toward nurses and those in the allied health professions. Like *Miller-Keane*, some of the entries are encyclopedic in nature; all have sentence definitions. Abbreviations and cross-references are actually alphabetized into the text. The book has more than 2,200 color photos and illustrations. There is a color atlas of human anatomy. The twenty appendixes cover such subjects as symbols and abbreviations, anatomy, Spanish-English-French commonly used phrases, health promotion, nutrition, herbs, complementary and allied health, nursing diagnoses, infection control, nursing interventions classification, and nursing outcomes classification. The layout and the typeface are clear and readable.

A Dictionary of Genetics has more than 7,500 definitions drawn from not only genetics, but from disciplines that are related to genetics such as molecular biology, cell biology, evolutionary studies, and so on. This edition includes more than 500 new entries. It is illustrated and cross-referenced. In addition to the dictionary portion, there are a number of useful appendixes, six of which have been heavily revised. Of note is a chronology section in which there are more than 1,000 entries for significant discoveries, events, and publications for genetics or genetics-related fields.

Campbell's Psychiatric Dictionary is targeted toward psychiatrists, but has the secondary goal of being accessible for those in the behavioral sciences and the health professions, and even a lay audience. In this it is successful. The entries are primarily encyclopedic. The latest edition has been expanded in size considerably. The book is cross-referenced.

Although *A Manual of Orthopaedic Terminology* is a dictionary, it is organized somewhat similarly to a textbook. Instead of a traditional A to Z arrangement, there are chapters on broad topics that are broken down further into subtopics. There is an index for easy location of a particular term. There are several appendixes, including one featuring orthopedic abbreviations and one on anatomic positions and directions. The seventh edition includes both print and online access.

8.26   Martin, Elizabeth A., and Robert S. Hine. *Dictionary of Biology*. 6th ed. Oxford, UK: Oxford University Press, 2008.

8.27   Lawrence, Eleanor, and Isabella Ferguson Henderson. *Henderson's Dictionary of Biology*. 15th ed. Harlow, UK: Benjamin Cummings, 2011.

The Dictionary of Biology, now in its sixth edition, has been heavily revised. It contains approximately 5,500 terms, of which 400 are new. The entries are clearly and concisely written. Topics receiving greater coverage include genetics, genomics, cell signaling, and molecular evolution. Several topics such as bioinformatics, genetically modified organisms, microarray technology, and RNA interference receive feature treatment and are covered in double-paged format. There are also several chronologies of topics such as biochemistry, cell biology, genetics, and microscopy. Some of the entries are linked to a companion website that contains additional details and is regularly updated.

Henderson's Dictionary of Biological Terms has more than 22,000 terms. More current than *The Dictionary of the Biological Sciences*, it is also directed at a similar audience. Acronyms are presented at the beginning of each letter; otherwise it is organized alphabetically. It is illustrated. Its coverage includes Latin and Greek derivations, units, structural formulae, as well as plant and animal classification tables. The latest edition includes chapters on bioinformatics, proteomics, and genomics.

Foreign-Language Dictionaries

Although there are plenty of generalized foreign-language dictionaries and online translation tools extant, the specialized nature of medicine and health care demands that there also be foreign-language medical dictionaries. For those treating the non-English speaker or looking for translation tools for other purposes, these are a selected sampling of some of the available sources.

8.28   McElroy, Onyria Herrera, and Lola L. Grabb. *Spanish-English, English-Spanish Medical Dictionary/Diccionario Médico Español-Inglés, Inglés-Español*. 4th ed. Philadelphia: Lippincott Williams and Wilkins, 2012.

8.29   Rogers, Glenn T. *English-Spanish, Spanish-English Medical Dictionary*. 3rd ed. New York: McGraw-Hill, 2007.

8.30   Sliosberg, Anatole. *Elsevier's Medical Dictionary in Five Languages: English/American, French, Italian, Spanish and German*. 2nd ed. rev. New York: Elsevier, 2004.

McElroy's *Spanish-English/English-Spanish Medical Dictionary* is an excellent example of what a foreign-language medical dictionary should be. With nearly 23,000 terms, its layout is a model of clarity. Every section of the book is presented in both languages. Some entries are illustrated. In addition to the terms, general abbreviations as well as medical abbreviations are included. There are extensive appendixes on patient communication, medical history, diagnosis, newborns, surgical procedures, anatomy, tests, consent forms, and trauma and emergency problems. It is available as an e-book.

The third edition of the *English-Spanish/Spanish-English Medical Dictionary* includes more than 5,000 new terms. These include medical and technical terms as well as slang and colloquialisms. If a word or phrase is specific to a particular Spanish-speaking nation, it is labeled as such. The book's small size makes this ideal for quick reference. There is also a section of sample conversations for interviews with patients on a number of topics.

Elsevier's Encyclopaedic Dictionary of Medicine has the advantage of presenting medical terms in five languages: English, French, German, Italian, and Spanish. Four volumes are available separately, consisting of general medicine; anatomy; biology; genetics and biochemistry; and therapeutic substances. The organization is the same throughout each volume. The first part is designated "the basic table," which is a list of the alphabetized entries in English. Every entry is numbered, possesses an English definition, and then lists the term in French, German, Italian, and Spanish. In the second section there are four indexes, one for each language. These indexes list the terms in that language; they are numbered as well. This number can be used to lead the user back to the entry in the basic table. The second edition adds 3,200 new entries and has a total of more than 20,000 terms.

Syndromes, Eponyms, and Quotations

A syndrome is a collection of symptoms or conditions that typify a certain disease. These can be significant as the presence of a sign or symptom can indicate a particular disease. Syndrome names are either eponymous, which means that they are named for the person who first reported the syndrome, or they are descriptive.

8.31   Magalini, Sergio I., and Sabina C. Magalini. *Dictionary of Medical Syndromes*. 4th ed. Philadelphia: Lippincott-Raven, 1997.

8.32   Jablonski, Stanley. *Jablonski's Dictionary of Syndromes and Eponymic Diseases*. 2nd ed. Malabar, FL: Krieger, 1991.

8.33   Bartolucci, Susan L. *Stedman's Medical Eponyms*. 2nd ed. Baltimore, MD: Lippincott Williams and Wilkins, 2005.

8.34   Enersen, Ole Daniel. *Whonamedit? A Dictionary of Medical Eponyms*. Oslo, Norway: OD Enerson, 2012. Available: http://www.whonamedit.com/.

Dictionary of Medical Syndromes contains nearly 3,000 terms that are listed in alphabetical order. Each entry lists synonyms; symptoms and signs; etiology; pathology; diagnostic procedures; therapies; and prognosis. A bibliography is also given and the index is cross-referenced. Despite its age, the well-designed layout of the syndromes makes this book very useful as a quick reference source.

Jablonski's Dictionary of Syndromes and Eponymic Diseases's self-expressed aim is to collect all eponymous diseases as well as all eponymous and noneponymous syndromes. Biographical information such as name, nationality, specialty, and birth and death dates is provided for eponymic entries where possible. Many entries, although not all, include symptoms, etiology, pathology, diagnoses, prognosis, and synonyms. Most entries include the original report for the syndrome or disease. Selected entries are illustrated.

Stedman's Medical Eponyms has more than 18,000 eponyms. Each entry contains brief biographical information such as full name, nationality, specialty, birth and death dates, and any associated terms. This is followed by the eponymous term and a short description. Terms are arranged alphabetically and are cross-referenced. The keyword index aids in retrieval when the eponym is not known.

Finding information about eponyms has been made significantly easier with the Internet. *Whonamedit? A Dictionary of Medical Eponyms* is an exemplary site. It is freely available with minimal distracting advertisements. *Whonamedit?* is published and maintained by Ole Daniel Enersen, a Norwegian medical historian. It is possible to search by eponym, by person, or by full text. There are also several indexes for those wishing to browse. One can browse the eponyms, the person, the country for the person originating the term, or a list of eponymous women.

8.35   Huth, Edward J., and T. Jock Murray. *Medicine in Quotations: Views of Health and Disease through the Ages.* 2nd ed. Philadelphia: American College of Physicians, 2006.

8.36   Strauss, Maurice B. *Familiar Medical Quotations.* Boston: Little, Brown, 1968.

8.37   McDonald, Peter. *Oxford Dictionary of Medical Quotations.* Oxford, UK: Oxford University Press, 2004.

Compilations of quotations not only serve to help those looking for suitable statements; they also present a historical perspective on the thoughts on medicine, health care, and disease. While there are quotation websites and Google searches, it is still sometimes simpler to locate appropriate quotations using books.

Medicine in Quotations: Views of Health and Disease through the Ages is an excellent source for finding applicable medical quotations. As it has been published more recently than the other books listed here, it has the advantage of currency. There is an extensive range of subjects. Quotations are arranged by topic and then alphabetically. Topic headings are broad and more standard so that the book can be accessible to a layman. The subject index is cross-referenced and should make up for any confusion.

One of the chief strengths of *Medicine in Quotations* is the author-citation index. Each of the 3,500 quotations is numbered. Where possible, the editors list the exact location of the quotation rather than just the name of the original source. This is an easy-to-use reference book that would be a helpful addition to most collections.

Familiar Medical Quotations contains more than 7,000 entries in the fields of medicine and an array of health-related topics. Each quotation is organized by theme and then chronologically. The entries include the author's birth and death years. There is both an author index and a keyword index. The latter provides paraphrases of the quotations. Where the entries were not verified, secondary sources are listed, making *Familiar Medical Quotations* an authoritative source.

The *Oxford Dictionary of Medical Quotations* has approximately 2,500 quotations from famous scientists, doctors, and others. Quotations are organized according to author. There is a topical index as well as a source bibliography.

CHAPTER 9

Handbooks and Manuals

KATHERINE SCHILLING

Handbooks and manuals are useful, quick-guide reference sources containing concise, factual data in the basic sciences and information for clinical diagnosis and treatment. Reviewed here are a variety of data books and popular resources for laboratory methods and evidence-based clinical decision making. This chapter organizes handbooks and manuals into four broad categories:

- Clinical diagnosis and treatment
- Disease classification and nomenclature
- Laboratory methods and laboratory diagnosis
- Scientific data books and compendia

Within each section, titles are listed alphabetically.

Clinical Diagnosis and Treatment

9.1 Domino, Frank J. *The 5-Minute Clinical Consult 2013*. 21st ed. Philadelphia: Lippincott Williams and Wilkins, 2012.

The 5-Minute Clinical Consult 2013 includes 900 medical conditions: their diagnosis, treatment, medications, follow-up, and associated conditions. This edition is evidence-focused, with evidence-based references for most topics. More than ninety-five new topics are included, such as Asherman syndrome, acute diarrhea, pulmonary fibrosis, hand-foot-mouth disease, Q fever, and many others.

Lippincott Williams and Wilkins publishes multiple individual titles in its *5-Minute* series, including *The 5-Minute Emergency Medicine Consult, The 5-Minute Pediatric Consult,* and titles on neurology, nurses' clinical consult, orthopedics, pain management, pediatrics, veterinary medicine, and others. The full collection is packaged as the *Lippincott Williams and Wilkins 5-Minute Clinical Consult Book Collection 2011. The 5-Minute Clinical Consult 2013* comprises the following titles overall:

5-Minute Anesthesiology Consult

5-Minute Consult: Clinical Companion to Women's Health

5-Minute Herb and Dietary Supplement Consult

5-Minute Neurology Consult

5-Minute Obstetrics and Gynecology Consult

5-Minute Orthopaedic Consult

5-Minute Pain Management Consult

5-Minute Pediatric Consult

5-Minute Sports Medicine Consult

5-Minute Toxicology Consult

5-Minute Urology Consult

Fleisher and Ludwig's 5-Minute Pediatric Emergency Medicine Consult

Gorbach's 5-Minute Infectious Diseases Consult

Lippincott Williams and Wilkins 5-Minute Clinical Consult Book Collection 2011 (full collection of 14 titles)

Nurse's 5-Minute Clinical Consult: Diagnostic Tests

Nurse's 5-Minute Clinical Consult: Diseases

Nurse's 5-Minute Clinical Consult: Multi-System Disorders

Nurse's 5-Minute Clinical Consult: Procedures

Nurse's 5-Minute Clinical Consult: Signs and Symptoms

Nurse's 5-Minute Clinical Consult: Treatments

Rosen and Barkin's 5-Minute Emergency Medicine Consult

Full contents of the 2013 edition, including access to twelve *5-Minute* titles, are currently available online via STAT!Ref (http://www.statref.com/), from OVID (http://www.ovid.com/), or for mobile devices from the publisher. The edition is also available online and for mobile devices via Unbound Medicine (http://www.unboundmedicine.com/products/5-minute_clinical_consult_5mcc).

9.2   Edge, Stephen B., David R. Byrd, Carolyn C. Compton, April G. Fritz, Frederick L. Greene, and Andrew Trotti. *AJCC Cancer Staging Manual*. 7th ed. New York: Springer, 2010.

The American Joint Committee on Cancer's *AJCC Cancer Staging Manual* compiles information on cancer staging based on anatomic site. Included is information on the etiology and pathology of cancer. The seventh edition has fifty-seven chapters, many with major revisions, as well as new site chapters for extrahepatic bile ducts, distal bile duct, cutaneous squamous cell carcinoma, Merkel cell carcinoma, and the adrenal gland. Also included is a more comprehensive section on ophthalmologic malignancies.

The *Manual* includes the principles and rules of TNM staging, including a summary of changes in the TNM classification. Full-color text highlights elements of the TNM, stage groupings, and prognostic factors. "Staging at a Glance" opens each chapter to provide an overview of staging and coding details. Available via STAT!Ref (http://www.statref.com/).

9.3   Bope, Edward T., and Rick D. Kellerman, eds. *Conn's Current Therapy 2013*. Philadelphia: W. B. Saunders, 2013.

Updated annually, *Conn's Current Therapy* is a handbook of diagnostics, therapeutics, and patient care, with descriptions of current therapeutic techniques for managing 300 common diseases and disorders. Disease conditions are referenced by body system. In the later editions, "current diagnosis" and "current therapy" boxes highlight key points in diagnosis and treatment, making for easy browsing. *Conn's Current Therapy* also covers herbal products, and recently approved and soon-to-be-approved drugs. The 2013 edition now includes further in-depth topics such as chest pain, pseudomembranous colitis, metabolic conditions, digestive diseases, skin disorders, and more.

Web-based access to the complete 2010 version is available (http://www.conns currenttherapy.com). Features of *Conn's Current Therapy* online include a frequently updated drug database, a variety of clinical algorithms and tables, chapter downloads in PDF format, and an option to download content onto mobile devices. The online chapters are organized by the body systems and particular conditions.

9.4   Papadakis, Maxine, Stephen J. McPhee, and Michael W. Rabow. *Current Medical Diagnosis and Treatment 2013*. 52nd ed. Los Altos, CA: Lange Medical Publishers, 2013.

Current Medical Diagnosis and Treatment (*CMDT*) presents signs, symptoms, epidemiology, etiology, and treatment options for more than 1,000 medical diseases and disorders. It is a useful tool for internal medicine clinicians. All primary topics are covered in alphabetical order, including dermatology, geriatrics, gynecology and obstetrics, neurology, ophthalmology, orthopedics, otolaryngology, palliative care, psychiatry, toxicology, and urology. Features include various figures and tables, drug treatment tables, *ICD-9* codes, "Essentials of Diagnosis" callouts, and references with (PubMed) PMID numbers.

The fifty-second revised edition of the *CMDT* includes a variety of updated and new sections, such as a new chapter on women's health, and revised chapters on viral infections, environmental factors in disease, blood disorders, peripheral artery aneurysms, and others. Also updated are the oncology sections, including breast cancer treatments, cervical cancer screening recommendations, and lung cancer screening protocols.

Well-organized and thorough tables of contents and indexes make this resource easy to browse. The index points users to primary discussions of each topic, tabular material, and figures. Drugs are listed by generic names.

Current Medical Diagnosis and Treatment is the flagship of the *Current* series from Lange Medical Publishers. The series includes these titles:

Current Emergency Diagnosis and Treatment

Current Geriatric Diagnosis and Treatment

Current Obstetric and Gynecologic Diagnosis and Treatment

Current Pediatric Diagnosis and Treatment

Current Surgical Diagnosis and Treatment

For more details about the series, see the Lange Medical Publishers website (http://www.langetextbooks.com/). As Lange Medical is an imprint of McGraw-Hill, many of the series titles are available for libraries through McGraw-Hill's Access Medicine (http://accessmedicine.com/).

9.5   *Guide to Clinical Preventive Services.* Washington, DC: U.S. Department of Health and Human Services, Agency for Healthcare Research and Quality, 2012.

The *Guide to Clinical Preventive Services* includes recommendations on screening, counseling, and preventive medication topics and clinical considerations from the U.S. Preventive Services Task Force (USPSTF), an independent panel of experts in primary care and prevention that provides systematic reviews of the evidence of effectiveness, and develops recommendations for clinical preventive services. The *Guide* comprises more than sixty preventive services, which now are presented in an easy-to-use, one-page summary table format. Clinical summaries are abridged versions of the USPSTF recommendations.

In addition, the *Guide* presents information on resources that clinicians can use to educate their patients on appropriate preventive services, as well as brief descriptions of and links to tools that they can use to improve their practices, including the electronic Preventive Services Selector, MyHealthfinder, and the Guide to Community Preventive Services.

The USPSTF Electronic Preventive Services Selector (ePSS) allows users to download the USPSTF recommendations to mobile devices, receive notifications of updates, and search and browse recommendations online. Users can search the ePSS for recommendations by patient age, sex, and pregnancy status (http://www.epss.ahrq.gov/).

9.6   Johns Hopkins Hospital, Kristin Arcara, and Megan Tschudy. *The Harriet Lane Handbook: A Manual for Pediatric House Officers*. 19th ed. Philadelphia: Mosby, 2012.

The *Harriet Lane Handbook* provides pediatric diagnostic, treatment, and management guidance, immunization schedules, procedures, recommended tests, and a comprehensive drug formulary. Features include drug efficacy and safety in children, and FDA Pregnancy Category notations, including the effects of drugs in breast milk. The *Handbook* also features emergency management protocols.

The nineteenth edition has been significantly reorganized to include an updated pediatric formulary, coverage of dermatology, eczema complications, lead poisoning, CDC immunization schedules, and full-color images to help detect child abuse. This edition is also more compact for easier pocket storage.

The pediatric formulary is continually updated online with dosing and drug information for children (http://www.expertconsult.com/). The *Harriet Lane Handbook* is available online and for mobile devices. Unbound Medicine (http://www.unboundmedicine.com/products/harriet_lane) also carries this title.

9.7   Bartlett, John G., Paul G. Auwaerter, and Paul A. Pham, eds. *Johns Hopkins ABX Guide: Diagnosis and Treatment of Infectious Diseases*. 3rd ed. Burlington, MA: Jones and Bartlett Learning, 2012.

The *Johns Hopkins ABX Guide 2012* is a pocket-sized handbook on anti-microbial agents, infectious diseases, and common pathogens. It is designed to be a point-of-care, evidence-based, decision support tool for preventing, diagnosing, and treating most infectious diseases. The *ABX Guide* is organized into four sections: "Anti-infectives," which includes prescribing information for a variety of drug categories. "Vaccines" provides agents used for immunization and prophylaxis. This section also includes information on diagnostic criteria, indications, administration, and adverse reactions. The "Diagnoses" section features common infectious diseases with diagnostic criteria, common pathogens, treatment regimens, and drug recommendations. "Pathogens" covers clinical information on bacteria, fungi, parasites, and viruses.

Each entry includes clinical relevance, sites of infection, treatment regimens, and general comments and references. The handbook also offers a variety of tables in a rear section and a fold-out chart covering the spectrum of activity for key drugs.

The *ABX Guide* is available for mobile devices (phone, iPad, Android), online free of charge from Johns Hopkins University (http://www.hopkins-abxguide.org/), or from OVID (http://www.ovid.com/). The guide is also available from Unbound Medicine (http://www.unboundmedicine.com/products/johns_hopkins_abx_guide).

9.8 Porter, Robert S., and Justin L. Kaplan, eds. *Merck Manual of Diagnosis and Therapy.* 19th ed. Whitehouse Station, NJ: Merck Research Laboratories, 2011.

The *Merck Manual of Diagnosis and Therapy,* first published in 1899, is a widely used medical handbook that gives the essentials of diagnosis and treatment of medical conditions and diseases in internal medicine. The small-format handbook is organized with thumb-tab access to twenty-two major sections organized by body system and medical specialty. More than 2,000 diseases and disorders are covered.

This edition includes fifteen new chapters, 300 new tables, and fifty-six new figures. A new sixteen-page color insert shows skin, eye, and oral disorders. Also new to this edition are sections on geriatric medicine. Appendixes include common drugs and key reference values. An extensive index is available.

The popular *Merck Manual* series has grown to include the *Merck Manual— Home Edition,* a lay version of *Merck Manual of Diagnosis and Therapy,* the *Merck Manual of Geriatrics*, the *Merck Index*, a chemical encyclopedia, as well as titles in children's health, women's and men's health, health and aging, and veterinary medicine.

Merck titles are available in print and online (http://www.merckmanuals.com/). The nineteenth edition (2011) is available online from STAT!Ref (http://www.statref .com/). Versions for mobile devices are available with or without an online account from the publishers (http://www.merckmanuals.com/).

9.9 Porter, Robert S., ed. *Merck Manual of Medical Information, Third Home Edition.* Whitehouse Station, NJ: Merck Research Laboratories, 2009.

The 2009 *Merck Manual of Medical Information, Third Home Edition* is a comprehensive consumer health version of the *Merck Manual of Diagnosis and Therapy* written in a lay-focused style and format. The online version contains photographs, audio, and video material not found in the print version.

The *Merck Manual of Medical Information, Third Home Edition* is available online and for mobile devices from Merck (http://www.merckmanuals.com/).

9.10 Oyelowo, Tolu. *Mosby's Guide to Women's Health: A Handbook for Health Professionals.* Geneva: Elsevier—Health Sciences Division, 2007.

Although not recently updated, *Mosby's Guide to Women's Health* is a useful clinical guide to managing common issues arising in women's health. Concise and well organized, this guide includes protocols for the diagnosis and treatment of a range of conditions. Traditional medical information is included, as is information on alternative treatments such as physical therapy, chiropractic, naturopathic therapies, nutrition, and herbs. The full 2007 edition is available online via ScienceDirect (http://www.sciencedirect.com/science/book/9780323046015).

9.11   Ackley, Betty J., and Gail B. Ladwig. *Nursing Diagnosis Handbook: An Evidence-Based Guide to Planning Care.* 9th ed. St. Louis, MO: Elsevier-Mosby, 2011.

The *Nursing Diagnosis Handbook* is designed to be used to build customized care plans based on individual patients' needs. It includes suggested nursing diagnoses for over 1,300 symptoms, diagnoses, procedures, surgical interventions, and clinical sites. The *Handbook* is organized alphabetically, with evidence-based practice information incorporated throughout. A step-by-step approach assists nurses in identifying a diagnosis and generating a care plan that includes the desired outcomes, interventions, and evidence-based rationales using a three-step process (assess, diagnose, and plan care).

This edition incorporates the 2009–2011 NANDA International (NANDA-I) approved nursing diagnoses, including twenty-one new and eight revised diagnoses. Color-coded boxes illustrate the problem-etiology-symptom format for formulating diagnostic statements. Three types of nursing diagnoses are explained, as are differences between actual and potential problems in performing assessments. A free-of-charge Care Plan Constructor website (http://evolve.elsevier.com/Ackley/NDH/) allows nurses to create customized care plans.[1]

9.12   Nicoll, Diana, Mark Lu Chuanyi, Michael Pignone, and Stephen J. McPhee. *Pocket Guide to Diagnostic Tests.* 6th ed. Norwalk, CT: Appleton and Lange, 2012.

The *Pocket Guide* is a useful, evidence-based resource that covers tests used in internal medicine, pediatrics, surgery, neurology, and obstetrics and gynecology. The guide is divided into ten sections, including diagnostic testing and medical decision making, point-of-care testing and provider-provided microscopy, common laboratory tests, therapeutic drug monitoring and pharmacogenetic testing, microbiology, diagnostic imaging by body system, electrocardiography and echocardiography, and differential diagnosis tables and algorithms.

New to this edition are more than twenty-four new or revised clinical laboratory test entries, microbiologic tests for new and reemerging pathogens and infectious agents, and more than two dozen new and revised tables and algorithms. A full index is included. Figures, tables, and an easy-to-read format make this a useful resource for students, nurses, and clinicians. The full sixth edition is available online through Access Medicine (http://www.accessmedicine.com/). Web and mobile versions are available through Unbound Medicine as well (http://www.unboundmedicine.com/products/pocket_guide_diagnostic_tests).

9.13   *Professional Guide to Diseases.* 10th ed. Philadelphia: Lippincott Williams and Wilkins, 2012.

The *Professional Guide to Diseases*, in its tenth edition in 2012, mirrors the *Merck Manual* in coverage and content. This handbook covers more than 600 disorders, including emerging diseases, antibiotic-resistant infections, and terrorist agents. It is organized around disease clusters. Each entry includes a descriptive overview and information on causes, incidence, signs, symptoms, diagnosis, treatment, and special considerations such as nutrition information, support referrals, or congenital abnormalities. Charts, new full-color illustrations, and anatomic drawings supplement the text. The tenth edition features improved sections focused on health promotion and disease prevention along with color charts and figures illustrating the pathophysiology of many conditions. This edition is now full-color, compared to the mostly black-and-white ninth edition. It is available via OVID (http://www.ovid.com/).

9.14   *Professional Guide to Signs and Symptoms.* 6th ed. Philadelphia: Wolters Kluwer/Lippincott Williams and Wilkins, 2011.

The *Professional Guide to Signs and Symptoms*, part of the "Professional Guide" series, is a useful and differential diagnostic manual for nurses, medical students, or clinicians. The revised sixth edition has more than 550 signs and symptoms, as well as 500 full-color illustrations, tables, and flowcharts. Approximately 300 of the most common and important signs and symptoms are organized alphabetically in the main text. Within each entry, users will find a description of the sign, emergency interventions, history and physical examination, causes, associated signs and symptoms, special considerations, pediatric pointers, geriatric pointers, and patient counseling. Emerging diseases are included as well. About 250 less common signs and symptoms are described in the appendixes, which also include a variety of English/Spanish translations. A thorough index is included. It is available online through OVID (http://www.ovid.com/) or for mobile devices from the publisher.

9.15   Hall, Brian J., and John C. Hall. *Sauer's Manual of Skin Diseases.* 10th ed. Philadelphia: Wolters Kluwer Health/Lippincott Williams and Wilkins, 2010.

Sauer's is a popular dermatology reference for clinicians. Presented here are instructions and algorithms for the diagnosis and treatment of all common skin conditions. Algorithms are based on site, type of lesion, and patient age. Its complete illustration library presents easy access to more than 700 full-color photographs. The tenth edition also includes a thorough dictionary/index of skin conditions, as well as new chapters on sexually transmitted infections, nonmelanoma skin cancer, vascular tumors, cutaneous T-cell lymphoma, ethnic skin diseases, obesity and dermatology, transplant patient skin diseases, and nutritional and metabolic skin diseases. This is available online via OVID (http://www.ovid.com/) or as a PDF download.

9.16   Ralph, Sheila S., and Cynthia M. Taylor. *Sparks and Taylor's Nursing Diagnosis Reference Manual*. 8th ed. Philadelphia: Wolters Kluwer Health/ Lippincott Williams and Wilkins, 2011.

Sparks and Taylor's Nursing Diagnosis Reference Manual presents care plan guidelines for all 2009–2011 NANDA International (NANDA-I) approved nursing diagnoses. Each NANDA-I diagnosis includes associated Nursing Interventions Classifications (NIC) and Nursing Outcomes Classifications (NOC). All related interventions, rationales, and measurable outcomes are included. The nursing process is integrated throughout.

The revised eighth edition is organized by life stages and types of care. Users can also browse nursing diagnoses by population, such as "adults," "pediatrics," "obstetrics," etc. Full-color coding makes content more easily searched by lifespan. New features include "Applying Evidence-Based Practice" content for each part of the book, and special icons pointing to online content. This feature includes content for "The Question," "Evidence-Based Resources," "Evaluating the Evidence," "Applying the Results and Making a Decision," and "Re-Evaluating Process and Identifying Areas for Improvement." A complete index is included, although users should be aware that in many cases, the online index points to the wrong page numbers. Available via STAT!Ref (http://www.statref.com/).

9.17   Washington University School of Medicine Department of Medicine, Corey Foster, Neville Mistry, Parvin F. Peddi, and Shivak Sharma. *Washington Manual of Medical Therapeutics*. 33rd ed. Philadelphia: Lippincott-Raven, 2010.

The *Washington Manual of Medical Therapeutics*, one of the texts formerly known as the "Spiral Manual Series," is a popular, quick-reference-style guide to a broad range of diseases and conditions. The thirty-third edition is organized into twenty-four easy-to-use chapters, and includes a complete index. New to this edition are color coding for better navigation, new decision support algorithms, and improved templates and bulleted formatting. Each symptom includes general principles (etiology, etc.), diagnosis (clinical presentation, history, physical examination, diagnostic testing, and differential diagnosis), and treatment options, all presented in bulleted formats. The *Washington Manual* is a copyright of the Washington University. Available via STAT!Ref (http://www.statref.com/) or OVID (http://www .ovid.com/). Versions for online and mobile devices are available from Unbound Medicine (http://www.unboundmedicine.com/products/washington_manual).

9.18   Klingensmith, Mary E., Abdulhameed Aziz, Ankit Bharat, Amy C. Fox,
        and Matthew R. Proembka, eds. *Washington Manual of Surgery*. 6th ed.
        Philadelphia: Wolters Kluwer/Lippincott Williams and Wilkins Health, 2012.

Also part of the former "Spiral Manual Series," the *Washington Manual of Surgery* presents a concise approach to the management of patients with a variety of common surgical conditions. The *Manual* is a useful tool for answering basic questions from pathology to epidemiology, prognosis, treatments, and so forth. It is particularly useful for students and new residents. The easy-to-use outline format enables quick access. The sixth edition includes full-color and updated diagnostic and treatment information of patients with surgical problems. No online version is available at present.

Disease Classification and Nomenclature

9.19   Schulte-Markwort, Michael, Peter Riedesser, and Kathrin Marutt, eds. *Cross-Walks ICD-10/DSM-IV: A Synopsis of Classifications of Mental Disorders*. Cambridge, MA: Hogrefe and Huber, 2003.

Although now dated, *Cross-Walks ICD-10/DSM-IV* is noteworthy for its easy comparisons between the still fairly current text revision (TR) editions of the *ICD-10* and *DSM-IV*. This manual is made up of tables comparing and contrasting the classifications, with "crosswalks" in both directions. The first half of the book presents tables from the *ICD-10* perspective; listing *ICD-10* mental disorders in the left column, the *DSM-IV-TR* diagnosis in the right column, with the cross-comparison in the center column. Included in these crosswalks are explanations of the correspondence between the codes, as well as differences or omissions in each of the coding systems. The second half of the book is organized similarly, but in reverse, with the *DSM-IV-TR* classification on the left and the *ICD-10* on the right. No indexes are available.

9.20   Abraham, Michelle. *Current Procedural Terminology: CPT 2013 Standard Edition*. Chicago: American Medical Association, 2013.

Current Procedural Terminology (*CPT*) includes hundreds of medical codes for identifying and describing all performed medical procedures that are used for reporting and billing Medicare or private insurers. *CPT* codes are published by the American Medical Association (AMA), and are updated annually. *CPT* is the nation's official, HIPAA-compliant code set for procedures and services.

Yearly editions of the book include code additions, changes, and deletions. Key features include an improved, comprehensive index to aid in locating codes related to specific procedures, services, anatomic sites, conditions, synonyms, eponyms, or abbreviations. The pathology and laboratory index entries include analytes, and new listings exist for proprietary test names for multi-analyte assays. Fourteen appendixes reference additional information and resources that cover such topics as modifiers, clinical examples, add-on codes, and vascular families.

The *CPT* is available from the American Medical Association (http://www.ama-assn.org/) and from STAT!Ref (http://www.statref.com/).

9.21   American Psychiatric Association. *DSM-5: Diagnostic and Statistical Manual of Mental Disorders.* 5th ed. Arlington, VA: The American Psychiatric Association, 2013.

The *DSM: Diagnostic and Statistical Manual of Mental Disorders*, by the American Psychiatric Association, contains descriptions, symptoms, and other criteria for diagnosing mental disorders. The *DSM* also establishes criteria for diagnosis that can be used in research on psychiatric disorders. No information about treatment is included in the *DSM*.

Released in 2013, the *DSM-5* is based on correcting issues and problems in the *DSM-IV*. Addressing symptom severity and co-occurring disorders are two priorities for the *DSM-5*, as are improving imprecise diagnostic criteria and reducing diagnoses currently contained in the "Not Otherwise Specified" section of the *DSM-IV*. *DSM-5* also includes assessment of common symptoms not currently addressed in the diagnostic criteria for specific illnesses. Goals also include making the *DSM-5* more developmentally focused. Ten categories are reduced to six specific personality disorder types (antisocial, avoidant, borderline, narcissistic, obsessive/compulsive, and schizotypal).

DSM-5 is organizationally different from *DSM-IV*. The latest manual's sixteen chapters are reordered based on underlying vulnerabilities and symptom characteristics. The chapters are arranged by general categories including neurodevelopment, "emotional and somatic to reflect the potential commonalities in etiology within larger disorder groups."[2] *DSM-5* will drop the traditional roman numbering. Subsequent editions will be numbered as *DSM-5.1, 5.2, 5.3*, and so forth.

The *DSM-IV* is available online from the publisher's site, PsychiatryOnline (http://dsm.psychiatryonline.org/). The online manual is organized into four primary sections beginning with details about organization and usage, followed by the DSM-IV-TR Classification, and a systematic list of codes and categories. The DSM-IV Multiaxial System for assessment is described. Finally, detailed diagnostic criteria for DSM-IV disorders are delineated along with descriptive text. A number of appendixes are also included.

9.22   Nomenclature Committee of the International Union of Biochemistry and Molecular Biology (NC-IUBMB) in consultation with the IUPAC-IUBMB Joint

Commission on Biochemical Nomenclature (JCBN). *Enzyme Nomenclature.* London: Department of Chemistry, Queen Mary University of London. Available: http://www.chem.qmul.ac.uk/iubmb/enzyme/.

The Enzyme Nomenclature database is a publicly available, web-based alternative to printed enzyme nomenclature tools (http://www.chem.qmul.ac.uk/iubmb/enzyme/). It covers 1992 through 2013. Data are presented in enzyme number order, giving a recommended name for each enzyme. EC numbers and details are given. Users can click on EC categories to identify specific enzymes, then click on the link to a detailed scope note for each enzyme.

9.23   Buck, Carol J. *HCPCS 2013 Level II Professional Edition.* Chicago: American Medical Association, 2012.

HCPCS—Level II is the *Healthcare Common Procedure Coding System.* The HCPCS manual represents medical services, items, supplies, and nonphysician services that are not covered by the AMA's CPT-4 codes. Medicaid and Medicare as well as private insurers use HCPCS standardized procedures and modifier codes for uniformity in claims and billing processing.

This spiral-bound edition includes the most current HCPCS codes and regulations. Each alphanumeric HCPCS code is followed by descriptive terminology that identifies a category of similar items. Other features include the American Dental Association's CDT dental codes, full-color drug tables with drug code annotations (brand and generic drug names), and full-color photographs and illustrations of medical equipment and related codes. This is available online; see the publisher website (http://www.ama.org/).

9.24   *ICD-9-CM: International Classification of Diseases, Ninth Revision, Clinical Modification.* 9th rev. ed. Washington, DC: U.S. Government Printing Office, 2011.

The *International Classification of Diseases* (*ICD*) is the standard international coding tool for diseases, injuries, and related health problems. It is broadly designed for morbidity and mortality information for statistical purposes. It also indexes hospital records by disease and operations for data storage and retrieval.

The *ICD-9-CM* is the official system for assigning hospital utilization codes to diagnoses and procedures. It is comparable to the *ICD-9*. The three-volume set includes a tabular list containing a numerical list of the disease code numbers in tabular format, and an alphabetical index to the disease entries. A classification system for surgical, diagnostic, and therapeutic procedures (alphabetic index and tabular list) is included.[3]

The complete October 2011 version of the *ICD-9-CM: International Classification of Diseases, Ninth Revision, Clinical Modification* is available on CD-ROM for Windows platforms only. The complete three-volume set can be purchased at the Government Printing Office for a minimal fee. The *ICD-9-CM for Physicians* (Volumes 1 and 2) is available via STAT!Ref (http://www.statref.com/).

9.25   Buck, Carol J., ed. *2014 ICD-9-CM for Hospitals, Professional Edition.* Vols. 1, 2, and 3. St. Louis, MO: Elsevier Saunders, 2013.

Available in a printed spiral-bound format, this reference offers the full three-volume set including both inpatient and outpatient codes. It includes anatomy artwork by *Netter's Atlas* and the *Official Guidelines for Coding and Reporting (OGCR)*. The online version has the "ITEMS" feature, which gives detailed information on common diseases and conditions. Symbols throughout the text also alert users to new, revised, or deleted codes. "Age and sex edits" alert users to codes limited to specific patient ages and genders. This edition is online through STAT!Ref (http://www.statref.com/).

9.26   World Health Organization. *ICD-10: International Statistical Classification of Diseases and Related Health Problems.* 10th ed. Vols. 1, 2, and 3. Geneva: World Health Organization, 2010.

The *ICD-10: International Statistical Classification of Diseases and Related Health Problems* is the U.S. clinical modification of the World Health Organization's *ICD-10*. It is used to classify mortality data from death certificates. The *ICD-10: International Statistical Classification* is also used for epidemiology, health management, and clinical purposes, and to monitor the incidence and prevalence of diseases and other health problems. The tenth edition is a three-volume set: (1) the tabular list, (2) related definitions, standards, rules and instructions, and (3) the alphabetical list. Volume 1 includes significant corrections for lymphomas and leukemias (neoplasms chapter), and clarification and more vigorous detail for some of the maternal conditions. Volume 2 includes clarification of definitions and rules regarding maternal causes of death, causes of pneumonia, and editing of the rules for coding of neoplasms in the cause of death. Volume 3 reflects changes to Volume 1. There are color illustrations and diagrams throughout. This edition also incorporates changes in the 2005 edition, which includes "common fourth and fifth digit subclassifications, and greater specificity in code assignment."[4]

The *ICD-10: International Statistical Classification* is available in print, with the 2010 edition online from the World Health Organization (http://apps.who.int/classifications/icd10/browse/2010/en). The most up-to-date releases are available for download in PDF format (http://www.cdc.gov/nchs/icd/icd10cm.htm). It is also available online via STAT!Ref (http://www.statref.com/).

Laboratory Methods and Laboratory Diagnosis

9.27   Vandenpitte, Jozef, K. Engbaek, and P. Rohner, eds. *Basic Laboratory Procedures in Clinical Bacteriology*. 2nd ed. Geneva: World Health Organization, 2003.

Basic Laboratory Procedures in Clinical Bacteriology provides World Health Organization guidelines on specimen sampling for lab investigation, bacteria identification, and antibiotics resistance testing. Part 1 covers bacteriological investigations of blood, cerebrospinal fluid, urine, stools, upper and lower respiratory tract infections, sexually transmitted diseases, purulent exudates, wounds and abscesses, anaerobic bacteriology, antimicrobial susceptibility testing, and serological tests. Part 2 covers key pathogens, media, and diagnostic reagents. It includes a list of media and reagents needed for the isolation and identification of the most common bacterial pathogens, together with an indication of importance for the laboratory.[5]

Instead of focusing on basic techniques of microscopy and staining, the handbook focuses on procedural issues related to quality control and assessment. The reference gives particular attention to the need for quality control in laboratory procedures, with step-by-step instructions for obtaining specimens, isolating and identifying bacteria, and assessing their resistance to antibiotics. *Basic Laboratory Procedures in Clinical Bacteriology* is available online through EBSCOhost Books (http://www.ebscohost.com/ebooks).

9.28   *Current Protocol Series*. Indianapolis, IN: John Wiley and Sons.

Current Protocols includes hundreds of research protocols and overviews for more than twenty primary areas: bioinformatics, cell biology, cell culture, chemical biology, cytometry, gene expression, genetics and genomics, imaging and microscopy, immunology, intermolecular interactions, laboratory organisms and animal models, magnetic resonance imaging, microbiology, molecular biology, mouse biology, neuroscience, nucleic acid chemistry, pharmacology and drug discovery, protein production, purification and analysis, proteomics, RNA, safety, stem cells, structural analysis of biomolecules, supporting lab techniques, and toxicology.

Each protocol contains a materials list with summaries that detail the purposes, applications, limitations, advantages, and other issues associated with each method. Commentary and guidelines are provided, along with a variety of illustrations, tables, data charts, and diagrams. *Current Protocol Series* titles are available in print, CD-ROM, or online via Wiley InterScience (http://www.currentprotocols.com/WileyCDA/). They are updated through 2012.

9.29   Van Leeuwen, Anne M. *Davis's Comprehensive Handbook of Laboratory and Diagnostic Tests with Nursing Implications*. 5th ed. Philadelphia: F. A. Davis, 2013.

Davis's Comprehensive Handbook of Laboratory and Diagnostic Tests with Nursing Implications is an easy-to-use laboratory handbook designed specifically for nurses. Content is arranged alphabetically by test, with critical considerations labeled with color-coded icons. *Davis's* includes explanations of each test, synonyms or acronyms for the test name, names of related tests, pre- and post-test considerations, types of specimens required, critical values, differences in age range and gender, rationale, indications, results, and factors affecting results. Search the index by abbreviation, synonym, disease/disorder, specimen type, or test classification.

The "Body Systems Appendix" includes a list of common laboratory and diagnostic tests for each body system, as well as nutrition-related lab tests. Nursing implications are presented for each test, including pre- and post-test preparation instructions for patients and families. The printed text comes with a one-year online subscription (unique access code). It is also available via STAT!Ref (http://www.statref.com/).

9.30   McPherson, Richard A., and Matthew R. Pincus, eds. *Henry's Clinical Diagnosis and Management of Laboratory Methods.* 22nd ed. Philadelphia: Saunders Elsevier, 2012.

The revised twenty-second edition of *Henry's Clinical Diagnosis and Management of Laboratory Methods* gives comprehensive, multidisciplinary coverage of laboratory test selection and results interpretation. It has good coverage of pathophysiology and diagnosis within different organ systems. Included in *Henry's* twenty-second edition is new and updated information on the chemical basis for analyte assays and common interfaces, lipids and dyslipoproteinemia, markers in the blood for cardiac injury evaluation and related stroke disorders, coagulation testing for antiplatelet drugs such as aspirin and clopidogrel, biochemical markers of bone metabolism, clinical enzymology, hematology and transfusion medicine, and others.[6] The full text and a complete image bank are available online (http://www.exertconsult.com/).

9.31   Chernicky, Cynthia C., and Barbara J. Berger. *Laboratory Tests and Diagnostic Procedures.* 8th ed. St Louis, MO: Elsevier Saunders, 2013.

The eighth revised edition of *Laboratory Tests and Diagnostic Procedures* is one of the more comprehensive laboratory test references. It includes over 900 tests and diagnostic procedures. Organized alphabetically with A-to-Z thumb tabs for easy browsing, it has two parts. Part 1 provides an alphabetical list of more than 600 diseases, conditions, and symptoms, and their corresponding diagnostic tests and procedures. Part 2 has key information on laboratory and diagnostic tests. Cross-referenced alternatives give test names and acronyms. Tests for toxic substances are included, along with "Panic Level Symptoms and Treatment" for dangerously elevated levels. Age and gender-specific norm, risks, and contraindications are included. Minimum volumes for blood samples are presented for patients for whom blood preservation is important. Special consent form requirements are indicated. Available via STAT!Ref (http://www.statref.com/).

9.32   Walker, John M., and Ralph Rapley. *Medical Biomethods Handbook*. Totowa, NJ: Humana Press, 2005.

The *Medical Biomethods Handbook* includes a large collection of molecular biology techniques. One of the strengths of this tool is that it can be effectively used by students, researchers, or clinicians who do not have advanced knowledge or expertise in laboratory methods. Arranged into seventeen chapters, the *Medical Biomethods Handbook* covers southern and western blotting techniques, electrophoresis, PCR, DNA and protein microarrays, liquid chromatography, in situ hybridization, karyotyping, flow cytometry, bioinformatics, genomics, and ribotyping. Included are the applications assays for mutation detection, mRNA analysis, chromosome translocations, inborn errors of metabolism, protein therapeutics, and gene therapy. Practical procedures, their applications, and underlying theories are described.[7]

9.33   Pagana, Kathleen D., and Timothy J. Pagana. *Mosby's Diagnostic and Laboratory Test Reference*. 11th ed. St. Louis, MO: Mosby, 2012.

The pocket-sized *Mosby's Diagnostic and Laboratory Test Reference* presents common clinical laboratory and diagnostic tests. Tests are listed by their complete names with abbreviations and alternate names. Test purposes and laboratory specimen source or location of procedure are described. There is also a test explanations and related physiology section. Normal findings are listed for infants, children, adults, and the elderly. Possible critical values are given. Where appropriate, values are separated into male or female. Contraindications, potential complications, procedure and patient care, and home care responsibilities are also overviewed. *Mosby's Diagnostic and Laboratory Test Reference* includes a "User's Guide to Test Preparation and Procedures." This guide for clinicians delineates their responsibilities for guaranteeing safe testing procedures and accurate results. Multiple appendixes list tests by body system, tests by type, disease and organ panels, and symbols and units of measurement. Available online; see the publisher's website (http://www.us.elsevierhealth.com/).

9.34   Pagana, Kathleen D., and Timothy J. Pagana. *Mosby's Manual of Diagnostic and Laboratory Tests*. 4th ed. St. Louis, MO: Mosby-Elsevier, 2010.

This popular manual references more than 700 commonly performed diagnostic and laboratory tests, identified via easy-to-use, color-coded tabs. Each chapter is alphabetically organized by test type, and begins with a list of the tests, followed by a test type overview with specimen collection techniques. Thirty new tests are included in this edition. Explanations of tests themselves, normal findings (including

SI units) and results, indications, contraindications and complications, interfering factors, procedures, patient care, clinical significance, and related tests are covered. Critical values alert clinicians to emergency situations.

The fourth edition includes full-color and 127 photographs and illustrations depicting procedures, equipment, techniques, and key concepts. Unique to *Mosby's Manual* are the "Test Results" and "Clinical Significance" sections, which explain pathophysiology and how test results may indicate certain disease processes. Also unique to *Mosby's* is the "Related Tests" sections, which list tests that provide similar information or evaluate the same body system, disease, or symptom. "Clinical Priorities" are contained in boxes, displaying information related to preparing patients for testing, performing tests, or evaluating results. Drug-related "Interfering Factors" brings attention to effects of various pharmacologic agents. Also included are "Patient Teaching" icons that present patient-focused information about each test, as well as "Home Care Responsibilities," which are used to prepare patients for testing. Finally, *Mosby's* includes unique "Age-Related Concerns" boxes that address special needs of pediatric and geriatric patients, and age-related variations in values. A comprehensive index with test names, synonyms, and relevant terms is included. This edition is available in multiple formats; see the publisher website (http://www.us.elsevierhealth.com/).

9.35   Williamson, M. A., and L. M. Snyder, eds. *Wallach's Interpretation of Diagnostic Tests*. Philadelphia: Wolters Kluwer Health/Lippincott Williams and Wilkins, 2011.

Now in its ninth edition, *Wallach's* is a practical clinical guide to common diagnostic tests. It is organized into two sections. The first lists common clinical laboratory tests in alphabetical order. Tests include sensitivity, specificity, and positive and negative probabilities (where applicable). Microbiology tests are listed separately. The second revised section covers disease states, including the patient's chief complaint and physical findings. It includes current molecular diagnostic testing and cytogenetics for selected diseases. Limitations of common tests are outlined. *Wallach's* also identifies appropriate tests for specific clinical presentations. References to pathophysiology and therapy are not included. This is available for mobile devices from the publisher and online via OVID (http://www.ovid.com/).

Scientific Data Books and Compendia

9.36   Bronzino, Joseph D., and Donald R. Peterson. *The Biomedical Engineering Handbook*. 4th ed. Vols. 1–4. Boca Raton, FL: CRC Press, 2013.

The Biomedical Engineering Handbook is a comprehensive and definitive manual of biomedical engineering for practicing biomedical engineers and students.

It was updated into three volumes in its third edition (2006), and is now a four-volume set. This set provides complete coverage of biomedical engineering fundamentals, medical devices and systems, computer applications in medicine, and molecular engineering. The 2013 edition has substantial revisions with all sections updated. New sections cover drugs and devices, personalized medicine, and stem cell engineering. Also included is a historical overview, as well as a special section on medical ethics.

Volume 1, *Biomedical Engineering Fundamentals* includes foundational concepts with coverage of physiologic systems, bioelectric phenomena, biomechanics, biomaterials, physiologic modeling, ethics, and neuroengineering. In Volume 2, *Medical Devices and Systems*, topics include sensor and imaging technologies, signal analysis, medical instrumentation, and many others. Volume 3, *Computer Applications in Medicine*, has chapters on biosignal processing, medical imaging, radiation imaging, ultrasound, MRI, infrared imaging, medical informatics, and physiological modeling. Volume 4 is dedicated to molecular engineering (molecular biology, transport phenomena and biomimetic, tissue engineering, artificial organs, and more).

9.37   CHEMnetBASE. Boca Raton, FL: CRC Press, 2013. Available: http://www.chemnetbase.com/.

CHEMnetBASE (http://www.chemnetbase.com/) is an online collection of products from CRC Press available via a site license to multi-user organizations only. One or all products can be licensed. The system is designed for locating unknown compounds and retrieving references for known compounds. The search interface allows only for each product to be searched independently. CHEMnetBASE includes the *Handbook of Chemistry and Physics*, *Properties of Organic Compounds*, and *Polymers: A Property Database*. *Polymers: A Property Database* provides scientific and commercial information on polymers. It is searchable by polymer, properties, trade name, application, and other fields. Several dictionaries are also available, including the *Combined Chemical Dictionary*, and the dictionaries of *Natural Products*, *Drugs*, *Commonly Cited Compounds*, *Inorganic and Organometallic Compounds*, *Marine Natural Products*, *Food Compounds*, *Carbohydrates*, and *Organic Compounds*.

9.38   Haynes, William M., ed. *CRC Handbook of Chemistry and Physics.* 94th ed. Boca Raton, FL: CRC Press, 2013.

The ninety-fourth edition of the *CRC Handbook of Chemistry and Physics* includes a broad range of physical scientific data commonly required by chemists, physicists, and engineers: properties of inorganic and organic compounds, chemical bonds, tables of isotopes, and scientific abbreviations and symbols. This edition includes new and updated tables (e.g., Appendix A: Mathematical Tables).

The *CRC Handbook of Chemistry and Physics* on CD-ROM contains the full, updated ninety-third edition in searchable PDF format. The full ninety-third edition is also available on the Web (hbcpnetbase.com). The online handbook now allows for searching by more than 10,000 chemical structures using the Marvin Sketch Java Applet from ChemAxon (http://www.chemaxon.com/products/marvin/marvin-sketch/). It also features interactive tables that can be sorted, filtered, and combined in various ways. The following tables are regularly updated and expanded online: Physical Properties of Inorganic Compounds, Enthalpy of Fusion, Bond Dissociation Energies, Table of the Isotopes (updated through 2005), Inorganic Ion and Ligand Nomenclature, Chemical Carcinogens, and Global Temperature Trend. Within these tables, substances can be searched by name, formula, or CAS Registry Numbers.[8]

9.39   Swartz, Michael E., and Ira S. Krull. *Handbook of Analytical Validation.* Boca Raton, FL: CRC Press, 2012.

The *Handbook of Analytical Validation* was written for practitioners in the drug and biotech industries. It contains current guidelines for analytical method validation, covering instrument qualification, method optimization, and validation basics, specification for different types of tests, validation of results for different methods, and implementation of new technologies. The *Handbook* compiles all of the appropriate regulatory steps required to get a drug through each stage of the validation process, including those coming from the USP. The guidelines apply to "both small molecules in the conventional pharmaceutical industry, as well as the biotech industry."[9] The current version is available in electronic format from the publisher (http://www.crcpress.com/).

9.40   Wild, David, ed. *The Immunoassay Handbook.* 4th ed. Oxford, UK: Elsevier Science, 2013.

The Immunoassay Handbook is a scientific text for immunoassay technology. Designed for a broad audience of pathologists, chemists, biochemists, and students, the *Handbook* covers a wide range of popular medical diagnosis and commercial immunoassay tests. The *Handbook* is organized into 77 chapters, including the useful introduction, "Immunoassay for Beginners." Chapters include brief guides to normal and disease states, with analytes described in depth. The revised fourth edition has nine major parts: Part 1 introduces the fundamentals of immunoassay theory, followed by a series of chapters related to immunoassay configurations in Part 2. Part 3 explores immunoassay components including antibodies, signal generation and detection systems, separation methods, conjugation methods, standardization and calibration, and calibration curve fitting. Part 4 discusses related techniques. Part 5 and Part 6 discuss immunoassay development and implementation, respectively. Part 7 introduces immunoassay product technology and explores topics such as clinical diagnostic testing. Part 8 looks at applications for immunoassay beyond clinical chemistry, and Part 9 explores twenty-three clinical applications of immunoassay for humans. An online version of the fourth edition is available through ScienceDirect (http://www.sciencedirect.com/science/book/9780080970370).

9.41   Versalovic, James, ed. *Manual of Clinical Microbiology*. 10th ed. Washington, DC: ASM Press, 2011.

The *Manual of Clinical Microbiology* is known primarily for its content in medical microbiology, diagnostic microbiology, and microbiological techniques. It includes all major diagnostic tests and therapeutic tests useful to clinical microbiologists, laboratory technologists, and infectious disease specialists in hospitals, clinics, and reference laboratories. The *Manual* includes laboratory test interpretations and comprehensive coverage of the taxonomy and classification of infectious microorganisms. The tenth edition is presented in two volumes comprising nine sections and 149 chapters on research findings, infectious agents, methods, practices, and safety guidelines.

Volume 1 is organized into multiple broad sections on diagnostic strategies and general topics, bacteriology, and antibacterial agents and susceptibility test methods. Volume 2 includes sections on virology, antiviral agents and susceptibility test methods, mycology, antifungal agents and susceptibility test methods, parasitology, and antiparasitic agents and susceptibility test methods.

The tenth edition of the *Manual of Clinical Microbiology* is available online via subscription (http://mcm10.asmpress.org/) or via STAT!Ref (http://www.statref .com/) Features of the ASM Press online edition include linked references, both within the product and to external databases such as PubMed and CrossRef, and PDF printing and saving options.

An online electronic image library includes all of the images in the printed edition plus more than 400 additional images. All of the images are tagged for easy searching. Color images replace the printed manual's black-and-white images.

9.42   Detrick, Barbara, Robert Hamilton, and James Folds, eds. *Manual of Molecular and Clinical Laboratory Immunology*. 7th ed. Washington, DC: ASM Press, 2006.

The revised seventh edition (2006) of the *Manual of Molecular and Clinical Laboratory Immunology* (formerly known as *Manual of Clinical Laboratory Immunology*) includes both standard and the latest immunological tests and procedures in clinical laboratory immunology. This immunology technique and diagnosis tool is organized into seventeen sections, each with chapters on topics including general methodology, laboratory management, molecular testing, clinical chemistry, hematopathology, medical microbiology, and others. Also included are more thorough sections on transplantation, allergic diseases, cancer, and others. Expanded treatment information has been added throughout.[10] It is available via STAT!Ref (http://www.statref.com/).

References

1. Ackley, Betty J., and Gail B. Ladwig. *Nursing Diagnosis Handbook: An Evidence-Based Guide to Planning Care*. 9th ed. St. Louis, MO: Elsevier-Mosby, 2011.

2. "DSM-5 Development." American Psychiatric Association. Last modified 2012. http://www.dsm5.org/Pages/Default.aspx.

3. *ICD-9-CM: International Classification of Diseases, Ninth Revision, Clinical Modification*. 6th ed. Los Angeles: Practice Management Information, 2006.

4. "ICD—Classification of Diseases, Functioning, and Disability." National Center for Health Statistics, Centers for Disease Control and Prevention. Last modified 2013, http://www.cdc.gov/nchs/icd.htm.

5. Vandenpitte, Jozef, K. Engbaek, and P. Rohner, eds. *Basic Laboratory Procedures in Clinical Bacteriology*. 2nd ed. Geneva: World Health Organization, 2003.

6. McPherson, Richard A., and Matthew R. Pincus, eds. *Henry's Clinical Diagnosis and Management of Laboratory Methods*. 22nd ed. Philadelphia: Saunders Elsevier, 2012.

7. Walker, John M., and Ralph Rapley. *Medical Biomethods Handbook*. Totowa, NJ: Humana Press, 2005.

8. Haynes, William M., ed. *CRC Handbook of Chemistry and Physics*. 94th ed. Boca Raton, FL: CRC Press, 2013.

9. Swartz, Michael E., and Ira S. Krull. *Handbook of Analytical Validation*. Boca Raton, FL: CRC Press, 2012.

10. Detrick, Barbara, Robert Hamilton, and James Folds, eds. *Manual of Molecular and Clinical Laboratory Immunology*. 7th ed. Washington, DC: ASM Press, 2006.

CHAPTER 10

Drug Information Sources

PENNY COPPERNOLL-BLACH and SHARON GIOVENALE

Librarians, as experts in keeping current with new information resources and technologies, face challenges in the rapidly evolving environment of drug information. Major factors driving changes in drug information include the emergence of pharmacogenomics, maturation of the Internet and mobile access, and changing roles of health-care practitioners. Drug information encompasses the fields of pharmacology (the study of the physiological actions of drugs), pharmacy (the compounding, manufacture, and dispensing of drugs), and toxicology (the study of hazardous effects of chemicals).

Pharmacogenomics, which accompanied the completion of the human genome project, involves the study of the genetic basis of drug and chemical actions in the body. Pharmacogenomics deals with genetic variations in individual responses to medications and promises a new era of personalized medicine. Health-care practitioners will have the ability to predict unique responses to drugs, either adverse or beneficial, in each patient. Pharmacogenomics impacts all areas of pharmacology and pharmacy, from drug design and development to education and practice. This adds complexity to drug information, not only by accelerating growth in the sheer volume of information, but by introducing new terminologies, new types of data, and new information resources.

The Internet has transformed scientific investigation and communications and contributed to the increasingly multidisciplinary nature of drug information.

Boundaries between disciplines are disappearing, and librarians may be called upon to access information not traditionally included in the category of drug information, such as DNA or protein sequences, chemical structures, and physical properties of drug molecules.

Clinical drug or therapy questions continue to proliferate with the changing roles of health-care professionals. Today's pharmacists function as integral members of health-care teams, partnering with physicians to customize drug regimens for individuals.[1] As high-level practitioners who are qualified to advise patients and physicians about drug therapies, they require drug information to support clinical decision making. With their professional responsibility for patient care, therapeutic outcomes, and medical standards of care requiring evidence-based practice, pharmacists rely heavily on timely and accurate drug information. Librarians serving this population are challenged to efficiently and effectively access current, relevant drug information in a highly dynamic field. While it may not be necessary for every health sciences librarian to master the use of research tools such as genetics databases, it will be important to maintain awareness of new developments in drug information resources.

Drug information questions are directed to librarians from a number of sources. A physician may want to know all adverse effects associated with the administration of a particular drug, or if the drug interacts with other drugs under specific physiological conditions. An occupational health specialist may ask if there is a relationship between a clinical symptom and daily exposure to a chemical in a work environment. A pharmacist may need the U.S. equivalent of a drug prescribed in another country. A nurse may want information about a drug being administered to a patient to assist in monitoring the patient's response to the drug. Increasingly complex drug information questions are also directed to librarians from patients. The Internet provides many sources of consumer health information, some more authoritative than others, and patrons often need help evaluating websites. Another factor affecting the scope of information needs is direct-to-consumer drug advertising. Armed with information from the Internet and drug company advertising, consumers and their families are questioning the recommendations of their physicians. As a result, patients may use the library to investigate questions about drugs they are taking or about additives in the foods they eat. Physicians and pharmacists may need drug information written in lay language to optimize their communications with patients.

The number of drugs (both prescription and nonprescription) available on the market has increased substantially in recent years. The use of herbal products and other alternative therapies has also expanded, due in large part to the empowerment of consumers with increased access to health information. With the increase in the number of drugs in use, there exists a proportional increase in the potential for adverse effects, and an exponential increase in the number of possible interactions between these drugs. As a result, iatrogenic (practitioner-induced) pathology continues to play a significant role in medicine today, and the need for reliable drug information sources is vital to reducing the incidence of medication errors.

Many of the drug information resources described in this chapter are now accessible using mobile applications (apps) for smartphones, iPads or tablets, and other mobile devices. Many apps are freely available, while others incur a charge. Some databases and websites use a browser mode that optimizes a full-screen application to fit a mobile device. Since apps are constantly evolving and changing, this chapter does not attempt to describe all apps that may be available for the drug resources.

Government Regulation and the Drug Approval Process

Government regulation adds another layer of complexity to drug information. The U.S. Food and Drug Administration (FDA) regulates all drugs in interstate commerce and is responsible for overseeing the labeling of drugs and ensuring that they are both safe and effective. These regulations are published in the *Code of Federal Regulations, Title 21: Food and Drugs* (available electronically through the U.S. Government Printing Office, Federal Digital System website at http://www.gpo .gov/fdsys/). The FDA requires pharmaceutical companies to notify prescribing physicians of contraindications, warnings, and adverse effects of drugs. In December 2000, the FDA proposed new requirements for drug packaging information, also known as "package inserts," to make them more user-friendly for physicians and patients (21 CFR part 201; 65 FR 81082, December 22, 2000). The agency gathered information through physician surveys, focus groups, and other communications to determine what information was most important, and developed a "Structured Product Labeling" format for the content of all drug labeling submitted to the FDA. The final rule, "Requirements on Content and Format of Labeling for Human Prescription Drug and Biological Products," appeared in the *Federal Register* (21 CFR parts 201, 314, and 71 FR 3922). Effective June 30, 2006, changes included the reorganization of information to include tables of contents and introductory sections titled "Highlights of Prescribing Information," which list the most important facts about the drug. Without these highlights, it can be difficult to extract the most relevant information because pharmaceutical companies are required to list all precautions and contraindications regardless of their probability. The National Library of Medicine (NLM) maintains a publicly available website, DailyMed, which includes current FDA-approved labeling of drugs (http://dailymed.nlm.nih.gov/dailymed/ about.cfm/). This is a useful resource for health-care practitioners to access essential information about the medications they prescribe and dispense (see 10.20).

In the industrial setting, the U.S. Department of Labor, Occupational Safety and Health Administration (OSHA) creates and enforces safety standards in the workplace. OSHA works together with the U.S. Department of Health and Human Services, National Institute for Occupational Safety and Health (NIOSH), which is responsible for conducting research and providing education and training for occupational safety. Both organizations were formed as a result of the Occupational Safety and Health Act of 1970. This chapter contains a section on adverse effects, toxicology, and poisoning, which includes information on drugs and other chemical substances. We also describe sources of government regulations, standards, and practices, as well as drug packaging information (see 10.19).

There are many stages of development before a drug gets to market, with investigators at each stage creating and accessing different kinds of information.[2] Understanding the stage of development associated with a drug-related question can be helpful in finding relevant drug information. In the drug discovery stage, various chemical and pharmacogenomics research methods and molecular modeling techniques are used to identify potential drug targets and to design new molecules optimizing the chemical interactions at those sites. Chemical literature from the Chemical Abstracts Service (see 10.55) is the best source of information about drugs in development. Next, in vitro and animal studies are conducted. In vitro tests usually involve the determination of drug concentrations that kill or inhibit the growth of various types of human cells in culture. Animal models are used to mimic human disease states for testing drug efficacy and determining appropriate therapeutic drug concentrations. In the next stage, routes of administration are chosen, prototype drugs are formulated, and formulations are evaluated for purity, stability, and toxicity in animal models. Information about in vitro and animal drug studies can be found in the biological literature through BIOSIS Previews (see chapter 4).

When a pharmaceutical company has a chemical entity that it believes has significant therapeutic value, it files an Investigational New Drug (IND) application with the FDA. The category of "new drugs" not only includes new chemical entities, but any existing drug proposed to be used in a way other than previously approved. IND applications are required for new dosage forms, routes of administration, and uses for new indications ("off-label" uses). The IND application must be reviewed and approved before clinical trials in humans can begin. The IND application includes preliminary safety data based on laboratory testing in animals; manufacturing, formulation, and chemical information about the drug; and detailed protocols for the proposed clinical trials. The IND approval process involves review by medical, chemical, pharmacological, and statistical experts to validate the preliminary data and to determine if there is sufficient evidence that it is safe to proceed with human testing. After the IND application is approved, the applicant must then conduct documented studies to demonstrate the therapeutic value and safety of the drug. Testing begins in very small groups (fewer than 100) of human volunteers (Phase 1 studies) to evaluate safety. Phase 1 studies may be conducted in patients, but usually are conducted in healthy volunteers. The studies are designed to generate information on drug metabolism, pharmacology, and side effects associated with high doses, and sometimes provide evidence on effectiveness. Phase 2 studies evaluate safety and dose range, as well as efficacy in patients (up to several hundred) with the disease the drug is intended to treat. If these trials show evidence of drug efficacy, the study moves into Phase 3, where the drug is given to a larger (several thousand) and more diverse population. When sufficient data have been collected, the pharmaceutical company submits another application to the FDA, a New Drug Application (NDA), with its data on the safety and effectiveness of the drug. The IND application becomes part of the NDA. Approval of the NDA means that the drug is approved for marketing and can be prescribed by licensed practitioners. Prior to this approval, the drug may be used only by certain physicians who have been approved to handle investigational drugs. As the drug is made available to potentially millions of patients, additional side effects may appear. For instance, some effects are idiosyncratic, occurring in a very small percentage of the population, and are often missed in the preclinical phases. Phase 4 studies, or post-marketing surveillance, investigate differences between drugs of the same type, or intended to treat the same condition, to determine advantages and disadvantages of one drug over another. Information on drugs in Phase 1 through 4 clinical trials can be found in the clinical literature through MEDLINE or PubMed (see Bibliographic Databases section of this chapter).

Information on drugs in development, prior to clinical trials and in the early phases of clinical trials, especially before they are patented, may be difficult to obtain. Clinical trials can be found in MEDLINE, the Clinical Trials website (http://clinicaltrials.gov/), and other professional organizations' websites such as World Health Organization and National Cancer Institute. Early studies on drug development appear in the chemical literature or the biological literature if it is a naturally derived substance. The biological literature is also a good place to search for early toxicity or carcinogenic animal studies performed before the IND application is submitted. The post-clinical trial NDA, with its documented evidence, never becomes a part of the public domain; it is considered to be proprietary information available only to the pharmaceutical company and the FDA. However the FDA's review of NDA content is available for most drugs at the Drugs@FDA Search website (http://www.accessdata.fda.gov/scripts/cder/drugsatfda/index.cfm/) (see 10.19). Also, researchers often publish their experiences with the drug during clinical trials in the journal and report literature.

After a drug patent expires, other companies may wish to market a generic equivalent. These companies must submit an Abbreviated New Drug Application (ANDA) to show that the generic drug has the same indications for use, active ingredients, routes of administration, dosage form, strength, bioavailability, and labeling.

Information on therapeutic equivalence of generic drugs is listed in the FDA publication, "Approved Drug Products with Therapeutic Equivalence," available on the Web (http://www.accessdata.fda.gov/scripts/cder/ob/).

This chapter describes many standard and new Web-based resources, reflecting the influence of the Internet on drug information organization and delivery, as well as essential print reference sources recommended for health sciences libraries. Many of the classic print resources described herein are now available online. Some of the information in this chapter articulates "universal truths" from earlier editions and that information has not been changed, so we extend our appreciation to Susan M. McGuinness, Nancy F. Stimson, and previous authors for their work. Other areas and newer resources are the current authors' contributions.

Guides to the Literature

Librarians and information professionals new to the drug information field can consult guides to the literature to put drug information in perspective. Current drug information bibliographies and comprehensive guides to the literature are few; however, Bonnie Snow's *Drug Information* compilation is essential to any collection. The fourth edition of *Drug Information: A Guide for Pharmacists* is designed for pharmacists and pharmacy students, but it is also suited to librarians. A more specialized list of resources is available from the American Association of Colleges of Pharmacy website.

10.1   Snow, Bonnie. *Drug Information: A Guide to Current Resources.* 3rd ed. New York: Neal-Schuman, 2008.

10.2   Malone, Patrick M., Karen L. Kier, and John E. Stanovich, eds. *Drug Information: A Guide for Pharmacists.* 4th ed. New York: McGraw-Hill, 2012.

10.3   American Association of Colleges of Pharmacy. *Basic Resources for Pharmacy Education.* August 2012 ed. Available: http://www.aacp .org/governance/SECTIONS/libraryinformationscience/Documents/ BasicResourcesAug2012.pdf.

The third edition of Snow's *Drug Information* provides good background and descriptive information supported by many resources in several areas. It covers drug nomenclature and identification, government regulations, adverse drug reactions and interactions, industrial pharmacy, competitive intelligence resources, sources for statistical information, plus online and Internet resources. A glossary and detailed index add to this guide's value.

Drug Information: A Guide for Pharmacists, states a goal "to educate both students and practitioners on how to efficiently research, interpret, evaluate, collate, and disseminate information in the most usable form." Chapter 3 is titled "Drug Information Resources." This textbook includes learning objectives, key concepts, and case studies for most chapters. The book also addresses issues such as the legal and ethical considerations of providing information, how to respond to requests for information, and how to determine what information should be made available. The book has an extensive appendix, glossary, and detailed index.

The American Association of Colleges of Pharmacy (AACP) website provides a detailed and lengthy list of resources for any collection involved with educating pharmacists. The AACP has an alphabetical and hierarchical listing of more than 800 sources; most books include price, and electronic resources include URLs.

Drug Nomenclature

One of the major problems in using the drug literature is recognizing the multiplicity of names for a given chemical compound and understanding how reference sources must be approached depending on the type of name. A thorough understanding of these names is essential (see figure 10.1). When a pharmaceutical company is investigating a large number of chemicals for possible therapeutic activity, it frequently assigns alphanumeric designations or code names. Often, a code name is the first designation in the primary literature.

The Chemical Abstracts Service (CAS) provides a unique Registry Number for each chemical compound, including drugs. One thing to remember about the Registry Number is that European countries commonly name the drug *for* the parent compound. In the United States, it is more usual to use the salt form (the compound formulated as a salt so that it will dissolve more easily in water), which will generally have a different Registry Number. Because indexes vary on whether the parent or salt Registry Number is used, the experienced searcher should try to identify both Registry Numbers for full retrieval.

The chemical name describes the chemical structure of a drug. There are a number of conventions for these chemical names, which are often very lengthy. Consequently, there is a need for a shorter, "common" name to describe a chemical. "Aspirin" and "tetracycline" are examples of these common names. Common names are also called "generic" and "nonproprietary" names. Names used by a manufacturer to describe marketed products are called "proprietary," "brand," or "trade" names. Proprietary names are registered trademarks, as are the color, shape, and markings of each pill or capsule. Two or more manufacturers may market the same generic drug, but each may also have its own trade name representing the specific product. These products may differ; although the active ingredients are the same, each manufacturer may use different ingredients in compounding the drug or in

FIGURE 10.1

Types of drug names

Research code designation:	U-18, 573
CAS Registry Number:	15687-27-1
Chemical names:	Benzeneacetic acid, α-methyl-4-2(methylpropyl) (±)-
	(±) p-isobutylhydratropic acid
	(±)-2-(p-isobutylphenyl) propionic acid
Generic name:	Ibuprofen
USAN, INN, BAN, JAN:	Ibuprofen
Proprietary names:	Advil (Whitehall-Robins)
	Midol 200 (Sterling Health U.S.A.)
	Motrin (Pharmacia and Upjohn)
	Nuprin Caplets and Tablets (Bristol-Meyers Products)
Molecular formula:	$C_{13}H_{18}O_2$

Structural formula:

holding it together. The composition of a pill, other than amounts of active ingredients, is proprietary or a trade secret, but the inactive ingredients for many drugs
are included with drug packaging information, which can be found in DailyMed.
Inactive ingredients are also sometimes listed in resources such a POISINDEX in
Micromedex's Healthcare Series of online databases (see 10.18).

Another source of confusion is the multiplicity of generic names. Two companies working with the same drug may call it by different generic names. In the past,
this practice has led to such confusion that now "official" generic names are designated. The United States Adopted Names (USAN) Commission has the authority
to declare a specific generic name as the officially recognized common name, the
"adopted name," in the United States. If another company wants to market a preparation of that drug, it will use this "official" generic name.

The nomenclature problem is compounded on an international scale. Other
countries also have authorized bodies to establish official names, Japanese Adopted

Names (JAN) and British Adopted Names (BAN), for example. The World Health Organization's International Nonproprietary Names (INN) attempts to unify official names in all participating countries, but differences still exist. These variations in nomenclature cause a range of difficulties. For instance, a patient taking a French drug travels to the United States and needs a refill of an American equivalent. A British doctor taking an American medical licensure exam finds "meperidine" on the examination questions rather than "pethidine," the name to which British doctors are accustomed. American researchers looking for information on the antiviral agent, "acyclovir," will miss sources that use the INN name, "aciclovir."

Librarians must understand the many types of names to use literature sources effectively. Some publications, particularly commercial sources, may be arranged by proprietary or trade name. Others, especially those from professional associations, are usually arranged by nonproprietary or generic name. Books published in other countries use their own official generic names, which are sometimes different from the American form. Some sources are limited to prescription drugs, while others include nonprescription (over-the-counter or OTC) medications. The librarian, presented with a drug name, may first need to determine the type of name and then go to appropriate reference sources. Descriptions of essential sources of drug identification follow.

Sources of Drug Names

Considering the many names that can be associated with a given drug, it is essential for libraries to have access to sources of proprietary and nonproprietary drug names. While there are increasing numbers of sources available in electronic drug information databases or on the Internet (see 10.17 and 10.18), the following key print sources are recommended for health sciences reference collections.

10.4   *American Drug Index.* St. Louis, MO: Wolters Kluwer Health, 1956– . Annual.

10.5   United States Pharmacopeial Convention and United States Adopted Names Council. *USP Dictionary of USAN and International Drug Names.* Rockville, MD: U.S. Pharmacopeial Convention, 1994– . Annual.

10.6   O'Neil, Maryadele J., ed. *The Merck Index: An Encyclopedia of Chemicals, Drugs, and Biologicals.* 14th ed., Whitehouse Station, NJ: Merck, 2006.

The *American Drug Index* is an ideal source to consult first when starting a search for drug names. This source has a comprehensive alphabetical listing of proprietary and nonproprietary names for both prescription and nonprescription drug products. The entries for proprietary names include the manufacturer's name, the nonproprietary (generic or chemical) name, composition and strength, pharmaceutical forms available, dosage, and a brief indication of use. The generic names frequently include the pronunciation, a designation of USP, USAN, or NF (National Formulary), a brief indication of use, and a "see" reference to the proprietary name. Useful appendixes at the back of this book include a list of medical abbreviations used in medical orders, tables of normal values for commonly requested laboratory tests, a medical terminology glossary, a list of telephone numbers and websites for drug manufacturers and distributors, and unique information such as oral dosage forms that should not be crushed or chewed and drug names that look alike and sound alike.

The *USP Dictionary* is updated annually and provides a compilation of the United States Adopted Names (USAN) since June 15, 1961. This source is very useful because it is a compilation and provides entries for earlier drug names. Each USAN entry lists the year the drug name was adopted, a pronunciation guide, molecular formula, molecular weight, chemical name, Chemical Abstracts Service (CAS) Registry Number, pharmacological or therapeutic activity, brand names under which the drug is marketed, manufacturer or distributor, and the structural formula. A detailed preface describes the purpose and history of the USAN Council and the procedures that establish a USAN. Several helpful appendixes are included, such as a listing of brand and nonproprietary names for the USAN names, a listing of molecular formulas and CAS Registry Numbers, and a grouping of USAN names by category, such as Analgesic, Antibacterial, Food Additive, and Ultraviolet Screen. Since this source also includes International Nonproprietary Names (INN), it should be noted that inclusion in this book does not necessarily mean that the drug is marketed in the United States; it only means that an official name has been designated. Frequently U.S. drugs are named around the time that they are patented and go into clinical trials. Thus, many years may pass before the drug receives final approval for marketing.

Another brief dictionary-type source is the *Merck Index*. This publication began in 1889 as a brief listing of drugs marketed by the Merck Company. Now in its fourteenth edition, it has grown to be a comprehensive encyclopedia of drugs, chemicals, and biological substances. The *Merck Index* should be considered an essential part of a basic drug information collection. Although this source is arranged alphabetically by chemical name, it is easier to use the index as the entry point into the descriptive paragraphs. There are several helpful listings of tables and chemical reactions at the end of this book, in addition to the in-depth indexes. The indexes that lead to the entries include Registry Numbers, therapeutic categories, molecular formulas, and chemical names. The entries in the *Merck Index* include Registry Number, chemical name, common names in some cases, molecular formula, molecular weight, and brief description of use, plus the added benefit of historical references, patent references, and preparation, synthesis, or review journal article references.

Comprehensive Treatises and Textbooks

In the medical or pharmacy library, questions frequently arise concerning the physical and chemical properties of drugs and associated mechanisms of biological activity. The librarian may begin with the sources in the previous section to obtain the necessary proprietary and generic drug names and brief information on pharmacological action. For more in-depth discussions, the following comprehensive sources are essential.

10.7   Brunton, Laurence L., John S. Lazo, and Keith L. Parker, eds. *Goodman and Gilman's The Pharmacological Basis of Therapeutics.* 12th ed. New York: McGraw-Hill Medical, 2011.

10.8   Dipiro, Joseph, Robert L. Talbert, and Gary C. Yee et al., eds. *Pharmacotherapy: A Pathophysiologic Approach.* 8th ed. New York: McGraw-Hill, 2011.

10.9   Remington, Joseph P., and Paul Beringer. *Remington: The Science and Practice of Pharmacy.* 22nd ed. Philadelphia: Pharmaceutical Press, 2013.

Goodman and Gilman's The Pharmacological Basis of Therapeutics, published since 1941, is still known as "the bible of pharmacology." A standard textbook on fundamental principles of drug action, it continues to be a valuable tool in medical and pharmacy schools. The book is divided into nine sections, beginning with general principles of pharmacology and proceeding with sections organized by modes of action on physiological systems, actions related to disease states and the pharmacology of special systems. New chapters cover drug invention, molecular mechanisms of drug action, drug toxicity and poisoning, principles of antimicrobial therapy, and pharmacotherapy of obstetrical and gynecological disorders. Each chapter provides in-depth discussions of pharmacologic mechanisms in terms of classes of drugs (e.g., hypnotics and sedatives), emphasizing the comparison between individual drugs of the same class and including many useful tables of drug names and properties. As in the previous edition, the appendixes include "Principles of Prescription Order Writing and Patient Compliance" and "Design and Optimization of Dosage Regimens: Pharmacokinetic Data." The detailed index allows the user to access information by a variety of keywords such as drug names, type of drug action, physiological systems, or symptoms. Online features in *Goodman and Gilman's* AccessMedicine version include frequent updates, "Grand Round" video lectures linked to the chapters, and animations illustrating such topics as the mechanisms by which antiplatelet drugs act to prevent thromboses.

Dipiro's *Pharmacotherapy* is known as a gold standard reference text for pharmacy and provides comprehensive information based on current practice standards on the pathophysiology and therapy for a wide range of disease states. Chapter authors are experts in their fields. The beginning of the book provides a foundation, with chapters on such important topics as pharmacoeconomics, health outcomes and quality of life, health literacy, cultural competency, pharmacogenetics, and palliative care. Each chapter begins with key concepts, highlighting the critical information. Many tables and figures summarize concepts and make the text easier to apply in practice. First-line therapies are clearly denoted. Clinical controversies are discussed. Each chapter is well referenced. This resource is available in McGraw-Hill's AccessPharmacy. The online version is frequently updated and includes videos that demonstrate the use of devices, such as nebulizers, and disease state risk assessments.

Remington: The Science and Practice of Pharmacy is a standard text of pharmaceutical science used by many pharmacy schools. With an emphasis on basic science, it covers a broad range of topics including pharmaceutical chemistry; pharmaceutical testing, analysis and control; pharmaceutical manufacturing; pharmacokinetics and pharmacodynamics; and many topics related to pharmacy practice. The latest edition of *Remington* has been divided into two volumes. Volume I covers the science of pharmacy and the monographs on specific "Pharmaceutical and Medicinal Agents." This source, and most other sources, use the designation "monographs" for the descriptive drug entries. These monographs generally include chemical names, formulas and molecular weights, as well as information on dosing, adverse effects, contraindications, and interactions with other drugs or food. The International Nonproprietary Names (INN) have been added to the monographs, as well as drug product names used in other countries. Volume II is divided into four sections related to the practice of pharmacy, covering the fundamentals and scope of pharmacy practice: social, behavioral, economic, and administrative sciences, and patient care. Since the last edition new chapters have been added: prodrugs; mass spectrometric methods; the entrepreneurial pharmacist; consultant pharmacy; pharmacists in academia, veterinary, pediatric, psychiatric, and transplant pharmacy; and pharmacogenomics, critical care, infectious diseases, and pain and palliative care in pharmacy practice; as well as the assessment of pharmacy-related quality of care. Each volume concludes with a comprehensive subject index.

Sources of Drug Information

The next two sources are produced by professional pharmacy organizations and provide authoritative information on drugs in terms of the disorders they treat, their specific activities, and formulations.

10.10   American Society of Health-System Pharmacists. *AHFS Drug Information.* Washington, DC: American Society of Health-System Pharmacists, 1959– . Annual.

10.11 Berardi, Rosemary R., et al. *Handbook of Nonprescription Drugs: An Interactive Approach to Self-Care.* 17th ed. Washington, DC: American Pharmaceutical Association, 2012.

Formerly known as the *American Hospital Formulary Service Drug Information*, *AHFS Drug Information* is produced and updated annually by the American Society of Health-System Pharmacists. Recommended by the National Association of Boards of Pharmacy as part of the standard reference library, it is the only comprehensive drug information resource published by a nonprofit professional organization. It is an authoritative source of evaluative information on drugs available in the United States. *AHFS* provides drug monographs arranged by therapeutic classification, such as anti-neoplastic agents, diagnostic agents, and gastrointestinal drugs. It also includes a section on vitamins. This organization by class enables the user to easily compare drugs from the same family. Each section begins with a listing of the generic names of drugs described in that section, with some sections divided into subcategories. Classification numbers are assigned to major sections and subsections. For example, "Anti-Infective Agents" (Section 8:00) includes subsections of amebicides (8:04), antibiotics (8:12) and more. The antibacterials subsection is further divided into ten subcategories, including cephalosporins (8:12.06). Individual drugs are not assigned classification numbers. These numeric classifications are important to pharmacists; the International Pharmaceutical Abstracts database, also published by the American Society of Health-System Pharmacists, enables searching by these classification numbers (see 10.53). Each *AHFS* section includes general statements on pharmacology and basic principles of drug action for that class of compounds. The descriptions of individual drugs (monographs) emphasize the critical evaluation of clinical drug data and include information on conventional, off-label, and investigational uses; preparations; dosages and administration; drug interactions and laboratory test interferences; mechanisms of action, pharmacokinetics, cautions, and contraindications. In cases where only the drug name is known, but not the drug classification, users may refer to the general index. The index contains both generic and proprietary names with useful cross references. *AHFS* is available in a variety of electronic formats, including online and mobile versions.

The *Handbook of Nonprescription Drugs: An Interactive Approach to Self Care,* published by the American Pharmacists Association, deals with over-the-counter drugs, including herbal remedies and dietary supplements. This information is extremely important, especially to users who may not be aware of risks associated with the use of nonprescription drugs. It is also useful to pharmacy students in developing problem-solving skills and to practitioners who interact with patients. The handbook is presented in textbook format beginning with introductory chapters on nonprescription drug therapy and followed by chapters on various disorders (mental disorders, dermatologic disorders, etc.). The chapter on home medical equipment covers self-testing and monitoring devices. Other chapters describe signs and symptoms, treatment approaches, and products that can be used in treatment. Also included are useful case studies, as well as treatment algorithms with assessment questions and answers. Each chapter has a bibliography at the end. New additions to the seventeenth edition include vaccine information and a chapter on self-care needs of patients with common chronic disorders. Appendixes on drug and natural product use during pregnancy and lactation and a general subject index are also provided. This volume is also available online through the APhA PharmacyLibrary database. There are frequent updates, and Web links related to the chapter topic are provided. In the online version, prior to the extensive references, each chapter has related cases for "organizing and applying acquired information to the solution of novel problems."

Numerous and varied sources exist that give information about specific drugs and pharmaceuticals. One mechanism by which the manufacturer informs physicians and the public about a specific product is the FDA-approved package insert, which includes the trade and chemical names; pharmacological action; indications and contraindications; warnings, precautions, and adverse reactions; dosage and overdosage; dosage forms; and, in most cases, references. The package insert is not necessarily complete or balanced. Although the FDA has agreed to the manufacturer's statements about the product and the manufacturer is legally responsible for the accuracy of the information included, the package insert remains a publicity and promotion mechanism for the manufacturer. A package insert does not compare or evaluate a given drug with other agents.

10.12   *Drug Facts and Comparisons.* 61st ed. St. Louis, MO: Wolters Kluwer Health, 2012.

10.13   *Red Book.* Montvale, NJ: Thomson PDR, 1896– . Annual.

Drug Facts and Comparisons is a comprehensive compendium of drug information. It is updated annually and is available as a bound volume, a loose-leaf format with monthly updates, and also online as Facts and Comparisons eAnswers. This source is arranged by drug therapeutic category; for example, nutritional agents, anticonvulsants, penicillins, immunologic agents, etc., are each grouped together in distinct sections. Each entry or group of entries in *Drug Facts and Comparisons* includes a product list, indications, dosing, pharmacology, pharmacokinetics, contraindications, warnings, interactions, adverse reactions, and patient information. Included are many useful tables that list comparisons between different brands, specific drug interactions, combinations, and supply methods. A thorough general index lists product brand names, generic names, synonyms, and therapeutic groups, for easy page reference to each entry. Additional indexes include a Canadian Trade Name index and a Manufacturers and Distributors index. Twelve useful appendixes

(FDA new drug classification, controlled substances, FDA pregnancy categories, etc.) are also included. This source is worth considering for any collection; it is quite current, comprehensive, and authoritative, with an Editorial Advisory Panel and a Contributing Review Panel of physicians and pharmacists and other health-care professionals from academic, private, and government institutions across the United States.

The *Red Book* is well known and trusted in the pharmaceutical marketplace. The print version of this resource ceased in 2010. The *Red Book* is more of a catalog of drug products than a comprehensive drug information text, and it is now available as a separate subscription as *Red Book Online* through *Micromedex 2.0*. This resource contains an alphabetical list of prescription drugs where each entry includes product names, supplier name, National Drug Code (NDC) numbers, route of administration, strength and quantity, Orange Book Code (OBC), and Average Wholesale Price and Direct Price. This is a good standard source for drug prices and some hard-to-find addresses.

10.14 *Physicians' Desk Reference: PDR.* Montvale, NJ: Thomson PDR, 1947– . Annual.

10.15 *PDR for Ophthalmic Medicines.* 35th ed. Montvale, NJ: Thomson PDR, 2006.

10.16 *PDR for Nonprescription Drugs, Dietary Supplements, and Herbs.* 28th ed. Montvale, NJ: Thomson PDR, 2006.

The *Physicians' Desk Reference* (*PDR*) is an annual compilation of package inserts. The introduction to this drug chapter discusses FDA requirements regarding package inserts. The *PDR* does not just contain package inserts. In addition, "for products that do not have official package circulars, *PDR* has asked manufacturers to provide comprehensive product information." In fact, it is difficult to tell which entries are official package inserts and which are not. The information in the *PDR* is arranged by company name. Most of the products marketed in the United States are listed in the *PDR*, making it a handy and frequently requested source. The *PDR* is useful for drug dosage, composition, contraindications, warnings, use, and adverse effects. The indexes included in the front of the *PDR* are a manufacturers' index, with addresses and contact information for most companies; a brand and generic name index; a product category index; and a product identification guide with color photographs of more than 1,600 tablets, capsules, and other dosage forms. Other resources to consider for visual drug identification are *Drug Facts and Comparisons*, Clinical Pharmacology, and Micromedex's IDENTIDEX, all available online (see 10.12, 10.17, and 10.18). Since the *PDR* is a source of manufacturer disclaimers, cautions, precautions, and side effects are enumerated in great detail, although there is sometimes no indication of the severity or frequency of the side effects.

The earliest editions of the *PDR* carried the subtitle "for the physician's desk only," and volumes were distributed free to physicians as a marketing tool. However, with the recent consumer movement in health care, this statement has been removed, and the *PDR* is now for sale throughout the country in bookstores. Librarians should be concerned about the public's reliance on the *PDR*. First, the information is not necessarily unbiased but represents only what the FDA has approved the manufacturer to disclose. Second, the coverage is selective, as drug companies are charged for inclusion. Therefore, not all drug companies participate, and those that do typically only include their more profitable drugs. Third, librarians should understand that the information included about drug use is not necessarily complete. Physicians can legally prescribe drugs for therapeutic applications which have not yet been approved by the FDA, and these off-label uses will not generally be addressed in the *PDR*. Finally, the information in the *PDR* is written in technical language and may be difficult for the general public to understand. Because rare side effects are included, the work may prove unnecessarily frightening to the nonprofessional reader. An ongoing challenge for the health sciences librarian is to channel members of the public from the *PDR* to more appropriate sources.

The popularity and success of the *PDR* have caused a whole series of *PDR* books to appear. Some of these titles are worth listing here; others will be covered in the following sections. The *PDR for Herbal Medicines* is discussed in more detail in the "Herbal Medicines and Natural Products" section of this chapter (see 10.39). Two complementary *PDR* publications that librarians may consider are the *PDR for Nonprescription Drugs* and the *PDR for Ophthalmic Medicines*. There is some overlap between these sources and the *PDR*, but there is also a lot of unique information that may be necessary for some collections.

Online Drug Resources

Today, electronic versions of standard print sources are proliferating. For example, Facts and Comparisons provides a suite of eleven reference books in a cross-searchable online format, many of which are described in this chapter. There are also some excellent electronic drug information resources that are not just electronic versions of books, but online full-text databases or freely available websites. This section describes online resources, either websites or drug information databases that have not already been covered in this chapter. Since these sources abound, a comprehensive list would soon be out of date. This section lists a few of the major, more reputable electronic resources and stable websites available at this writing. Many of these resources also have mobile versions available.

Full-Text Databases

10.17 Clinical Pharmacology. Elsevier/Gold Standard. Available: http://www
.clinicalpharmacology.com/. Mobile version: https://cpmobile.mobi/.

10.18 Micromedex. Ann Arbor, MI: Truven Health Analytics. Available:
http://www.Micromedex.com/. Mobile version [mobileMicromedex]
is available in their App Store.

Clinical Pharmacology is an excellent source of authoritative, full-text drug information, and it is available for both workstations and mobile devices. Information on all U.S. prescription, over-the-counter, herbal, new, and investigational drugs can be found using either generic or proprietary names. Upon entering a drug name, the system retrieves an alphabetical list of drug names and formulations, from which the user can select specific products. For a given product, the user can access a broad range of information through links to a variety of sources. The Drug Information section includes monographs similar to the print sources described in this chapter, with lists of alternative names and discussions of indications, dosages, adverse effects, drug interactions, product photographs, manufacturing information, and costs. Drug monographs present highlighted keywords in context. Clinical Pharmacology also contains several useful tools for identifying and comparing drugs. The Product Comparison tool allows the searcher to enter any number of ingredients to build comparison tables of available drugs containing the ingredients. The Drug IDentifier tool allows the user to enter characteristics such as color, shape, and imprint to identify drug products. This is very useful in the clinical setting where patients often keep their medications in containers other than the original labeled package, and the health-care practitioner needs to identify the medications. The Clinical Comparison Report tool generates summaries of known interactions, adverse effects, or IV compatibility for combinations of drugs. Patient information is available in English and Spanish. Convenient links provide navigation between these tools from all sections of the database. Clinical Pharmacology can be licensed by institutions, or the mobile version can be purchased for individual access.

Micromedex offers a variety of environmental health, toxicology, and drug information through its online Clinical Knowledge Suite and Patient Connect Suite. It includes full-text electronic books such as *Martindale: The Complete Drug Reference*, Detailed Drug Information for the Consumer, *Index Nominum*, and the *PDR,* as well as sets of drug monographs, product lists, dosing calculators, drug interactions, alternative medicine, and information for patients. The drug interactions tool is particularly useful, allowing the user to build a profile, add drugs to the profile, and display drug interactions. Micromedex resources can be purchased in various combinations or as a complete set. Examples of available databases include:

DRUGDEX—evaluative and comparative drug information for the health-care professional, including FDA-approved, investigational, nonprescription, and international drugs

AltMedDex—peer-reviewed information on herbal, vitamin, mineral, and other dietary supplements

DISEASEDEX—evidence-based disease information for general and emergency medicine

POISINDEX—product identification and toxicological information on over 1 million drugs and chemicals

REPRORISK—reproductive risk information for males, females, and unborn children including the full text of Shepard's *Catalog of Teratogenic Agents* (see 10.26)

Micromedex has the capability to search across all databases or by a specific database. Search results are grouped into sets retrieved from each database. Each link leads to a more specific, narrower category while indicating the hierarchical path. Links to product information are also provided if there are products associated with the search term. Considering the depth of information contained in this system, navigation is relatively simple due to the hierarchical organization. An app called mobileMicromedex is available for mobile access with smartphones.

Websites

10.19   U.S. Food and Drug Administration, Drugs. Available:
http://www.fda.gov/drugs/.

10.20   DailyMed. Bethesda, MD: National Library of Medicine. Available:
http://dailymed.nlm.nih.gov/.

10.21   RxList: The Internet Drug Index. New York: WebMD. Available:
http://www.rxlist.com/.

The FDA Drugs website offers essential information such as public health alerts and warnings, drug information pages, patient information, and clinical trials. Unique to this site are drug approval histories and reports, therapeutic equivalents to drugs, and drug safety announcements and drug recalls. This site includes the *Approved Drug Products with Therapeutic Equivalence Evaluations/Orange Book,* which provides information on therapeutic equivalence for generic drugs. The drug information pages list therapeutic equivalents where appropriate.

DailyMed, maintained by NLM, is a database of all approved labeling of drug products as submitted to the FDA and currently in use. Free to the public, it provides easy access to a collection of more than 45,000 package inserts for medications. It is updated daily and includes RSS feeds of updates.

The RxList website is part of the WebMD network, with content written by pharmacists and physicians. It contains an alphabetical listing of drug monographs, which include information on pharmacology, adverse effects, and many of the same categories of information provided through other drug resources. It also includes herbs, vitamins, dietary supplements, and natural products. There is a pill identification tool. Because it is free, this is a good site to recommend to users who do not have access to the other drug information reference books and licensed resources described in this chapter.

Official Compendia

In the drug information field, an official book of legal pharmaceutical standards is known as a pharmacopeia. Pharmacopeias are published in different countries to define the accepted purity and standards of chemicals used in therapy. Many pharmacopeias also include information on chemical tests and assay preparation.

10.22   United States Pharmacopeial Convention and United States Pharmacopeial
         Convention Committee of Revision. *The United States Pharmacopeia/
         The National Formulary: USP-NF.* Rockville, MD: U.S. Pharmacopeial
         Convention, 1979– . Annual.

In the United States, the two official compendia are the *U.S. Pharmacopeia* and the *National Formulary*. These two publications have been producing official standards since 1820 and 1888, respectively, although under different sponsorship. Beginning in 1979 the *U.S. Pharmacopeia* and the *National Formulary* were published in one volume, because the *National Formulary* was acquired by the *U.S. Pharmacopeia* after the publication of its fourteenth edition. There is a note at the beginning of the *National Formulary* monographs stating that although both compendia, the *United States Pharmacopeia* and the *National Formulary*, currently are published under one cover, they remain separate compendia. The latest combined edition (*USP 36–NF 31*) is a three-volume set due to the increase in content. The first volume includes the mission statement and lists of people involved (e.g., board of trustees, Council of Experts, executive committees, collaborators, and members of the U.S. Pharmacopeia Convention); new drug admissions and revisions; tests and assays; reagents, indicators and solutions; reference tables; dietary supplement monographs; and *NF* monographs. The second volume includes *USP* monographs

A–I, and the last volume contains *USP* monographs J–Z. All three volumes contain the full index. Although the *NF* monographs and *USP* monographs differ in terms of the entry elements, most contain information about packaging and storage, labeling, identification, properties (e.g., pH, viscosity, and solubility), and other standards information.

It should be noted that the need to collect pharmacopeias from other countries is often misinterpreted. Most drug questions relate to therapeutic use or to the general identification of a drug, rather than to official standards of purity as given in these compendia. Caution should always be exercised in evaluating any title with the word *pharmacopeia* in it, since most sources using that term may not be pharmacopeias in the true sense of the word if they are not listings of legal standards.

Adverse Effects, Toxicology, Poisoning

Some of the most commonly asked questions in the field of drug information deal with adverse effects of drugs and chemicals. What are the side effects of Prozac? Does tamoxifen cause hair loss? What is the lethal dose of aspirin? Many of the sources previously described provide information on adverse effects, drug interactions, toxicity, and poisoning, and the following sources focus specifically on this area. Since it is not possible, or ethical, to randomize patients to receive potentially toxic doses of medications, the drug toxicology literature is based primarily on case studies. Sometimes adverse effects are discovered during clinical trials, but more often these effects do not become apparent until a drug has been on the market and administered to large numbers of patients. Generally the older the drug, the more information will be available on toxicity. The following sources are compilations of observed adverse effects of drugs.

10.23 Aronson, Jeffrey K. *Meyler's Side Effects of Drugs: The International Encyclopedia of Adverse Drug Reactions and Interactions.* 15th ed. Amsterdam: Elsevier, 2006.

10.24 Van Boxtel, Christoffel Jos, and Jeffrey K. Aronson, eds. *Side Effects of Drugs.* Amsterdam: Elsevier, 1977– . Annual.

10.25 Klaassen, Curtis D., ed. *Casarett and Doull's Toxicology: The Basic Science of Poisons.* 7th ed. New York: McGraw-Hill Medical, 2008.

10.26 Shepard, Thomas H., and Ronald J. Lemire. *Catalog of Teratogenic Agents.* 13th ed. Baltimore, MD: Johns Hopkins University Press, 2010.

10.27 Briggs, Gerald G., Roger K. Freeman, and Sumner J. Yaffe. *Drugs in Pregnancy and Lactation: A Reference Guide to Fetal and Neonatal Risk.* 9th ed. Philadelphia: Lippincott Williams and Wilkins, 2011.

10.28   Goldfrank, Lewis R., et al. *Goldfrank's Toxicologic Emergencies.* 9th ed. New York: McGraw-Hill Medical, 2011.

10.29   Lewis, Richard J., Sr. *Sax's Dangerous Properties of Industrial Materials.* 12th ed. New York: J. Wiley, 2012.

10.30   Lewis, Richard J., Sr. *Hazardous Chemicals Desk Reference.* 6th ed. New York: J. Wiley-Interscience, 2008.

10.31   TOXNET. Bethesda, MD: National Library of Medicine. Available: http://TOXNET.nlm.nih.gov/.

Meyler's Side Effects of Drugs is an encyclopedia of comprehensive articles that summarize adverse drug reactions and interactions. Its presentation of data organized by drug classification enables the user to easily review a family of drugs as a whole. Each chapter describes a broad class of drugs, such as central nervous system stimulants, and is divided into monographs on drug families such as amphetamines. Each monograph provides an overview of the toxic effects and patterns of adverse reactions, specific effects on organs and systems, withdrawal effects, overdosage information, patient susceptibility factors, and brief reviews of individual drugs belonging to that family. With the fifteenth edition, *Meyler's Side Effects of Drugs* has gone from one volume to a six-volume set and is also available online. A complementary guide to *Meyler's* is the *Side Effects of Drugs Annual,* which provides a survey of the latest developments in this field. Chapter titles correspond to those in *Meyler's*, enabling the user to easily combine the general encyclopedic information with annual updates. Libraries should retain the full series because both sources refer to earlier editions.

Casarett and Doull's Toxicology serves as the gold standard in the field of toxicology. This text is organized into the following units: history and general principles of toxicology; paths and mechanisms that the poisons pass through the body and the related transformations and kinetics; carcinogens, genetic and developmental toxicology; target organ toxicity; toxic agents; environmental toxicology; and applications of toxicology, including food, forensic, clinical, and occupational toxicology. Each chapter is very thoroughly referenced.

Teratology, the study of the adverse effects of drugs on the fetus, is a widely recognized area of concern. Shepard's *Catalog of Teratogenic Agents* covers fetal exposure to more than 3,200 drugs and other agents. It also includes gene mutations known to cause congenital defects. Entries are organized alphabetically by the chemical name, and include synonyms, Chemical Abstracts Service Registry Numbers where available, descriptions of teratogenicity, and references. Author and subject indexes are also provided. This book is available in electronic format, through Micromedex (see 10.18).

As its name implies, *Drugs in Pregnancy and Lactation* includes information on possible harm to the fetus from drugs taken during pregnancy, or possible harm to breast-feeding infants from drugs present in breast milk. Summaries of drug toxicity, in encyclopedic format, are listed alphabetically by generic drug name. Risk factors, defined in the "Instructions for Use of the Reference Guide" section, are assigned to each drug, allowing the user to quickly assess toxicity. Each entry lists the generic name, drug class, risk factor, summaries of fetal risk and breast-feeding risk, recommendations for pregnancy and lactation, and references. There is an appendix classifying drugs by pharmacologic category. This is helpful for identifying drugs of the same class. The subject index lists both generic and proprietary names.

Goldfrank's Toxicologic Emergencies is a comprehensive textbook of medical toxicology covering basic principles; biochemical, molecular, and pathophysiologic foundations; and chapters on specific agents such as prescription and nonprescription drugs, drugs of abuse, household toxins, heavy metals, pesticides, and other environmental and occupational toxins. Chapters on toxins describe classes of compounds, followed by specific information related to individual chemicals. Each chapter offers a history and epidemiology, pharmacology, clinical manifestations, management and antidotes, summaries, and references. A subject index is also included. An online learning center is available (http://www.goldfrankstoxicology.com/) and includes case studies and a database of multiple choice questions that allow the creation of a custom test for review and study.

An essential source of authoritative data on environmental health and safety, *Sax's Dangerous Properties of Industrial Materials* (*DPIM*) provides detailed toxicity information on over 28,000 chemicals found in the workplace, including drugs, food additives, pesticides, dyes, lubricants, soaps, plastics, and more. Each item is encoded with a unique identifier, the DPIM entry code, consisting of three letters followed by three numbers. Chemicals are listed in alphanumeric order by code. For example, the entry for acethion amide (AAT000) precedes the entry for acetic acid (AAT250). The synonym cross index of 108,000 chemical names refers to DPIM codes, and this is the best entry point for the user searching for substances by name. The online version, in which users can browse articles by the common name of the chemical, is more user-friendly. Each chemical listing provides the DPIM code, the chemical name, Chemical Abstracts Service Registry Number where available, and the U.S. Department of Transportation (DOT) Hazard Code. DOT codes are recognized internationally and are used in regulating shipping and labeling of hazardous materials. Also included are the molecular formula, molecular weight, and other physical properties such as solubility and flammability data. Numeric coded toxicity data are listed next, including skin and eye irritation, acute toxicity, mutagenic, teratogenic, carcinogenic, and other lethal or nonlethal effects. All toxicity data include citations to the scientific literature. These citations consist of a journal "CODEN" character code, followed by the number of the volume, the page number of the first page of the article, and a two-digit number referring to the year of publication. Each chemical entry also lists standards and recommendations from U.S government or expert groups including the Occupational Safety and Health Administration (OSHA). Safety profiles, which verbally summarize toxicity and hazard data, are also provided with each entry. Consensus reports are included where applicable. The *DPIM* is a five-volume set, the first volume containing indexes needed to translate the chemical listings of toxicological information in the second through fifth volumes. Volume 1 provides instructions for using the *DPIM*, a key to abbreviations, a cross-index of DOT hazard codes with DPIM codes, a cross-index of Chemical Abstracts Service Registry Numbers with DPIM codes, the synonym cross index, detailed descriptions, and definitions of the toxicity data found in Volumes 2 through 5. Volume 1 also includes a bibliography of cited references listed in order of CODEN and including journal titles with publishing information. The *Hazardous Chemicals Desk Reference* is a condensed version of this work. This more manageable single volume lists only the most relevant substances, according to the U.S. Environmental Protection Agency's Toxic Substances Control Act (TSCA) Chemical Substance Inventory.

The National Library of Medicine produces TOXNET, a set of databases with information on toxicology, hazardous chemicals, and environmental health. These databases are freely available worldwide online (http://toxnet.nlm.nih.gov/). Four categories of information are available: toxicology databanks on toxicity and additional hazards of chemicals; toxic release information; chemical information, with nomenclature, identification, and structures; and toxicology literature, including scientific studies, reports, and other bibliographic material. The toxicology databanks include the Hazardous Substances Data Bank (HSDB), Integrated Risk Information System (IRIS), Chemical Carcinogenesis Research Information System (CCRIS), GENE-TOX (Genetic Toxicology), and LactMed. HSDB contains emergency handling procedures, human health effects, detection methods, OSHA standards and other regulatory requirements for more than 5,000 potentially harmful chemicals. Records are divided into categories including human health effects, emergency medical treatment, pharmacokinetics, and many others. This enables users to quickly navigate to specific topics. IRIS provides information from the EPA about the potential health effects of environmental pollutants, including carcinogenic and noncarcinogenic health risk information for more than 500 chemicals. CCRIS contains scientifically evaluated data from the National Cancer Institute (NCI) on carcinogenicity, mutagenicity, tumor promotion and tumor inhibition tests for more than 9,000 chemicals. GENE-TOX contains information from the EPA on more than 3,000 potentially DNA-damaging chemicals. LactMed is a database of drugs and other chemicals, with information on levels in breast milk and infant blood, possible alternatives to drugs that are contraindicated in breast-feeding, recommendations from the American Academy of Pediatrics, and references to primary literature.

TOXNET's Toxics Release Inventory (TRI) database provides annual estimates on release of specific toxic chemicals and their management as waste, as reported to EPA by U.S. industrial and federal facilities. The database is searchable by chemical name, company name, or geographic region (including by ZIP code). ChemID*plus* contains more than 390,000 chemical records, of which more than 300,000 include chemical structures, and it is searchable by subject, chemical generic or proprietary name, CAS Registry Number, molecular formula, and structure. The bibliographic sources in TOXNET are reviewed in the section on Bibliographic Databases. Users may search all TOXNET databases simultaneously or may select individual sources.

Drug Interactions

With the popularity of herbal supplements, nutritional supplements, and other over-the-counter products and with the proliferation of advertising about drugs, health-care providers are facing a complex and growing problem of drug interactions. There is overwhelming evidence that the pharmacological action of a drug can be affected by the administration of other drugs, foods, alcohol, and even environmental factors, such as excessive exposure to sun or chemicals. Depending on the interaction and the chemicals involved, a drug's intended action could be minimized or increased, absorption and metabolism rate changed, toxicity levels raised, and other untoward effects could occur. For example, a person taking a monoamine oxidase inhibitor antidepressant should avoid cheese, since eating tyramine-rich foods could bring about life-threatening hypertension. Similarly, a person prescribed a tetracycline or quinoline antibiotic should be warned to avoid dairy products or anti-acids in certain circumstances, since these substances can reduce or negate the effectiveness of the antibiotic.

This is a very important and challenging area of drug information. Sources of information on drug interactions are proliferating, but the following trusted sources continue to rise to the top. There is some overlap but unique material is found in each, so librarians should collect a variety of well-balanced sources to meet their users' needs.

10.32   Pronsky, Zaneta M. *Food-Medication Interactions.* 17th ed. Birchrunville, PA: Food-Medication Interactions, 2012.

10.33   *Drug Interaction Facts.* St. Louis, MO: Wolters Kluwer Health, 1998– . Annual.

10.34   *Hansten and Horn's Drug Interactions Analysis and Management.* St. Louis, MO: Wolters Kluwer Health, 2002– . Loose-leaf, updated quarterly.

10.35   Baxter, Karen, ed. *Stockley's Drug Interactions: A Source Book of Interactions, Their Mechanisms, Clinical Importance and Management.* 9th ed. London: Pharmaceutical Press, 2010.

Food-Medication Interactions is a pocket-sized spiral-bound handbook. A useful guide for using this book is located inside the front cover. Medications are listed by generic and trade names. Each generic drug listing includes: the most prescribed FDA indications; related drugs with similar pharmacologic properties; reported effects, where specific minimum percentage reported effects are indicated by underlining and/or capitalization; standard categories including proper oral administration, specific dietary recommendations, effects that alter nutritional status, alerts, FDA pregnancy category, alterations in laboratory values, and recommendations for specific monitoring of patients. After the monograph section there are many tables, including laboratory values, nutritional assessment standards for adults, drug-alcohol interactions, caffeine content of foods and beverages, Vitamin K sources, and drugs not compatible with tube feeding. This book is also available as software for personal computers, pocket PCs, and smartphones.

Drug Interaction Facts has been published since 1983 by Facts and Comparisons, then a division of J. B. Lippincott Co., and now part of Wolters Kluwer Health. This source is in loose-leaf format due to frequent updates. The introduction states, "*Drug Interaction Facts* attempts to present all drug-drug and drug-food interactions that have been reasonably well documented to occur in humans. Recently we began including significant and well-documented interactions with herbal products as well. Simple additive or antagonistic effects that are anticipated to occur based on known pharmacological activity are not necessarily included." This is considered an authoritative source due to its reliance on current biomedical literature and on a review board of physicians, pharmacologists, and clinical pharmacists. The comprehensive index is essential as it lists entries by generic drug name and drug class name, with frequent cross-references for product trade names. The index also notes the significance of the interaction using a numeric code. Each entry is about one page in length with the interaction significance number listed first (i.e., the onset, severity, and interaction documentation), then the effects, mechanism, and management, with a brief discussion and references at the end. This source is relatively easy to use, and it seems to be widely accepted and consulted in most health sciences libraries.

Hansten and Horn's Drug Interactions Analysis and Management is also published by Facts and Comparisons. This source has been in publication for more than thirty years, and the authors, Philip D. Hansten and John R. Horn, have been recognized as experts in the field of drug interactions for many years. *Hansten and Horn's* is updated quarterly and is available in loose-leaf binder format. Drugs are listed first alphabetically by generic name, and then by the interacting drug name. For this reason, the index is the key to using this source. Each combination of drug and interacting drug has a number listed beside it. This number indicates the "intervention needed to minimize the risk of the interaction" (e.g., 1 = avoid combination, 2 = usually avoid combination, 3 = minimize risk, 4 = no action needed, and 5 = no interaction). Each entry includes a brief summary, risk factors, clinical evaluation, related drugs, and references. There is also a very useful and easy-to-spot "Management Options" boxed section in each entry that is helpful for clinicians and pharmacists, with headings such as "consider alternative," "circumvent/minimize," and "monitor." This source is very similar to *Drug Interaction Facts*. In some cases the clinical evaluation section (called discussion section in *Drug Interaction Facts*) lists the same clinical trial or evidence, with the same references. There are some differences in the index entries. Often *Drug Interaction Facts* lists more drug interactions for a particular drug than *Hansten and Horn's*. For example, more than 100 drug entries are listed under "Aspirin" in *Drug Interaction Facts*, while there are only about fifty listed in the same index category in *Hansten and Horn's*. One reason that *Drug Interaction Facts* sometimes has more index entries for a particular drug appears to be that it includes more therapeutic drug categories. However, it should be noted that some interactions are unique to each of these sources.

Stockley's Drug Interactions is an excellent secondary source for the circulating collection of a pharmacy school or large health sciences library. Its purpose is to "inform busy doctors, pharmacists, nurses, and other health-care professionals, about drug interactions." It contains more than 3,400 monographs that briefly describe the clinical evidence, mechanism, importance, and management of proven drug interactions. All of the monographs include references, and many have lengthy reference lists. After an informative introduction, the chapters address drugs in broad therapeutic categories (e.g., analgesics and NSAIDS, anticoagulants, beta-blockers, calcium channel blockers, immunosuppressants, etc.), with the drugs that cause reactions in each category. The final chapter deals with "Miscellaneous Drugs." This is a valuable resource but may not be for every collection.

Of course, drug interactions can also be checked in online resources such as Facts and Comparisons eAnswers, Clinical Pharmacology, and Micromedex (see 10.12, 10.17, and 10.18). It is important to check more than one source, since these sources may not provide identical information in terms of the drugs included and the severity of the interactions.

International Drugs

Questions about foreign drugs are particularly challenging. For example, spelling may vary in different languages. Users often have insufficient information, and the librarian begins a search looking for the proverbial needle in a haystack. Whenever possible, the requestor should be queried for further information: Do you have the generic or chemical name and the exact spelling? For what purpose is the drug used? Do you know the manufacturer? The *USP Dictionary of USAN and International Drug Names*, with INN, JAN, and BAN is a good place to start if the patron knows the generic or USAN name (see 10.5). The *Merck Index* is useful because of its broad international coverage and its inclusion of many chemical, generic, and even trade names (see 10.6). Maintaining a collection to include every country would be impractical for most libraries, and key sources will depend on geographic location and ethnicity. In the United States, Canadian and European sources are often particularly useful. These three sources are helpful for international drug information.

10.36   Sweetman, Sean C., ed. *Martindale: The Complete Drug Reference*. 37th ed. London: Pharmaceutical Press, 2011.

10.37   Swiss Pharmaceutical Society. *Index Nominum: International Drug Directory*. 20th ed. Stuttgart, Germany: Medpharm Scientific, 2011.

10.38   *Compendium of Pharmaceuticals and Specialties: The Canadian Drug Reference for Health Professionals*. Toronto: Canadian Pharmaceutical Association, 1974– . Annual.

Martindale: The Complete Drug Reference is extremely valuable for its wide coverage of European drugs and extensive indexing under trade names. It provides comprehensive information similar to *Goodman and Gilman*'s, but with international coverage, less emphasis on basic pharmacology, and more specific information on individual drugs. The major part of this work is "Monographs on Drugs and Ancillary Substances." Each chapter gives a general description of a class of drugs, with particularly useful discussions of the drugs' indications. For example, the chapter on analgesics defines analgesia and pain, and describes the drugs of choice for various categories of pain such as headache, low back pain, labor pain, and more. The chapters include detailed descriptions of drugs belonging to that class, including adverse effects, drug interactions, preparations, and countries of origin for each drug. Because regulations regarding new drugs are not as stringent in other countries as in the United States, *Martindale's* coverage includes many drugs not available in the United States. It provides international equivalents of drugs marketed in this country. Drug monographs list British Adopted Names (BANs) first, followed by International Nonproprietary Names (INNs) and United States Adopted Names (USANs) where available. Also listed are chemical formulas, molecular weights, and Chemical Abstracts Service (CAS) Registry Numbers. References are provided at the end of each monograph. "Supplementary Drugs and Other Substances" contains shorter monographs of similar format on herbals and other preparations. There is an index of proprietary preparations from a number of countries. Records generally include proprietary names, manufacturers or sources, and ingredients, as well as page references to the complete monographs. A directory of manufacturers is included at the back of the book, in addition to the general index. The directory lists manufacturers in alphabetical order using abbreviations. The general index includes both generic and proprietary drug names, as well as synonyms and chemical names. Diseases and associated terms are also listed. The Micromedex Healthcare Series of databases includes the contents of *Martindale* and is therefore an excellent source of international drug information, providing proprietary names used worldwide for both FDA-approved and investigational drugs (see 10.18 and 10.36).

The *Index Nominum* is published in English, with introductory information also provided in German and French. This resource describes more than 5,000 drugs and drug derivatives, arranged in alphabetical order by International Nonproprietary Name (INN) in English. Each entry lists German, French, Spanish, and Latin names, as well as the World Health Organization's ATC (Anatomical Therapeutic Chemical) code. Also included are therapeutic classifications (e.g., "calcium antagonist"), Chemical Abstracts Service Registry Numbers, chemical names, molecular formulas, chemical structure diagrams, and lists of proprietary names used in different countries. At the end of each entry is an alphabetical list of drug derivatives, salts for example. The twentieth edition is divided into two volumes. Volume One starts with an alphabetical listing of therapeutic categories, a list of ATC classification codes, a list of abbreviations and symbols, and a list of country codes, followed by the drug monographs. Volume Two consists of a variety of indexes, including an extensive index of proprietary names and synonyms. This index is the primary starting access point for patrons seeking drug information with only a proprietary foreign name. Other indexes include drugs and their corresponding ATC codes, veterinary drugs and their ATCvet codes, and reverse indexes for each.

The Canadian *Compendium of Pharmaceuticals and Specialties,* a guide to drugs available on the Canadian market, is divided into several sections. There is a useful brand and generic name index. This is followed by a therapeutic guide listing drugs by disease state, for example "hiccoughs, persistent." There is a product identification table with color photographs of drug products. The "Clin-Info" section contains information for clinicians on selected topics including dosing and monitoring tools, drug use guides and summaries of therapeutic interventions, and drug interactions. There is also a directory of Canadian poison control centers, health organizations, and pharmaceutical manufacturers. The major portion of the book is devoted to product monographs, listed in alphabetical order by brand name. This information is voluntarily submitted by manufacturers and may include either the complete or abridged versions of the drug package inserts. Each entry describes pharmacology, indications for use, contraindications and other precautions, drug interactions, adverse effects, and dosing information. Unlike many of the resources described in this chapter, this book lists drugs in alphabetical order by proprietary name. Appendixes contain supplemental information such as new reports of adverse drug events. Glossaries include medical and pharmaceutical abbreviations, nomenclature for microorganisms, and Latin prescription terms. The sections of this book are color coded for convenient access.

Herbal Medicines and Natural Products

In these days of increased interest and usage of herbal and natural preparations, a few authoritative sources are a must for any collection. These resources may be located in the pharmacy and pharmacology sections or in the complementary medicine area. These sources are especially important because consumers often do not realize that herbal medicines and natural products can have harmful effects and interactions with prescription drugs. The following selections are representative of increasing numbers of excellent reference works in this field.

10.39   *PDR for Herbal Medicines.* 4th ed. Montvale, NJ: Thomson PDR, 2007.

10.40   *Herbal Medicines.* 4th ed. London: Pharmaceutical Press, 2013.

10.41   Duke, James A. *Handbook of Medicinal Herbs.* 2nd ed. Boca Raton, FL: CRC Press, 2002.

10.42   *Mosby's Handbook of Herbs and Natural Supplements.* 4th ed. St. Louis, MO: Mosby Elsevier, 2010.

10.43   *Natural Medicines Comprehensive Database.* 13th ed. Stockton, CA: Therapeutic Research Faculty, 2013. Available: http://www .naturaldatabase.therapeuticresearch.com/.

10.44   Natural Standard. Somerville, MA: Natural Standard. Available: http://www.naturalstandard.com/.

10.45   National Center for Complementary and Alternative Medicine (NCCAM). Bethesda, MD: National Institutes of Health. Available: http://nccam.nih.gov/.

As with other PDR publications, the *PDR for Herbal Medicines* has several helpful indexes in the front of the book. After the informative foreword, there is an in-depth alphabetical index of all the scientific, common, and brand names included in this source. There are also indexes by therapeutic categories, indications, homeopathic indications, an Asian Indications Index, side effects index, drug/herb interactions guide, and safety guide. This edition contains more than 700 botanicals, as well as nutritional supplements. There is also an extensive herb identification guide with color photographs of more than 400 common medicinal plants, followed by the herbal monographs arranged in alphabetical order. The monographs include common name, genus species, description, actions and pharmacology, clinical trials, indications and usage, contraindications, precautions and adverse reactions, dosage, and references.

Herbal Medicines, published by Pharmaceutical Press, contains impartial information on 180 of the most commonly used herbal medicinal products. The lengthy monographs, written by experts in the field, are extensively referenced, detailing photochemical, pharmacological, and clinical aspects of each herb. Use, dosage, adverse effects, interactions, toxicology, and contraindications are included. Chemical structures and color photographs of the plant are presented where available. Numerous appendixes, such as Potential Drug-Herb Interactions, and an extensive index are included. *Herbal Medicines* is an invaluable reference text for pharmacists and other health-care professionals who require evidence-based information on herbal medicines used for treatment and prevention of health problems.

The Handbook of Medicinal Herbs describes more than 1,000 herbs used for medicinal purposes. In the introduction the author states that he has tried to cover most of the important and widely used medicinal plants. He also states, "Unlike Commission E and the Herbal PDR, which seem to stress European and American traditions, I include proportionately more herbs from the older African, Ayurvedic, and Chinese traditions as well, not wanting to slight any major medicinal plant from any major tradition." The herbs are listed in alphabetical order with a scientific name index and a common name index at the end of the book. Each herb entry lists the scientific name in parentheses after the common name, and a safety rating system (the safety score is explained in the introduction). Many entries include an illustration of the plant, and there are some color plates in the center of the book. The entry descriptions include many abbreviations, some of which are listed in the Abbreviations section in the beginning. The entries include synonyms, activities, indications, dosages, contraindications, interactions, and side effects. This source is very comprehensive and extensive, but it is not as easy to interpret due to the abundance of abbreviations in the descriptions.

Mosby's Handbook of Herbs and Natural Supplements contains detailed, unbiased monographs of 300 herbs and natural supplements. There are appendixes, such as Herb/Drug Interactions and Pediatric Herbal Use, a glossary, and an index, all designed to be easy to use by both consumers and health professionals.

Natural Medicines Comprehensive Database is an important resource because it is based on scientific evidence gathered and evaluated by a team of medical and pharmacy professionals. In many cases the uses of herbal products are based on tradition, rather than science. *Natural Medicines Comprehensive Database* describes the available evidence; in cases where scientific data is lacking, this is clearly stated. There are more than 1,100 herbal and nonherbal natural products listed in this source. The print version arranges products alphabetically by their most common name, with an index at the end to help provide cross-references from other names. Each entry starts with a section labeled "Also Known As" to include other names and synonyms for the herbs, plus scientific names, usage, safety, effectiveness, mechanism of action, adverse reactions; interactions with herbs, dietary supplements, drugs, foods, and lab tests; and dosage and comments. All references cited in various paragraphs appear at the end of the entries, arranged in numerical order by citation number. Also included is a section on brand name natural products and the ingredients they contain. This is a print source worth considering if the online version's cost is prohibitive.

The online version of *Natural Medicines Comprehensive Database* is more current, interactive, and comprehensive than the print product. Updated daily, it is easy to browse by product name or disease/condition name. The product records include ingredients, effectiveness, adverse effects, and interactions with drugs, herbs, food, lab tests, or diseases. When searching a disease or condition, the results include products known to have been used to treat or improve that condition. For example, a search of "leukemia" retrieves a record on arsenic, describing how it has been suggested to be effective for treatment of acute promyelocytic leukemia. The online version also includes an interactions checker where interaction between natural products or drugs and natural products can be found. This online resource is worth considering due to comprehensiveness and relative low cost.

Natural Standard is edited and compiled by an international, multidisciplinary group of experts who use a systematic grading system to evaluate the evidence underlying uses of complementary and alternative therapies. The website includes a thorough description of how the scientific evidence is evaluated. Natural Standard covers not only herbs and supplements, but other "alternative" treatments such as acupuncture, and health and wellness activities such as yoga. It also has an interactions checker. Natural Standard is a nice complement to *Natural Medicines Comprehensive Database.* It is worth considering subscribing to multiple sources of complementary and alternative medicine because of the quickly changing applications of these therapies, as well as the constantly mounting evidence supporting or opposing their uses.

The NCCAM is an authoritative website published by the National Institutes of Health. It includes informative pages defining and describing complementary and alternative medicine. It is searchable by disease or condition, and treatment or therapy. Very consumer friendly, the entries on treatments or therapies include sections on "what the science says" and "side effects and cautions." The records also include references to primary literature.

Drug Information for Patients and the Public

With the proliferation of websites claiming to offer consumers the best in health-care information and attempting to sell them health-care products and drugs, it is hoped that some consumers will still choose to consult authoritative sources for reliable information on medications and products they are taking. To this end, librarians should have a basic collection of easy-to-understand, authoritative, print drug information sources, as well as being able to point consumers to trustworthy online resources. Any information given to patients should be accompanied by encouragement to consult with health-care professionals for help in interpreting and evaluating the information obtained.

10.46   Griffith, H. Winter, and Stephen Moore. *Complete Guide to Prescription and Nonprescription Drugs.* New York: Penguin Group. Annual.

10.47   *PDR Consumer Guide to Prescription Drugs.* Montvale, NJ: PDR Network, 2011.

10.48   "Drugs, Supplements and Herbal Information" (part of MedlinePlus). Bethesda, MD: National Library of Medicine. Available: http://www.nlm .nih.gov/MEDLINEplus/druginformation.html/. Mobile version: http:// m.medlineplus.gov/.

10.49   *PDRhealth, Physicians' Desk Reference.* Montvale, NJ: Thomson Healthcare. Available: http://www.pdrhealth.com/drugs/.

10.50   "Consumer Reports Best Buy Drugs." Yonkers, NY: Consumers Union. Available: http://www.crbestbuydrugs.org/.

10.51   SafeMedication.com. Bethesda, MD: American Society of Health-System Pharmacists. Available: http://www.safemedication.com/.

H. Winter Griffith's *Complete Guide to Prescription and Nonprescription Drugs* provides information on more than 6,000 brand name drugs and more than 1,000 generic name drugs. Griffith is the author of twenty-five medical books for consumers. His name is well known and respected enough that he is listed as the primary author for this book even though he died in 1993. The last few editions of this book, which is updated annually, have been "revised" by Stephen W. Moore. Each entry in the book includes up to thirty-three elements, including some information not included in similar works such as whether the drug is habit forming, time lapse before the drug works, frequency of symptoms in people who take the drug, considerations for people over age sixty, and warnings about premature discontinuation of the drug. Drugs are listed alphabetically by generic name, and there are also some entries for categories of drugs such as "anticoagulants" and "antihistamines." In the front of the book, there is a listing of "medical conditions and their commonly used drugs." At the back, there is a brand name directory, listing of "additional drug interactions," glossary, and extensive index that includes both generic and brand names. The 2013 edition contains revised information on new FDA changes and also comprehensive coverage of lifestyle drugs such as skin aging, obesity, and sexual dysfunction.

PDR Consumer Guide to Prescription Drugs covers more than 400 of the most commonly prescribed medicines. Written by PDR's staff of pharmacists, this 650+- page book provides answers to such questions as side effects, drug interactions, and pregnancy complications. The text is written in patient-friendly language, with the ever-popular PDR full-color images of pills included for easy identification.

MedlinePlus, produced by National Library of Medicine, is the most comprehensive, understandable, and authoritative website for consumer health information. The "Drugs, Supplements and Herbal Information" section of the website includes drug information from *AHFS Consumer Medication Information*, American Society of Health-System Pharmacists. Herb and supplement information is from *Natural Medicines Comprehensive Database*. Drugs, herbs, and supplements are listed alphabetically by both generic and brand name. Each drug entry includes information about why the drug is prescribed, how it should be used, special precautions, special dietary instructions, what to do if a dose is missed, side effects, storage, what to do in case of overdose, and brand names.

Another good resource, *PDRhealth*, is written in lay terms and is based on the FDA-approved drug information found in the *PDR*. There are links to information about prescription drugs, over-the-counter drugs, herbal medicines, and nutritional supplements, all organized alphabetically. The drug entries contain most of the same types of information as MedlinePlus. Interestingly, a search box allows searching by drug name, health condition, or disease.

The Consumers Union, creator of the *Consumer Reports* magazine and renowned for its expertise, independence, and lack of bias, has created a series of *Consumer Reports Best Buy Drugs* reports. More than 700 reports compare prescription drugs by category and also combine an expert review of the scientific evidence with pricing information. Current topics include antidepressants, beta blockers for heart disease and high blood pressure, statins for high cholesterol and heart disease, nonsteroidal anti-inflammatory drugs (NSAIDSs) for osteoarthritis, sleeping pills for insomnia, and several other drug categories. The reviews of the scientific evidence are conducted by teams of physicians and researchers at several medical schools, under the auspices of the Drug Effectiveness Review Project (DERP). Reports can be located by report title, drug name, or disease. Each report, written in lay language, includes a recommendations page, table of generic and brand names, discussion of what the drugs do and who needs them, "Best Buy Picks," and a discussion of the evidence. Drug cost information is also included. The full text of the reports (about 15–20 pages in length), in English, and two-page summaries, in English and Spanish, are available in PDF format. There are also more than 100 guides available for commonly used supplements, such as St. John's wort and ginkgo biloba, with some of the information coming from American Society of Health-System Pharmacists.

SafeMedication.com is an authoritative source geared to consumers and developed by the American Society of Health-System Pharmacists (ASHP). It includes drug news, patient information, and a searchable database based on ASHP's *AHFS Consumer Medication Information*. The website features easy-to-read information in about 1,000 monographs on more than 12,000 drug products that are approved by the FDA, both prescription and over-the-counter medications. The monographs include information on side effects, special precautions, and overdose.

In addition to the above sources, *Detailed Drug Information for the Consumer* is available through Micromedex and is an accepted authoritative source for consumers. This was formerly Volume II of the *USP DI*, titled *Advice for the Patient, Drug Information in Lay Language*. Print publication of the *USP DI* ceased in 2007. *Detailed Drug Information for the Consumer* is written at the 12th grade literacy level for the informed patient. Generic and brand names, descriptions of the medication, proper use, precautions, and side effects are all included. The drug monographs include information on storage of the medication, pregnancy, and breast-feeding, and information for different age groups.

Currently, fifty-seven poison control centers offer free, private, confidential medical advice twenty-four hours a day, seven days a week. The Poison Help Line for the nearest center is 1-800-222-1222. The American Association of Poison Control Centers also maintains a website (http://production-aapcc.dotcloud.com/).

Bibliographic Databases

This section focuses on bibliographic databases that are specific to drug information, or that contain considerable drug information. For more general indexing services and sources, and in-depth descriptions, please refer to chapter 4.

MEDLINE, and its most popular interface, PubMed, is a key bibliographic database for drug information. It is important for librarians to be aware of effective strategies in using the National Library of Medicine's Medical Subject Headings (MeSH) to find drug information. MeSH terms for drugs are generic names, with the U.S. Adopted Names (USAN) as the standard. Entry terms include many, but not all brand names, and also Chemical Abstracts Service (CAS) Registry Numbers when known. Therefore, MeSH users may often need tools such as the *American Drug Index* (see 10.4) or *USP Dictionary of USAN and International Drug Names* (see 10.5) to convert trade names to generic names. A number of MeSH subheadings are especially useful in searching for drug information. MeSH terms for diseases and conditions always include the subheadings "drug therapy" and "chemically induced." MeSH terms for drugs include the use of these subheadings: administration and dosage, adverse effects, chemical synthesis, contraindications, metabolism, pharmacokinetics, poisoning, therapeutic use, and toxicity.

MeSH has shown a dramatic increase in its inclusion of drug names since its inception. Originally, drug entries in MeSH were grouped under the "Chemicals and Drugs" branch of the MeSH tree structure and were organized by chemical classification. For example, aspirin, introduced in 1965, falls under salicylates. Since 1996, the NLM assigns pharmacologic actions to the MeSH records. The MeSH heading for aspirin includes five pharmacologic actions including "anti-inflammatory agents, non-steroidal." The pharmacologic action field [pa] is a powerful tool because users often need to find lists of drugs belonging to a particular class. For example, healthcare professionals or consumers may seek alternatives to a prescribed drug because of an adverse effect, allergy, cost, or other reasons. In the MeSH database, a search for a pharmacologic action (e.g., antihypertensive agents [pa]) will yield a list of drugs indexed with that same pharmacologic action.

With increasing numbers of drug names needing to be indexed, the NLM added "substance names" as supplementary concepts, which map to MeSH headings. Concept mapping is transparent to the user searching PubMed; for instance, a search for the keyword aspirin, maps to aspirin [MeSH], and a search for a newer drug, Celebrex, maps to Celecoxib [supplementary concept]. Generally, new drug name entries are added to MeSH as substance names, unless there is a significant amount of literature on analogs and derivatives, which fit well in the chemically oriented MeSH hierarchy. Substance name records include pharmacologic actions, but they do not include subheadings. If a subheading is needed for a substance name, the searcher may use a floating subheading. Also, because substance names map to a MeSH heading, the searcher can select "Heading Mapped to" from a substance name MeSH record, or from any citation indexed with a substance name, and add that concept, with the desired subheading, to their search. For example, a search for adverse effects of atorvastatin could include the terms "atorvastatin" [Supplementary Concept], "adverse effects" [Subheading], and "Heptanoic Acids/adverse effects" [MeSH]. Librarians should become familiar with drug-related MeSH subheadings and the best methods for working with MeSH terms and supplementary concepts for drugs.

NLM is also developing RxNorm, a new drug vocabulary. RxNorm is a more granular vocabulary than MeSH; the concepts it describes are "clinical drugs," which are the actual drug products used in patients. A clinical drug concept includes the active ingredient, strength, and dosage form of the drug. Part of the Unified Medical Language System (UMLS) Metathesaurus, RxNorm provides normalized names and unique identifiers for medicines and drugs. Its goal is to allow computer systems to communicate drug-related information efficiently and unambiguously. Librarians should be aware of RxNorm because it will have impact on hospital information systems used in patient care.

All of the databases mentioned below are available online. As with all resources, licensing costs vary. Different vendors' search interfaces can also vary considerably, so librarians should be careful in selecting the most appropriate, cost-effective resource possible. Almost all vendors allow trial access to their products, which makes it easier to decide which vendor and interface to choose. Most libraries have noticed a significant decrease in the number of patrons coming through their doors and have shifted their collections to mainly electronic resources that can be accessed remotely. Since users are so self-reliant, it is important to select user-friendly search interfaces whenever possible.

10.52   TOXNET. Bethesda, MD: National Library of Medicine. Available: http://TOXNET.nlm.nih.gov/. Mobile version: http://toxnet.nlm.nih.gov/pda/.

10.53   International Pharmaceutical Abstracts. Bethesda, MD: American Society of Health-System Pharmacists.

10.54   Embase. Amsterdam: Elsevier B.V. Available: http://www.embase.com/.

10.55   Chemical Abstracts. Columbus, OH: American Chemical Society, Chemical Abstracts Service. Available: http://www.cas.org/.

TOXNET (see also 10.31) includes two literature databases: TOXLINE and the Developmental and Reproductive Toxicology/Environmental Teratology Information Center (DART/ETIC). TOXLINE is a collection of more than 4 million bibliographic citations on drugs and other chemicals. DART/ETIC covers teratology and other aspects of developmental and reproductive toxicology. It contains more than 100,000 references to literature published since 1965.

International Pharmaceutical Abstracts (IPA) has been produced in print and electronic versions by the American Society of Health-System Pharmacists since 1964; in 2005 it was purchased by Thomson Reuters. IPA covers a substantial volume of worldwide pharmacy practice literature not indexed in MEDLINE (note that the print version of IPA does not contain as many abstracts as the online version). IPA covers drug use and development literature from 1971 to the present and includes meeting abstracts of the American Society of Health-System Pharmacists, International Pharmaceutical Federation, and American Association of Colleges of Pharmacy. Journals unique to IPA include state journals of health system pharmacy, and other journals such as *Journal of Herbs, Spices and Medicinal Plants* and *WHO Drug Information*. In addition to the typical searchable fields found in electronic bibliographic databases, IPA can be searched by Chemical Abstracts Service Registry Number or AHFS therapeutic drug classification. The latter is especially useful for accessing information on entire families of drugs. For example, a search of "4.00" in the therapeutic class field retrieves articles on antihistamines. IPA is a useful supplement to MEDLINE for any library supporting pharmacy education or practice. IPA is available currently from seven vendors.

Embase is produced in the Netherlands and is an international database concentrating on pharmaceutical and biomedical literature. It is often considered to be the "European MEDLINE," but it includes many unique references not duplicated in MEDLINE. Embase covers more than 7,600 current peer-reviewed journals, including more than 2,300 titles not available in MEDLINE.[3] These unique Embase titles are 82 percent from publishers outside North America.

Embase offers unusually thorough indexing of the world's drug-related literature. In fact, 12 percent of the Embase records are Pharmacology and Toxicology subjects. The Emtree Thesaurus includes chemical names, trade names, and laboratory/research codes as well as generic names when known for more than 30,000 drugs and chemicals. Emtree also covers all new International Nonproprietary Names (INNs) for drugs registered with the World Health Organization (WHO), as well as all U.S. Adopted Names and NDAs (New Drug Approvals) listed by the Food and Drug Administration (FDA) and European Medicines Agency (EMA). Trade names belonging to major pharmaceutical companies are covered as well. All MeSH terms from MEDLINE are linked to Emtree terms. Embase covers more than 25 million articles going back to 1947, and it is currently growing at over a million records per year. The database is available directly from Elsevier or via a number of vendors.

Chemical Abstracts is also a useful source of drug information. When searching for chemical or physical properties of drugs, such as solubility, or information on chemical synthesis and product formulations, searching Chemical Abstracts is often more efficient and effective than searching the biomedical literature. Chemical Abstracts also includes abstracts from patents, dissertations, technical reports, and other document types, in addition to journal articles. Since it indexes more than 10,000 journals and patents from sixty-three patent authorities worldwide, it offers a broader scope than MEDLINE/PubMed or Embase. Because of its great breadth, Chemical Abstracts is often used to locate citations not indexed elsewhere. Patents describing the manufacture of a specific drug fall into this category. Although the emphasis is not primarily on clinical medicine, extensive research material is included, and there is substantial coverage of drugs in research. It is therefore very important to remember this source in order to be comprehensive in searching for drug information outside of purely clinical topics. When using Chemical Abstracts as an electronic database, the CAS Registry Number for the compound may provide one of the most efficient ways of searching a drug with multiple names. SciFinder Scholar is an easy-to-search interface for Chemical Abstracts and is licensed by many large institutions so that users can do their own chemical, structure, and patent

searching. There is a mobile version of SciFinder Scholar available as well (https://
scifinder.cas.org/mobile/).

Drug Information Centers

More than seventy-five pharmacist-run drug information centers (DICs) are operating today in the United States, although the numbers have been steadily decreasing
since 1986.[4] These services are usually affiliated with hospitals, medical centers,
and schools of medicine and pharmacy. These centers provide specialized consultation on a variety of questions related to patient care. Topics may include drug
identification, prescribing, prevention and management of adverse effects, and drug
interactions. Drug information centers have access to specialized resources often
found only in medical libraries, and pharmacists may analyze literature and provide
expert advice where conflicting information exists. However, it is difficult to make
general observations because services vary from place to place. Some may offer
services only to medical and nursing staffs, while others may extend their services
to the community. Fees for service also vary, with some DICs offering services free
of charge.

The International Drug Information Center at the Arnold and Marie Schwartz
College of Pharmacy and Health Sciences, Long Island University, has published
directories of drug information centers since 1974. These authors periodically conduct surveys to obtain names and addresses of centers, hours of operation, and contact information. Their next survey is planned for 2013.

Librarians should be aware of nearby drug information centers and make efforts
to build relationships with staff and collaborate on delivering the best possible services to users.

References

1. Keely, J. L., and American College of Physicians–American Society of Internal
   Medicine. "Pharmacist Scope of Practice." *Annals of Internal Medicine* 136, no. 1
   (2002): 79–85.
2. "Development and Approval Process (Drugs)." U.S. Food and Drug Administration,
   Center for Drug Evaluation and Research. Accessed January 4, 2013. http://www
   .fda.gov/Drugs/DevelopmentApprovalProcess/.
3. "What Is Embase? Journals Coverage." Embase Biomedical Answers. Accessed
   January 15, 2013. http://www.embase.com/info/what-is-embase/coverage/.
4. Rosenberg, J. M., S. Schilit, J. P. Nathan, T. Zerilli, and H. McGuire. "Update on the
   Status of 89 Drug Information Centers in the United States." *American Journal of
   Health-System Pharmacy* 66, no. 19 (2009): 1718–22. doi:10.2146/ajhp080563.

CHAPTER 11

Consumer Health Sources

MARY L. GILLASPY and MARY O'CONNOR PRANICA

An Overview of Consumer Health Information

Individuals have always sought information about their health. From ancient times, shamans and other healers within cultures have provided treatments of varying efficacy to relieve disease and suffering, and the recipients of this traditional (or folk) medicine have welcomed their interventions, or at least accepted them in the absence of any better alternative. Patients in every age have also talked with others who have shared the same or a similar experience and sought their counsel and support. When Web browsers began providing easy access to the World Wide Web in the 1990s, early adopters—both searchers and content managers—recognized the power of the new medium for posting information about health and wellness.

MedlinePlus arrived as part of the first generation of the World Wide Web, or Web 1.0. By 2004 the Web had matured into what came to be called Web 2.0, the primary components of which enable users to create and share information digitally. Interactive sites like YouTube, Facebook, Angie's List, and others have transformed the way many Americans organize their social lives, purchase products and services, and share content. Such a revolution in communication of course included health care.

One of the nonlibrarian thought leaders in the use of Web 2.0 technology as it pertains to health is Matthew Holt, a health information technology professional for twenty-five years. He began writing *The Health Care Blog* in 2003 and cofounded

Health 2.0 in 2007. Health 2.0 not only hosts events around the world to showcase new health-care technologies, but the organization also runs a competition for innovative technological approaches to solving various problems in health care; consults with companies to implement technology; and encourages the formation of chapters around the world (at least fifty local chapters, from Amsterdam to Beijing to East Tennessee to Mumbai, are currently active).[1]

The ubiquity of smartphones and other technologies has spawned thousands of "apps," and other technologies to help a tech-savvy segment of the population track health markers for themselves or a loved one. In fact, according to a 2013 Pew Research Center study, nearly seven in ten Americans track at least one health indicator (weight, blood pressure, exercise, etc.) for either themselves or someone else, and one in five of these people track the indicator using some sort of technology.[2]

All of this activity fits in well with an increasing governmental and institutional focus on patients, families, and caregivers. Government regulations from both the Centers for Medicare and Medicaid Services and the Patient Protection and Affordable Care Act have driven hospitals and individual providers to adopt electronic health records and to establish policies regarding patient safety and quality. To provide a standard measure against which consumers can compare hospitals based on *patient perception* of care, the data are gathered through the use of the HCAHPS (Hospital Consumer Assessment of Healthcare Providers and Systems) survey and reported via the Hospital Compare website.[3]

Well into the second decade of the twenty-first century, consumer access to health information is more critical than ever because of changes in delivery of health care, the growth of personalized medicine, the largest elder population in United States (and world) history, and the unprecedented number of unpaid caregivers, estimated by the Family Caregiver Alliance to be 65.7 million people or 29 percent of the U.S. population[4] providing some level of care to an ill, disabled, or aged individual. New technology offers a means of facilitating access to the information people need, at the time that they need it; however, the use of the technology assumes that information seekers can afford the required device, understand how to use it, and are literate enough to understand and apply the results they retrieve. The "digital divide" and low literacy threaten to deny access to critical health information,[5] even as it becomes less expensive for institutions and providers to relay it to patients. Medical librarians working in public libraries, community-based organizations, some colleges and universities, clinics, and hospitals can assist individuals who need help accessing or understanding health information that may be critically important for them.

Changes in the Delivery of Health Care

The Patient Protection and Affordable Care Act may currently be the most discussed change in the environment of health care but is actually only the most recent. Health-care access and delivery constantly evolve, partly because of local and regional responses to needs and partly because of regulations, laws, and judicial decisions. For librarians, electronic health records (EHRs) represent perhaps the most salient change in health-care delivery. EHRs usually contain a patient education component, a personal chart so that patients can view test results online, and a way to e-mail a provider directly, though individuals and institutions do not always choose to activate all of the available applications. While at first glance EHRs might seem to bypass librarians, in reality they offer new opportunities. First, education or information orders can be part of any EHR system, making it possible to refer patients to a library just as they are referred to physical therapy or other services. Second, even if patients can see a report of a test, they may still have questions about vocabulary or other aspects of the document. Some of these questions can appropriately be handled by a librarian. Finally, consumers have hardly ever had as much access to their own medical records as they potentially do with an EHR. Some of them will want to do further research but be uncertain how best to proceed. Librarians are the perfect guides in these cases.

Genomics and the Era of Personalized Medicine

By 2003, the sequencing of the human genome, accomplished ahead of schedule, was changing the face of medicine and its clinical practice. At the end of 2004, federal government agencies, corporations, venture capital firms, patient advocacy organizations, research and educational institutions, and various other groups combined to launch the Personalized Medicine Coalition (PMC). Personalized, or predictive, medicine combines genomic science, information technology, and empowered patients[6] to transform the practice of clinical medicine and the physician-patient relationship. It is an approach that "uses molecular analysis to achieve optimum medical outcomes in the management of . . . disease"[7] or a predisposition to disease and holds great promise for the future of patient care and the ability to reduce risk and sometimes prevent disease in the first place. By 2011, PMC had released the third edition of *The Case for Personalized Medicine* and reported that seventy-two products were commercially available, up from just thirteen in 2006.[8]

Pharmacogenomics represents perhaps the most intense area of research, since the goal of the discipline is to identify which genes are responsible for the "wide variability in people's responses to many common drugs."[9] The earliest research focused on tests to determine how an individual would respond to common chemotherapy drugs as well as antidepressants, anticoagulants, and other medications that can either build up to toxic levels in some individuals or be flushed from the body too quickly in others, preventing a therapeutic effect. The emerging science promises that eventually physicians will test patients during their office visit; on the basis of the information obtained, the doctor will know whether a given medication is safe for that person and the dose that will be most effective. Designer drugs will have left the street and become part of the practice of medicine. As noted in *The Case for Personalized Medicine,* the future has arrived in some cases, especially for some relatively common cancers like melanoma.

On the consumer side, the website 23andMe launched in late 2007 with a mission of taking "the genetic revolution to a new level by offering a secure, web-based service where individuals can explore, share and better understand their own genetic information."[10] In 2011 the database surpassed the 100,000 user mark. As is common with technology, the price of the service has gone lower and lower. The original charge was $999, for which consumers received fourteen reports; in 2013 the charge was $99, for which users received more than 200 reports on health and traits as well as some genetic ancestry information. As of late 2012, there was no subscription fee. Moreover, users' profiles are updated when new studies are completed.

Since 2010, 23andMe has received funding from the National Institutes of Health, and since 2008, the research team has worked to better understand the genetics of Parkinson's disease. Other diseases, both common and rare, are part of the research agenda. This Web 2.0 initiative involves ordinary citizens in "bleeding edge" genetic research and helps them understand some aspects of their own genetic profile. Health sciences librarians can answer questions about this program and other personal genomic services and the results, once users receive them. One of the most important services a librarian can provide is a reminder that biology is not destiny; genetic indicators describe risk and are usually not a diagnosis. It is unknown where all of this sensitive information online will lead, even behind secure passwords, in the hands of laypeople, but surely librarians have a role to play as increasing numbers of individuals satisfy their curiosity to know more about themselves at the molecular level.

Aging Population

According to the Federal Interagency Forum on Aging-Related Statistics, in 2010 the population aged sixty-five and over accounted for 13 percent of the total U.S. population, or 40 million people. The "oldest old," those aged eighty-five and over, totaled 5.5 million. As the generation known as the baby boomers age, the population aged sixty-five and older is projected to comprise 20 percent of the U.S. population by 2030, with the "oldest old" group projected to expand rapidly after 2030. In fact, the U.S. Census Bureau estimates that the group aged eighty-five and older will grow from 5.5 million in 2010 to 19 million by 2050.[11] Continued improvements in health care would mean that the "oldest old" population could grow even more rapidly. The report *Global Health and Aging* categorically states: "The world is facing a situation without precedent: We soon will have more older people than children and more people at extreme old age than ever before."[12]

Unpaid Caregivers

These aging populations, especially the "oldest old," usually require assistance at various levels, from transportation to medication management to actual nursing care. The situation is exacerbated by the expense of professional care, whether in the home or in some form of special housing; the lack of adequate personal financial resources in most families set aside to cover these expenses; and the exponential growth in age-related dementia,[13] rendering care of the elderly even more problematic. The Alzheimer's Association reports that nearly half of all people who live beyond age eighty-five will develop some form of dementia, compounding the challenges presented by the world's aging population to a decreasing number of younger people who carry more than their share of not only the financial burden of this demographic but also some part of the day-to-day burden of care. This perfect storm of factors surrounding the aging population of the entire world provides unique opportunities for librarians to provide support through information to caregivers.

Scientific Literacy in the United States

Besides the many opportunities and questions that these factors raise, however, the remarkable scientific advances and social challenges are unfortunately colliding with a crisis in literacy, including scientific literacy, among some segments of the U.S. population. The National Center for Education Statistics (NCES) measured health literacy among adults in the United States in a 2003 assessment. Literacy levels were described as below basic, basic, intermediate, or proficient. The study found that 53 percent of adults had intermediate literacy, while only 12 percent measured proficient. An alarming 14 percent had below basic literacy, while 22 percent measured at the basic level.[14] In a report issued in 2004, the Institute of Medicine (IOM) put the number of Americans who have difficulty both comprehending and using health information provided to them by physicians, nurses, and pharmacists at 90 million, or nearly half the adult population.[15] The majority of people with limited health literacy are Caucasian and born in the United States; however, a disproportionate number live in rural areas, are socioeconomically disadvantaged, are part of ethnic or racial minorities, or are elderly.[16] By any standard, literacy rates generally, and health literacy rates specifically, must improve for people to understand the kinds of information and make the kinds of choices regarding their care that are on the near horizon. For librarians as well as for physicians and nurses, the best approach may be "to assume that all patients experience some degree of difficulty in understanding health information . . . [so] we should adopt the perspective of 'universal precautions' and use plain language, communication tools . . . and 'teach back.'"[17]

Medical Library Association and Health Literacy

The Medical Library Association (MLA) translated their concern about health literacy among consumers into action more than a decade ago when they developed a brochure titled *Deciphering Medspeak*. In 2002, they added links to the "top ten most useful websites" to MLANet. In 2006, three additional brochures became available to help laypeople understand terms associated with breast cancer, diabetes, and heart disease. In September 2006 the National Library of Medicine awarded a two-year, $250,000 contract to MLA to determine the degree to which hospital providers and administrators are aware of health literacy issues and their value to patient care.[18] Curricula for librarians and some constituencies are available as a result of this original funding, and MLA is still active in the health literacy arena.

The very first objective of the MLA Health Information Literacy Research Project was the following: "To demonstrate whether or not hospital administrators favor funding consumer health information resource centers over hospital libraries targeted for health-care providers."[19] Hospitals that have been in the forefront of offering "learning centers" to their patients and families, and sometimes to the public, include such institutions as the Mayo Clinic in Minnesota, Stanford Hospitals and Clinics, Children's Hospital of Philadelphia, Northwestern Memorial Hospital in Chicago, Salem Health in Salem, Oregon, the Beth Israel Deaconess and Brigham and Women's hospitals in Boston, cancer centers throughout the United States, Planetree clinics, and others; many other institutions have set aside an area of traditional medical libraries for consumers. (MedlinePlus devotes a section of its website to libraries that provide services to health consumers; as complete a list as is available can be found there).[20] With the growing use of electronic resources for health-care professionals, and the need for educating patients and families, hospital libraries may continue a trend toward providing more physical space for laypeople and increased programming for consumers.

Increasing Use of Online Health Information

The Pew Internet and American Life Project has been tracking Internet use among U.S. adults since 2000. The *Online Health Search 2006* reported several

interesting findings. First, the number of Internet users searching for health information remained constant over four years—63 percent in 2002, 66 percent in 2004, and
64 percent in 2006—despite the increase in Internet connectivity and the ubiquity
of broadband access. Two-thirds of health information seekers begin their search
at a search engine rather than at a trusted source, such as MedlinePlus. One fourth
reported feeling "overwhelmed" by the quantity of what they found, and 18 percent
reported feeling "confused" by the information they accessed. Only one-third of
users discussed their findings with their physician, and more than half (56 percent)
reported feeling "relieved or comforted" by their findings.[21]

Health Online 2013 reflects significant changes from the 2006 report. The number of U.S. adults who used the Internet for any reason in 2012 was 81 percent, with
72 percent stating that they had searched for health information. The focus is somewhat different, in that the researchers sought to quantify the number of Internet users
who have gone online to attempt a self-diagnosis and what they do with the information. No longer did Pew researchers track the number of Internet users; instead, they
based their numbers on the entire U.S. adult population. Of that group, 59 percent
reported having looked online for health information in the past twelve months, and
fully 35 percent say that they have used the Internet to try to figure out a health condition that either they or someone they know might have. Forty-six percent of these
searchers sought professional medical advice as a result of the online information,
and 41 percent of these reported that the professional confirmed their self-diagnosis.
Thirty-eight percent of these searchers stated that their condition was something
they could take care of at home. Noting the importance of understanding what the
numbers do and do not signify, Fox and Duggan state: "Historically, people have
always tried to answer their health questions at home and made personal choices
about whether and when to consult a clinician. Many have now added the internet to
their personal health toolbox, helping themselves and their loved ones better understand what might be ailing them."[22] The number of users who begin their search for
health information at a search engine rather than a portal or other site has increased
from two-thirds to 80 percent. Moreover, the researchers report that "the social life
of health information is a steady presence in American life."[23] One-fourth of U.S.
adults have turned to others with the same condition, a number that has remained
constant since Pew's 2010 survey. A mere 11 percent of Internet users report having
registered for e-mail updates or alerts regarding health issues, and despite the ubiquity of governmental, institutional, and commercial sites offering reviews of health
products, services, and providers, fewer than 20 percent of consumers have made
use of these reviews and rankings. The notion of feeling "overwhelmed" or "confused" by information found online was not even part of the survey for this report,
perhaps indicating that people who use the Internet have become much more comfortable with the medium than they were a decade ago.

In a companion report, Pew researchers surveyed people aged sixty-five and older to determine their use of the Internet, mobile technology, and social networking. A stark divide exists between seniors aged sixty-five to seventy-four and those aged seventy-five and older. For the first time since the project began in 2000, more than half of all seniors in the United States, or 53 percent, use the Internet. Among the older group, however, use of the Internet is only 34 percent. Sixty-nine percent of seniors report owning a mobile phone, and approximately one-third use a social networking site like Facebook. E-mail use is much more common, with nearly 90 percent of seniors who use the Internet reporting having an account.[24]

Provision of Consumer Health Information in Libraries

Consumer health libraries are no longer the "new kid on the block" of medical libraries. They have rapidly matured into sophisticated entities, with their reach expanded across communities through innovative partnerships of all kinds. Indeed, consumer health librarianship is now recognized as its own specialty, and the Medical Library Association offers a credential in the provision of such information.[25] Following are some particulars to remember when providing services through these types of information centers.

Differences between Consumer Health Information and Traditional Medical Reference

Providing health information to laypeople differs considerably from traditional medical reference. First, though the information may be delivered in a hospital or academic health science library setting, the venue may also be a storefront, public library, or community-based organization. Personnel providing the information may also be different from those in traditional settings; it could be a nurse, a trained volunteer, a librarian, a health educator, or some other person who interacts with the consumer. Most important of all, the information needs and information-seeking behaviors of a health consumer are usually quite different from those of a physician, researcher, nurse, or allied health professional. Consumers vary widely in their level of literacy, for example, and they often seek narratives that describe the experience of others who have faced the same issues.

Information Needs of Health-Care Consumers

While clinicians and researchers exhibit somewhat predictable information needs, the same cannot be said for the health-care consumer. Arguably, their needs are often more difficult to meet, since they frequently are unsure of how to frame their questions and may be distraught from the gravity of a diagnosis, sudden financial stress, grief, or other stressors associated with negotiating the health-care system. The responsibility lies with the information professional to (1) select and make available the best resources in a variety of formats; (2) assess the consumer's level of need and willingness to learn; and (3) stage the information correctly so that the person can learn incrementally and move as far along a continuum of health information need as she or he wishes, using resources appropriate to the individual's learning style. Literacy level must also be determined and taken into account when providing health information to consumers.

Successful librarians possess finely honed interpersonal skills, and in no field are these skills more important than in consumer health. Providing health information to the public has in the past been the purview of physicians and nurses. This situation has begun to change, but the first and most important thing that any librarian working in consumer health in a hospital, clinic, or academic medical center must do is gain the trust of the providers in the institution. Once that hurdle has been overcome, providers are grateful for the support of a well-run consumer health information center, because they simply do not have the time to meet the increasing health information needs of their patients. Trust and respect for the librarian, other staff, and volunteers must be earned and carefully nurtured with all providers for the consumer health library program to prosper.

Critical Role of Librarians in Consumer Health

Genomics and personalized medicine, scientific literacy among consumers—what does all this have to do with medical librarians? Medical librarians who work with the public are uniquely positioned to make a positive impact on patients' understanding of and compliance with medical instructions, their health and lifestyle decision making, and their navigating not only a complicated, multitier health-care system but also a bewildering array of new technologies.

Librarians working in consumer health will rely more and more heavily on Internet- and technology-based applications for their customers. As physicians and other primary-care providers become more accustomed to using electronic health records, they will attach information directly to communications with their patients. Consumers seeking health information outside of a primary care environment (e.g., individuals searching for a relative or neighbor who has a new diagnosis of cancer, diabetes, Parkinson's disease, etc.) will increasingly use their own devices and searching skills to acquire the information, bypassing traditional library services. Is there a place still for consumer health librarians in this electronically connected world? Absolutely there is, for the simple reason that not everyone can afford or use a computer, smartphone, or other electronic device, nor can everyone be certain of information they find for themselves. For example, a news item from MedlinePlus in January, 2013, highlights a study from *JAMA Dermatology* finding that smartphone apps for detecting skin cancer risk are unreliable.[26]

Despite the complexity of the subjects, millions of people every day search for topics ranging from tests and procedures, to drug information, to information about a new diagnosis. Profound scientific advances and an emphasis on translational applications—moving research more quickly from the bench to the bedside—mean that people have even more pressing decisions to make about their health. The volume of information and its increasing complexity provide an ideal niche for health science librarians to work directly with patients, families, and interested laypersons as they navigate an ever more complicated health-care landscape.

The role of the information professional in the provision of health information to the public includes all of the following factors: emphasizing the importance of and defining trusted sources of health information; knowing when to consult a physician; understanding the nuances of communicating with physicians, nurses, and pharmacists; and using authoritative information to make decisions about testing, treatment, and risk reduction. Medical librarians can guide laypeople in all of these directions. Their role is a critical one as the information becomes not only easier to locate but also more complex in its content and presentation. The references discussed in the remainder of this chapter represent the best resources available to guide health-care consumers through the complicated maze of information they face in the medical environment.

General Reference Sources for Consumer Health Information

Consumer health information encompasses a broad spectrum of resources, from easy-to-read to medical textbooks and journal articles. The most important principle regarding reference sources for consumers is to provide an array of resources, at an array of levels, in multiple formats to match individual learning styles. Literally thousands of books and websites are available today for consumer health information. What is listed here is not meant to be comprehensive. The references that are discussed are ones that have been found in consumer health settings to be the most authoritative and useful to laypeople and the librarians and educators who help them satisfy their health information needs.

In some cases, core medical textbooks are included as key consumer health references. The use of such resources may be controversial; however, in the case of consumers seeking information on rare conditions, medical textbooks often provide the only alternative to complex journal articles. Though the number of their subjects was very small, Baker and Gollop devised a study that indicated some of "the problems involved in reading medical materials," even among well-educated users, and they identified some of the factors of which librarians and educators should be aware as they "help laypeople in their quest to read and understand medical terminology." They concluded that "library and information science professionals should test the reading comprehension of medical textbooks so that they can tailor medical and health material to the specific needs of their communities."[27]

Is there a place for print in this new world? To a lesser extent than in previous times, yes, there is, because a large segment of the population still prefers paper to a website, especially if they are already dealing with illness and the many stressors that accompany it. Moreover, certain types of information lend themselves better to print than to reading online. Consequently, the remainder of this chapter will include both print and electronic references. With more than 13,000 apps for health and fitness to be had,[28] it will be impossible to list even a small sampling of all that is available. The sites included are primarily key portals to specific categories of information. The criteria for including an electronic reference include the following:

- Reference is created and maintained by a reputable, noncommercial source such as the American Diabetes Association, the U.S. government, an academic institution, or a well-known hospital or health system.
- Reference is designed specifically for consumers and has an overall reading level of eighth grade or lower.

Guides to the Literature

11.1   Consumer and Patient Health Information Section (CAPHIS) of the Medical Library Association. Chicago: CAPHIS. Available: http://caphis.mlanet.org/.

Here are found several key documents for consumer health, as well as an article describing how to establish and manage a consumer health library.

11.2   Healthnet: Connecticut Consumer Health Information Network, Lyman Maynard Stowe Library, University of Connecticut. "Recommended Books for a Consumer Health Reference Collection." Farmington, CT: University of Connecticut. Available: http://library.uchc.edu/departm/hnet/pdf/corelist.pdf.

This excellent resource includes a core bibliography for consumer health reference from the Lyman Maynard Stowe Library at the University of Connecticut Health Center. Items recommended for basic consumer health collections in public libraries of any size are marked with a double asterisk (**), with a single asterisk

(*) denoting titles for large public libraries or any library with a heavy emphasis on consumer health information.

Directories

Many of the directories that were once essential are now marginal purchases, since so much of this type of information is available on the Web. However, some directory information, such as that in the database from the American Board of Medical Specialties, is available only for an annual subscription fee; yet when available, it is frequently used by consumers.

11.3   *AHA Guide.* Chicago: American Hospital Association. 1997– . Annual.

This annual publication lists all hospitals in the United States alphabetically by state and includes utilization data, hospital organization structure, and a great deal of other useful information. A companion resource, also published annually by the AHA, is *AHA Hospital Statistics,* a reference source for analysis and comparison of historical trends in community hospitals across the United States. Both are available electronically for a fee. Special pricing is available for institutional members.

11.4   *The Official ABMS Directory of Board Certified Medical Specialists.* St. Louis, MO: Saunders, 1992– . Available: http://www .abmsdirectory.com/.

Once available as a multivolume print reference, the ABMS Directory is now entirely electronic. An abbreviated directory for consumers is available at no charge. Institutions can subscribe to the full database, which is now updated quarterly rather than annually.

11.5   *Medical and Health Information Directory.* Detroit: Thomson Gale, 1977– .

This multivolume work includes (1) organizations, agencies, and institutions; (2) publications, libraries, and other information resources; and (3) health services, which includes such items as sleep disorder clinics, sports medicine clinics, transplant centers, and more. In 2013 the twenty-eighth edition appeared. This is also available electronically from Gale Cengage Learning.

11.6   AMA Doctor Finder. Chicago: American Medical Association. Available: http://ama-assn.org/doctorfinder/home.jsp.

More than 814,000 licensed medical doctors and osteopaths are included in this database, which can be searched by name and city or state, or by medical specialty and city or state. This Internet database and several other similar ones of health professionals are also available from MedlinePlus at http://www.nlm.nih.gov/medline plus/directories.html.

Dictionaries

Even with good online medical dictionaries available, print editions continue to be valuable and necessary in a consumer health setting. Following are the most important titles.

GENERAL MEDICAL DICTIONARIES

11.7   *Dorland's Illustrated Medical Dictionary.* Philadelphia: Elsevier/Saunders, 2012.

Often considered the most venerable resource in its field, *Dorland's* is an optional selection for a consumer health collection. The definitions are written using sophisticated medical vocabulary, and users are directed from common names (e.g., Bell's palsy) to the name of the nerve and to the entry for *palsy*. This text is best for sophisticated users and staff. It is also available via CD-ROM or online.

11.8   *Stedman's Dental Dictionary: Illustrated.* 2nd ed. Philadelphia: Wolters Kluwer Health/Lippincott Williams and Wilkins, 2012.

The last print edition of *Stedman's Illustrated Medical Dictionary* was published in 2006. The dental dictionary provides useful information in an area where few resources for consumers exist.

11.9   *Stedman's Medical Dictionary for the Health Professions and Nursing.* 7th ed. Philadelphia: Wolters Kluwer/Lippincott Williams and Wilkins, 2012.

Accessible definitions, illustrations, and additional materials make this a helpful consumer resource.

11.10   Venes, D., ed. *Taber's Cyclopedic Medical Dictionary.* 22nd ed. Philadelphia: F. A. Davis, 2013.

Clearly written entries make this an exceptional resource for consumer use. Its many illustrations (some in color), and extensive appendixes are also helpful. In a consumer health setting, Taber's is the print dictionary of choice.

SPECIALTY DICTIONARIES

11.11   Cancer dictionaries. Bethesda, MD: National Cancer Institute, National Institutes of Health. Available: http://www.cancer.gov/dictionary.

The best resource for cancer terminology is the website of the National Cancer Institute (NCI). On this website, users will have access to the *NCI Dictionary of Cancer Terms*, the *NCI Dictionary of Genetics Terms*, a *Glossary of Statistical Terms*, and *Terminology Resources*. The *NCI Drug Dictionary* is also available (http://www .cancer.gov/drugdictionary). For each drug searched, a link to both active and closed clinical trials is available.

11.12   Jablonski, Stanley. *Jablonski's Dictionary of Medical Acronyms and Abbreviations*. 6th ed. Philadelphia: Saunders/Elsevier, 2009.

This edition includes explanations of molecular biology terms in an approachable format. Also included is an expanded symbols section that includes unusual and seldom-used symbols. It is available in online, CD-ROM, or print formats.

11.13   *Stedman's Abbreviations, Acronyms, and Symbols*. 4th ed. Philadelphia: Wolters Kluwer/Lippincott Williams and Wilkins, 2008.

Besides this work, Stedman's also produces an entire series of "wordbooks," including such titles as *Stedman's Radiology Words*, *Stedman's Alternative and Complementary Medicine Words*, and *Stedman's Surgery Words*, which also includes anesthesia and pain management. A complete listing of these resources can be found online (http://www.lww.com/). All are available either online or in print.

11.14   Costello, Elaine. *Random House Webster's Unabridged American Sign Language Dictionary*. 2nd ed. New York: Random House Reference, 2008.

This is an excellent resource for consumers who are learning American Sign Language (ASL), for schoolchildren who are writing reports about it, and for hearing-impaired individuals and their families as well.

11.15   Valli, Clayton, ed. *Gallaudet Dictionary of American Sign Language*. Washington, DC: Gallaudet University Press, 2006.

This resource includes a DVD showing how to form each of the more than 3,000 signs included in the book. The work also features examples of idioms in American Sign Language (ASL) and an article about the place of ASL in the deaf community.

Encyclopedias

Gale Cengage Learning (formerly Thomson Gale) products, available electronically as well as in print, are the best general consumer health encyclopedias on the market. They are plainly written, well-illustrated, updated in a timely manner, and provide introductions to most common diseases and conditions as well as some rare ones. Information is easy to find because of multiple access points within each set, and biographical and historical sidebars in all the volumes enrich understanding. A resource list is included at the end of every entry. Entries in all volumes are arranged alphabetically, with an index in the final volume. The list of titles continues to grow. They are available in both print and electronic formats.

11.16   Fundukian, Laurie J., ed. *The Gale Encyclopedia of Medicine*. 4th ed. Detroit: Gale Cengage Learning, 2011.

This set was first published in 1999. Cross-references have improved in successive editions. The content is excellent. There are entries for diseases and disorders as well as tests and treatments. In the first category, the entries typically include definitions, descriptions, causes and symptoms, diagnosis, treatments, alternative treatments (if any), prognosis, and prevention. Entries for tests and treatments include definitions, purposes, precautions, descriptions, preparation, aftercare, risks, and normal and abnormal results.

11.17   Fundukian, Laurie J., ed. *The Gale Encyclopedia of Genetic Disorders.* 3rd ed. Detroit: Gale, 2010.

This resource brings much of the work of the Human Genome Project to the medical consumer at the place they care about, the disorders themselves. Relatively common disorders (epilepsy, cystic fibrosis) are included, as well as much rarer ones (Fahr disease, Li-Fraumeni syndrome). Articles include definitions, descriptions, genetic profile, demographics, signs and symptoms, diagnosis, treatment and management, and prognosis.

11.18   Longe, Jacqueline L., ed. *Gale Encyclopedia of Children's Health: Infancy through Adolescence.* 2nd ed. Detroit: Gale, 2011.

This resource follows the format of other sets in the series. A part of most of the articles is "Parental Concerns," a very helpful guide for both parents and librarians assisting them.

11.19   Longe, Jacqueline L., ed. *The Gale Encyclopedia of Cancer: A Guide to Cancer and Its Treatments.* 3rd ed. Detroit: Gale Cengage Learning, 2010.

Included in this set are entries on 120 different cancers, common cancer drugs, traditional and alternative treatments, and diagnostic procedures. The drug section entries are quite helpful. They appear in the encyclopedia under generic name but are indexed under both brand and generic names, with a cross-reference from the brand name to the generic. Most helpful of all, treatment acronyms like MOPP and EVA are explained, and the names of all the drugs included in the combination therapies and the types of cancer for which they are administered are also included in the entry. These articles, generally about one-and-one-half pages long, are an approachable adjunct to *The Chemotherapy Sourcebook* (4th ed., Baltimore, MD: Lippincott Williams and Wilkins, 2007), an excellent but technical reference. Articles on specific therapies are lengthy; for example, the "Chemotherapy" article is nine pages long, while "Radiation Therapy" is four pages in length. Terms commonly used in cancer and cancer treatment—such as adjuvant chemotherapy—are clearly explained, and when several terms are used for the same procedure, like internal radiation therapy, all of them are named and described. The fourth edition will be available in 2014.

11.20   Key, Kristin, ed. *The Gale Encyclopedia of Mental Health*. 3rd ed. Detroit: Thomson Gale, 2012.

Entries for most of the 150 disorders classified in the *Diagnostic and Statistical Manual of Mental Disorders* (*DSM*) (see 11.95) are included in this very approachable and useful work. Medications—prescription, alternative, and over-the-counter—are discussed in detail. Selective serotonin reuptake inhibitors (SSRIs), a large class of frequently prescribed drugs, have their own entry. Therapies beyond pharmaceutical agents, like electroconvulsive therapy, are included, as are alternative therapies and diagnostic tools like electroencephalography.

11.21   Gale editors. *The Gale Encyclopedia of Neurological Disorders*. 2nd ed. Detroit: Gale Cengage Learning, 2012.

Because of the serious nature and unfortunately common occurrence of neurological disorders, a separate title for this class of diseases and conditions is warranted. It follows the same format as other titles by this publisher. Nervous system aspects of diseases and syndromes that may have neurological components, such as HIV disease, are discussed in detail. Pharmaceuticals that are commonly prescribed for neurological disorders are also included.

11.22   Key, Kristin, ed. *The Gale Encyclopedia of Diets: A Guide to Health and Nutrition*. 2nd ed. Detroit: Gale, 2013.

Nutrition and diet therapy comprise one of the most frequent areas of inquiry in consumer health settings. This encyclopedia helps users understand the basics of the Zone, Atkins, Pritikin, and other diets about which they hear in the media.

11.23   Longe, Jacqueline L., ed. *The Gale Encyclopedia of Senior Health: A Guide for Seniors and Their Caregivers*. Detroit: Gale Cengage Learning, 2009.

Half of this encyclopedia is dedicated to the aging body and diseases that can affect it. Treatment options for diseases common to this population are addressed. Remaining sections discuss nutrition and exercise guidelines for seniors as well as transportation, housing, adaptive equipment, and other issues impacting quality of life for seniors.

11.24   Longe, Jacqueline L., ed. *The Gale Encyclopedia of Fitness*. Detroit: Gale Cengage Learning, 2012.

This encyclopedia offers articles, illustrations, and photographs to enhance understanding of body systems, exercise, sports, and preventive health. It also addresses health conditions associated with extreme fitness activity and details government initiatives in the United States and throughout the world designed to promote healthy lifestyles and combat obesity.

11.25   Gale editors. *The Gale Encyclopedia of Environmental Health*. Detroit: Gale Cengage Learning, 2013.

Entries for specific environmental disasters explain how each event occurred, its impact on health, and how to identify and treat related conditions. Additional articles cover diseases and conditions related to environmental catastrophes, legal statutes and policy issues, and biographies of key leaders in environmental health.

11.26   Gale editors. *The Gale Encyclopedia of Public Health*. Detroit: Gale Cengage Learning, 2013.

Provides broad coverage of public health topics such as epidemics and pandemics, chronic conditions (e.g., malnutrition, cancer), and social issues impacting health (e.g., obesity, bullying). Entries detail the origins of each public health issue, public and government response, treatment and preventive measures, and resources for additional information.

11.27   Albrecht, Gary L., ed. *Encyclopedia of Disability*. Thousand Oaks, CA: Sage, 2006.

Nothing else matches this five-volume compendium of information. Black-and-white illustrations depict disability as it has appeared in art and film. The final volume makes available in one place important primary source documents on disability, which are arranged chronologically. Noted individuals, such as the cellist Jacqueline du Pré; events having to do with disability, such as Paralympics; and special situations, such as children of disabled parents and issues of sexuality in this population, are all covered in well-written articles.

11.28   Albrecht, Gary L., ed. *Reference Series on Disability: Key Issues and Future Directions*. Thousand Oaks, CA: Sage, 2013.

This series includes nearly 3,000 pages in eight volumes, the topics of which comprise the following: ethics, law, and policy; arts and humanities; employment and work; education; disability through the life course; health and medicine; assistive technology and science; and rehabilitation interventions. Albrecht's work is essential in any library that serves individuals with disabilities or people learning more about the many topics associated with physical disabilities.

Handbooks and Manuals

11.29   Beers, Mark H., et al., eds. *Merck Manual of Medical Information*. 2nd ed. Whitehouse, NJ: Merck, 2004–2007. Available: http://www.merck.com/mmhe/index.html.

11.30   Beers, Mark H., et al., eds. *Merck Manual of Health and Aging.* Whitehouse Station, NJ: Merck, 2005. Available: http://www.merck.com/pubs/mmanual_ha/contents.html.

The first and most important resources in the area of handbooks and manuals are these two Merck manuals, which should be used in their online versions because the websites contain corrections and changes from the original or current print editions. The date of the "last full review/revision" is posted at the bottom of each topic page. The online versions also provide multimedia enhancements that can be very helpful to consumers' understanding of a topic, especially if literacy is a barrier to learning. For example, technical terms are pronounced correctly with a single click, and a comprehensive table provides trade names for drugs positioned next to the generic name. Photographs, animations, and video files are also included.

11.31   Rakel, Robert E., and Edward T. Bope, eds. *Conn's Current Therapy.* Philadelphia: Saunders, 1984– . Annual.

11.32   Tierney, Lawrence M., ed. *Current Medical Diagnosis and Treatment.* New York: Lange Medical Books/McGraw-Hill, 1974– . Annual.

The Lange and Conn series of handbooks have long been used by consumers and by reference librarians helping consumers answer questions. Before there were many quality consumer health resources available, except for pamphlets from organizations, these two series offered a gateway to medical knowledge that helped patients understand what was happening to their bodies and what to expect from treatment.

Today they are the middle ground between materials written specifically for consumers and medical textbooks. For the literate consumer who wants to go beyond the basic information offered by an encyclopedia article or printouts from a website, these handbooks are a good choice. They delve more deeply into actual disease processes than the consumer material and allow a deeper understanding of the actual medical problem. The reading level of both resources, however, is very high. Baker and Gollop found that the reading ease (Flesch reading ease score) for Conn was 13.56, while that for Lange was 13.80, where the score range is from zero (very difficult to read) to 100 (easy to read). (See reference 27.) As in all cases, librarians must know their users and make appropriate resources available. Where education and literacy rates are high, Conn and Lange may be helpful.

(Also available in the Lange series are titles for cardiology, critical care, emergency medicine, family medicine, geriatrics, neurology, obstetrics and gynecology, orthopaedics, otolaryngology-head and neck surgery, pain, pediatrics, psychiatry, pulmonary medicine, and rheumatology. These specialized volumes are less helpful in the consumer health realm than the more general one. All are available electronically.)

Key Medical Series Written for the Consumer

Certain institutions and publishers have developed consumer health information series that, like the Thomson Gale encyclopedias, follow a similar format and exhibit a recognizable "look and feel." In alphabetical order by producer or sponsoring institution, the best of the best include the following. The website, if available, follows the name of the organization, publisher, or series.

11.33   American Academy of Pediatrics. AAP Online Bookstore. Elk Grove Village, IL: American Academy of Pediatrics. Available: http://www.aap.org/bst/index.cfm?DID=15.

Click on a topic under "Parent Resources" to find authoritative publications in a variety of formats (e.g., handbooks, DVDs, illustrated card decks). One of the best features of these resources is that they are frequently updated; moreover, many publications are available in both English and Spanish. Click on the "Parenting Corner" tab to visit HealthyChildren.org, a free website offering expert information on children's health topics, guidance on parenting issues, and access to the guidelines and policies of the American Academy of Pediatrics.

11.34   Harvard Medical School Guides. Available: http://www.health.harvard.edu/books/.

Several dozen titles are available in this outstanding series.

11.35   Johns Hopkins University Press. Available: http://www.press.jhu.edu/books/health_med.html.

Click on "consumer health" to find more than 100 titles. Some of the most important consumer health resources, such as *The 36-Hour Day*, are published by this press.

11.36   Mayo Clinic books for consumers. Available: http://store.mayoclinic.com/productList.cfm?mpt=1.

Excellent references on common diseases and conditions, from arthritis to vision and eye health. Some or all of them should be available for reference in consumer health libraries.

11.37   Omnigraphics Health Reference Series. Available: http://www.omnigraphics.com/category_view.php?ID=3.

Nearly 150 volumes are available in this series, and all of them are frequently updated. The series directed toward adolescents, the Teen Health Series, is well worth including in a consumer health collection that serves teenagers, as the format is engaging and the titles address important concerns of this age group. More than two dozen titles are available in the Teen Health Series.

11.38   Roizen, Michael F., and Mehmet C. Oz. YOU Manuals [various titles].
      New York: Free Press, 2006– .

Beginning with *YOU: The Smart Patient* in 2006, these two well-known physicians have written nine titles in this series (as of 2013), some of which they have updated and expanded. They offer sound advice on topics from diet to parenting to stress management to pregnancy. These volumes tend to be very popular with the public.

Category-Specific Reference Resources for Consumer Health Information

Category 1: General Health and Medical References

Librarians who serve the public may find that in order to answer the questions asked of them, they need access to a core set of medical textbooks, even though the material will not necessarily be understood in depth without medical training. On a continuum of resources (an array of levels) running from materials written at a fourth to sixth grade reading level on up the scale, these works are the upper end of the collection. Today they may be obtained either in print or in an electronic database or both. In a large consumer health collection, including the current edition of a core medical textbook in most specialty areas is a sound practice.

11.39   Longo, Dan, Anthony S. Fauci, Dennis L. Kasper, Stephen L. Hauser,
      J. Larry Jameson, and Joseph Loscalzo, eds. *Harrison's Principles of Internal Medicine*. 18th ed. New York: McGraw-Hill Professional, 2011.

11.40   Goldman, Lee, and J. Claude Bennett, eds. *Goldman's Cecil Medicine*.
      22nd ed. Philadelphia: Saunders, 2004.

These two works are sometimes called the "bibles" of internal medicine. Ideally, a consumer health collection would have both.

Many excellent portals to consumer health information are available today on the Internet. All of the various institutes and centers of the National Institutes of Health feature extensive websites for patients and consumers. Some of the information is available in more than one language, and easy reading pamphlets are sometimes present. Many private organizations (like the Alzheimer's Association, American Heart Association, American Diabetes Association, and American Cancer Society, among many others) have excellent information as well. The first consumer health portal from the federal government, Healthfinder.gov, is continually enhanced and is particularly easy to use—because of its clean, bright format—for seniors or persons with poor vision. KidsHealth.com, MayoClinic.com, and many other sites provide particular inducements. However, by going to MedlinePlus, the site described below, consumers are directed to an enormous array of resources, including everything available through the federal government as well as the independent sites listed previously. MedlinePlus truly offers one-stop shopping for consumer health reference information.

11.41   MedlinePlus. Bethesda, MD: National Library of Medicine. Available: http://medlineplus.gov/.

MedlinePlus is the premier free portal to consumer health information on the Web. Beginning with pages devoted to fewer than fifty health topics in 1998, the site has grown to include well more than 1,000. It also includes the A.D.A.M. medical encyclopedia, drug information, health check tools, and more than 150 interactive health tutorials covering common diseases and conditions, diagnostic tests and procedures, surgeries and surgical procedures, and prevention and wellness information.

CONSUMER NEWSLETTERS

Most of the newsletters listed below are available electronically, but in a consumer health library setting, clients enjoy having the print available as well.

Cleveland Clinic Arthritis Advisor, Cleveland Clinic Heart Advisor, Cleveland Clinic Men's Health Advisor

Environmental Nutrition

Harvard Health Letter, Harvard Heart Letter, Harvard Men's Health Watch, Harvard Mental Health Letter, Harvard Women's Health Watch

Johns Hopkins Medical Letter: Health After 50

Mayo Clinic Health Letter

Mind, Mood and Memory (from the Massachusetts General Hospital)

Nutrition Today

UC Berkeley Wellness Letter

From the Massachusetts Medical Society, publishers of the *New England Journal of Medicine*, relevant *Journal Watch* titles for specialties and topics are very helpful for consumers who want to stay current with the medical literature in a simplified form.

Category 2: Procedures, Therapies, Symptoms, and Manifestations

DRUG INFORMATION

Consumers expect to see a current *Physicians' Desk Reference* in a health library, though online resources are more authoritative (because of frequent updates) and generally much easier to use. Drug information from the American Society of Health System Pharmacists is available online for free from MedlinePlus.

11.42   Clinical Pharmacology. Tampa, FL: Gold Standard Multimedia. Available: http://goldstandard.com/.

Clinical Pharmacology, produced by Gold Standard Multimedia (a division of Elsevier), is a very attractive product that provides technical monographs as well as patient education handouts, available in several languages besides English. The database includes all Food and Drug Administration–approved prescription and over-the-counter pharmaceuticals, investigational drugs that are being investigated at Phase III or IV, and dietary supplements for which evidence of benefit or harm exists.

11.43   Micromedex. Greenwood Village, CO: Thomson Reuters (Healthcare). Available: http://www.micromedex.com/.

Micromedex and Thomson Reuters produce a comprehensive patient education/consumer health resource called CareNotes that includes drug information written for laypeople. A subset of Micromedex, POISINDEX, is the gold standard product for poisoning and toxicology information. Most well-supplied emergency departments keep POISINDEX as part of their online toolbox.

Most patient education/consumer health information packages that may be purchased by hospitals, such as Krames StayWell or Micromedex's CareNotes, include some drug information.

DIAGNOSTIC TESTS

11.44   Fischbach, Frances T., et al. *Manual of Laboratory and Diagnostic Tests.* 8th ed. Philadelphia: Wolters Kluwer Health/Lippincott Williams and Wilkins, 2009.

The Fischbach book is a core title that will provide background for material written specifically for the consumer. It is available electronically.

11.45   American Association for Clinical Chemistry. Lab Tests Online. Available: http://labtestsonline.org/.

Lab Tests Online is the primary source that MedlinePlus uses for their laboratory tests page and is by far the most authoritative free online site for reading about diagnostic or screening tests. Users can employ pull-down menus to search by the name of the test, condition for which the test is being performed, or screening guidelines by age. A general search box is also available. A special section titled "Understanding Your Tests" provides information about reference ranges, genetic testing, pharmacogenomics, and more. Another section called "Inside the Lab" affords users a glimpse of different types of laboratories, who works in them, who provides oversight, and many more details. Absent institutionally approved patient education for specific tests, *Lab Tests Online* is the place to start to provide this sort of information to consumers.

GENETICS

11.46   Genetics Home Reference. Bethesda, MD: National Library of Medicine. Available: http://ghr.nlm.nih.gov/.

Outstanding resource for consumers that continues to grow as scientists uncover more and more of the secrets of the human genome. Users may search under genetic conditions, genes, or chromosomes for specific information regarding diseases or conditions. A handbook, glossary, and links to additional information about genetics are also included.

11.47   MedlinePlus, "Genetics/Birth Defects." Bethesda, MD: National Library of Medicine. Available: http://nlm.nih.gov/medlineplus/geneticsbirth defects.html.

Links to specific diseases and conditions as well as to entire pages devoted to genetic testing, genetic counseling, and gene therapy.

11.48   *A Science Primer*. Bethesda, MD: National Center for Biotechnology Information. Available: http://ncbi.nlm.nih.gov/About/primer/.

For the consumer who would like to explore genetic topics in more depth, this primer offers an excellent quick course in the most important technologies currently being explored.

SYMPTOMS AND MANIFESTATIONS

11.49   Margolis, Simeon. *Johns Hopkins Complete Home Guide to Symptoms and Remedies*. New York: Black Dog and Leventhal, 2004.

Many health-care consumers use a library service to "check out" symptoms prior to seeing a physician. This book is an authoritative answer to such an information need. The first half of the book lists symptoms, such as "swallowing difficulty," with three columns of information: associated symptoms, possible diagnosis, and distinguishing features. The possible diagnoses are listed in alphabetical order. The second half of the book is an alphabetical arrangement of disorders, with each article explaining the condition and the cause, prevention, diagnosis, treatment options, and when to call a doctor. A textbox with each article provides cross-references to symptoms.

MedlinePlus also offers a way to investigate symptoms such as abdominal pain or fever, but the Margolis book is more comprehensive.

See also *Fitzpatrick's Color Atlas and Synopsis of Clinical Dermatology* (11.96) for diagnostic information.

NUTRITION AND DIET THERAPY

11.50   Hornick, Betsy, Roberta L. Duyff, and Alma A. Flor. *American Dietetic Association Complete Food and Nutrition Guide.* 4th ed., revised and updated. New York: Houghton Mifflin Harcourt, 2012.

This outstanding, very well-written resource provides important nutrition information for consumers. The fourth edition is organized completely differently from the previous three and includes topics of great interest and discussion today, including food choices and shopping, food safety guidelines, and chapters on food for different stages of life, from infancy to the elder years. Chapters on special dietary issues of athletes, those with food sensitivities, and specific conditions like osteoporosis and diabetes are also included. This is a must purchase for any consumer health collection.

11.51   Mahan, L. Kathleen, Sylvia Escott-Stump, and Janice L. Raymond, eds. *Krause's Food and the Nutrition Care Process* (formerly *Krause's Food, Nutrition, and Diet Therapy*). 13th ed. Philadelphia: Elsevier/Saunders, 2011.

Krause is the most authoritative resource available on diet therapy. The reference offers tables and illustrations for individual diseases and conditions and how they can be managed through diet.

11.52   Pennington, Jean A. T. *Bowes and Church's Food Values of Portions Commonly Used.* Philadelphia: Lippincott Williams and Wilkins, 2005.

This resource answers many typical consumer questions regarding the specific nutrient content of certain foods and even indexes items by brand name.

ALTERNATIVE, COMPLEMENTARY, AND INTEGRATIVE MEDICINE

As in so many other instances, current, authoritative information for alternative, complementary, and integrative medicine is better found online than in print, though two important print resources are included here. Two proprietary databases offer evidence-based information, while additional information is available at various government and institutional websites. The following listing begins with the two products that require purchase, followed by authoritative free resources on the Web.

11.53   *Natural Medicines Comprehensive Database.* Stockton, CA: Therapeutic Research Faculty. Available: http://www.naturaldatabase.therapeuticresearch.com/.

Produced and maintained by the same company that publishes *Pharmacist's Letter* and *Prescriber's Letter*, *Natural Medicines Comprehensive Database* offers access to evidence-based information about more "natural" products than any other single source. A natural product/drug interaction checker enables users to determine very quickly if any known ingredients in specific products may interact harmfully with a pharmaceutical. Safety and effectiveness ratings, based on available evidence, are noted along a continuum that ranges from unsafe, possibly unsafe, likely unsafe, possibly safe, likely safe, and safe, with the same scale for efficacy. Information regarding potential interactions with laboratory or diagnostic tests is also included. Searches may also be performed by disease or medical condition. Both professional and consumer monographs are available for hundreds of products, and the company has recently introduced a special consumer version of the database. The patient monographs are available for free through MedlinePlus.

11.54   Natural Standard. Cambridge, MA: Natural Standard. Available:
        http:// www.naturalstandard.com/.

Natural Standard, "The Authority on Integrative Medicine," features a very attractive interface and uses grades of A, B, C, D, or F to rate safety and effectiveness for the substances evaluated and the disease or condition for which its use is suggested. The grades, which are easy for laypeople to understand, reflect the level of evidence available to support each claim. The interface also features "bottom line" monographs in both English and Spanish and a "flash card" that serves as a patient handout. Color photographs of varying quality picture the herbals in natural habitats. The Natural Standard integrative medicine database represents an international research collaboration composed of more than one hundred institutions.

11.55   MedlinePlus, "Complementary and Alternative Therapies." Available: http://
        www.nlm.nih.gov/medlineplus/complementaryandalternativetherapies.html.

This site contains a number of pages with links to authoritative sources. Lacking access to one of the sources listed above, this is the best place to begin for information about integrative medicine.

Other authoritative sites providing information on alternative, complementary, and integrative medicine include the following:

11.56   National Center for Complementary and Alternative Medicine (NCCAM).
        National Institutes of Health. Available: http://nccam.nih.gov/.

11.57   Office of Cancer Complementary and Alternative Medicine. National
        Institutes of Health. Available: http://cancer.gov/cancertopics/cam.

11.58   Integrative Medicine Program. University of Texas MD Anderson Cancer
        Center. Available: http://www.mdanderson.org/education-and-research/
        departments-programs-and-labs/programs-centers-institutes/integrative
        -medicine-program/index.html.

11.59 "About Herbs, Botanicals and Other Products." Memorial Sloan-Kettering Cancer Center. Available: http://www.mskcc.org/cancer-care/integrative -medicine/about-herbs-botanicals-other-products.

11.60 Klein, Siegrid, Robert Rister, and Chance Riggins, aus. and eds. *The Complete German Commission E Monographs: Therapeutic Guide to Herbal Medicines*. Austin, TX: American Botanical Council, 1999.

11.61 Blumenthal, Mark, ed. *Herbal Medicine: Expanded Commission E Monographs*. Newton, MA: Integrative Medicine Communications, 2000.

These two books are authoritative sources for information on herbals used as medicine. They are also available in CD-ROM format.

SURGERY

11.62 MedlinePlus. "Surgery and Rehabilitation." Available: http://www.nlm.nih.gov/medlineplus/surgeryandrehabilitation.html.

This portal offers easy access to a number of organizations' patient websites, such as the American Academy of Orthopaedic Surgeons. Videos of some surgeries are also available here.

11.63 Brunicardi, F. Charles, ed. *Schwartz's Principles of Surgery*. 9th ed. New York: McGraw-Hill, 2009.

11.64 Mulholland, Michael W., et al. *Greenfield's Surgery: Scientific Principles and Practice*. 5th ed. Philadelphia: Lippincott Williams and Wilkins, 2010.

These two general surgery textbooks may be useful in a consumer health setting. As well, many trade books are available about both reconstructive and aesthetic surgery, which represent two very different aspects of plastic surgery. Having at least a book about breast reconstruction, for breast cancer patients, and one that explains the pros and cons of aesthetic surgery are important in consumer health collections. Librarians should weigh what is available against customer needs to make the best purchase decision.

Category 3: Anatomy and Physiology

11.65 Page, Martyn, ed. *The Human Body: An Illustrated Guide to Every Part of the Human Body and How It Works*. New York: Dorling Kindersley, 2001.

Beautiful illustrations, coupled with detailed yet lucid text, make this book an outstanding reference for laypersons, despite its age. A section on the human life cycle describes changes occurring in the body from conception to old age. Very general medical conditions, such as infections and cancer, are also described, with the emphasis on exactly what goes wrong inside the body when one of these conditions is present.

11.66   Netter, Frank H. *Atlas of Human Anatomy*. 5th ed. New York: Saunders, 2010.

The magnificent illustrations in this volume make it an essential purchase for any library that has a biomedical collection.

11.67   Patton, Kevin T., and Gary A. Thibodeau. *The Human Body in Health and Disease*. 6th ed. St. Louis, MO: Mosby, 2013.

A text written for students in health professions programs, this volume is a very good choice for a mid-level resource in anatomy and physiology. Clear illustrations and helpful tables make this text approachable and useful for literate users.

Category 4: Selected Disorders and Conditions

BONES, JOINTS, AND MUSCLES

11.68   Klippel, John H., et al., eds. *Primer on the Rheumatic Diseases*. 13th ed. New York: Springer, 2008.

This is an excellent mid-level resource that discusses individual rheumatic diseases, what is known about the role of genetics in these diseases, rehabilitation, self-management, the economic consequences of rheumatic disease, and much more. Illustrations and tables enhance the text. Appendixes include criteria for the classification and diagnosis of specific rheumatic diseases, guidelines for management, drugs, and supplements.

BRAIN AND NERVOUS SYSTEM

11.69   *The Gale Encyclopedia of Neurological Disorders* (see 11.21).

11.70   Rowland, Lewis P., and Timothy A. Pedley, eds. *Merritt's Neurology*. 12th ed. Philadelphia: Lippincott Williams and Wilkins, 2010.

Straightforwardly written, this text can answer many involved neurology questions posed by a consumer. It is available in electronic and print formats.

ALZHEIMER'S DISEASE AND OTHER DEMENTIAS

11.71   Mace, Nancy L., and Peter V. Rabins. *The 36-Hour Day: A Family Guide to Caring for People Who Have Alzheimer Disease, Related Dementias, and Memory Loss*. 5th ed. Baltimore, MD: Johns Hopkins University Press, 2011.

For more than thirty years, this book has been central to the lives of family members and friends caring for a loved one afflicted by any kind of dementia or severe memory loss. The most current information, especially research advances, is incorporated into this newest edition.

11.72 Robinson, Anne, Beth Spencer, and Laurie White. *Understanding Difficult Behaviors: Some Practical Suggestions for Coping with Alzheimer's Disease and Related Illnesses.* Ypsilanti, MI: Eastern Michigan University, 2007.

This helpful book lists common behaviors exhibited by people with dementia (including hallucinations, wandering, repetitive actions, agitation, and problems with activities of daily living) and then provides strategies for coping with the behaviors. Causes for the behaviors are also listed, so that, if possible, these can be removed from the patient's environment. Tips for communication with the patient are also included. (See also 11.122.)

PARKINSON'S DISEASE AND OTHER MOVEMENT DISORDERS

11.73 Weiner, William J., Lisa M. Shulman, and Anthony E. Lang. *Parkinson's Disease: A Complete Guide for Patients and Families.* 2nd ed. Baltimore, MD: The Johns Hopkins University Press, 2006.

Although this book needs to be updated, it is still a useful manual for patients and families, especially if it is supplemented with referral to key websites like We Move (http://www.wemove.org/), the National Parkinson Foundation (http://www.parkinson.org/), and the National Institute for Neurological Disease and Stroke, or NINDS (http://www.ninds.nih.gov/). The Michael J. Fox Foundation for Parkinson's Research sponsors the Fox Trial Finder to encourage patient participation in clinical trials and to help patients find trials available in their area.

CANCERS

11.74 *Gale Encyclopedia of Cancer* (see 11.19).

11.75 DeVita, Vincent T., Theodore S. Lawrence, and Steven A. Rosenberg, eds. *Cancer: Principles and Practice of Oncology.* Philadelphia: Lippincott Williams and Wilkins, 2011.

The core medical textbook in its field, this is an essential reference for researching cancer questions.

Many other excellent books have been written regarding specific types of cancer, especially common ones like lung, breast, and prostate cancer. Today the first stop is one of the websites outlined below and specific guides or patient narratives of the cancer experience.

11.76 Thiboldeaux, Kim, and Mitch Golant. *Reclaiming Your Life After Diagnosis: The Cancer Support Community Handbook.* With a foreword by Mehmet C. Oz. Dallas, TX: BenBella Books, 2012.

In 2009, the two most prominent providers of cancer-support care in the United States, The Wellness Community and Gilda's Club Worldwide, merged to form the Cancer Support Community, or CSC. Both in-person and online support is provided through these centers throughout the cancer journey, from diagnosis to survivorship. This handbook provides excellent advice and resources for all psychosocial aspects of cancer as well as matters such as clinical trials. The program and recommendations are based on a 2007 Institute of Medicine report, *Cancer Care for the Whole Patient: Meeting Psychosocial Health Needs.*[29]

11.77   Cancer.gov: Cancer Information. Bethesda, MD: National Cancer Institute. Available: http://cancer.gov/cancertopics.

Cancer.gov contains comprehensive cancer treatment information from the National Cancer Institute. The site covers all aspects of cancer and should be a first stop for information about this disease. It also links out to other sources of information. Treatment documents are updated whenever new information is available.

11.78   Cancer.net. Alexandria, VA: American Society of Clinical Oncology (ASCO). Available: http://www.cancer.net/.

Cancer.net is more consumer friendly than Cancer.gov, with pleasing graphics, multimedia, and helpful resources for coping and survivorship. All content is overseen by practicing oncologists who subscribe to the notion, stated on the website, that "the best cancer care starts with the best cancer information. Well-informed patients are their own best advocates and invaluable partners for physicians."[30]

11.79   Cancer.org. Atlanta: American Cancer Society. Available: http://www.cancer.org/.

The American Cancer Society is one of the most respected charities in the United States. With local chapters throughout the country, this organization brings significant services to cancer patients. For example, they may provide transportation, free or reduced price lodging, wigs, and other necessities to patients undergoing treatment. Their information resources are excellent, with many available in print as well as online.

11.80   Leukemia and Lymphoma Society. White Plains, NY. Available: http://www.lls.org/.

For patients of any age fighting a blood cancer, the Leukemia and Lymphoma Society offers invaluable information and support.

11.81   American Brain Tumor Association. Chicago, IL. Available: http://abta.org/.

The American Brain Tumor Association offers excellent information and support to patients of any age and their caregivers.

DIABETES

11.82   American Diabetes Association. *American Diabetes Association Complete Guide to Diabetes*. Alexandria, VA: American Diabetes Association, 2011.

Clearly written and well organized, this book is an essential reference because of the prevalence of Type II diabetes. Type I diabetes is covered as well. Visit the association's website (http://www.diabetes.org/) or an online bookstore to view the many other resources available. Cookbooks, sources for carbohydrate counting, and many other materials are available. This organization produces outstanding resources for patients.

11.83   Levin, Marvin E., and Michael A. Pfeifer, eds. *Uncomplicated Guide to Diabetes Complications*. 3rd ed. Alexandria, VA: American Diabetes Association, 2009.

This resource, also available from the American Diabetes Association, is an essential reference that will answer many consumer questions about peripheral neuropathy, hypoglycemia, and much more that can affect the health and quality of life of diabetic patients.

For the best video resources for diabetes, visit Milner-Fenwick (http://www.milner -fenwick.com/). Since 1994, patient educators at this company have been developing video-based education with the American Association of Diabetes Educators. The products are brief, well presented, and accurate to a fault. More than thirty titles are available in various formats.

CAREGIVING

Three general categories of resources on caregiving are important to include in any collection: care of the caregiver; "how-to" materials to help nonprofessional caregivers, e.g., how to help patients safely transfer from bed to wheelchair, infection control procedures in the home, medication safety, etc.; and dying at home. Many resources exist on these topics; caregiving is a crowded field. With the aging population growing so rapidly, both the number and the need for resources will expand. Some of the best resources in each category follow.

Care of the caregiver. Many nonprofit organizations (such as the Alzheimer's Association) that deal with specific diseases or categories of diseases have sections of websites or print materials devoted to caregivers. MedlinePlus offers a general page about caregivers as well as specific pages for Alzheimer's caregiving, elder care, and others. The Family Caregiver Alliance and the Caregiver Action Network may also be helpful; check their websites.

11.84   Carter, Rosalynn, and Susan Golant. *Helping Yourself Help Others: A Book for Caregivers*. New York: Three Rivers Press, 1995.

Although this work by Rosalynn Carter and Susan Golant is almost twenty years old, the information contained in it is timeless. They remind readers of the four kinds of people in the world: those who have been caregivers, are currently caregivers, who will be caregivers, or who will need caregivers.[31]

11.85   Abramson, Alexis, and Mary Anne Dunkin. *The Caregiver's Survival Handbook (Revised): Caring for Your Aging Parents without Losing Yourself.* New York: Perigee Trade, 2011.

Although this book speaks to parent care and female caregivers, there is good material for all sorts of care provided by individuals of both genders included.

11.86   Kane, Robert L., MD. *The Good Caregiver: A One-of-a-Kind Compassionate Resource for Anyone Caring for an Aging Loved One.* New York: Avery Trade, 2011.

This book includes a section on self-care for caregivers but much more besides, including advocacy.

"HOW-TO" GUIDES FOR NONPROFESSIONAL CAREGIVERS

11.87   Karpinski, Marion. *Quick Tips for Caregivers.* 2nd ed. Clackamas, OR: Medifecta Healthcare Training, 2000.

Comprehensive work covers details of basic nursing care that family caregivers must learn in order to provide safe in-home care for a loved one. The book accompanies an extensive series of DVDs, including fall prevention, body mechanics and back safety, transfers, personal care, nutrition, infection control, and more.

11.88   Meyer, Maria M., and Paula Derr, RN. *The Comfort of Home: A Complete Guide for Caregivers.* San Francisco: CareTrust Publications, 2007.

Comprehensive guide to most aspects of providing safe care for patients in the home environment, including discussions of challenges caregivers will face and financial issues.

11.89   Capossela, Cappy, Sheila Warnock, and Sukie Miller. *Share the Care: How to Organize a Group to Care for Someone Who Is Seriously Ill.* Revised and updated ed. New York: Touchstone, 2004.

This is a useful resource for caregivers of patients at any age. For example, parents with an injured child may face months of performing movement exercises to help the child regain mobility. Or, a cancer patient may need transportation, meals, and household help that are too extensive for one person to provide. This book offers a means of avoiding caregiver burnout through the construction of an "alternate family" to assist with care.

11.90   Goldberg, Stan. *Leaning into Sharp Points: Practical Guidance and Nurturing Support for Caregivers*. New York: New World Library, 2012.

Stan Goldberg uses the counterintuitive idea of embracing the "sharp point," or fear, of providing care for a loved one who is very ill or dying rather than avoiding it. This metaphor informs the useful advice imparted to readers throughout.

END OF LIFE

11.91   Sankar, Andrea. *Dying at Home: A Family Guide for Caregiving*. Rev. ed. Baltimore, MD: Johns Hopkins University Press, 1999.

For nonprofessional caregivers who have never experienced the dying process, this book is a must. It clearly explains the signs of impending death and compassionately addresses the needs of the family and caregiver.

11.92   Kübler-Ross, Elisabeth. *On Death and Dying*. New York: Scribner, 1997.

First published in 1969, this classic work should be included in any collection that addresses the issue of caregiving. Kübler-Ross addresses the fear of death, attitudes toward dying and death, and the famous stages that she first articulated: denial, anger, bargaining, depression, and acceptance.

11.93   Boerstler, Richard W., and Hulen S. Kornfeld. *Life to Death: Harmonizing the Transition: A Holistic and Meditative Approach for Caregivers and the Dying*. Rochester, VT: Healing Arts Press, 1995.

This work provides comfort and coping strategies for caregivers and families and offers instruction in comeditation that can help ease the suffering of the dying patient.

MENTAL HEALTH AND BEHAVIOR

11.94   *The Gale Encyclopedia of Mental Health* (see 11.20).

11.95   *DSM-5: Diagnostic and Statistical Manual of Mental Disorders*. 5th ed. Washington, DC: American Psychiatric Association, 2013.

This is an essential reference for any biomedical collection. Family members, friends, and caregivers of individuals diagnosed with a mental illness will find this resource very helpful, since it lists the diagnostic criteria for all recognized mental disorders. The previous edition was *DSM-IV-TR: Diagnostic and Statistical Manual of Mental Disorders, Fourth Edition, Text Revision,* published in 2000. *DSM-5* includes a great deal of new material and diagnostic criteria for various conditions.

Look also for current works on specific disorders, especially depression, bipolar disorder, schizophrenia, eating disorders, and self-mutilation.

SKIN, HAIR, AND NAILS

11.96   Wolff, Klaus, Thomas Fitzpatrick, Richard A. Johnson, and Richard Suurmond. *Fitzpatrick's Color Atlas and Synopsis of Clinical Dermatology: Common and Serious Diseases.* 7th ed. New York: McGraw-Hill Professional, 2013.

The table of contents and excellent index make this reference easy to use. Brief articles include an illustration of the disorder, with textual content organized by description, epidemiology, pathogenesis, history, physical examination, differential diagnosis, laboratory tests, diagnosis, prognosis, and management.

11.97   Baumann, Leslie. *Cosmetic Dermatology: Principles and Practice.* 2nd ed. New York: McGraw-Hill Professional, 2009.

Although this is a textbook, it offers a comprehensive reference source for questions many consumers have regarding topics such as chemical peels, dermal fillers, and laser therapy, among many others.

11.98   Bouillon, Claude, and John Wilkinson. *The Science of Hair Care.* New York: Informa/Taylor and Francis, 2006.

While written for dermatologists, this book is a good one to have for patients with disorders affecting their hair or for anyone who simply wants to know whether one shampoo is as good as any other. Included is a chapter that discusses occupational disorders in hairdressers.

SKIN CANCERS

11.99   Lacouture, Mario E. *Dr. Lacouture's Skin Care Guide for People Living with Cancer.* Foreword by Cornelia Dean and Steven T. Rosen. Cold Spring Harbor, NY: Harborside Press, 2012.

This is an expert guide for patients undergoing cancer treatment and experiencing side effects that affect their skin, hair, or nails. It includes practical suggestions for avoiding or coping with the effects of treatment-related toxicities.

11.100   American Cancer Society. *QuickFACTS: Basal and Squamous Cell Skin Cancer: What You Need to Know—NOW.* Atlanta: American Cancer Society, 2012.

This consumer health book provides key information about the most common of all cancers in the United States, as well as associated but rarer maladies like actinic keratosis and Merkel cell carcinoma. All risk factors are clearly explained. A volume in the same QuickFACTS series is available for melanoma and most other types of cancer.

11.101   Wang, Steven Q. *Beating Melanoma: A Five-Step Survival Guide.* Baltimore, MD: Johns Hopkins University Press, 2011.

This book offers excellent information for patients who want to understand their diagnosis of melanoma or people who want to avoid this most deadly of skin cancers.

WELLNESS

11.102   MedlinePlus, "Health and Wellness." Available: http://www.nlm.nih.gov/medlineplus/healthtopics.html.

11.103   Familydoctor.org. Health Information for the Whole Family: Healthy Living and Smart Patient Guide. Available: http://familydoctor.org/online/famdocen/home/healthy.html and http://familydoctor.org/online/famdocen/home/pat-advocacy.html.

The American Academy of Family Physicians (AAFP) has compiled a lengthy list of their Web publications for individuals to maintain the healthiest life possible and to use the health system effectively.

11.104   Roizen, Michael F., and Mehmet C. Oz. *YOU: The Owner's Manual: An Insider's Guide to the Body That Will Make You Healthier and Younger.* New York: HarperCollins, 2005.

11.105   Roizen, Michael F., and Mehmet C. Oz. *YOU: The Smart Patient: An Insider's Guide for Getting the Best Treatment.* New York: Free Press, 2006.

Roizen and Oz have written a series of books since 1999 based on a concept they call "real age." The information they provide represents sound research and common sense. (See also the note at 11.38.)

Category 5: Demographic Groups

CHILD AND TEEN HEALTH

11.106   HealthyChildren.org—From the American Academy of Pediatrics [some Spanish]. (See also 11.33.) Available: http://www.healthychildren.org/.

Health information for ages 0–21 is available at this comprehensive site.

11.107   Omnigraphics Teen Health Series. (See also 11.37.) Available: http://omnigraphics.com/category_view.php?ID=46.

11.108   MedlinePlus, "Toddler Health." Available: http://www.nlm.nih.gov/medlineplus/toddlerhealth.html.

MedlinePlus offers separate pages on toddler development, nutrition, and toilet training.

11.109   MedlinePlus, "Children's Health." Available: http://www.nlm.nih.gov/
medlineplus/childrenshealth.html.

MedlinePlus offers a page just for children as well as separate sites on child mental health, development, behavior disorders, and much more.

11.110   MedlinePlus, "Teen Health." Available: http://www.nlm.nih.gov/
medlineplus/teenhealth.html.

MedlinePlus also offers a page just for teens as well as separate sites on teen sexual health, mental health, development, and more.

11.111   Familydoctor.org, "Kids." Available: http://familydoctor.org/familydoctor/
en/kids.html.

The American Academy of Family Physicians (AAFP) has compiled articles relating to children's health, including behavior, nutrition and exercise, and home safety. Tabs on this website lead to similar pages for pregnancy and newborns, teens, and seniors.

11.112   American Academy of Child and Adolescent Psychiatry. Available:
http://www.aacap.org/.

At one time the AACAP published books on emotional, behavioral, and cognitive development for both children and teens. That information is now on their website.

SENIORS' HEALTH

11.113   *Merck Manual of Health and Aging* (see 11.30).

11.114   MedlinePlus, "Seniors' Health." Available: http://www.nlm.nih.gov/
medlineplus/seniorshealth.html.

11.115   Familydoctor.org: Health Information for the Whole Family, "Seniors."
Available: http://familydoctor.org/familydoctor/en/seniors.html.

The American Academy of Family Physicians (AAFP) has compiled a lengthy list of their Web publications for seniors on this page. Items as diverse as urinary incontinence, memory loss, driving skills, as well as much more, are covered here. A special section, "Managing Your Healthcare," offers information on health-care reform, health insurance, and more.

11.116   Terra Nova Films. Available: http://terranova.org/.

Terra Nova Films is the only company anywhere devoted solely to the production and distribution of films, videos, and other educational material concerning the aging process. Many of the films have won awards. Their products include every

relevant aspect of aging, dementia, family caregiving, societal attitudes, staff training, and end-of-life issues.

MEN'S HEALTH

11.117   MedlinePlus, "Men's Health." http://www.nlm.nih.gov/
medlineplus/men.html.

Hundreds of books are available that focus on various aspects of men's health.
Fitness is a popular topic among this population, so building a small collection of
excellent titles in this area is a good idea. So are works in any format that focus on
African American, Latino, and other groups of men, since they have very specific
health issues.

WOMEN'S HEALTH

11.118   MedlinePlus, "Women's Health." Available: http://www.nlm.nih.gov/
medlineplus/women.html.

11.119   Boston Women's Health Book Collective and Judy Norsigian. *Our Bodies,
Ourselves*. New York: Touchstone, 2011.

In 1973, *Our Bodies, Ourselves: A Book by and for Women* appeared. Women had
never before seen such a work devoted just to them and their health. In the ensuing
decades the work has been updated several times. Several other books have been published by this group as well. For a complete list of titles and to learn more about the
organization and its work, visit their website at http://www.ourbodiesourselves.org/.

As is true with men's health, many hundreds of books exist that address all
aspects of women's health, from adolescence through the child-bearing years through
old age.

INDIVIDUALS WITH DISABILITIES

11.120   *Encyclopedia of Disability* (see 11.27).

11.121   MedlinePlus, "Disabilities" and "Developmental Disabilities." Available:
http://www.nlm.nih.gov/medlineplus/disabilities.html and http://www.nlm
.nih.gov/medlineplus/developmentaldisabilities.html.

Much progress continues to be made in the area of all disabilities, from hearing
loss to prosthetics. Disability ethics is currently an area of great interest as well. The
Donnelley Ethics Program at the Rehabilitation Institute of Chicago (http://www
.ric.org/resources/ethics/) is a renowned center for studying these issues, as is the
Institute on Disability and Rehabilitation Ethics at the University of Iowa (http://
www2.education.uiowa.edu/services/idare/).

Category 6: Patient Narratives

A very important area for any consumer health collection is patient narratives. With the explosion of memoir publishing in the past twenty years, thousands of titles exist, ranging along all points of a continuum from poor to excellent. Following are a few that have become classics.

11.122   Bayley, John. *Elegy for Iris.* New York: Picador, 1999.

Iris Murdoch routinely appears on lists of "100 greatest" authors of the twentieth century. Trained in both classics and philosophy, she remains best known for her novels, of which she wrote more than twenty-five. She was stricken with Alzheimer's disease at age seventy-five. This memoir, written by her husband, John Bayley, chronicles her descent as a result of this disease and his struggle to care for her.

11.123   Harpham, Wendy S. *When a Parent Has Cancer: A Guide to Caring for Your Children.* New York: HarperCollins, 1997.

A physician who was stricken with cancer, Wendy Harpham has written several books designed for patients to help them cope with their diagnosis and treatment. This title includes a children's book, *Becky and the Worry Cup.*

11.124   Havemann, Joel. *A Life Shaken: My Encounter with Parkinson's Disease.* Baltimore, MD: Johns Hopkins University Press, 2002.

An updated paperback edition, published by JHU Press in 2004, is also available.

11.125   Jamison, Kay R. *An Unquiet Mind: A Memoir of Moods and Madness.* New York: Knopf, 1995.

This is the acclaimed memoir by a woman who, despite her bipolar illness, has achieved a faculty position at a major university and a MacArthur "genius" grant.

11.126   Solomon, Andrew. *The Noonday Demon: An Atlas of Depression.* New York: Touchstone, 2001.

This work won the National Book Award in 2001.

11.127   Styron, William. *Darkness Visible: A Memoir of Madness.* New York: Random House, 1990.

One of the great American authors of the twentieth century describes in harrowing detail his periodic descents into suicidal depression.

11.128   Taylor, Jill Bolte. *My Stroke of Insight: A Brain Scientist's Personal Journey.* New York: Penguin Group, 2006.

Readings

Besides the items in the References list, the following articles provide useful insights and some historical perspective on consumer health information reference services.

Anonymous. "The Librarian's Role in the Provision of Consumer Health Information and Patient Education." *Bulletin of the Medical Library Association* 84, no. 2 (1996): 238–39.

Baker, L. M., and K. E. Pettigrew. "Theories for Practitioners: Two Frameworks for Studying Consumer Health Information-Seeking Behavior." *Bulletin of the Medical Library Association* 87, no. 4 (1999): 444–50.

Calabretta, N. "The Hospital Library as Provider of Consumer Health Information." *Medical Reference Services Quarterly* 15, no. 3 (1996): 13–22.

Calabretta, N., and S. Cavanaugh. "Education for Inpatients: Working with Nurses through the Clinical Information System." *Medical Reference Services Quarterly* 23, no. 2 (2004): 73–79.

Calabretta, N., S. Cavanaugh, M. Malone, and B. J. Swartz. "A Hospital-Based Patient and Family Education Center: If You Build It, Will They Come?" *Medical Reference Services Quarterly* 30, no. 1 (2011): 19–30.

Calvano, M., and G. Needham. "Public Empowerment through Accessible Health Information." *Bulletin of the Medical Library Association* 84, no. 2 (1996): 253–56.

Calvin, K. L., and B. T. Karsh. "A Systematic Review of Patient Acceptance of Consumer Health Information Technology." *Journal of the American Medical Informatics Association* 16, no. 4 (2009): 550–60.

Cosgrove, T. L. "Planetree Health Information Services: Public Access to the Health Information People Want." *Bulletin of the Medical Library Association* 82, no. 1 (1994): 57–63.

Fox, N., and K. Ward. "Health Identities: From Expert Patient to Resisting Consumer." *Health (London, England: 1997)* 10, no. 4 (2006): 461–79.

Goodchild, E. Y., J. A. Furman, B. L. Addison, and H. N. Umbarger. "The Chips Project: A Health Information Network to Serve the Consumer." *Bulletin of the Medical Library Association* 66, no. 4 (1978): 432–36.

Homan, J. M., and J. J. McGowan. "The Medical Library Association: Promoting New Roles for Health Information Professionals." *Journal of the Medical Library Association* 90, no. 1 (2002): 80–85.

Huber, Jeffrey T., and Mary L. Gillaspy. "Knowledge/Power Transforming the Social Landscape: The Case of the Consumer Health Information Movement." *The Library Quarterly* 81, no. 4 (2011): 405–30.

Lindner, K. L., and L. Sabbagh. "In a New Element: Medical Librarians Making Patient Education Rounds." *Journal of the Medical Library Association* 92, no. 1 (2004): 94–97.

Marill, J. L., N. Miller, and P. Kitendaugh. "The MedlinePlus Public User Interface: Studies of Design Challenges and Opportunities." *Journal of the Medical Library Association* 94, no. 1 (2006): 30–40.

Perryman, C. "*Medicus deus*: A Review of Factors Affecting Hospital Library Services to Patients between 1790–1950." *Journal of the Medical Library Association* 94, no. 3 (2006): 263–70.

Pifalo, V., S. Hollander, C. L. Henderson, P. DeSalvo, and G. P. Gill. "The Impact of Consumer Health Information Provided by Libraries: The Delaware Experience." *Bulletin of the Medical Library Association* 85, no. 1 (1997): 16–22.

Spatz, M. A. "Providing Consumer Health Information in the Rural Setting: Planetree Health Resource Center's Approach." *Bulletin of the Medical Library Association* 88, no. 4 (2000): 382–88.

Tattersall, R. L. "The Expert Patient: A New Approach to Chronic Disease Management for the Twenty-First Century." *Clinical Medicine: Journal of the Royal College of Physicians of London* 2, no. 3 (2002): 227–29.

Vega, Laurian C., Tom DeHart, and Enid Montague. "Trust between Patients and Health Websites: A Review of the Literature and Derived Outcomes from Empirical Studies." *Health and Technology* 1, no. 2–4 (2011): 71–80.

Zipperer, L. "Clinicians, Librarians and Patient Safety: Opportunities for Partnership." *Quality and Safety in Health Care* 13, no. 3 (2004): 218–22.

Zipperer, L., and J. Sykes. "The Role of Librarians in Patient Safety: Gaps and Strengths in the Current Culture." *Journal of the Medical Library Association* 92, no. 4 (2004): 498–500.

Zipperer, Lorri, Mary Gillaspy, and Roxanne Goeltz. "Facilitating Patient Centeredness through Information Work: Seeing Librarians as Guests in the Lives of Patients." *Journal of Hospital Librarianship* 5, no. 3 (2005): 1–15.

References

1. "Health 2.0." San Francisco: Health 2.0. Accessed April 9, 2013. http://www.health 2con.com/.
2. Fox, S., and M. Duggan. "Tracking for Health." Washington, DC: Pew Research Center. Last modified January 28, 2013; accessed April 9, 2013. http://www .pewinternet.org/~/media//Files/Reports/2013/PIP_TrackingforHealth%20with%20 appendix.pdf.
3. "HCAHPS Fact Sheet." Washington, DC: Agency for Healthcare Research and Quality. Last modified May 2012; accessed April 9, 2013. http://www.hcahpson line.org/files/HCAHPS%20Fact%20Sheet%20May%202012.pdf.
4. "Fact Sheet: Selected Caregiver Statistics." San Francisco: Family Caregiver Alliance. Accessed April 9, 2013. http://www.caregiver.org/caregiver/jsp/content _node.jsp?nodeid=439.

5. Huber, J. T., R. M. Shapiro II, and M. L. Gillaspy. "Top Down versus Bottom Up: The Social Construction of the Health Literacy Movement." *The Library Quarterly* 82, no. 4 (2012): 429–51.

6. Millenson, M. L. "Personalized Medicine: Finding the Patient's 'Doctor Within.'" New York: Medscape General Medicine. Last modified May 5, 2006; accessed April 9, 2013. http://www.medscape.com/viewarticle/530922.

7. Personalized Medicine Coalition. "New Report Cites Emerging Impact of Personalized Medicine on Healthcare." Washington, DC: Personalized Medicine Coalition. Last modified November 14, 2006; accessed April 9, 2013. http://www.personalizedmedicinecoalition.org/communications/press-releases/2006-11-14.

8. Personalized Medical Coalition. *The Case for Personalized Medicine.* 3rd ed. Washington, DC: Personalized Medicine Coalition, November 16, 2011. Accessed April 9, 2013. http://www.personalizedmedicinecoalition.org/sites/default/files/files/Case_for_PM_3rd_edition.pdf.

9. Collins, F. S. "Personalized Medicine: A New Approach to Staying Well." Boston: Boston Globe. Last modified July 17, 2005; accessed April 9, 2013. http://www.boston.com/news/globe/editorial_opinion/oped/articles/2005/07/17/personalized_medicine/.

10. "23andMe Launches Web-Based Service Empowering Individuals to Access and Understand Their Own Genetic Information." Mountain View, CA: 23andMe. Last modified November 19, 2007; accessed April 9, 2013. http://mediacenter.23andme.com/press-releases/23andme-launches-web-based-service-empowering-individuals-to-access-and-understand-their-own-genetic-information/.

11. "2012 Older Americans." Washington, DC: Federal Interagency Forum on Aging-Related Statistics. Accessed April 9, 2013. http://www.agingstats.gov/Main_Site/Data/2012_Documents/Population.aspx.

12. National Institute on Aging and World Health Organization. *Global Health and Aging.* Washington, DC: National Institute on Aging. Last modified March 27, 2012; accessed April 9, 2013. http://www.nia.nih.gov/research/publication/global-health-and-aging/preface.

13. Alzheimer's Association. "2013 Alzheimer's Disease Facts and Figures." *Alzheimer's and Dementia* 9, no. 2 (2013): 208–45.

14. Kutner, M., E. Greenberg, Y. Jin, and C. Paulsen. "The Health Literacy of America's Adults: Results from the 2003 National Assessment of Adult Literacy." NCES 2006-483. Washington, DC: U.S. Department of Education, National Center for Education Statistics. Last modified September 6, 2006; accessed April 9, 2013. http://nces.ed.gov/pubsearch/pubsinfo.asp?pubid=2006483.

15. Nielsen-Bohlman, L., A. M. Panzer, and D. A. Kindig, eds. "Health Literacy: A Prescription to End Confusion." Washington, DC: Institute of Medicine. Last modified April 8, 2004; accessed April 9, 2013. http://www.iom.edu/Reports/2004/Health-Literacy-A-Prescription-to-End-Confusion.aspx.

16. Kutner et al., "Health Literacy of America's Adults."

17. Baker, D. W. "The Meaning and Measure of Health Literacy." *Journal of General Internal Medicine* 21, no. 8 (2006): 878–83.
18. "Health Information Literacy." Chicago: Medical Library Association. Accessed April 9, 2013. http://www.mlanet.org/resources/healthlit/.
19. Shipman, J. P., and C. Funk. "MLA Health Information Literacy Project: Overview." Chicago: Medical Library Association. Accessed April 9, 2013. http://www.mlanet.org/resources/healthlit/hil_project_overview.html.
20. "MedlinePlus: Find a Library." Bethesda, MD: National Library of Medicine. Accessed April 9, 2013. http://www.nlm.nih.gov/medlineplus/libraries.html.
21. Fox, S. "Online Health Search 2006." Washington, DC: Pew Internet and American Life Project, October 29, 2006. Available: http://www.pewinternet.org/PPF/r/190/report_display.asp.
22. Fox, S., and M. Duggan. "Health Online 2013." Washington, DC: Pew Internet and American Life Project, January 15, 2013. http://www.pewinternet.org/Reports/2013/Health-online.aspx.
23. Ibid., 18.
24. Zickuhr, K., and M. Madden. "Older Adults and Internet Use." Washington, DC: Pew Internet and American Life Project, June 6, 2012. http://www.pewinternet.org/Reports/2012/Older-adults-and-internet-use.aspx.
25. "Consumer Health Information Specialization Program." Chicago: Medical Library Association. Accessed April 9, 2013. http://www.mlanet.org/education/chc/index.html.
26. Preidt, R. "Smartphone Apps for Skin Cancer Risk Aren't Reliable, Study Finds." Bethesda, MD: MedlinePlus. Last modified January 16, 2013; accessed April 9, 2013. http://www.nlm.nih.gov/medlineplus/news/fullstory_133138.html.
27. Baker, L. M., and C. J. Gollop. "Medical Textbooks: Can Lay People Read and Understand Them?" *Library Trends* 53, no. 2 (2005): 336–47.
28. Freudenheim, M. "More Using Electronics to Track Their Health." *New York Times.* Last modified January 27, 2013. http://www.nytimes.com/2013/01/28/health/electronic-health-tracking-increasingly-common-researchers-say.html [available online only to subscribers].
29. *Cancer Care for the Whole Patient: Meeting Psychosocial Health Needs, Consensus Report.* Washington, DC: Institute of Medicine. Last modified October 15, 2007; accessed April 9, 2013. http://www.iom.edu/Reports/2007/Cancer-Care-for-the-Whole-Patient-Meeting-Psychosocial-Health-Needs.aspx.
30. "Cancer.net." Alexandria, VA: American Society of Clinical Oncology. Accessed May 1, 2013. http://www.cancer.net/about-us.
31. Carter, Rosalynn, and Susan K. Golant. *Helping Yourself Help Others: A Book for Caregivers.* New York: Three Rivers Press, 1995, 3.

CHAPTER 12

Medical and Health Statistics

BARRIE HAYES and JENNIFER DARRAGH

As an information professional, one does not need to be a statistician or well versed in statistical methods to recommend appropriate datasets, statistical aggregators, or analytic tools to patrons. One uses the skills one has developed in conducting the tried-and-true reference interview combined with an understanding of how empirical research is conducted to determine patrons' needs. Many researchers collect their own data in order to test hypotheses (treatment outcomes, propensity for disease, health-care disparities, etc.). However, they often need secondary sources of data from national surveys, government agencies, research organizations, and other research projects to better inform (and often strengthen) their analysis. It is these secondary sources of data that this chapter will be covering.

When assisting a researcher with a "data" question, it is important to determine what type of data is needed to answer the question. A researcher looking for a distinct number—such as how many people die each year from heart disease—is looking for statistical information. Statistical information is finite information already analyzed or aggregated with no additional statistical analysis needed. It can be presented as a single number (e.g., percent) or as a group of information in a table, chart, or graph. On the other hand, a doctor investigating heart disease risk factors in women, and what effect various prevention strategies may have, may want to analyze an available national-level dataset before committing to collect her own data. In the simplest of terms, one must determine if one needs the short answer (static information) or the long answer (test various conditions to determine significance of outcome).

With increasing Web technologies, statistics that used to be found only in reference books and on webpages as static numbers/charts/tables are now being made available through statistical aggregators that allow for customized presentation of statistical information based on user-selected criteria. These statistical aggregators pull information from formatted datasets behind the Web interface (typically referred to as the "back end"). Aggregators have helped to make data more accessible and useable to a broader audience; from patient, to student, to seasoned researcher. Some of the most commonly used tools will be highlighted and reviewed later on in the chapter.

The Open Data Movement has also made a large impact on the availability of data to the general public. The U.S. government now has Data.gov, the World Bank Group has its Open Data Catalog, and Kenya is one of many countries outside the United States providing an open portal to their data (http://opendata.go.ke). One important thing to note is that while more and more troves of data are being opened, the data are not always formatted for immediate use, and some data are just not released publicly via the Web (sensitive information, geographic identifiers, etc.).

Conducting the Data-Centric Reference Interview

When a researcher is looking for statistics, he or she is typically looking for evidence to strengthen his or her case as to why more and/or different research needs to be done in a particular area. Statistics are often part of the exploration process and are reported in the literature review section of a journal article, conference poster, or as "scene-setting" information in a book chapter.

Empirical research begins with a hypothesis, based on the identification of problem. Predictions are then made as to under what conditions the problem is alleviated and/or changed. Empirical evidence collected through observed and/or measurable phenomena in the problem setting determine whether the hypothesis is supported or refuted—in other words, the prediction was correct or incorrect.[1] In the case of empirical research analyzing secondary datasets, we are primarily talking about the search for significant measureable phenomena, as no direct or indirect observations can be made firsthand. The determination of significance is based on the statistical analysis of independent (specific condition) and dependent variables (phenomena that changes based on the specific condition involved).

So, with all of that being said, previous editions of this work have outlined a logical strategy when searching for statistics and data,[2] which I have adapted as follows:

1. Determine if the researcher needs the short answer (statistics) or the long answer (datasets).

2. Identify the variables needed to answer the question. Typically the variables will fall into these categories: demographic (race, sex, age, population group), location (national, state, local, and country), time (current, historic, or longitudinal), and specific problem/condition/issue(s) (health condition, cost of health care, facilities, personnel, treatment intervention, etc.).

3. As mentioned previously, there are many sources of statistical information, and depending on the need for current data, information direct from the source may be preferable to a vendor-repackaged product. There will always be a lag between when something is released from the source until it is ingested and prepared by a vendor for release via the vendor's interface. Sometimes it is preferable to wait for the vendor because the vendor often adds value to the data (creates customized statistics, maps or provides statistical package ready-formatted data). It is important to keep in mind that large, national-level datasets can be a year or more behind because of the time it takes to clean up the data for public release.

4. When it appears that the patron's statistics query cannot be answered by any readily available statistical resources (Web or print), check the secondary literature to see if a particular study has been done that addresses the patron's question and includes statistical tables and graphs. Another option is to ask the patron if he or she is comfortable working with a full dataset—there are times where the needed statistic can still be pulled from a dataset using a spreadsheet application or statistical package.

5. When it appears that the patron's dataset query cannot be fulfilled due to data not being readily available, it might be worthwhile to consider restricted-use datasets (more detail later in the chapter) as well as combing through the secondary literature to see if a particular study has been done where the raw data has not been published, but the principal author can be contacted about data availability for secondary analysis.

As one converses with the patron throughout the reference interview, one may be able to broaden (or narrow) the query to find at least some numeric information that can help inform the patron's research. As always, with any resource found on the Internet, one needs to evaluate its authority, currency, references/citations to source material, and any potential bias. However, when it comes to sources of data and statistics, one will want to look for a few other things as well, such as clear description of methodology (of data collection or statistical construction), representativeness (what kind of sample?), and documentation (if full dataset, need variable names, labels, etc.). Statistics and data are only useful if they can be properly interpreted and/or analyzed, otherwise they are just numbers.

Changes in the Collection of Demographic Information by the U.S. Census Bureau

Anyone who conducts research on the U.S. population typically uses demographic data from the Census Bureau—primarily from the decennial census, and now from the American Community Survey. It is important to be aware of and understand the recent changes in how the Census Bureau collects data, especially if one works with public health professionals and epidemiologists utilizing a geographic information system (typically referred to as GIS—more on that following this section).

In 1940, the first probability sampling design was applied to the decennial census.[3] This allowed more detailed questions (such as veteran status, parents' birthplace, and language), to be asked of 5 percent of the population without overburdening respondents or data processors. This practice was upheld for the decennial census, allowing collection of both full and sample data (known as the long-form data), up to, and including, the 2000 Census (though methods and sample sizes did of course change over time as techniques became more sophisticated). Some may have heard about the various "summary files" that the Census Bureau used to release for the latter part of the twentieth century—summary files 1 and 2 were 100 percent count data, and summary files 3 and 4 were based on sample data from the long-form census. While the sample data allowed a richer understanding of the nation's population, it still only provided a snapshot view.

The idea of continuous measurement as an alternative to the long-form census was first proposed as early as 1990, but the need for greater understanding of sampling, survey methods, and deliverable data products delayed implementation until after the 2000 Census.[4] After more than eleven years of testing, the first nationwide American Community Survey was conducted in 2005. With the successful launch of the American Community Survey (also called the ACS), the 2010 Census was slated to be a short-form only census,[5] with only basic demographic information collected in ten questions.

An important thing to be aware of is that the sample size of the American Community Survey (1 in 40 households) is much smaller than the sample size of the population who received the census long form (1 in 6 households).[6] While the sample size is smaller, the ACS with its rolling sample design provides continual, current estimates of poverty, education, employment, and many other variables. The schedule of data release being in one-year, three-year, and five-year files makes it possible to increase the sample size over time, reducing sampling error, and providing data for smaller geographic units with each release. The first full five-year release was the 2005–2009 ACS, and now each year of collection results in a new five-year dataset.

12.1   American Fact Finder. Washington, DC: U.S. Census Bureau. Available:
http://factfinder2.census.gov/faces/nav/jsf/pages/index.xhtml.

The American Fact Finder (AFF) system is the main access point for data collected and published by the United States Census Bureau. This includes data from
the last two decennial censuses (2000 and 2010) and the American Community
Survey (ACS one-year, three-year, and five-year samples). A few important points
to note about the system are to always choose the geography level first, and then the
dataset or topic, as not all data is available at every level of geography. The AFF system is the first point of release for ACS data, and is very useful for looking up quick
demographic facts at the national, state, and local level. However, if one wishes to
download a data file from this site, please be advised that it is not optimally formatted for statistical packages or ArcGIS, each table is provided as a separate file, and a
considerable amount of editing will need to be done. There has been mention that the
AFF system is set for another redesign, but an official announcement has not been
made at the time of this writing.

Geographic Information Systems and Health

Whether it is investigating child nutrition by determining green grocery density
and accessibility within cities or tracking the transmission of cholera across India,
geographic location plays an important part in both public health and epidemiology
research. Geographic information analysis is a method of analyzing data by using
spatial visualization techniques. Using a geographic information system (GIS),
most notably ESRI's ArcGIS software, researchers are able to conduct spatial analysis and create thematic maps, 3D models, and animated maps (e.g., for tracking
spread of disease over time). Many researchers who work with a GIS collect their
own data using surveys (interviewer or respondent-reported geography) and/or portable GPS units.

In order to build a map utilizing a GIS, researchers need an authoritative base
map that they join their tabular data to using matching geographic coordinates.
The U.S. Census Bureau collects, defines, and maintains boundaries for more than
twenty-nine different geographic areas, and has set the statistical geographic standard that other government data producers follow. In order to work seamlessly
with GIS software, the Census Bureau has created and provides the Topologically
Integrated Geographic Encoding and Referencing (TIGER)/Line Shapefiles.[7] These
files can be downloaded directly from the Web based on the geographic area needed
for analysis (e.g., Baltimore City Census Tracts), unzipped and added to ArcGIS,
and then joined with the researcher's data based on a matching location code.

Geospatial analysis is typically conducted using smaller area geographies like census block groups, tracts, Zip Code Tabulation Areas (ZCTAs), and counties as opposed to states or the entire nation so that subtle trends can be identified. American Community Survey five-year data is often used as baseline demographic information, which is then combined with investigator-collected data and joined with the GIS shapefile(s). Smaller area geographies pose a challenge if the researcher wants to use existing health data for research, as data at lower-level geographies are often not released publicly because of a higher risk of deductive disclosure (more on limited datasets later in the chapter). To learn more about how a GIS and health data work together, it is worthwhile to take a look at the ESRI Press book *GIS Tutorial for Health*, Fourth Edition.[8]

Common Terminology

When conducting the reference consultation and the subsequent search, it is important to understand some of the general analytic and health statistical jargon one will encounter. At the end of this chapter is an appendix that includes many commonly appearing terms broken into two parts—the first being general analytic/statistical terms followed by health data–centric terms. As mentioned in previous editions of this work, one will come across the term *rate* quite often.[9] It is used as an expression of how often a phenomenon occurs within a specific population over a certain period of time. *Rate* is often used for births (natality), deaths (mortality), and occurrence of specific phenomena such as disease (incidence/prevalence). As Rankin and Burgess have stated previously, "[t]he use of rate rather than raw numbers is essential for the comparison of experience between populations at different times, different places, or among different classes of persons."[10] A rate is constructed as shown in figure 12.1.

In order to measure the effect of various teenage pregnancy prevention programs over the past ten years, one would want to see if the pregnancy rate has declined during this time (this is actually the case for the example in figure 12.2).[11]

FIGURE 12.1
Formula for calculating rate

Numerator = Number of Events in a Specific Period × 10 (100, 1,000, 10,000, etc.)
Denominator = Population Number during the Specific Period

The multiplier is used to determine the rate per x number of cases (10 cases, 100 cases, 1,000 cases, etc.). In the case of national-level studies, "per 1,000" is a common grouping.

> **FIGURE 12.2**
> ## Formula for calculating teen birthrate
>
> In 2010, there were 367,678 live births for females aged 15–19.* In 2010, official Census counts put the population for females aged 15–19 at 10,736,677. To determine the 2010 "teen" birthrate, construct the formula as follows:
>
> 367,678 / 10,736,677 × 1,000 (rate is per 1,000 females) = teen pregnancy rate of 34.2
>
> ---
>
> *Martin, J. A., B. E. Hamilton, S. J. Ventura, M. J. K. Osterman, E. C. Wilson, and T. J. Mathews. "Births: Final Data for 2010." *National Vital Statistics Reports* 61, no. 1 (2012). Centers for Disease Control and Prevention. http://www.cdc.gov/nchs/data/nvsr/nvsr61/nvsr61_01.pdf.

Where to Search for Health Statistics and Data

When beginning to search for statistics or datasets many options are available, both free and subscription-based. As one learns to navigate these resources, one will find oneself in an "alphabet soup," as many organizations and their resultant studies/datasets are referred to by their acronyms. In addition, empirical research articles are also a valuable source of statistical information, and, in some cases, serve as a connection point for researchers who may need access to unpublished data.

12.2   PubMed. Bethesda, MD: National Institutes of Health, National Library of Medicine, National Center for Biotechnology Information. Available: http://www.ncbi.nlm.nih.gov/pubmed.

PubMed is an essential research tool for anyone conducting medical research, be it MDs, epidemiologists, public health researchers, or geneticists. Full-text access to the majority of articles in PubMed (excluding those in PubMed Central) are facilitated by institutional subscriptions to journals and are relayed to the user using a link resolver (such as SFX). As mentioned previously, empirical research articles are a great source of very specific statistical information, and sometimes can lead to access of unpublished, raw data. Beyond PubMed, NCBI provides a set of databases, software, and downloads for genetic and chemical data. See http://www.ncbi.nlm.nih.gov/guide/data-software/.

12.3   ClinicalTrials.gov. Bethesda, MD: National Institutes of Health. Available: http://clinicaltrials.gov/ct2/home.

ClinicalTrials.gov is a registry of publicly and privately supported clinical studies of human participants all over the world. It is a valuable resource to both clinicians and public health researchers. The registry is easy to browse by primary topic, and can be refined using additional limiters. An important thing to note about data from clinical trials is that results are not always posted. Studies with results are clearly indicated in the results list as "Has Results," which can then be viewed in their own tab. In cases where studies have been completed but results have not been posted, information is given as to who served as the principal investigator (direct contact information not provided but name and location are given). In the United States it was only as of 2008 that results from clinical trials were provided (see http://clinicaltrials.gov/ct2/about-site/history). At present, results are not required to be provided for all trials, but this may change in the future.

National Health Demographics

12.4   National Center for Health Statistics. Hyattsville, MD: U.S. Department of Health and Human Services, Centers for Disease Control and Prevention, National Center for Health Statistics. Available: http://www.cdc.gov/nchs.

If one is looking for national-level health information for the United States, the best place to start is the National Center for Health Statistics (commonly referred to by its acronym, NCHS). In short, NCHS's mission is to compile statistical information for the public in order to better their own health and to guide public health policy. NCHS collects a variety of information about the nation's population through administrative records (such as birth, death, and medical records), surveys and interviews, direct physical exams, and laboratory testing. Surveys cover the health status of the population including illnesses (physical and mental), injuries, nutrition, pregnancy, immunizations, health hazards (such as obesity or smoking), and on the use of health services and facilities (with some cost and use information as well as manpower figures). NCHS provides prepared statistical information, access to some online analytic aggregation tools, and full dataset downloads. An important thing to note is that most public-use data files do not provide any detailed geography (Census region may be all that is available). In addition, some surveys are collected annually, but others only periodically. NCHS also provides additional services such as access to linked data (links NCHS surveys with datasets collected by other agencies), the National Death Index, and a Research Data Center to which researchers can apply to obtain restricted-use confidential data (which often does have greater geographic detail). Due to the large amount of data collected, there is often a lag of a year or more until a dataset is released for public-use.

12.5   Surveys and Data Collection Systems. Hyattsville, MD: U.S. Department of Health and Human Services, Centers for Disease Control and Prevention, National Center for Health Statistics. Available: http://www.cdc.gov/nchs/surveys.htm.

TABLE 12.1

Data collections for use in statistical analyses

NAME	DESCRIPTION
National Health Interview Survey (NHIS)	The principal source of information on the health of the civilian, noninstitutionalized population of the United States since 1957, this survey provides data on health status, access to and use of health services, health insurance coverage, immunizations, risk factors, and health-related behaviors.
National Health and Nutrition Examination Survey (NHANES)	This is NCHS's most in-depth data collection effort, combining personal interview, physical exams, diagnostic procedures, and laboratory testing via mobile testing sites across the country. NHANES collects information about undiagnosed and diagnosed conditions, child growth and development, diet and nutrition, weight, health risk factors, and environmental exposures.
National Health Care Surveys	These surveys involve gathering information from health-care providers and health settings based on type of care (inpatient, nursing homes, etc.). Data are collected from the establishments and their records rather than from the patients themselves. The specific surveys included are National Ambulatory Medical Care Survey (NAMCS), National Hospital Ambulatory Medical Care Survey (NHAMCS), National Survey of Ambulatory Surgery (NSAS), National Hospital Discharge Survey (NHDS), National Nursing Home Survey (NNHS), National Hospital Care Survey (NHCS), National Nursing Assistant Survey (NNAS), National Home and Hospice Care Survey (NHHCS), National Home Health Aide Survey (NHHAS), and National Survey of Residential Care Facilities (NSRCF).
National Vital Statistics System (NVSS)	The nation's official vital statistics are based on the collection and registration (at both state and local levels) of birth and death events. Full datasets are available for births, deaths, fetal death, maternal and infant health, and linked birth and infant death. Marriage and divorce statistics are provided in the *National Vital Statistics Reports*, but no longer in microdata format (suspended in 1996). The NVSS data are used to examine teenage birthrates, prenatal care and birth weights, pregnancy health risks, infant mortality, life expectancy, and leading cause of death.

(cont.)

TABLE 12.1   Data collections for use in statistical analyses (cont.)

NAME	DESCRIPTION
National Survey of Family Growth (NSFG)	This national survey collects data on family life, marriage and divorce, pregnancy, infertility, use of contraception, and men's and women's health.
National Immunization Survey (NIS)	The purpose of the NIS study is to monitor immunization coverage for children between the ages of 19 and 35 months living in the United States (at the time of the interview). The method of collection is an initial telephone survey and then a mailed survey sent to children's immunization providers.
Longitudinal Studies of Aging (LSOA)	The LSOA is a collaborative project of the National Center for Health Statistics (NCHS) and the National Institute on Aging (NIA). The study universe is adults 70 years of age and older. Its purpose is to measure changes in health, functional status, living arrangements, and health services utilization over time.

All of the data collections listed in table 12.1 are available as raw data for use in statistical analyses but also include links to published reports on the data. NCHS provides access to aggregate statistics and online analysis tools that utilize data from these surveys as well. Some of these aggregators and tools follow.

12.6   FASTSTATS A to Z. Hyattsville, MD: U.S. Department of Health and Human Services, Centers for Disease Control and Prevention, National Center for Health Statistics. Available: http://www.cdc.gov/nchs/fastats/.

FASTSTATS is an alphabetized topical list of quick links to statistical information on a wide range of health topics. This is a helpful place to start when one isn't immediately aware of a particular dataset or statistical report on a particular subject. On each of the resultant topic pages, links are provided to publications that include the statistics presented, to sources of more data for deeper analysis, and to related webpages. FASTSTATS also includes a State and Territory Data subsite with a clickable map.

12.7   Health Data Interactive. Hyattsville, MD: U.S. Department of Health and Human Services, Centers for Disease Control and Prevention, National Center for Health Statistics. Available: http://www.cdc.gov/nchs/hdi.htm.

The Health Data Interactive is an aggregating tool that facilitates building customizable tables (by age, gender, race/ethnicity, and geography) of national health statistics for infants, children, adolescents, adults, and older adults.

12.8   VitalStats. Hyattsville, MD: U.S. Department of Health and Human Services, Centers for Disease Control and Prevention, National Center for Health Statistics. Available: http://www.cdc.gov/nchs/VitalStats.htm.

VitalStats is an interactive exploration tool for vital statistics products including tables, data files, and reports. It provides both prebuilt tables and the option to delve deeper into the data using the National Vital Statistics System online analysis tool.

12.9   Health Indicators Warehouse. Hyattsville, MD: U.S. Department of Health and Human Services, Centers for Disease Control and Prevention, National Center for Health Statistics. Available: http://healthindicators.gov/.

The Health Indicators Warehouse (HIW) is a collaborative venture among various government agencies (such as the Centers for Medicare and Medicaid Services and the Health Resources and Services Administration) and offices within the Department of Health and Human Services. The purpose of this Internet-based warehouse is to provide a single point of access to authoritative health status and determinants at the national, state, and local level. Users can choose to select indicators based on topic, geography, or particular government initiative (such as Healthy People 2020). Once an area has been selected in which to search, the interactive filtering capacity makes it possible to further narrow indicator options (e.g., Health Risk Behaviors → Alcohol → Adults Binge Drinking [%]). The clickable "i" next to each indicator opens a metadata (source information) window. When the indicator link is clicked, an overview of how the indicator was constructed is provided. Next to the Overview is a Data tab. This view offers researchers an interactive table, chart, or map view (map when available). If a researcher wants more options for analytics, he or she can then use the Download tab to get the raw data in either an Excel or Comma Separated Values (CSV) file.

12.10 HealthData.gov. Washington, DC: U.S. Department of Health and Human Services. Available: http://www.healthdata.gov/.

The result of the Health Data Initiative (http://www.hhs.gov/open/initiatives/hdi/index.html), the DHHS has "liberated" its trove of data from multiple offices to provide wider access to health policy makers, innovators, and researchers. As of 2012, the site is still a work in progress with collections added and interface changes made quite often. The HealthData.gov site serves as a union catalog of government-produced health data. Metadata records provide links to where the data actually "lives," which means that once someone finds something he or she wishes to access, he or she will leave the HealthData.gov site. One of the main goals of this site is to "unleash the power of private-sector innovators and entrepreneurs to utilize HHS data to create applications, products, services and features that help improve health and health care—while also helping to create jobs of the future at the same time."[12] With that being said, the site can sometimes be a bit difficult for the average user to navigate, and not as comprehensive as needed for the seasoned researcher. As the site is still reasonably new, it is likely more enhancements will be made over time to accommodate varying levels of user skills.

State and Local Health Demographics

For local and state health statistics, often the best sources of statistical information are local and state health departments. For example, the Baltimore City Health Department (http://baltimorehealth.org/dataresearch.html) provides statistics that are especially relevant to the city's population (the growing Hispanic population and health disparities, food security, and alcohol outlet density). The Maryland Department of State and Mental Hygiene (http://dhmh.maryland.gov/SitePages/Home.aspx) provides statistical reports on public health issues that are of importance in Maryland (access to care, nutrition, and food safety). To find the local health department, a simple Web search for one's area name and health department will often yield a link. If not, one can look for one's state health department to see if it has statistics for that local area. The National Center for Health Statistics does provide some access to state-level statistics, but most public-use datasets only provide region as a geographic variable.

12.11   FASTSTATS, "State and Territorial Data." Hyattsville, MD: U.S. Department of Health and Human Services, Centers for Disease Control and Prevention, National Center for Health Statistics. Available: http://www.cdc.gov/nchs/fastats/map_page.htm.

This is a subset of the FASTSTATS site. Rather than organized alphabetically by topic, the user is presented with a clickable map of the United States (text links to states are also available). Once clicked, users are taken to the resultant state's page where links are provided to publications that include birth, death, marriages and divorces, and to sources of more data available at the state level for deeper analysis (for example, the Behavioral Risk Factor Surveillance System), and a link to the state's health department.

12.12   Behavioral Risk Factor Surveillance System. Hyattsville, MD: U.S. Department of Health and Human Services, Centers for Disease Control and Prevention, National Center for Health Statistics. Available: http://www.cdc.gov/brfss/.

The Behavioral Risk Factor Surveillance System (BRFSS) collects information on health risk behaviors, preventive health practices, and health care related to chronic disease and injury. Data are collected monthly in all fifty states, Washington,

DC, Puerto Rico, the U.S. Virgin Islands, and Guam, with more than 350,000 adults interviewed each year. BRFSS data are used to establish and track health objectives and legislation, identify emerging health problems, and develop and evaluate public health policies and programs. In some states, the BRFSS is the only source of timely and accurate health-based data.

12.13   Kaiser State Health Facts. Menlo Park, CA: Henry J. Kaiser Family
         Foundation. Available: http://www.statehealthfacts.org/index.jsp.

State Health Facts provides timely, easy-to-use, freely accessible data on more than 700 health topics. The Kaiser Family Foundation is a nonprofit organization that focuses on major health-care issues in the United States as well as the role the U.S. plays in global health policy. The site can be browsed by topic category (such as health insurance or minority health) or by particular state. A state vs. nation or state vs. state comparison is also available.

Health Care Facilities

12.14   Area Resource File. Rockville, MD: U.S. Department of Health and Human
         Services, Health Resources and Services Administration, National Center for
         Health Workforce Analysis. Available: http://arf.hrsa.gov/.

The Area Resource File (ARF) provides county-level information on health facilities and health professions, measures of resource scarcity, health status, health training programs, and socioeconomic and environmental characteristics. The ARF used to only be available on CD-ROM and for an 800-dollar fee. It is now freely available for download and on CD-ROM (an ASCII text file and Access Database version are available). One can also easily search the online variable database to see if it contains the information needed for analysis.

12.15   Healthcare Cost and Utilization Project and HCUPnet. Rockville, MD:
         U.S. Department of Health and Human Services, Agency for Healthcare
         Research and Quality. Available: http://www.hcup-us.ahrq.gov/ and
         http://hcupnet.ahrq.gov/.

The Healthcare Cost and Utilization Project (HCUP) is a suite of health-care datasets that bring together the data collection efforts of state organizations, hospital associations, private data organizations and the federal government to create a national longitudinal information resource of patient-level health-care data. These data facilitate research on health policy issues, including cost and quality of health services, medical practice patterns, access to health-care programs, and outcomes of treatments at the national, state, and local levels. HCUP databases (which are available as formatted text datasets) include the Nationwide Inpatient Sample (NIS), the Kids' Inpatient Database (KID), the Nationwide Emergency Department Sample (NEDS), the State Inpatient Databases (SID), the State Ambulatory Surgery Databases (SASD), and the State Emergency Department Databases (SEDD). Full datasets may be applied for, but the researcher will likely have to do that himself or herself as a formal data use agreement with signatures and project purpose is required. In addition, there is an associated cost for the data depending on what the researcher needs. HCUPnet is the freely available, online HCUP database query system which presents customizable data tables from the HCUP databases. Please note some information may be suppressed if the cell counts are too small.

12.16   AHA Data/Healthcare DataViewer. Chicago: American Hospital Association (AHA). Available for purchase: http://www.ahadataviewer.com/.

The American Hospital Association's Healthcare DataViewer offers one-stop access to AHA's proprietary information from the AHA Annual Survey of Hospitals, IT Supplement Survey, and AHA membership data. This is a subscription-based or pay-as-you-go resource. There are some limited free queries, but the full benefit of access to this resource is in its paid services.

12.17   AHA Hospital Statistics. Chicago: American Hospital Association (AHA). Available for purchase: http://www.ahadataviewer.com/book-cd-products/ AHA-Statistics/.

An essential for most medical library reference collections since 1946, the annual AHA Hospital Statistics publication (with supplemental data tables on CD) provides hospital trends on utilization, personnel, and finances for U.S. community hospitals. Trend data are provided at the national level, U.S. Census division, by state and hospital bed count brackets.

Health Care Utilization and Costs

All of the resources numbered 12.14–12.17 are also useful resources when looking for health-care costs and health-care utilization. Here are a few additional resources that can also be consulted when looking for this information.

12.18   Medical Expenditure Panel Survey. Rockville, MD: U.S. Department of Health and Human Services, Agency for Healthcare Research and Quality. Available: http://meps.ahrq.gov/mepsweb/.

The Medical Expenditure Panel Survey (MEPS) surveys households, their medical providers, and employers across the United States. It is the most complete source of data on the cost and use of health care and health insurance coverage. The survey also includes information on employment, health conditions, long-term care, and other specific medical service use events. Full dataset download capabilities are available for multiple years (ASCII text data with STATA, SAS, and SPSS programming statements) and customized tables can be created through an online tool, MEPSNet. Static tables are also available for quick look-up information.

12.19   Medicare Current Beneficiary Survey (MCBS), "Data Tables." Baltimore, MD: Centers for Medicare and Medicaid Services. Available: http://www .cms.gov/Research-Statistics-Data-and-Systems/Research/MCBS/ Data-Tables.html.

The Medicare Current Beneficiary Survey (MCBS) is a continuous survey of a nationally representative sample of the Medicare population collected by the Centers for Medicare and Medicaid Services. The survey collects information on expenditures and sources of payment for all services used by Medicare beneficiaries, including co-payments, deductibles, and noncovered services. It is also used to determine all types of health insurance coverage and match coverage to sources of payment. The MCBS is also used to track processes over time, such as changes in health status, "spending down" to Medicaid eligibility, and the impacts of program changes, as well as satisfaction with and source of care. The MCBS raw data files are limited use, and must be applied for in order to obtain the data. However, aggregate statistics in the form of data tables from the MCBS are freely accessible online for download and use in research (e.g., 2010 Characteristics and Perceptions of the Medicare Population).

12.20   "Health Insurance." Washington, DC: U.S. Census Bureau. Available: http://www.census.gov/hhes/www/hlthins/.

The U.S. Census Bureau collects information on health insurance via three different surveys: the Current Population Survey's Annual Social and Economic Supplement (CPS ASEC), the American Community Survey (ACS), and the Survey of Income and Program Participation (SIPP). The surveys differ in sample, geography, length, and content. Depending on what is needed, one survey may be more appropriate than another if the researcher wants to work with raw data. The Health Insurance webpage on the Census Bureau site acts as a gateway to all three surveys, and also as a hub for the collection of reports and tables related to health insurance coverage and expenditures for the U.S. population.

Health Care Workforce

12.21   National Center for Health Workforce Analysis. Rockville, MD: U.S. Department of Health and Human Services, Health Resources and Services Administration, Bureau of Health Professions. Available: http://bhpr.hrsa.gov/healthworkforce/index.html.

The primary goal of the National Center for Health Workforce Analysis is "to become the leading source of comprehensive health workforce data to inform public policies and private sector investments in the workforce arena." HRSA is attempting to meet this goal by focusing on several priority areas: Expanding and Improving the Health Workforce Data, Health Workforce Data Compilation and Dissemination, Improved Health Workforce Projections, Collaboration with States, International Health Workforce, and Health Workforce Research and Collaboration. The center's website links to three data sources: the Area Resource File (mentioned earlier as 12.14 under Health Facilities), which has a wealth of information on health professions and health professions training at the county level; a Health Workforce Statistics interactive map, which provides a visual representation of the number of health professionals across all fifty states (data comes from the Bureau of Labor Statistics Occupational Employment Statistics Survey [OES]); and the Health Resources County Comparison Tool, which allows researchers to compare health status indicators and health resources across counties (or county equivalents). The Center also publishes reports that contain findings from various health workforce surveys (such as the National Sample Survey of Registered Nurses).

12.22   Health Workforce Information Center. Rockville, MD: U.S. Department of Health and Human Services, Health Resources and Services Administration, Bureau of Health Professions, National Center for Health Workforce Analysis. Available: http://www.hwic.org/.

The Health Workforce Information Center (HWIC) provides a "one-stop shop" for the latest information on health professions. The site includes a multitude of resources that can be used for teaching, training, and research including audio/video, directories, exams, and (of course) statistics. The best way to navigate and find statistics by specific profession is to use the Resources tab, select the profession of interest, and then narrow further (using the Narrow Results by) Topic → Research and Data Collection Methods. To browse resources by state, click on the States tab, select the state of interest, and look for the Workforce Statistics and Data Sources section on the resultant state page.

12.23   *Physician Characteristics and Distribution in the U.S.* Chicago: American Medical Association (AMA), 1963– . Annual. Available for purchase from the AMA Bookstore: https://catalog.ama-assn.org/Catalog/.

This book contains current and historical data on more than 1 million physicians in the United States. The latest edition (2013) includes the new category of group and physician positions data by size, specialty, and state; as well as data on physician trends, characteristics, and distribution, analyses of professional activity, primary care specialties, and data on more than 67,000 osteopathic physicians. It is published annually and is available in both print and e-book format.

12.24   National Sample Survey of Registered Nurses. Rockville, MD:
U.S. Department of Health and Human Services, Health Resources and
Services Administration. Available: http://datawarehouse.hrsa.gov/
nursingsurvey.aspx.

The National Sample Survey of Registered Nurses (NSSRN) has been conducted every four years since 1977. There are two types of data files that are provided
for public use—state-based and county-based. The data collected include nursing
education (initial and post-licensure), employment setting, job title, hours worked,
level of care, patient population, clinical specialty, earnings, employment intentions
(whether currently working in the nursing profession), employment outside nursing,
job satisfaction, reasons for changing jobs, and general respondent demographics.
Downloadable datasets for every year the survey has been given are available via the
link above (HRSA Data Warehouse). The latest reports based on the data are accessible through the National Center for Health Workforce Analysis (http://bhpr.hrsa.
gov/healthworkforce/) under "Reports by Discipline."

12.25   Occupational Employment Statistics (OES) Survey, "May 2012
Occupational Profiles." Washington, DC: Bureau of Labor Statistics,
Division of Occupational Employment Statistics. Available:
http://www.bls.gov/oes/current/oes_stru.htm.

The Occupational Employment Statistics (OES) Survey collects employment
and wage estimates for more than 800 occupations. Estimates are provided for the
number of people employed in certain occupations, and the wages paid to them. Self-
employed persons are not included. Employment estimates are available at national
and state levels, and also for metropolitan and nonmetropolitan areas. Data are presented for professions by Standard Occupational Classification (SOC) Code, which
are presented in hierarchy (for example, 29-0000 is for all Healthcare Practitioners
and Technical Operations; 29-1062 is for all Family and General Practitioners).

Health Education Statistics

12.26   *AAMC Data Book: Medical Schools and Teaching Hospitals by the
Numbers.* Washington, DC: Association of American Medical Colleges,
2013. Annual. Available for purchase: https://www.aamc.org/data/
databook/.

The Association of American Medical Colleges (AAMC) annually publishes
a compilation of statistics on medical education programs at accredited medical
schools and teaching hospitals. The statistics in this book are gathered from member
schools and also from government and educational sources. The *AMC Data Book*
is available as both a print publication and by online subscription (advantage for

subscribing online is that information is updated as it becomes available over the course of the year). The book covers twelve main topics: accredited medical schools; medical school applicants and students; medical school faculty; medical school revenue; graduate medical education; tuition, aid, and debt; teaching hospitals; healthcare financing; research expenditures; physicians; faculty compensation; and general/historical price indexes. Information provided about medical students includes mean admissions test scores, enrollment demographics, geographic location choices upon graduation, and choice of specialization. For faculty, information on status (full-time, part-time, and volunteer) and distribution across academic department are included. In addition to the book, the AAMC provides access to some of its most frequently requested data via FACTS tables online: https://www.aamc.org/data/facts/.

12.27 Health Workforce Information Center. Grand Forks, ND: U.S. Department of Health and Human Services, Health Resources and Services Administration, Bureau of Health Professions (funders), Center for Rural Health at the University of North Dakota School of Medicine and Health Sciences (site developers). Available: http://www.hwic.org/.

The Health Workforce Information Center (HWIC) is a clearinghouse for information related to health professions. It covers a multitude of topics with a set of associated resources, organizations, funding, events, and news including practical learning tools, research and data collection methods, and trends and emerging issues. Education and training is a selectable topic area, and its library contents may be browsed by state, profession, or by common topics. By selecting "trends and emerging issues" as a common topic, one is presented with current reports such as Diversity in Medical Education: Facts and Figures 2012, and A Snapshot of the New and Developing Medical Schools in the U.S. and Canada.

12.28 *Medical Education Issue, JAMA: Journal of the American Medical Association.* Chicago: American Medical Association. Published annually (though not in 2012), typically in September. Available via subscription: http://www.jama.com/.

Prior to 2012 (Medical Education Issue not published at the time of review), this issue was normally released sometime in September. It provides a view into the state of medical education in the United States and the issues/experiences of students over the course of the previous year (or two). At the end of the journal issue is an appendix that includes extensive statistical tables on U.S. Medical Schools (enrollment, full-time faculty numbers, discipline, and academic rank of faculty) and Graduate Medical Education (resident demographics, residents by specialty, completions).

International Statistics

International health statistics and data can be found through a variety of online resources. Perhaps the most prominent source is the World Health Organization (WHO), followed closely by the World Bank. Many individual countries also have their own ministries of health or public health offices as well as statistical/data bureaus. What can make working with international statistics very challenging is the unavailability of longitudinal data, unavailability of data for geographies below country level, and the inconsistency of data across countries for comparative analysis.

12.29 Global Health Observatory (GHO) Data Repository. Geneva: World Health Organization. Available: http://apps.who.int/gho/data/?theme=main.

The GHO Data Repository provides access to more than fifty datasets on high-priority health topics including mortality and burden of diseases, the Millennium Development Goals (child nutrition, child health, maternal and reproductive health, immunization, HIV/AIDS, tuberculosis, malaria, neglected diseases, water, and sanitation), noncommunicable diseases and risk factors, epidemic-prone diseases, health systems, environmental health, violence and injuries, and social determinants of health care (equity). The GHO also provides electronic access to WHO's annual World Health Statistics report. Users may select data using the faceted menu on the left side of the page or by using the search feature. Data are presented as interactive statistical tables (which allow for filtering) and can then be downloaded as Excel tables or comma-separated values files (.csv) which can be loaded into any spreadsheet or statistical software package. The former WHO Statistical Information System (WHOSIS) has been absorbed into the GHO in order to provide both more data, and more analytic options.

12.30 World Bank Data. Washington, DC: World Bank Group. Available: http://data.worldbank.org/.

In 2010, the World Bank joined the Open Data movement by removing pay walls and fully opening its trove of data for public access. The World Bank collects and distributes (most notably) the World Development Indicators (WDI), Global Development Finance, and the Africa Development Indicators. The website provides a gateway to World Bank data via the Databank (a Web aggregating tool) and full dataset downloads (when possible) in Excel and XML format. Users may opt to view a full Data Catalog (indicated as such), or browse by country, topic, particular WDI indicator, or microdata availability (analyzable data from surveys). Health topics include adolescent fertility rates, birthrates, malnutrition, life expectancy at birth, malaria incidences, sanitation, and health expenditures. The Databank feature is a guided aggregation tool that allows users to choose the database, countries they wish to view data for, analyzable data topics and time frame. If one selects a topic or country first on the website and then chooses to use the Databank, some choices will already be selected automatically. In the next iteration of the Databank (currently in Beta), users will be able to create a personal login in order to save and export both reports and data.

12.31   Regional Health Observatory. Washington, DC: Pan American Health Organization, World Health Organization. Available: http://new.paho.org/ hq/index.php?option=com_content&view=category&layout=blog&id =2395&Itemid=2396&lang=en.

The Pan American Health Organization (PAHO) is an arm of the World Health Organization that has been working for the past 110 years to improve health and living standards across the countries of the Americas. Like the WHO's Global Health Observatory, the PAHO has a Regional Health Observatory that serves as a gateway to databases, statistics, and reports on countries spanning the Americas. Statistics for countries include information such as general population demographics, mortality, immunizations, physician ratio, socioeconomics, and health risk factors. The primary report generated by this agency is the *Health Situation in the Americas: Basic Indicators* (annual), and it is available in full text online as a downloadable PDF. Databases such as Summary of Reported Deaths by Demographic Variables provide access to interactive tables where filters for summary years, country, and gender can be applied. The Regional Health Observatory is not quite as technologically developed as the Global Health Observatory (hence the long URL), but it will likely improve in the future.

12.32   Demographic and Health Surveys (DHS). Calverton, MD: MEASURE DHS. Available: http://www.measuredhs.com/.

The Monitoring and Evaluation to Assess and Use Results (MEASURE) Demographic and Health Surveys project has provided technical assistance on the deployment of more than 260 surveys in more than ninety countries thereby advancing the global understanding of health and population trends in developing countries. MEASURE DHS is renowned for collecting and disseminating accurate, nationally representative data on fertility, family planning, maternal and child health, gender, HIV/AIDS, malaria, and nutrition. There are multiple standardized surveys across all participating countries, which collect primarily quantitative, but also qualitative data. Geospatial data is also included in more than 100 DHS surveys across forty-five countries and can be downloaded on request. DHS datasets are fairly complex, and do require adequate analytic experience in order to successfully work with the data. However, there is a statistical aggregating tool called the STATcompiler, which creates customized tables from a large pool of demographic and health indicators across more than seventy countries. In addition to tables, users can also create charts, scatter plots, line graphs, and thematic maps to visualize statistics.

12.33   UNdata. New York: United Nations Statistics Division. Available:
        http://data.un.org/.

UNdata is an online gateway to all United Nations databases and select statistical databases from an extensive list of partner agencies—UNESCO, WHO, ILO, IMF (the full list can be viewed here: http://data.un.org/Partners.aspx). Users may search for data on a particular topic or browse by topic area. Statistical profiles are provided for member countries (small link to the right of the country name), but even more helpful are the links provided to member country data services offices. Quite often researchers will want statistical information for smaller areas within countries such as provinces, municipalities, villages, etc., and this information is often only available (if available at all) from the data service within the country. In order to use the customized table features, click on the View Data option. Users are able to filter data by country or year, and specify sort order. When it is appropriate for the table, a pivot table option is available. Tables can be downloaded as comma-, tab-, or pipe-delimited text files that can then be imported into spreadsheet or statistical software.

Subscription Databases

The availability of statistical information and data through various subscription resources is a huge benefit to users who are affiliated with medical, research, and academic libraries. Some databases do have a bit of a learning curve, but once mastered, become essential reference and analytic tools. In addition, some subscription tools make it far easier to work with data than it would be to download the same data from the original source.

12.34   LexisNexis Statistical Insight and Statistical Datasets. Los Angeles:
        LexisNexis. Subscription information: http://www.lexisnexis.com/en-us/
        products/statistical-datasets.page; http://cisupa.proquest.com/ws_display
        .asp?filter=Statistical%20Datasets%20Overview.

LexisNexis Statistical has long been used by libraries as an index to statistical publications and tables from government agencies all over the world. In its latest interface (which works best via Internet Explorer), they have added the ability for users to begin typing a search and have suggested subject terms appear below the search box and a massive set of optional filters once a result set has been returned. Therefore, the most efficient way to search is to start small with a primary topic and then refine results using the filters. The types of results include an abstract, PDF document, published tables (GIF file), and even Excel spreadsheets. When an item is abstract only, it is often because it is an older document. Full citation information is given, however, which makes it possible to check one's library catalog or WorldCat to determine availability.

LexisNexis Statistical Datasets is a newer product, having come online in the past ten years. It was recently sold to ProQuest (and, in early 2013 a new vendor, Data-Planet, is also going to be providing access to this resource, see http://home page.data-planet.com/data-planet-statistical-datasets). It provides a way to create aggregate data tables from a variety of sources both public and private. With regard to health data, there are multiple categories such as allergies, asthma, blood pressure, physical activity, cause of death, and health insurance coverage. As an example, for asthma, one can build an aggregate table and chart out asthma attacks in the past twelve months by year (data is released in three-year intervals from 2000–2009 thus far), by specific age groups or all ages (age-adjusted or crude rates), by race/ethnicity, and by gender. One can then download that table as a PDF or Excel file. One can also export full references into RefWorks (citation management tool) or download an XML file. While much of these data do come from publicly available sources, the value-added features of centralized location, level of coverage, and sophistication of aggregation may make it worthwhile for purchase in one's library.

12.35   Social Explorer. New York: Oxford University Press. Subscription information: http://www.oup.com/online/us/socialexplorer/?view=usa.

Social Explorer is a very useful online tool for downloading data from the decennial census of the United States (from the very first census to the present) and the American Community Survey in formats friendly for use in both statistical and geospatial analysis. When American FactFinder, the Census Bureau's primary data extraction and aggregation tool was redesigned, the download capabilities unfortunately did not recover to their previous level, resulting in a lot of extra work to make files useable—especially large files with lower-level geographies and multiple tables. As census data is so important for baseline population demographics, Social Explorer became the primary tool that many data and GIS librarians opted to purchase and use to download well-formatted data. In addition to well-formatted data, users are easily able to create thematic maps at varying levels of census geography for various census surveys (including the earliest censuses).

12.36   SimplyMap. New York: Geographic Research. Subscription information: http://geographicresearch.com/simplymap/.

SimplyMap provides a way for researchers who do not have access to GIS desktop software to create thematic maps on thousands of variables including demographics, market segments, consumer expenditures, and public health (primarily from sample data). In addition to maps, users can also create tabular reports comparing multiple variables across locations, or make a ranking table based on a particular variable by location. A few important things to note about SimplyMap are (1) the mapping, while vivid and easily exportable, is only available for one variable at a time, and (2) while the data provided are available at lower levels of geography than would be from the source (for example, the government-collected Consumer Expenditure Survey), users need to be aware that these are still estimated projections. SimplyMap is able to provide data at lower levels of geography due to their relationship with a company called EASI (Easy Analytic Software Inc.) which has developed a sophisticated, proprietary model to make projections and estimates at those lower levels. SimplyMap's primary benefits are that GIS software is not needed to create very rich maps, and that greater location granularity is offered. A particular example of health-specific research made possible by this resource is the ability to investigate economic and racial health disparities and the relationship between the two (e.g., look at all census tracts in Baltimore City, add household health-care spending average [descending order], average household income by race [e.g., black] and percent black population). For more sophisticated tables such as these, users are able to export the table as a .dbf file to conduct deeper spatial analysis using GIS software.

12.37   Inter-University Consortium for Political and Social Research (ICPSR). Ann Arbor, MI: University of Michigan, Institute for Social Research. Membership information: http://www.icpsr.umich.edu/icpsrweb/content/membership/index.html.

ICPSR is a membership-based consortium of more than 700 academic institutions and research organizations. It is a long-standing (est. 1962) leader in facilitating access to research data through its primary and partner data archives/collections. In addition, ICPSR provides intensive statistical and data curation training via the annual ICPSR Summer Program (see http://www.icpsr.umich.edu/icpsrweb/sumprog/), and encourages the use of social science data across the undergraduate curriculum.

The ICPSR archive collection currently has more than 500,000 research files. Of particular interest to medical and public health researchers are the AHRQ Multiple Chronic Conditions Research Network Data Archive (MCC), Center for Population Research in LGBT Health, Health and Medical Care Archive (HMCA), Collaborative Psychiatric Epidemiology Surveys (CPES), Integrated Fertility Survey Series (IFSS), National Addiction and HIV Data Archive Program (NAHDAP), National Archive for Computerized Data on Aging (NACDA), and the Substance Abuse and Mental Health Data Archive (SAMHDA). The majority of the data files provided via ICPSR are available as SAS, SPSS, and Stata data files, as well as ASCII text with statistical set-up files (again for SAS, SPSS, and Stata). In addition, ICPSR also provides online analytic capabilities using the SDA (Survey and Documentation Analysis) program developed by researchers and technologists at the University of California, Berkeley. SDA offers more sophisticated online analysis than many online tools due to its ability to perform specific statistical operations (cross-tabs, correlations) as well as providing subsetting capabilities (very useful for large, national-level datasets).

Health Sciences Library Statistics

In order to effectively secure funding and programmatic support, academic, hospital, and specialized health libraries need to provide both qualitative and quantitative evidence of both successes and gaps to stakeholders.[13] Comparative data across institutions are especially useful in this regard as they provide a perspective on performance among peers. There are many ways to collect data within one's own library—gate counts, circulation statistics, instruction requests, reference transactions, collection dollars, and via patron satisfaction surveys. This section contains references to sources of health library statistics as well as some materials to consult in order to develop an assessment program.

12.38   *Annual Statistics of Medical School Libraries in the United States and Canada.* Seattle: Association of Academic Health Sciences Libraries. Available for purchase: http://www.aahsl.org/annual-statistics.

This publication is put together by the Association of Academic Health Sciences Libraries (AAHSL). Member libraries are able to access the Annual Statistics through the Member Center on the AAHSL Website. Nonmember libraries are able to purchase the statistics for 500 dollars. The Annual Statistics provide comparative data on medical school library collections, expenditures, personnel, and services. Every five years information is provided on space allocations and reporting structure. This compendium of statistics has proven to be a valuable benchmarking tool to medical school administrators and medical library directors.

12.39   *Academic Health Sciences Library Statistics.* Washington, DC: Association of Research Libraries. Available: http://www.arl.org/stats/annualsurveys/med/index.shtml.

The Association of Research Libraries also collects and provides statistics on member institutions that have dedicated Academic Health Science Libraries. Published annually (though there is a lag in release time), these statistics are also comparative, and include data on collections, expenditures, staff, and user services. Access to this title is provided in electronic format through the ARL Website. Statistical reports from year 2004–2005 and earlier are freely accessible. From 2005–2006 up to the latest available year (2009–2010 at the time of this writing), access is only available through a paid subscription to the ARL Statistics Collection or a one-time purchase of electronic download.

12.40   "Benchmarking and Library Standards." Chicago: Medical Library Association (MLA). Available: http://www.mlanet.org/resources/index.html#bench.

Professional associations offer valuable networking, advocacy, and educational opportunities for librarians of all types. The Medical Library Association is the association supporting medical librarians in hospitals, medical schools, and other specialized health library settings. On their website, MLA provides a link to their latest Health Science Library Statistics and Benchmarking Interactive Reports. Participants in the survey are able to access the reports for free; MLA members and nonmembers must pay a fee in order to obtain a copy (MLA Members do get a discount). The MLA Benchmarking Network is also a valuable source for comparative assessment. Attending conferences in person whenever possible is also essential for building knowledge about the current landscape of the field.

Statistical Software and Analytic Training Resources

Many librarians who become tasked with assisting patrons on data queries wonder if they should dive into a statistical methods course in order to learn statistical software and analysis methods. If one has a personal interest in learning, it certainly does not hurt to do so. However, I have found that it is not necessary to become a statistics guru even as a full-time data librarian. What's most important is to understand empirical research methods, what patrons truly need (the short answer or long answer), and what some common statistical operations and terms mean (see the appendix at the end of this chapter). To develop skills in these areas, librarians have several options; audit a research methods course or basic biostatistics class, read empirical research articles that are on a topic of interest, and/or consult any number of books and online tutorials. If one's library subscribes, Safari Books Online (http://www.safaribooksonline.com/) is a great resource for the ins and outs of statistical software as well as other computer programs.

The current front-runner statistical tools in biostatistics courses are Stata (http://www.stata.com/), a commercial product, and R (http://www.r-project.org/), an open source product. R is gaining popularity due to its extensibility (infinite potential as syntax is user-defined), cost (it is free), and its ability to create publication-ready tables and charts. Stata is not all that different than other programs such as SAS or SPSS (which are still used, and if familiar with either of these, one can likely adapt). With regard to capabilities across different statistical software platforms, the true difference is in the syntax—none are the same across platforms. The flavor of software that a researcher uses is usually due to their level of comfort with the syntax and the program's interface (or graduate student's comfort level/skill as many have research assistants).

The ability to troubleshoot reading data into a statistical package with existing syntax (often called "canned" as it comes with the data) is a very useful skill to learn—essentially understanding where file paths originate, where output goes, and what type of punctuation is needed in order to make the program run smoothly. Another useful skill is developing some comfort with text data (comma-, tab- or pipe-delimited), recognizing what format it is in (if not clearly stated), and how to import it into different packages. A lot of datasets are still made available as Excel spreadsheets and Access databases, but files from either can be exported into formats compatible with more sophisticated statistical applications. Finally, if one anticipates working with multiple data formats, a statistical software package called StatTransfer (http://www.stattransfer.com/) is an essential tool for converting files from one format into another without having to work with the original files' native software (legacy program versions do sometimes cause problems).

Limited or Restricted-Use Data

Data derived from personally identifiable health information (PIH) necessary for medical and public health research is subject to the *Standards for Privacy of Individually Identifiable Health Information* (in short, known as the Privacy Rule) under the Health Insurance Portability and Accountability Act of 1996 (HIPAA) and the HIPAA Security Rule before it can ever be released for research purposes.[14] HIPAA and the Privacy Rule can be somewhat complicated to understand in full, but for the purposes of this section, how it affects researchers in the form of limited data sets and data use agreements will be discussed.

A limited data set excludes certain direct/unique identifiers (names, addresses, phone numbers, social security, etc.),[15] but may include geographic information (level may vary) and other nonunique characteristics. A limited data set is released for research under a data use agreement between data provider, the researcher, the researcher's employer, and supplemental research team members. Elements of a typical data use agreement application include a specific research proposal, a data protection plan (computing and physical security clearly outlined), and a binding legal agreement requiring an institutional signature from the researcher's employer and from the researcher. The agreement typically stipulates that the data will be used solely for the purposes outlined in the proposal and by only those named in the agreement; that the team will not attempt to directly or indirectly disclose subjects' identities; will disclose any violations of the agreement; and will adhere to all safeguards described in the data protection plan. There may be additional stipulations in the agreement, such as how data should be rounded when presented in table cell counts, or that all publications must be reviewed by the data provider prior to being submitted for publication.

Beyond PIH and limited datasets, some survey data may also be considered restricted use due to an elevated risk of deductive disclosure. This means that while indirect identifiers are not present in the data, there may be enough unique characteristics such as low-level geography, detailed racial categories, single years of age, or specific income, which, when combined, could result in the possibility of a respondent being identified.

Some important things to be aware of when a researcher approaches you about the possibility of accessing restricted-use data is that he or she typically already must have a PhD/MD (students need faculty guidance and backing); a department or unit head is not an acceptable institutional signer (it must be someone who has authority to sign for the entire university); data and computers cannot be moved from one location to another without approval (and laptops are often not permissible); and researchers are not allowed to take the data with them when they change institutions. Restricted-use data support is a very specialized service, and is not offered by many libraries.

Data Sharing and Data Management

The practice of sharing data among colleagues to allow new research has long been a common practice in educational settings and across certain disciplines. However, this has been more informal and a "common good" type of activity rather than a requirement for being allowed to do the research. The National Institutes of Health do have a formal Data Sharing Policy (http://grants.nih.gov/grants/policy/data _sharing/) which has been in place since 2003. In essence, the NIH promotes the idea of providing access to data from all research funded by NIH whenever possible, but a data-sharing plan is only required of grant applications asking for more than $500,000 in direct costs per year or if stipulated in the funding opportunity announcement.

As of January 2011, the National Science Foundation (NSF) began requiring that all NSF grant applications include a two-page data management plan.[16] Requiring data management plans of all applications was a bold move made by the agency in favor of the open data movement. Many universities have responded by adding new data management librarian positions and some (such as my home institution, Johns Hopkins) have added a new support unit to assist faculty and research scientists in developing data management plans and formal archiving and preservation of data from NSF-funded projects.

As of February 2013, the United States Office of Science and Technology Policy (OSTP) released an official memorandum on expanding access to results from all federally funded research (both publications and data).[17] As a health sciences librarian, it will be important to watch how NIH's existing data-sharing policy evolves, and to determine how one and one's library can assist researchers in preparing data management plans for health-related data.

Genetic and Other Microbiology Data Sources

Data sources on health behaviors and conditions can be found in multiple locations, but the most authoritative source when assisting a patron who requires data for genetic or other human microbiology research is the National Center for Biotechnology Information (NCBI) within the National Library of Medicine (NLM).

12.41　National Center for Biotechnology Information (NCBI). Bethesda, MD: National Institutes of Health, National Library of Medicine. Available: http://www.ncbi.nlm.nih.gov/.

Within NCBI, researchers are able to mine for data using specialized software such as The Basic Local Alignment Search Tool (BLAST). BLAST allows researchers to look for similarities in nucleotide or protein sequences and determine if there is any statistical significance (i.e., is there an evolutionary relationship between sequences). NCBI also provides tools for three-dimensional structure analysis of genetic sequences. In addition to the software provided, NCBI also provides access to Entrez, which is a linked database retrieval system. The type of information that can be pulled from Entrez includes a wide array of genetic information for a number of organisms in addition to human.

12.42　DRYAD. Raleigh, NC: National Evolutionary Synthesis Center, University of North Carolina Metadata Research Center, and additional partners. Available: http://www.datadryad.org/pages/members. Site built and maintained by North Carolina State University. Available: http://datadryad.org/.

Dryad's mission is "to promote the availability of data underlying findings in scientific literature for research and educational reuse." With partner journals, publishers, and scientific society backing, Dryad has become a robust archive of data in the basic and applied biosciences that did not otherwise have a discipline archive home. Dryad is being included as a trusted repository in the upcoming Data Citation Index (a Thomson Reuters product—http://wokinfo.com/products_tools/multidisciplinary/dci/) and NCBI is a partner repository. The types of data researchers may locate and use in the repository include ecological and conservation, evolutionary, quantitative, and population genetics.

References

1. Williams, Frederick, and Peter R. Monge. *Reasoning with Statistics: How to Read Quantitative Research.* 5th ed. Belmont, CA: Thomson Wadsworth, 2001.
2. Rankin, J. A., and M. L. Burgess. "Medical and Health Statistics." In *Introduction to Reference Sources in the Health Sciences*, 5th ed., edited by Jeffrey T. Huber, Jo Ann Boorkman, and Jean C. Blackwell, 249–302. New York: Neal-Schuman, 2008.

3. Gauthier, Jason G., and U. S. Census Bureau. *Measuring America: The Decennial Censuses from 1790 to 2000*. Rev. ed. Washington, DC: U.S. Department of Commerce, Economics and Statistics Administration, U.S. Census Bureau, 2002.

4. Eggers, Frederick J., K. R. Copeland, J. H. Thompson, and U. S. Census Bureau. *A Compass for Understanding and Using American Community Survey Data: What Federal Agencies Need to Know*. Washington, DC: U.S. Government Printing Office, 2008. http://www.census.gov/acs/www/Downloads/handbooks/ACSFed.pdf.

5. McGinn, L. S., L. M. Blumerman, and D. H. Griffin. "American Community Survey: Design and Methodology, Unedited Version." Technical Paper No. 67. Washington, DC: U.S. Government Printing Office, 2006.

6. Lowe, S. "How the American Community Survey Improves Census Statistics." U.S. Census Bureau. Last modified 2010; accessed November 15, 2012. http://www.census.gov/newsroom/releases/pdf/10ACS_improve.pdf.

7. "TIGER Products." U.S. Census Bureau. Last modified 2012. http://www.census.gov/geo/maps-data/data/tiger.html.

8. Kurland, Kristen Seamens, and Wilpen L. Gorr. *GIS Tutorial for Health*. 4th ed. Redlands, CA: ESRI Press, 2012.

9. Rankin and Burgess, "Medical and Health Statistics."

10. Ibid., 256.

11. Martin, J. A., B. E. Hamilton, S. J. Ventura, M. J. K. Osterman, E. C. Wilson, and T. J. Mathews. "Births: Final Data for 2010." *National Vital Statistics Report* 61, no. 1 (2012). Centers for Disease Control and Prevention. http://www.cdc.gov/nchs/data/nvsr/nvsr61/nvsr61_01.pdf.

12. "Unleashing the Power of Data and Innovation to Improve Health." HealthData.gov. Accessed February 25, 2014. http://www.healthdata.gov/unleashing-power-data-and-innovation-improve-health.

13. Rankin and Burgess, "Medical and Health Statistics."

14. "Understanding Health Information Privacy." U.S. Department of Health and Human Services. Accessed December 13, 2012. http://www.hhs.gov/ocr/privacy/hipaa/understanding/index.html.

15. "HIPAA Privacy Rule and Its Impacts on Research: Limited Data Set and Data Use Agreement." National Institutes of Health. Accessed December 13, 2012. http://privacy uleandresearch.nih.gov/pr_08.asp#8d.

16. "NSF Data Management Plan Requirements." National Science Foundation Directorate for Engineering. Accessed December 13, 2012. http://www.nsf.gov/eng/general/dmp.jsp.

17. "Expanding Public Access to the Results of Federally Funded Research." Office of Science Technology and Technology Policy. Last modified 2013. http://www.whitehouse.gov/blog/2013/02/22/expanding-public-access-results-federally-funded-research.

Appendix

The terms listed in table 12.2 are largely from the previous edition of this book (see reference 2). Newly added terms are indicated with an asterisk.

TABLE 12.2

Common general statistical and health statistical terms

GENERAL	
Cases*	Also known as the "N" or "n." This is the number of subjects in a study or in a subset of that study. An individual subject record is referred to as a single case.
Civilian, Noninstitutionalized Population	Civilian noninstitutionalized population is the civilian population not residing in institutions. Institutions include correctional institutions, detention homes, and training schools for juvenile delinquents; homes for the aged and dependent (e.g., nursing homes and convalescent homes); homes for dependent and neglected children; homes and schools for the mentally or physically handicapped; homes for unwed mothers; psychiatric, tuberculosis, and chronic disease hospitals; and residential treatment centers.
Cohort*	All study subjects share a commonality—be it a particular event, circumstance, health condition, age, location, etc. Often a set time period is also included. For example, all babies born in California in May 2010 could be considered a birth cohort.
Cohort Study	A cohort study is a longitudinal study of the same group of people over time. See Cohort definition.
Cross Tabulation*	Commonly called crosstabs, this fairly simple statistical technique is used to determine the number of cases per variable(s). It is used often during exploratory analysis to determine if a study sample has adequate data available for more sophisticated significance testing.
Demography/ Demographics	A demographer studies entire population groups—typically with respect to births, marriages, deaths, employment, migration, and health.
Descriptive Statistics*	Also simply referred to as descriptives, these include means, medians, standard deviation, frequencies, ranges, and some simple scatter plots. Different statistical packages offer various statistics as descriptives, but the above are the most commonly included.

Ethnic Group	An ethnic group is a designation of a population subgroup having a common cultural heritage, as distinguished by customs, characteristics, language, and common history.
*Exploratory Analysis**	During exploratory analysis, a researcher runs some simple descriptive statistics and preliminary crosstabs to determine if a secondary dataset would be useful for his analysis.
*Frequencies**	A grouping of the data where the number of cases is given per potential condition or response. Often also presented with a percentage, where *x*% of the total *N* responded or fit in to that particular condition.
*Geography Level**	The level of geography is especially important for studies using geospatial analysis (see pp. 305–306 for more detail). The levels of geography for the United States are set by the U.S. Census Bureau. The most common units are nation, region, state, MSA or CSA, County, Place, Census Tract, and Block Group. Depending on the country, international official geographic units for statistical analysis can be more difficult to discern, and even more difficult to obtain.
*Machine Readable Data/Formatted Data**	Any data that is provided in digital format. Typically one wants data that is not only machine readable, but also formatted in some way so that it can be read by a spreadsheet program (such as Microsoft's Excel) or a statistical software program (such as Stata). One can tell how a file is formatted either by the file extension (.csv is a comma-separated values file, .sav is an SPSS data file) or by opening the text file and looking for spaces (tab-delimited) or | symbol (pipe-delimited). Conducting a Web search of a file extension will also often tell one what the file is if one hasn't encountered it before.
*Margin of Error and Confidence Intervals**	Margin of error is often something one hears presented by news media, but the Census Bureau also reports it with American Community Survey (ACS) data.[a] When one pulls a random sample from a population, it is not an exact mirror to the population drawn from (see Sampling Error, p. 333). Because data producers want to be as accurate as possible, they set a limit to how often they are "wrong." They do this by determining the confidence interval.[b] Typically, a 95% confidence interval is used, but some calculate based on 99%, and some use 90% (Census Bureau uses 90). The confidence interval involves finding the upper and lower

GENERAL (cont.)	
Margin of Error and Confidence Intervals* (cont.)	boundaries of where sample means could fall. A margin of error range can then be determined using the CI, and reported as a +/- (the Census provides detailed information on how they derive the margin of error for ACS estimates).
Meta-analysis	Meta-analysis refers to the analysis of analyses, that is, the statistical analysis of a large collection of analysis results from individual studies for the purpose of integrating the findings.
Metadata*	Metadata is information about a dataset or collection. It can be thought of in similar terms to a bibliographic record. Metadata can be either descriptive (e.g., title, producer, variable names) or structural (e.g., a defined XML schema).
Over Sample	An over sample procedure is designed to give a demographic or geographic population a larger portion of the representation in the sample than the population's proportion of representation in the overall population.
Race	In 1977, the Office of Management and Budget issued standards for ethnicity/race for federal government statistics and administrative reporting in order to promote comparability of data among federal data systems. The 1977 standards called for the federal government's data systems to classify individuals into the following four racial groups: American Indian or Alaska Native, Asian or Pacific Islander, black, and white. Depending on the data source, the classification by race was based on self-classification or on observation by an interviewer or other person filling out the questionnaire. In 1997, new standards were announced for classification of individuals by race within the federal government's data systems. The 1997 standards have five racial groups: American Indian or Alaska Native, Asian, black or African American, Native Hawaiian or other Pacific Islander, and white. These five categories are the minimum set for data on race for federal statistics. The 1997 standards also offer an opportunity for respondents to select more than one of the five groups, leading to many possible multiple race categories. As with the single race groups, data for the multiple race groups are to be reported when estimates meet agency requirements for reliability and confidentiality. The 1997 standards allow for observer or proxy identification of race but clearly state a preference for self-

	classification. The federal government considers race and Hispanic origin to be two separate and distinct concepts. Thus, Hispanics may be of any race. Federal data systems were required to comply with the 1997 standards by 2003.
Sampling Error*	Sampling error is the calculated estimate of how often random sample characteristics deviate from population characteristics.[c]
Statistical Significance*	When something is statistically significant, this means that the calculated statistics from the data support the research hypothesis. There are multiple tests that can be used to determine significance depending on the data and the research question.
Study Sample (not to be confused with biospecimen)*	Nearly all social science surveys use a sample of the population rather than surveying the entire population (really not feasible). There are multiple methods of sampling. The most well-known and used is the random sample; in short, everyone in a given population has an equal chance of being selected as a research subject.
Subset/Variable Subset*	A subset is a smaller cut of a larger research dataset. Subsets are often created when a researcher is working with a large national dataset with tens of thousands of cases. A subset can be created by selecting specific variables of interest or for subjects only meeting specific criteria.
Universe*	The universe is the population that is being studied. For example, the National Health Interview Survey universe is the civilian, noninstitutionalized population of the fifty states and the District of Columbia.[d]
Value Label*	Like variable labels, value labels provide context for coded values. This is also something that requires someone to write the code to include the labels in a statistical package. An example would be where only 1 or 2 appears in the data field; the variable view in IBM's SPSS says 1 = male, 2 = female.
Variable Label*	A variable label is a descriptive label for a variable in a study. This is something that most statistical programs make possible—researchers and statistical programmers write code in order to better describe the data when they are working as most statistical programs only allow variable names to be a certain length. So a variable that is MAR124C could actually be labeled "How often have you used marijuana in the past year?"

HEALTH SPECIFIC	
Acute Condition	An acute condition is a type of illness or injury that ordinarily lasts less than three months, was first noticed less than three months before the reference data of the interview, and was serious enough to have had an impact on behavior. Pregnancy is also considered to be an acute condition despite lasting longer than three months.
Age-Adjusted Death Rates	Age-adjusted death rates are calculated using age-specific death rates per 100,000 population rounded to one decimal place. Adjustment is based on 11 age groups: under 1 year, 1–4 years, 5–14 years, 15–24 years, 25–34 years, 35–44 years, 45–54 years, 55–64 years, 65–74 years, 75–84 years, and 85 years and over. The exceptions to these groupings are: (1) the age-adjusted death rates for black males and black females in 1950 are based on nine age groups, with "under 1 year" and 1–4 years of age combined as one group, and 75–84 years and "85 years of age and over" combined as one group; (2) the age-adjusted death rates by educational attainment for the age group 25–64 years are based on four 10–year age groups (25–34 years, 35–44 years, 45–54 years, and 55–64 years); and (3) the age-adjusted rates for "years of potential life lost" (YPPL) before age 75 years are based on eight age groups: under 1 year, 1–14 years, 15–24 years, and 10-year age groups through 65–74 years.
*Age-Adjusted Rates**	The New York State Health Department provides a wonderfully succinct explanation; "[a]ge-adjustment is a statistical process applied to rates of disease, death, injuries or other health outcomes which allows communities with different age structures to be compared."[e] Age adjustment is important because different diseases and health outcomes occur at varying levels of frequency among different aged populations.
*Bioindicator**	Bioindicators are self-reported health conditions, for example, if someone reports in a national survey that he or she has asthma.
*Biomarker**	Biomarkers are data that are obtained through laboratory results such as blood glucose levels, thyroid function, etc.
*Biomeasure**	Biomeasures are measureable phenomena such as height, weight, BMI, or blood pressure.

Biometry	Biometry is statistics applied to the living world. Statistical methods are applied to the study of numerical data based on biological observations and phenomena. It includes demography, epidemiology, and clinical trials.
Birthrate/Natality Rate	Birthrate is the number of births occurring in a stated population during a stated period of time, usually a year. The rate may be restricted to births to women of specific age, race, marital status, or geographic location (specific rate) or it may be related to the entire population (crude rate). It is calculated by dividing the number of live births in a population in a year by the mid-year resident population.
Birthweight	Birthweight is the first weight of the newborn obtained after birth. • Low birthweight is defined as less than 2,500 grams or 5 pounds 8 ounces. • Very low birthweight is defined as less than 1,500 grams or 3 pounds 4 ounces.* --- *Before 1979, low birthweight was defined as 2,500 grams or less and very low birthweight 1,500 grams or less.
Cause-of-Death	Cause-of-death is also known as multiple-cause-of-death. For the purpose of national mortality statistics, every death is attributed to one underlying condition, based on information reported on the death certificate and using the international rules for selecting the underlying cause-of-death from the conditions stated on the death certificate. The World Health Organization defines underlying cause of death as the disease or injury that initiated the train of events leading directly to the death or the circumstances of the accident or violence that produced the fatal injury. Generally, more medical information is reported on death certificates than is directly reflected in the underlying cause of death. The conditions that are not selected as underlying cause of death constitute the non-underlying cause-of-death.
Cause-of-Death Ranking	Cause-of-death ranking is when selected causes-of-death, which are determined to be of public health and medical importance, are tabulated and ranked according to the number of deaths assigned to these causes. The top-ranking causes determine the leading causes of death.

HEALTH SPECIFIC (cont.)	
Chronic Condition	A chronic condition refers to any condition lasting longer than three months or more or to a condition classified as chronic regardless of its time of onset (for example, diabetes, heart conditions, emphysema, and arthritis).
Chronic Disease	A chronic disease is a disease that has one or more of the following characteristics: • Is permanent; • Leaves residual disability; • Is caused by nonreversible pathological alteration; • Requires special training of the patient for rehabilitation; or • May be expected to require a long period of supervision, observation, or care.
Clinical Trial	A clinical trial is a research activity that involves the administration of a test regimen to humans to evaluate its efficacy and safety. The term is subject to wide variation in usage, from the first use in humans without any control treatment to a rigorously designed and executed experiment involving test and control treatments and randomization. Several phases of clinical trials are distinguished: • Phase I trial—The first introduction of a candidate vaccine or a drug into a human population to determine its safety and mode of action. • Phase II trial—Initial trial to examine efficacy usually in 200 to 500 volunteers. Usually, but not always, participants are randomly allocated to study and control groups. • Phase III trial—Complete assessment of safety and efficacy. It involves larger numbers, perhaps thousands of volunteers, usually with random allocation to study and control groups, and may be a multi-center trial. • Phase IV trial—Includes research to explore a specific pharmacological effect, to establish the incidence of adverse reactions, or to determine the effects of long-term use. Ethical review is required for Phase IV clinical trials.
Communicable Disease	Communicable disease is a disease that can be communicated by an infectious agent or its products from an infected person, animal, or reservoir to a susceptible host.

Comparability Ratios	Comparability ratios measure the effect of changes in classification and coding rules. About every 10–20 years the International Classification of Diseases (WHO, 1992) is revised to stay abreast with advances in medical science and changes in medical terminology. Each of these revisions produces breaks in the continuity of cause-of-death statistics. Discontinuities across revisions are due to changes in classification and rules for selecting underlying cause of death. Classification and rule changes impact cause-of-death trend data by shifting deaths away from some cause-of-death categories and into others.
Death Rate/Mortality Rate	The number of deaths occurring in a population during a given period, usually a year, as a proportion of the number in the population. Usually the mortality rate includes deaths from all causes and is expressed as deaths per 1,000. Death rate and mortality rate are used interchangeably.
Disability	Disability is the general term that refers to any long- or short-term reduction of a person's activity as a result of an acute or chronic condition.
Disease Classification	The *International Classification of Diseases (ICD)* (WHO, 1992) provides the ground rules for disease classification. The *ICD* is developed collaboratively through the World Health Organization and ten international centers (one of which is housed at the U.S. National Center for Health Statistics in Hyattsville, Maryland). The purpose of the *ICD* is to promote the international comparability in the collection, classification, processing, and presentation of health statistics. Since the beginning of the century, the *ICD* has been modified about once every ten years, except for the twenty-year interval between *ICD-9* and *ICD-10*.
Epidemic	An epidemic is the occurrence of an illness, specific health-related behavior, or other health-related event(s) that is prevalent and rapidly spreading among many individuals in a community or region at the same time and clearly in excess of normal expectancy.
Epidemiology	Epidemiology is the branch of medicine that investigates all the elements contributing to the occurrence or nonoccurrence of a disease, specific health-related behavior, or other health-related events in a population, and the application of this study to the control of health problems.

Fertility Rate	Fertility rate is the total number of live births, regardless of age of mother, per 1,000 women of reproductive age, 15–44 years.
Health Facilities	Collectively, all buildings and facilities used in the provision of health services.
Health Resources	Health resources are the resources (human, monetary, or material) used in producing health care and services.
Health Statistics	Health statistics are the aggregated data describing and enumerating attributes, events, behaviors, services, resources, outcomes, or costs related to health, disease, and health services. The data may be derived from survey instruments, medical records, administrative documents, or a combination thereof. Vital statistics are a subset of health statistics.
Health Status	Health status is a measure of the nature and extent of disease, disability, discomfort, attitudes, and knowledge concerning health and of the perceived need for health care.
Health Workforce	Health workforce (also called health manpower) is the collective of all men and women working in the provision of health services whether as individual practitioners or as employees of health institutions and programs, whether or not professionally trained, and whether or not subject to public regulation. Facilities and manpower are the principal health resources used in producing health services.
Hispanic Origin	Hispanic origin includes persons of Mexican, Puerto Rican, Cuban, Central, and South American and other unknown Latin American or Spanish origins. Persons of Hispanic origin can be of any race (see Race, p. 332, for more information).
Hospice Care	Hospice care as defined by the National Home and Hospice Care Survey is a program of palliative and supportive care services providing physical, psychological, social, and spiritual care for dying persons, their families, and other loved ones. Hospice services are available at home and in-patient settings.
Incidence	Incidence is the number of cases of disease having their onset during a prescribed period of time. It is often expressed as a rate (e.g., the incidence of measles per 1,000 children 5–15 years of age during a specified year). Incidence is a measure of morbidity or other events that occur within a specified period of time.

Incidence Rate	Incidence rate is a rate expressing the number of new events or new cases of a disease in a defined population at risk, within a specified period of time. It is usually expressed as cases per 1,000 or 100,000 per annum.
Incubation Period	The incubation period is the time interval between invasion by an infectious agent and appearance of the first sign or symptom of the disease in question.
Instrumental Activities of Daily Living	Instrumental activities of daily living (IADL) are activities related to independent living and include preparing meals, managing money, shopping for groceries or personal items, performing light or heavy housework, and using a telephone.
Leading Health Indicators	The Leading Health Indicators are used to measure the health of the nation in ten-year intervals. The current Leading Health Indicators can be found on the Healthy People 2020 Website—http://www.healthypeople.gov/2020/LHI/default.aspx. The Leading Health Indicators were selected on the basis of their ability to motivate action, the availability of data to measure progress, and their importance as public health issues.
Life Expectancy	Life expectancy is the average number of years of life remaining to a person at a particular age and is based on a given set of age-specific death rates, generally the mortality conditions existing in the period mentioned. Life expectancy may be determined by race, sex, or other characteristics using age-specific death rates for the population with that characteristic.
Life Table	A life table provides a comprehensive measure of the effect of mortality on life expectancy. It is composed of sets of values showing the mortality experience of a hypothetical group of infants born at the same time and subject throughout their lifetime to the age-specific mortality rates of a particular period, usually a given year.
Morbidity	Morbidity is any departure, subjective or objective, from a state of physiological or psychological well-being. In this sense, sickness, illness, and morbid condition are similarly defined and synonymous. Morbidity is usually stated in terms of incidence rate and prevalence rate.

HEALTH SPECIFIC (cont.)	
National Health Expenditures	National health expenditures estimate the amount spent for all health services and supplies and health-related research and construction activities consumed in the United States during the calendar year. Detailed estimates are available by source of expenditures (e.g., out-of-pocket payments, private health insurance, and government programs), type of expenditures (e.g., hospital care, physician services, and drugs), and are in current dollars for the year of report. Data are compiled from a variety of sources.
Notifiable Disease	A notifiable disease is one that, when diagnosed, health providers are required, usually by law, to report to state or local public health officials. Notifiable diseases are those of public interest by reason of their contagiousness, severity, or frequency.
Occupancy Rate	The American Hospital Association defines hospital occupancy rate as the average daily census divided by the average number of hospital beds during a reporting period. Average daily census is defined by the AHA as the average number of in-patients, excluding newborns, receiving care each day during a reporting period. The occupancy rate for facilities other than hospitals is calculated as the number of residents reported at the time of the interview divided by the number of beds as reported. In the CMS administrative Medicare and Medicaid Online Survey Certification and Reporting database, occupancy is the total number of residents on the day of certification inspection divided by the total number of beds on the day of certification.
Parity	Parity is defined as the total number of live births ever had by a woman.
Prevalence/ Prevalence Rate	Prevalence/prevalence rate is the number of cases of a disease, infected persons, or persons with some other attribute present during a particular interval of time, divided by the population at risk of having the attribute or disease at this point in time or midway through the period.
Randomized Control Trial	A randomized control trial is an epidemiologic experiment in which participants in a population are randomly allocated into groups, usually called study and control groups, to receive or not to receive an experimental preventative or therapeutic procedure, maneuver, or intervention.

a. Eggers, Frederick J., K. R. Copeland, J. H. Thompson, and U. S. Census Bureau. *A Compass for Understanding and Using American Community Survey Data: What Federal Agencies Need to Know.* Washington, DC: U.S. Government Printing Office, 2008. http://www.census.gov/acs/www/Downloads/handbooks/ACSFed.pdf.

b. Thornton, R. J., and J. A. Thornton. "Erring on the Margin of Error." *Southern Economic Journal* 71, no. 1 (2004): 130–35.

c. Linneman, Thomas John. *Social Statistics: The Basics and Beyond.* New York: Routledge, 2010.

d. U.S. Department of Health and Human Services, Centers for Disease Control and Prevention, National Center for Health Statistics. "National Health Interview Survey, 2009." ICPSR28721-v2. Ann Arbor, MI: Inter-university Consortium for Political and Social Research [distributor], 2010-08-26. doi:10.3886/ICPSR28721.v2.

e. "Age-Adjusted Rates—Statistics Teaching Tools." New York State Department of Health. Last modified 1999; accessed November 15, 2012. http://www.health.ny.gov/diseases/chronic/ageadj.htm.

CHAPTER 13

History Sources

LUCRETIA W. McCLURE

Updated and revised by
MICHAEL A. FLANNERY

"The library is the historian's laboratory," and in health sciences libraries, the historian may be a resident, a student, a physician, or an individual interested in a particular topic or person in the fields of medicine or science. Gnudi goes on to say the historian must have the scholarly reference works that form the "working apparatus" of this laboratory.[1]

The purpose of this chapter is to provide a sampling of the resources that hold the information necessary to the users seeking historical facts and knowledge. The earlier editions of this book included chapters on history sources by Judith A. Overmier.[2] They continue to be relevant and useful. This chapter focuses on new resources as well as those that may be found in a general collection. Many libraries in the health sciences do not have formal history of medicine departments or collections, yet users come with history-related questions. There are a surprising number of books, journals, materials in electronic format, and so forth that may be useful in answering questions of a historical nature. Librarians must develop a creative mode of thinking when searching for answers in general works.

The Nature of Questions

Many of the questions fall into these categories: biographical, bibliographical, dates and facts, and illustrations. These are the "Who was it?," "What did he do?," "When did it happen?," and "Do you have a picture of it?" questions. The Internet brings an indispensable dimension to the librarian's ability to find historical information. Once it was necessary to have the volumes at hand in order to search. Today, the library can supplement its print resources with an array of digital locations. Because the Internet changes rapidly, only a sample of websites will be provided because new URLs appear and disappear daily.

The librarian in a small medical, hospital, or special library now has more opportunity than ever to search for the answers to historical questions. When the search of print resources proves unfruitful, the Web opens doors to the homepages of libraries with spectacular history of medicine collections. These libraries often have librarians with extensive knowledge of the history of medicine who may provide assistance. History-of-medicine organizations also have websites as well as electronic discussion lists, and all may be tapped for guidance and help.

Biographical Sources

One of the most frequently asked questions is about the individual physician or scientist. Often the person asking has superficial information at best. Knowing the dates of birth or death, an institution from which the individual was graduated or taught, or a medical specialty can give the librarian a lead to an obituary or an announcement of an honor. The following are examples of resources of biographical information.

13.1   Bynum, William F., and Helen Bynum, eds. *Dictionary of Medical Biography.* Westport, CT: Greenwood Press, 2006. 5 vols.

13.2   Hafner, Arthur W., ed. *Directory of Deceased American Physicians, 1804–1929; a genealogical guide to over 149,000 medical practitioners providing brief biographical sketches drawn from the American Medical Association's Deceased Physician Masterfile.* Chicago: American Medical Association, 1993. 2 vols.

13.3   *The New York Times Obituaries Index.* New York: New York Times, 1970–1980. Vol. 1, 1858–1968; vol. 2, 1969–1978.

13.4   Magill, Frank N., ed. *The Nobel Prize Winners: Physiology or Medicine.* Pasadena, CA: Salem Press, 1991– . Vol. 1, 1901–1944; vol. 2, 1944–1969; vol. 3, 1969–1990.

13.5   *JAMA: The Journal of the American Medical Association.* Chicago: American Medical Association, 1919– . Vol. 1– .

13.6   Sammons, Vivian O. *Blacks in Science and Medicine.* New York: Hemisphere, 1990.

13.7   Bullough, Vern L., Olga M. Church, and Alice P. Stein. *American Nursing: A Biographical Dictionary.* New York: Garland, 1988–1992. 2 vols.

13.8   Scrivener, Laurie, and J. Suzanne Barnes. *A Biographical Dictionary of Women Healers: Midwives, Nurses, and Physicians.* Westport, CT: Oryx Press, 2002.

13.9   Thacher, James. *American Medical Biography.* Boston: Richardson and Lord, 1828. 2 vols. in 1. Reprint: New York: DaCapo, 1967.

13.10 Atkinson, William B. *The Physicians and Surgeons of the United States.* Philadelphia: Robson, 1878.

13.11 Kelly, Howard A. *Cyclopedia of American Medical Biography; comprising the lives of eminent deceased physicians and surgeons from 1610–1910.* Philadelphia: Saunders, 1912. 2 vols.

13.12 Kelly, Howard A., and Walter L. Burrage. *American Medical Biographies.* Baltimore, MD: Norman, Remington, 1920.

13.13 Kelly, Howard A., and Walter L. Burrage. *Dictionary of American Medical Biography.* New York: Appleton, 1928.

13.14 Kaufman, Martin, Stuart Galishoff, and Todd Lee Savitt, eds. *Dictionary of American Medical Biography.* Westport, CT: Greenwood Press, 1984. 2 vols.

13.15 Holloway, Lisabeth M. *Medical Obituaries: American Physicians' Biographical Notices in Selected Medical Journals before 1907.* New York: Garland, 1981.

13.16 Morton, Leslie T., and Robert J. Moore. *A Bibliography of Medical and Biomedical Biography.* 3rd ed. Burlington, VT: Ashgate, 2005.

Each of these tools provides information for those seeking biographical material. The *Dictionary of Medical Biography* provides 1,100 biographies of major medical practitioners in all times and cultures. Practitioners of alternative medicine as well as major figures from traditional Chinese, Indian, and Islamic medicine are included. Some 3,000 images as well as bibliographies for further reading on these individuals and their work are also provided. The AMA *Directory of Deceased American Physicians* includes indexes of African-American practitioners, female practitioners, and self-designated eclectic, homeopathic, and osteopathic practitioners. *The New York Times Obituaries Index* provides the date of death and location of an obituary. Finding the death date of an individual is often the key to locating further information (i.e., an obituary, and so forth). Comprehensive information on a laureate's life and career is presented along with description of the speeches and commentary that accompany the awarding of the Nobel Prize in the series on the Nobel Prize winners in physiology or medicine.

One of the most useful sources for information is the *Journal of the American Medical Association* (*JAMA*). The journal indexes list names of physicians under the terms Deaths or Obituaries, leading to brief obituaries that provide basic information. Specialty journals often have extensive obituaries of their noted members, and the transactions of many societies write elaborate memoirs of cherished members.

More than 1,500 African-American physicians, scientists, and other professionals are listed in *Blacks in Science and Medicine*. The first biographical dictionary to be published since Kelly and Burrage published the DAMB in 1928, it was the work of the same name published in 1984. The work covers the seventeenth through twentieth centuries and in addition to physicians and surgeons, included representative blacks and women, biochemists, medical educators, and hospital administrators. The coverage is through 1976. Bullough's *American Nursing* directory includes biographies of 175 women and two men in nursing who were deceased or born before 1890. The *Dictionary of Women Healers* is another source for information on women in a variety of health professions.

The biographical tools for American physicians of an earlier age began with Thacher. His work was followed by Atkinson, Kelly, and others. All are of value when searching for biographies and/or portraits of important practitioners. Holloway's work includes brief biographical information as well as sources of obituaries for some 17,350 physicians deceased before 1907. *A Bibliography of Medical and Biomedical Biography* is limited to works published in book form in the English language during the nineteenth and twentieth centuries. It includes those who have made significant contributions to the related biomedical sciences, making it broader than Thornton's *Select Bibliography of Medical Biography*.

13.17   Rosen, George, and Beate Caspari-Rosen, coll. and arrang. *400 Years of a Doctor's Life*. New York: Schuman, 1947.

13.18   Comroe, Julius H., Jr. *Retrospectroscope: Insights into Medical Discovery*. Menlo Park, CA: Von Gehr Press, 1977.

Popular biographies or sources such as Rosen's *400 Years* portray physicians through short sketches or personal experiences. Other titles such as Comroe's *Retrospectroscope* offer background information concerning various discoveries, thus shining light on the scientist or physician seeking answers.

Good biographical information may be found in alumni directories, local newspapers, and historical society publications. Major textbooks often have biographical information concerning those who developed a treatment or device or who made significant breakthroughs in medicine or science. The standard medical, nursing, and dental directories are also useful in finding basic information about individuals. Databases such as MEDLINE as well as the print *Index Medicus* for earlier years are good sources for obituaries of well-known individuals in science and medicine. The

Journal of Medical Biography, started in 1993 by the Royal Society of Medicine in London, has biographies of both patients and physicians.

Biographical Websites

With the advent of the Internet, a whole realm of resources has been developed. Never before has so much information been available at the touch of a keyboard. The caveat is, of course, to be certain of the creator of the information and to view all sites with healthy skepticism. Among the useful sites are the following:

13.19   Biography and Genealogy Master Index. Farmington Hills, MI: Gale Group. http://galenet.gale.com/a/acp/db/bgmi.

13.20   Whonamedit.com. Oslo, Norway: Whonamedit.com. Available: http://www.whonamedit.com/.

13.21   Profiles in Science. Bethesda, MD: National Library of Medicine. Available: http://www.profiles.nlm.nih.gov/.

13.22   The Social Security Death Index. Provo, UT: MyFamily.com. Available: http://ssdi.genealogy.rootsweb.com/.

13.23   American National Biography Online. New York: Oxford University Press, 2000. Available: http://www.anb.org/.

13.24   Bois, Danuta. Distinguished Women of Past and Present. Available: http://www.distinguishedwomen.com/.

13.25   Women Physicians' Autobiographies. Available: http://research.med.umkc .edu/teams/cml/WomenDrs.html.

The Web tools listed above offer a great variety of coverage. The Gale resource lists persons from all time periods, geographical locations, and fields of endeavor. The Whonamedit source lists eponyms from A to Z, includes biographies by country, lists female entries, traces the eponym to the article by the named author, and identifies the source of an obituary.

The National Library of Medicine produces the Profiles in Science database, listing prominent twentieth-century biomedical scientists. The listing may be reviewed chronologically or alphabetically and many have pictures and papers. The Death Index lists more than 70 million names, including dates of birth and death, social security number, last known residence, and date of last benefit. The American National Biography includes more than 18,700 men and women who have influenced and shaped American history and culture. A recent collaboration between the ANB and the National Portrait Gallery will link these entries with an "accurate likeness for the subject." With 2,700 illustrations currently, the ANB will add many more as a result of the new partnership.

Two websites that provide biographies of women in science and medicine are the Distinguished Women of Past and Present that includes women from the fourth through the twentieth centuries and Women Physicians' Autobiographies that grew out of a project begun by Dr. Marjorie S. Sirridge including medical school graduates 1849–1920.

There are many such sources on the Internet today, and it is likely that many more will become available. A search may start with putting an individual's name on a search engine to bring forth an array of sites. Comparing the information with one of the standard biographical tools is one way to ensure that the information is accurate.

One last but important general source for biographical information on the Web is the Harvard Library Resource Guide for the History of Science (http://guides.library .harvard.edu/content.php?pid=140185&sid=3166031&gid=4877). Clicking on the appropriate tab will also link the researcher with information in public health, nursing, and the pharmaceutical sciences.

Portraits and Illustrations

While many of the biographical sources include portraits of the individuals, there is need for resources that point to the printed source or institutional location of portraits of widely known scientists, physicians, nurses, or others in the health field. Several works that include anatomical illustrations are also listed.

13.26 *Portrait Catalog of the Library of the New York Academy of Medicine.* Boston: G. K. Hall, 1960. 5 vols. Suppl. 1, 1959–1965; suppl. 2, 1966–1970; suppl. 3, 1971–1975.

13.27 Berkowitz, Julie S. *The College of Physicians of Philadelphia Portrait Catalogue.* Philadelphia: The College, 1984.

13.28 Burgess, Renate. *Portraits of Doctors and Scientists in the Wellcome Institute of the History of Medicine: A Catalogue.* London: Wellcome Institute for the History of Medicine, 1973.

13.29 Roberts, Kenneth B., and J. D. W. Tomlinson. *The Fabric of the Body: European Traditions of Anatomical Illustrations.* New York: Clarendon Press, 1992.

31.30 Porter, Roy. *The Cambridge Illustrated History of Medicine.* Cambridge, UK: Cambridge University Press, 1996.

13.31   Netter, Frank H. *The Ciba Collection of Medical Illustrations: A Compilation of Pathological and Anatomical Paintings.* Summit, NJ: Ciba Pharmaceutical Products, 1959–1993.

13.32   Sournia, Jean-Charles. *The Illustrated History of Medicine.* London: Harold Starke, 1992.

13.33   Naythons, Matthew. *The Face of Mercy: Photographic History of Medicine at War.* New York: Random House, 1993.

The New York Academy of Medicine Library's catalog is the most comprehensive source for portraits. Included are the library's holdings of more than 14,000 original portraits, paintings, woodcuts, engravings, and photographs. In addition, it provides nearly 300,000 citations to portraits in journals and books, both primary and secondary sources. The College of Physicians and the Wellcome catalogs are examples of sources for portraits or paintings from these institutions.

Illustrations of a medical nature are often requested by historians, scholars, writers, and students. *The Fabric of the Body* is an anthology of anatomical illustrations from the medieval period to the present day. It includes text about the anatomists, their collaborators, and their books. It is also about the context in which anatomical illustrations were prepared and distributed. The work features some of the most beautiful and renowned anatomical illustrations. Porter's work uses illustrations to further describe the sections on disease, hospitals and surgery, medical science, and so forth. The Ciba collection includes eight volumes, some with many parts, illustrating various parts of the body such as nervous system, respiratory system, reproductive system, and so forth. The English translation of Sournia's *Illustrated History of Medicine* as well as the French original have excellent illustrations. *The Face of Mercy* depicts medicine at war images on the Web. The Internet offers a wide range of sites with images and portraits. One has only to enter the words "medical illustrations" in a search engine to find dozens of possibilities. The National Library of Medicine has two important offerings.

13.34   Images from the History of Medicine (IHM). Bethesda, MD: National Library of Medicine. Available: http://www.nlm.nih.gov/hmd/36.

13.35   The Visible Human Project. Bethesda, MD: National Library of Medicine. Available: http://www.nlm.nih.gov/research/visible/visible_human.html.

13.36   Online Portrait Gallery of the Moody Medical Library, University of Texas Medical Branch at Galveston. Galveston, TX: University of Texas. Available: http://www.utmb.edu/.

13.37   History of Medicine. London: Wellcome Trust. Available: http://www.wellcome.ac.uk/.

13.38   The Whole Brain Atlas. Cambridge, MA: Harvard School of Medicine. Available: http://www.med.harvard.edu/aanlib/home.html.

13.39   Index of Medieval Medical Images with Illustrations (IMMI). Los Angeles: UCLA Library. Available: http://digital.library.ucla.edu/immi/.

13.40   Anatomia 1522–1867. Toronto: University of Toronto. Available: http://link .library.utoronto.ca/anatomia/application/index.cfm.

13.41   Historical Anatomies on the Web. Bethesda, MD: U.S. National Library of Medicine. Available: http://www.nlm.nih.gov/exhibition/historicalanatomies/ browse.html.

13.42   Medical Photographic Library. London: Wellcome Trust. Available: http:// medphoto.wellcome.ac.uk/ixbin/hixclient.exe?_IXDB_=wellcome&_IXSE.

13.43   Images.MD. Springer. Available: http://www.springerimages.com/ imagesMD/.

13.44   Public Health Image Library (PHIL). Atlanta: Centers for Disease Control and Prevention. Available: http://phil.cdc.gov/phil/.

The National Library of Medicine's database has approximately 70,000 images from the Library's historical and photographs collection. It includes portraits, photographs, fine prints, caricatures, genre scenes, posters, and other graphic art illustrating the social and historical aspects of medicine from the Middle Ages to the present. The Visible Human Project is the creation of complete, anatomically detailed, three-dimensional representations of the normal male and female bodies.

Many libraries have mounted portraits and images from their collections on the Web. Two examples are more than 40,000 high-quality images relating to the history of the biomedical sciences in the Moody Medical Library and the Wellcome Trust's site that includes a medical photographic library with exquisite images from the library's collections.

The Whole Brain Atlas produced by Keith A. Johnson and J. Alex Becker is a source providing central nervous system imaging that integrates clinical information with magnetic resonance, computed tomography, and nuclear medicine images.

Many libraries are digitizing interesting and rare images from their collections. A variety of examples include the following. The IMMI comprises 509 images from thirteen medieval manuscripts up to the year 1500 owned by six institutions in this country. The 4,500 full-page plates in the *Anatomia* were taken from the Thomas Fisher Rare Book Library at the University of Toronto. The illustrations, taken from ninety-five titles, are fully cataloged. The National Library of Medicine's Historical Anatomies on the Web includes images from some thirty-five anatomical atlases in NLM's collections. The Wellcome Trust's Medical Photographic Library has more than 250,000 historical and contemporary images. More than 50,000 images from ninety collections and 2,000 contributors are offered through Images.MD. The Centers for Disease Control and Prevention provides a wide range of photographs, illustrations, and multimedia files on topics of interest in all areas of public health.

Medical Instruments

Libraries receive many requests to identify medical instruments as well as to provide illustrations of scalpels, obstetric tools such as forceps, artificial hearts, and so forth. The following tools offer valuable resources on these topics.

13.45   Edmonson, James M. *American Surgical Instruments: The History of Their Manufacture and a Directory of Instrument Makers to 1900.* San Francisco: Norman Publishing, 1997.

13.46   Shultz, S. M. *Sources for Identification of Antique Medical Instruments in Print and on the Internet.* York, PA: WellSpan Health. Available: http://www.priory.com/homol/ant.htm.

13.47   Truax, Charles H. *The Mechanics of Surgery; comprising detailed descriptions, illustrations, and lists of the instruments, appliances, and furniture necessary in modern surgical art.* Chicago: Hammond Press, 1899.

13.48   Kirkup, John. *The Evolution of Surgical Instruments: An Illustrated History from Ancient Times to the Twentieth Century.* Novato, CA: Historyofscience .com, 2006.

13.49   Bennion, Elisabeth. *Antique Medical Instruments.* Berkeley, CA: University of California Press, 1979.

13.50   Rosenthal, J. William. *Spectacles and Other Vision Aids: A History and a Guide to Collecting.* San Francisco: Norman Publishing, 1996.

Edmondson's work is a comprehensive directory of surgical instrument makers in the United States prior to 1900 with some 280 illustrations. The website includes a bibliography of books and articles on antique instruments, Internet sites, catalogs, and dealers. Truax provides a wealth of descriptions of instruments prior to the twentieth century. The Kirkup book begins with ancient times and includes the nineteenth century. Although more than thirty years old, many curators will find the Bennion source quite useful, and Rosenthal provides an excellent guide to glasses and optometry objects.

Readers should be cautioned to note the copyright restrictions for use of images from both print and Web sources. That said, there are a number of useful Web resources for researching medical instruments and artifacts. Antiquespectacles.com, Medicalantiques.com, and Museumofvision.org are just a few.

Discoveries/Chronologies

Questions concerning medical discoveries and happenings are among the most frequent. These questions take the form of who made a scientific discovery, when did an event take place, and were there controversies. The following tools provide answers.

13.51   Morton, Leslie T., and Robert J. Moore. *A Chronology of Medicine and Related Sciences.* Aldershot, Hants, UK: Scolar Press, 1997.

13.52   Friedman, Meyer, and Gerald W. Friedland. *Medicine's 10 Greatest Discoveries.* New Haven, CT: Yale University Press, 1998.

13.53   Schmidt, Jacob E. *Medical Discoveries: Who and When: A Dictionary Listing Thousands of Medical and Related Scientific Discoveries in Alphabetical Order.* Springfield, IL: Charles C Thomas, 1959.

13.54   Simmons, John G. *Doctors and Discoveries.* Boston: Houghton Mifflin, 2002.

Morton's work begins with 3000 BC and runs through 1996. Only 236 pages brings one to 1850; from 1851 to 1996 requires 430 pages. The Friedman work is a more detailed review of major discoveries whereas Schmidt's work is an easy-to-use dictionary with brief statements. The Simmons book provides brief biographies that focus on the discoveries of the individuals that have helped to shape medicine as we know it today.

Chronology Websites

There are scores of Internet sites devoted to medical discoveries, both general and by specialty. The following example is from the National Institutes of Health:

13.55   NIH Chronology of Events. Bethesda, MD: National Institutes of Health. Available: http://www.nih.gov/about/almanac/historical/chronology_of_events.htm.

Bibliographies/Library Catalogs

The advent of the Internet and the ease and speed of citation retrieval has changed the way individuals search for information. While the MEDLINE database is a boon to searchers for literature from 1957 onward, historians and scholars as well as students need resources that cover the literature of earlier centuries. Medicine has an array of resources that serve users well.

13.56 *Index-Catalogue of the Library of the Surgeon-General's Office.*
Washington, DC: Government Printing Office, 1880. 61 vols. in 5 series:
1880–1895; 1896–1916; 1913–1932; 1936–1955; 1959–1961. IndexCat.
Available: http://indexcat.nlm.nih.gov/.

13.57 *Current Work in the History of Medicine.* London: Wellcome Institute for the
History of Medicine, 1954–1999. Available: http://library.wellcome.ac.uk/.

13.58 Norman, Jeremy, ed. *Morton's Medical Bibliography: An Annotated Check-
List of Texts Illustrating the History of Medicine (Garrison and Morton).* 5th
ed. Aldershot, Hants, UK: Gower, 1991.

13.59 Hoolihan, Christopher, comp. and annot. *An Annotated Catalogue of the
Edward C. Atwater Collection of American Popular Medicine and Health
Reform.* Rochester, NY: University of Rochester Press, 2001– .

13.60 Washington University (Saint Louis, MO), School of Medicine Library.
Catalog of the Bernard Becker, M.D. Collection in Ophthalmology. 2nd ed.
St. Louis, MO: Washington University School of Medicine Library, 1983.

13.61 Wygant, Larry J., comp. *The Truman G. Blocker, Jr., History of Medicine
Collections: Books and Manuscripts.* Galveston, TX: University of Texas
Medical Branch, 1986.

13.62 Wellcome Historical Medical Library. *A Catalogue of Printed Books in the
Wellcome Historical Medical Library.* New York: Martino Publishers, 1995– .

The publications of the National Library of Medicine, the largest medical
library in the world, are the most comprehensive for users working in the history of
medicine. The *Index-Catalogue* is the monumental work established by John Shaw
Billings in 1880 that includes the holdings of the Surgeon-General's Library, now the
National Library of Medicine. The dates of the volumes do not reflect the dates of
the items; the first three series cover the books, articles, pamphlets, and dissertations
from 1500 through 1926. The project to digitize the *Index-Catalogue* was completed
in 2004. Researchers will rejoice to have access to IndexCat, a catalog of more than
4.5 million references from 3.7 million bibliographic items. Included are journal
articles, books, pamphlets, reports, dissertations, and portraits, dating from antiquity
through 1950.

The *Index Medicus,* the index to the most important and most used journals
in medicine, is also useful in the search for articles of an earlier time. Published
under various titles, this print source includes obituaries. A complete description of
Index Medicus is found in chapter 4. It should be noted that MEDLINE does include
the citations formerly in the Histline database. The print version of Histline, the
Bibliography of the History of Medicine, was published by NLM from 1964 to 1993.

Current Work in the History of Medicine is an index to periodical articles on the history of medicine and includes a list of books received in the Wellcome Library. The Wellcome Library now publishes *Current Work in the History of Medicine* as the *Wellcome Bibliography for the History of Medicine* on its website.

In addition to the bibliographies cited above, there is a definitive bibliography now in its fifth edition. *Morton's Medical Bibliography* is a heavily used resource listing nearly 9,000 publications, classed by subject, that were of significance in the development of Western medicine. Translations and reprint editions are noted. The first four editions were produced by Leslie T. Morton, beginning in 1943. He based the work on a list of milestones in the development of medicine compiled by Fielding H. Garrison in the *Index-Catalogue,* volume 17:89–178, 1912. Morton undertook the task of expanding and updating the list after Garrison's death, hence the designation Garrison and Morton.

Many libraries have published catalogs of collections on special topics that can be of great help to historians and others searching for works on one subject. The Atwater collection on popular medicine and the Becker collection on ophthalmology are good examples of topical bibliographies. The Wellcome and the Blocker catalogs reflect the holdings of the libraries.

Histories

Histories of medicine provide a wide range of information. Some are general, covering the entire realm; others focus on an aspect or specific time period. Following are examples of a variety of histories.

13.63   Kiple, Kenneth F., ed. *The Cambridge World History of Human Disease.* New York: Cambridge University Press, 1993.

13.64   Bynum, William F., and Roy Porter, eds. *Companion Encyclopedia of the History of Medicine.* 2 vols. New York: Routledge, 1993.

13.65   Kohn, George C. *Encyclopedia of Plague and Pestilence.* New York: Facts on File, 1995.

13.66   Major, Ralph H. *History of Medicine.* 2 vols. Springfield, IL: Charles C Thomas, 1954.

13.67   Sigerist, Henry E. *A History of Medicine.* 2 vols. New York: Oxford University Press, 1951–1961.

13.68   Castiflioni, Arturo, and E. B. Krumbhaar, trans. *A History of Medicine.* 2nd ed., rev. and enl. New York: Alfred A. Knopf, 1958.

13.69 Garrison, Fielding H., ed. *An Introduction to the History of Medicine, with Medical Chronology, Suggestions for Study, and Bibliographic Data.* 4th ed., reprinted. Philadelphia: Saunders, 1966.

13.70 Duffin, Jacalyn. *History of Medicine: A Scandalously Short Introduction.* 2nd ed. Toronto: University of Toronto Press, 2010.

Histories abound in the fields of medicine and science. The Cambridge volume includes essays on distribution of diseases, medical traditions, various organs, and organ systems as well as a section on "Major Human Diseases Past and Present" arranged alphabetically by disease. The *Companion Encyclopedia* is a two-volume work arranged by topics whereas the *Encyclopedia of Plague and Pestilence* outlines and provides a timeline for specific epidemics.

Many older volumes of history continue to be of use. While they vary in style and organization, all serve as a starting point for those interested to learn from and about the past. The titles by Major, Sigerist, and Castiglioni have served generations of readers. The Garrison history includes a medical chronology and suggestions for study; it is a great book for anyone who wishes to use such a resource as a study guide with answers. Duffin's history was written in response to her medical students' request for an introductory text in the history of medicine. Her purpose is to raise awareness of history in order to understand the present and to instill a sense of skepticism with regard to the "dogma" of the medical curriculum.

History-of-Medicine Journals

Many journals contain historical articles along with their general topics. There are also journals devoted to the history of medicine. A number of the titles are now online.

13.71 *Bulletin of the History of Medicine.* Baltimore, MD: Johns Hopkins University Press, American Association for the History of Medicine, 1939– . 7– . Available: http://www.press.jhu.edu/journals/bulletin_of_the_history_of_medicine/.

13.72 *Gesnerus.* Basel: Schwabe; Swiss Society of the History of Medicine, 1943– . 1– . [Not online.]

13.73 *Isis.* Chicago: University of Chicago Press for the History of Science Society, 1913– . 1– . Available: http://www.journals.uchicago.edu/Isis/home.html.

13.74 *Journal of the History of Medicine and Allied Sciences.* London: Oxford University Press, 1946– . 1– . Available: http://jhmas.oxfordjournals.org/.

13.75 *Medical History.* London: Wellcome Trust Centre for the History of Medicine, 1957– . 1– . Available: http://pubmedcentral.gov/.

13.76   *Canadian Bulletin of Medical History.* Waterloo, ON: Wilfrid Laurier
University Press, 1984– . 1– . Available: http://www.cbmh.ca/.

13.77   *Social History of Medicine.* London: Oxford University Press, 1970– . 1– .
Available: http://shm.oxfordjournals.org/.

History-of-medicine journals provide the works of today's medical and scientific historians. All of the journals cited contain articles and book reviews. The *Journal of the History of Medicine and Allied Sciences* also carries a list of recent dissertations in the history of medicine. The titles cover the social, cultural, and scientific aspects of medical history as well as the other disciplines that impinge on it. Readers should note that many of the titles are available online through various vendors. Dates of availability vary widely, but one of the major aggregators of online access is Project Muse, a subscription journal site with access to more than 250 from over 40 publishers operated by the Johns Hopkins University Press.

Tools for the Librarian

With libraries and Google digitizing books, journals, and other resources, a proliferating range of full-text titles is available on the Internet. The Google scanning project with a number of university libraries, including Harvard, Oxford, Stanford, Princeton, and the universities of California, Michigan, Wisconsin, and the New York Public, will provide millions of titles in the public domain.

This rich resource will be a boon to historians, scholars, and students around the world. As libraries plan digitizing projects, the following will be of great use to those involved in the planning and digitizing.

13.78   Mugridge, Rebecca. *Managing Digitization Activities.* Washington, DC: Association of Research Libraries, 2006.

13.79   Koelling, Jill M. *Digital Imaging: A Practical Approach.* Walnut Creek, CA: AltaMira Press, 2004.

13.80   *Building and Sustaining Digital Collections: Models for Libraries and Museums.* Washington, DC: Council on Library and Information Resources, 2001.

13.81   Sitts, Maxine K., ed. *Handbook for Digital Projects: A Management Tool for Preservation and Access.* Andover, MA: Northeast Document Conservation Center, 2000.

Librarians must deal with questions concerning the book as a physical object as well as the content it contains. Many questions arise about the cost of books and other publications as well as how to care for books, determination of quality over time, and how to become a collector. Librarians must know and understand the structure of bibliography and be prepared to answer questions concerning collations, watermarks, signatures, and so forth. Medical publishing and medical literature are topics of great interest to historians and scholars, and the library will find the following array of sources to be a good basis for collecting in this area.

13.82 *American Book Prices Current.* Washington, CT: Bancroft-Parkman, 1894/1895– . Vol. 1– . 110. CD-ROM 1975-2005.

13.83 *Bookman's Price Index.* Detroit: Gale, 1964– . Vol. 1– .

13.84 Carter, John. *ABC for Book Collectors.* 8th ed. New Castle, DE: Oak Knoll Press, 2004.

13.85 McKerrow, Ronald B. *An Introduction to Bibliography for Literary Students.* New Castle, DE: Oak Knoll Press, 1994.

13.86 Thornton, John L. *Thornton's Medical Books, Libraries, and Collectors: A Study of Bibliography and the Book Trade in Relation to the Medical Sciences.* 3rd rev. ed. Aldershot, Hants, UK: Gower, 1990.

13.87 Blake, John B., and Charles Roos. *Medical Reference Works, 1679–1966: A Selected Bibliography.* Chicago: Medical Library Association, 1967. Three supplements: 1970–1975.

Library users as well as librarians are interested in the prices of book they wish either to purchase or donate. The *American Book Prices Current* and *Bookman's Price Index* are useful for this purpose as are recent catalogs from rare-book dealers. The world of the "book," its production, description, format, and terminology are identified in Carter's *ABC for Book Collectors* and in McKerrow's classic work on bibliography. The development of medical literature and the book trade are examined in Besson's revision of Thornton's *Medical Books.* Blake and Roos provide the standard list of medical reference works dating from 1679 through 1975.

13.88 Brooks, Constance, and Pamela W. Darling. *Disaster Preparedness.* Washington, DC: Association of Research Libraries, 1993.

13.89 Kahn, Miriam. *First Steps for Handling and Drying Water-Damaged Materials.* Columbus, OH: MBK Consulting, 1994.

13.90 Waters, Peter. *Procedures for Salvage of Water-Damaged Library Materials.* 2nd ed. Washington, DC: Library of Congress, 1979.

13.91 Harvey, D. R. *Preservation in Libraries: Principles, Strategies, and Practices for Librarians.* New York: Bowker-Saur, 1993.

13.92   Horton, C. *Cleaning and Preserving Bindings and Related Materials.* 2nd ed. rev. Chicago: Library Technology Program, American Library Association, 1969.

13.93   Harvey, Douglass R. *Preserving Digital Materials.* Munchen: Saur, 2005.

13.94   Schweidler, Max. *The Restoration of Engravings, Drawings, Books, and Other Works on Paper.* Translated, edited, and with an appendix by Roy Perkinson. Los Angeles: Getty Conservation Institute, 2006.

13.95   Adcock, Edward P., comp. and ed. *IFLA Principles for the Care and Handling of Library Materials.* Washington, DC: International Federation of Library Associations and Institutions, Core Programme on Preservation and Conservation, 1998.

13.96   Long, Jane S. *Field Guide to Emergency Response.* Washington, DC: Heritage Preservation, 2006.

13.97   Halsted, Deborah D., Richard P. Jasper, and Felicia M. Little. *Disaster Planning: A How-To-Do-It Manual for Librarians with Planning Templates on CD-ROM.* New York: Neal-Schuman, 2005.

13.98   Ogden, Sherelyn. *Preservation of Library and Archival Materials: A Manual.* 3rd ed., rev. and exp. Andover, MA: Northeast Document Conservation Center, 1999. Available: http://www.nedcc.org/home.php.

Acquiring is only the first step in collection management. The volumes held in both special and general collections must be housed, handled, and, when necessary, repaired or restored. Preservation is an essential part of the library's responsibility for its collections. The books on disaster preparedness, water damage, and preservation are full of information to help librarians deal with the protection of their collections. The Northeast Document Conservation Center has produced a website that includes leaflets on specific topics that are freely available to all.

Rare book librarianship has many facets because of the great variety of formats collected in history of medicine libraries. Users of the collections are also varied as individuals interested in history and historical research range from students to scholars, laymen to health professionals, and historians of medicine to those in different disciplines.

Good overviews of the kinds of work expected from rare book/history librarians as well as the wide range of resources needed can be found in the series of handbooks published by the Medical Library Association. The titles given in the "Readings" section following will acquaint librarians with background and guidelines.

The electronic world in which we work with and for the users in our libraries offers endless resources undreamed of by our predecessors. With the click of a mouse, the librarian can retrieve medical and health-related books and journals that range from antiquity to the present. Susan E. Lederer writes that the craft of the historian (and I would add of the librarian) "has many parallels with the craft of the diagnostician. History, like diagnostics, is an interpretive activity in which one attempts to construct an intelligible narrative, based on elements from diverse possible choices."[3] She goes on to say that historical narrative, like the physician's diagnosis, is always subject to change: Just as an expert diagnostician incorporates cues from the patient's words, affect, and clothes, the historian "uses texts, films, literature, and the visual arts" to elucidate and describe the past.[4]

Readings

Annan, G. L. "Rare Books and the History of Medicine." In *A Handbook of Medical Library Practice*, edited by Janet Doe, 265–370. Chicago: American Library Association, 1943.

Cavanagh, George Stanley T. "Rare Books, Archives, and the History of Medicine." In *Handbook of Medical Library Practice*, 3rd ed., edited by G. L. Annan and J. W. Felter, 254–283. Chicago: Medical Library Association, 1970.

Zinn, Nancy W. "Special Collections: History of Health Science Collections, Oral History, Archives, and Manuscripts." In *Handbook of Medical Library Practice*, 4th ed., edited by Louise Darling, 469–572. Chicago: Medical Library Association, 1988.

References

1. Gnudi, M. T. "Building a Medical History Collection." *Bulletin of the Medical Library Association* 63, no. 1 (1975): 42–46.
2. Overmier, Judith A. "History Sources." In *Introduction to Reference Sources in the Health Sciences*, edited by Fred W. Roper and Jo Anne Boorkman, 257–70. Chicago: Medical Library Association, 1994.
3. Lederer, Susan E., E. S. More, and J. D. Howell. "Medical History in the Under-graduate Medical Curriculum." *Academic Medicine* 70, no. 9 (1995): 770–76.
4. Ibid.

CHAPTER 14

Directories and Biographical Sources

TRACY SHIELDS

Directories, both in print and electronic formats, provide information about individuals, groups, and organizations. Biographical sources provide biographical information on individuals, both historical and contemporary. These ready reference tools can be invaluable resources for health and medical libraries. Depending on the information needs, the librarian must consider a variety of factors when selecting a directory or biographical source, including authority, currency, accuracy, accessibility, and relevancy. Added to this is the choice of electronic or print sources. Print sources will be dependent on the collection; electronic or online sources may be more accessible and abundant, as they are not limited by physical space, but could be restricted because of subscriptions or other paywalls.

The authority of print directories and biographical sources at times can be more easily ascertained than some electronic or online sources. Proprietary, subscription-based electronic resources may have more obvious authority than their open-access, freely available counterparts, with potential information overlap between the two types. Currency of information can be a major issue. Online and electronic directories may be frequently updated (e.g., weekly database uploads, quarterly CD-ROMs), whereas print resources may be less often updated (e.g., annual editions). Both print and electronic resources could have problems with accuracy. The nature of electronic media may allow for more timely correction of misinformation; print inaccuracies will persist until the next edition. The accessibility of print materials is only limited by collection holdings (although interlibrary loan offers to alleviate that) and physical constraints. Even with the perceived ease of use with electronic or online information (the "just Google it" mentality), some of it could be restricted through lack of subscriptions to the resource or by paywalls. An older printed directory easily found in the collection may be more reliable, faster, and more accurate than an electronic resource.

In light of these concerns, the information professional is burdened with choice—which type of resource, in what form (print or electronic), timeliness of retrieval, and what option best meets the patron's needs for this information. Familiarity with the pros and cons of media forms, along with the content of resources, is essential for selecting the most appropriate resource.

Directories

Health-care providers and consumers alike may ask for information on medical and health-related organizations (including those for special populations), health education centers, or medical and scientific publishing. These requests often require basic contact information (phone number, address, etc.), although more detailed data can also be found. Following are selected resources that are helpful in addressing these information needs.

Organization Directories

14.1   DIRLINE. Bethesda, MD: U.S. National Library of Medicine. Available: http://dirline.nlm.nih.gov/.

14.2   MedlinePlus Directories. Bethesda, MD: U.S. National Library of Medicine. Available: http://www.nlm.nih.gov/medlineplus/directories.html.

Maintained by the National Library of Medicine (NLM), DIRLINE: Directory of Health Organizations includes information on health and medical organizations, agencies, institutions, professional societies, referral centers, and other resources. This online source is of interest for professionals and consumers. Records include mailing addresses, phone numbers, e-mail addresses, Web addresses, abstracts, type of organization, and date of last review. The database can be browsed or searched by name or acronym, MeSH heading, or keyword. Search results may be saved and/or downloaded. This resource is notable for being curated and freely available.

MedlinePlus, a consumer-oriented health information resource also curated by the NLM, offers multiple directories on hospitals and clinics, doctors and other health-care providers (also noted in later sections), and special services (e.g., mental health facilities, vision testing, rehabilitation, etc.). The MedlinePlus list of directories replaces the no longer supported Go Local initiative, which was discontinued in 2010. Both NLM resources offer curated, authoritative resources for health-related directories for consumers and providers.

Gale publishes several directories of potential interest. All Gale resources described here are subscription-based electronic resources or print editions.

14.3   Health and Wellness Resource Center (HWRC). Detroit: Gale.

The Health Organization Directory (offered through the Health and Wellness Resource Center from Gale) is a searchable database of health-care agencies, organizations, health-care facilities, and medical schools. Like DIRLINE, records include contact information, phone numbers, and e-mail and Web addresses, as well as a citation on where the information was retrieved.

14.4   *Encyclopedia of Associations: National Organizations of the US.* Detroit: Gale. Irregular publication 1961–1973, then annually 1975– .

The *Encyclopedia of Associations* (*EA*) is a three-volume resource of nonprofit membership organizations. The main volume lists those U.S.-based organizations with a national scope and includes contact information (address, phone number), founding date, purpose, associated conferences, membership numbers, website address, affiliates, publications, and other relevant data. The companion volumes include details on geographic and executive indexes (volume 2) and updated contact information and newly identified associations (volume 3). It is available in print or electronic formats. The *EA* includes subset publications such as Regional, State, and Local Organizations; National Organizations; and International Organizations.

14.5   *Encyclopedia of Medical Organizations and Agencies.* 15th ed. Detroit: Gale, 2006.

The *Encyclopedia of Medical Organizations and Agencies* includes details on organizations, foundations, state and federal government agencies, research centers, and medical education institutions (medical and allied health). This resource contains more than 18,000 entries and a cross-index, along with the typical alphabetical name and keyword indexes.

14.6   *Research Centers Directory.* 42nd ed. Detroit: Gale, 2012.

Gale also publishes the *Research Centers Directory*, detailing programs, facilities, publications, and other information on universities and nonprofit research institutes in North America.

Hospitals and Other Health-Care Facilities

14.7   *AHA Guide.* Chicago: Health Forum, 2013.

The American Hospital Association (AHA) annually publishes (print and electronic formats) a directory based on membership, its survey of hospitals, and other sources. The AHA Guide includes information on 6,500 hospitals, more than 400 health-care systems, networks, and alliances, 700 health-care organizations and associations, 700 government agencies, and 3,000 accredited providers. As noted previously, NLM's MedlinePlus online directories include links to hospitals and clinics (general and specialized), and other health-care facilities and services.

14.8   *American Hospital Directory.* Louisville, KY: American Hospital Directory, 2013. Available: http://www.ahd.com/.

The subscription-based (although some limited free searching is available) online American Hospital Directory provides data on more than 6,000 hospitals in the United States. Record details include addresses (physical and online), contact information, clinical services offered, Joint Commission accreditation status, some utilization statistics, and other hospital-specific data. Updates to the information are noted on the site.

14.9   Joint Commission Certified Organizations. Terrace, IL: Joint Commission, 2013. Available: http://www.qualitycheck.org/consumer/searchQCR.aspx.

The Joint Commission (JC; formerly known as the Joint Commission on Accreditation of Healthcare Organizations, or JCAHO), which accredits health-care organizations in the United States, provides a search of its directory of JC-certified organizations. The site offers real-time data for download, along with searching for disease-specific care. Unfortunately, data are limited to type of program, location, and date of certification; data will most likely need to be supplemented from other sources for a broader picture.

Physicians and Other Health Providers Directories

There are a plethora of resources—print or electronic/online—that list physicians and other health providers. Some authoritative sources to find physician directories include individual hospitals or health-care facilities; local and state health departments or licensing bodies; insurance (public and private) company coverage lists; specialty board certification groups; professional organizations and associations; and national directories. Listing all these is beyond the scope of this text; a few general resources follow—some free, some subscription- or fee-based—that provide a good starting point for physician and health provider directory information. Many physician and health provider directories have a consumer-health focus. MedlinePlus (see

14.2) offers many resources to find doctors, dentists, and other health-care providers (e.g., physical therapist, dietitian, etc.) with links to organizations and groups who provide the data.

14.10   AMA DoctorFinder. Chicago: American Medical Association, 2013. Available: http://extapps.ama-assn.org/doctorfinder/home.jsp.

The American Medical Association's online DoctorFinder offers a national, U.S.-based directory of physicians (although limited to those physicians with AMA membership). Geared toward a consumer audience, the directory offers a search by name or by specialty, and limits to state, city, and zip code. A "sounds-like" option is helpful as well. Of note, the information contained is self-designated; that is, physicians select their specialty or subject area independent of any certification. If one needs to search by certification or specialty as granted by specific groups and boards, there is the directory of the American Board of Medical Specialties, which is subscription-based and online.

14.11   ABMS Directory of Board Certified Medical Specialists. Chicago: American Board of Medical Specialties, 2013. Available: http://www.abmsdirectory.com/abms/static/home.htm.

14.12   Find a DO. Chicago: American Osteopathic Association; 2013. Available: http://www.osteopathic.org/osteopathic-health/find-a-do/Pages/default.aspx.

14.13   ADA Find-A-Dentist. Chicago: American Dental Association; 2013. Available: http://www.mouthhealthy.org/find-a-dentist.aspx.

14.14   Find an NCCAOM Certified Practitioner. Jacksonville, FL: National Certification Commission for Acupuncture and Oriental Medicine, 2013. Available: http://www.nccaom.org/fap.

Other directories for health-care providers include the American Osteopathic Association's Physician Database, to find osteopathic physicians; the American Dental Association's Find a Dentist search, which allows for searching by name, specialty, and area by distance; and the National Certification Commission for Acupuncture and Oriental Medicine's Certified Practitioner directory, which allows for searching by name, location, and certification. Again, not all directories for finding a health-care provider are listed herein, so one should consider other sources depending on the information needs.

Special Population Directories

As previously mentioned, the directory listing of MedlinePlus (see 14.2) offers resources for specific groups, based on disease or condition. Other online or electronic sources to consider would be professional organizations or groups that may provide data on members or affiliates; these lists may or may not be curated, authoritative, accurate, or current. As with any resource selection, these factors should be considered when using them.

14.15   Medicare Directory. Baltimore, MD: Centers for Medicare and Medicaid Services, 2013. Available: http://www.medicare.gov/forms-help-and -resources/find-doctors-hospitals-and-facilities/quality-care-finder.html.

The federally run Medicare program has a directory of doctors, hospitals, nursing homes, suppliers, and other providers that serve Medicare patients. The directory has a simple search, usually by location or name.

14.16   Mental Health Treatment Facility Locator. Rockville, MD: SAMHSA, 2013. Available: http://findtreatment.samhsa.gov/MHTreatmentLocator/faces/ quickSearch.jspx.

The U.S.-based Substance Abuse and Mental Health Services Administration (SAMHSA) offers a locator directory of mental health treatment facilities and providers. The resource allows searching by location and name; it includes substance abuse treatment centers, buprenorphine physician locator, and other facilities.

14.17   *The National Directory of Mental Health and Addiction Services.* Salt Lake City, UT: Dorland Health, 2012.

14.18   *The National Directory of Children, Youth and Family Services.* Salt Lake City, UT: Dorland Health, 2012.

14.19   *The National Directory of Adult and Senior Services.* Salt Lake City, UT: Dorland Health, 2012.

As for print options, Dorland Health publishes several national directories focused on special populations. These resources include directories for mental health and addiction services; children, youth, and families services; and adult and senior services.

Medical and Scientific Publishing Directories

14.20   Ulrich's Knowledgebase. Serials Solutions, 2013. Available: http://ulrichsweb.serialssolutions.com/.

Ulrich's Periodicals Directory (in print; available electronically as Ulrichsweb) is the main resource for those seeking a directory of subscription-based and open-access medical and scientific literature publishers. The online version includes records for more than 300,000 periodicals, noting details such as publisher and contact information for publisher; country of origin; format; ISSN; frequency of publication; language; referred status (i.e., peer-reviewed), subject areas; pricing data; abstracting and indexing databases; and other features specific to the journal. It is an invaluable resource for collection development and information on scientific, technical, and medical publishing. The database includes popular magazines, newspapers, and newsletters, both domestic and international, and all subject areas, not just science and medicine. The online resource is updated weekly for users.

14.21   DOAJ: Directory of Open Access Journals. Available:
         http://www.doaj.org/. No subscription required.

Founded in 2003, the Directory of Open Access Journals (DOAJ) contains those scientific and scholarly periodicals that publish under "open access," defined as using a funding model that does not charge readers or their institutions for access. At the time of this writing, DOAJ contains more than 9,900 journals from 120 countries. DOAJ's goal is to increase visibility and ease of use for open-access-published journals and increase their impact. Included journals—which are not limited to medical and scientific areas, but cover any academic discipline—must be open access, peer reviewed, or have editorial quality control, report primary results of research or review research results for a scholarly audience, and be serial in nature. An editorial board and advisory board provide quality control and maintain the directory.

Education Directories

MEDICAL

14.22   AAMC resources. Available: http://www-aamc-org/. The CE Directory can
         be found under Initiatives; CIR under Data and Analysis; CurrMIT and CE
         Directory (via the MedEdPORTAL) under Services.

14.23   *AAMC Data Book.* Washington, DC: Association of American Medical
         Colleges, 2013.

The online Association of American Medical Colleges (AAMC) Curriculum Directory, which provided searchable information on medical school programs in the United States and Canada, has been incorporated into the Curriculum Inventory and Reports (CIR) resource. Much of the information found previously in the Curriculum Directory, such as information on medical school requirements, courses, and degree programs, can be found in the CIR. A list of medical schools can be found using the AAMC member search, limited to medical school organization type.

The AAMC also has the Curriculum Management and Information Tool (CurrMIT), which offers detailed comparisons of curricula, trends in medical education, and other information specific to U.S.- and Canadian-based medical schools.

The AAMC annually publishes much of this information in the *AAMC Data Book*. Also of potential interest is AAMC's Continuing Education (CE) Directory, which assists physicians in finding evidence-based online activities for CE credit.

14.24   *Directory of American Medical Education*. Washington, DC: Association of American Medical Colleges, 2013.

The AAMC annually publishes the Directory of American Medical Education, which lists administrators, department and division chairs, faculty information, and some basic data on enrollment and facilities.

14.25   *Graduate Medical Education Directory 2012–2013*. Chicago: American Medical Association, 2013. Available: http://freida.ama-assn.org/.

14.26   *Medical Specialty Information*. Chicago: American Medical Association, 2013. Available: http://www.ama-assn.org/ama/pub/about-ama/our-people/member-groups-sections/medical-student-section/membership-services/choosing-medical-specialty/specialty-information.page.

The American Medical Association (AMA) publishes Graduate Medical Education Directory annually. Also known as "the Green Book," this text gives details on more than 9,000 graduate medical education programs including residencies, fellowships, combined programs, and other programs. Additionally, the AMA offers information on medical specialties, including links to medical specialty societies through its website.

14.27   Residency Directory. Alexandria, VA: Society of General Internal Medicine. Available: http://www.sgim.org/career-center/public-health-training-directory/residency-directory.

14.28   Fellowship Directory. Alexandria, VA: Society of General Internal Medicine. Available: http://www.sgim.org/career-center/public-health-training-directory/fellowship-directory.

14.29   Public Health Training Directory. Alexandria, VA: Society of General Internal Medicine. Available: http://www.sgim.org/career-center/public-health-training-directory.

The Society of General Internal Medicine (SGIM) provides directories for residencies and fellowships. A Public Health Training Directory is also available. This online resource includes Internal Medicine programs that offer specialized training in domestic public health issues.

14.30   Avicenna Directory. Copenhagen, Denmark: University of Copenhagen, 2013. Available: http://avicenna.ku.dk/database/medicine.

14.31   International Medical Education Directory (IMED). Foundation for Advancement of International Medical Education and Research, 2013. Available: http://imed.faimer.org/.

The Avicenna Directory offers those seeking international information on medical education details on the world's medical schools. Based on the World Health Organization (WHO) World Directory of Medical Schools, the Avicenna Directory, which is currently in beta, updates the WHO directory and as of 2008 acts as a replacement for the WHO directory. It contains contact information, admission requirements, program descriptions, and accreditation status.

The International Medical Education Directory provides similar information to the Avicenna Directory—including historical data on former and current medical schools, as well as current contact details—on medical schools, searchable by region or country.

DENTAL

14.32   Dental Assisting, Hygiene and Lab Technology Programs. Chicago: American Dental Association, 2013. Available: http://www.ada.org/5500 .aspx.

14.33   DDS/DMD Programs. Chicago: American Dental Association, 2013. Available: http://www.ada.org/267.aspx.

14.34   Advanced Dental Programs. Chicago: American Dental Association, 2013. Available: http://www.ada.org/5502.aspx.

The American Dental Association (ADA) provides a list of all accredited dental education programs in the United States, for doctoral (DDS/DMD), advanced (postdoctoral), and allied health (dental assistant and dental laboratory technology) education levels.

14.35   *ADEA Official Guide to Dental Schools.* Washington, DC: American Dental Education Association, 2013. Available: http://www.adea.org/publications/ Pages/OfficialGuide.aspx.

Updated annually, the American Dental Education Association publishes an official guide to dental schools. The book outlines the dental school application process, information on accredited schools in the United States and Canada, their admission requirements, and financial aid details, and offers comparisons of schools on those data points.

MISCELLANEOUS DIRECTORIES

14.36   Europa World of Learning. London: Routledge/Taylor and Francis Group, 2013. Available at http://www.worldoflearning.com/.

Covering a broader scale, the subscription-based Europa World of Learning gives information on address, phone numbers, e-mail addresses, personnel, activities, and publications for more than 30,000 universities, colleges, libraries, art and music schools, museums and art galleries, and other educational learning institutions around the world.

14.37   Local Poison Centers. Alexandria, VA: American Association of Poison Control Centers, 2013. Available: http://www.aapcc.org/centers.

14.38   World Directory of Poison Centres. Geneva: World Health Organization. Available: http://www.who.int/gho/phe/chemical_safety/poisons _centres/en/.

The American Association of Poison Control Centers provides a list of all centers in the United States, with a central toll-free phone number help line (1-800-222-1222). The WHO has an interactive map for locations of domestic and international poison centers.

14.39   Find a Clinic. Atlanta: Centers for Disease Control and Prevention, 2013. Available: http://wwwnc.cdc.gov/travel/page/find-clinic.

The U.S. Centers for Disease Control and Prevention (CDC) offers a directory of state health departments and sources for private travel medicine clinics.

14.40   Websites of U.S. Embassies, Consulates, and Diplomatic Missions. U.S. Department of State, 2013. Available: http://www.usembassy.gov/.

Those in search of information on health-care providers, facilities, and other health-care needs may find the list of embassies from the U.S. Department of State a valuable resource; consular services for U.S. citizens include reporting births and deaths abroad, along with other services.

14.41   USA.gov: The U.S. Government's Official Web Portal. Available: http://usa.gov/.

When retrieving U.S.-based government information of all types—list of agencies, topics such as health and nutrition, and benefit information—the USA.gov website offers a one-stop-shop approach. The Web portal is an extensive online resource for citizens. Specific organizations can be found via the main search box.

14.42   Foundation Directory Online. New York: Foundation Center. Available: http://fconline.foundationcenter.org/.

The Foundation Directory Online is a subscription-based site that offers searches to find grant opportunities. The information—pulled from IRS returns, annual reports, application guidelines, and various other sources—is updated weekly. Users can search by grantmakers, companies, and grants.

14.43   Directory of Special Libraries and Information Centers. 38th ed. Detroit: Gale, 2010.

14.44   NN/LM Members Directory. Bethesda, MD: National Library of Medicine, 2013. Available: http://nnlm.gov/members.

There are several library and information science–centric directories that may be of interest. The *Directory of Special Libraries and Information Centers* from Gale (subscription-based electronic resource, or in print) details the contact information (address, phone, e-mail, etc.), person in charge, founding date, subscriptions, holdings, special collections, publications, and other data on more than 34,500 international libraries and centers. The National Network of Libraries of Medicine provides a directory of members for domestic libraries.

Biographical Sources

Biographical questions and the associated reference requests can be unexpectedly complicated. What may seem like a straightforward question (e.g., "Who is James Burns Amberson, and why does he have a lecture named after him?") could require extensive searching in multiple sources for accurate, complete information. Incomplete or inaccurate details from the questioner ("At least, I think that is his name . . ."), which is not uncommon, further complicate the issue. Authoritative sources, along with data judged accurate and current, are essential. While a quick Google search may find a Wikipedia article on the person, its authority and accuracy should be suspect. Choosing the better biographical source in the beginning can save time and provide more reliable answers. The following sources include some more general biographical sources as well as those focused on physicians and scientists.

14.45   *Encyclopedia of World Biography.* 2nd ed. Detroit: Gale, 1997. Additional volumes and yearly supplements, 1998– .

The *Encyclopedia of World Biography* is a multivolume resource (17 volumes at the time of this writing), which also has an electronic version, of more than 7,000 entries on notable people. It was completely revised and updated in 1997; the electronic version includes annual supplemental volumes and high-resolution photographs.

14.46   *Marquis Biographies Online.* Berkeley Heights, NJ: Marquis Who's Who, 2013. Available: http://www.marquiswhoswho.com/online-database.

Another broad biographical resource is the Marquis Who's Who. This subscription-based online database includes more than 1.5 million comprehensive profiles, and includes digitized biographies from the Who's Who archives, from 1607 to the present. Multiple subsets may be included with a subscription. Biographic profiles include details such as education, certifications, career highlights, memberships, and other affiliations. It should be noted that listings in Who's Who are available on a for-purchase basis, so librarians may wish to consider the authority of this resource before committing to a subscription.

14.47   *American Men and Women of Science.* Detroit: Gale, 2012.

14.48   *Who's Who in Medicine and Healthcare.* 8th ed. Berkeley Heights, NJ: Marquis Who's Who; 2011.

There are several science- and medicine-focused biographical sources that are handy tools in the ready reference toolbox. *American Men and Women of Science* (print and electronic) contains biographical information on more than 120,000 living persons in the physical, biological, and related science fields. Data includes birthdate and place, specialty field, education and degrees, professional and career details, memberships and affiliations, awards, and contact information. Another print option is the Who's Who in Medicine and Healthcare, which contains the biographies of more than 27,000 medical professionals, administrators, educators, researchers, clinicians, and industry leaders, mostly from the United States (see also 14.36). Like the other resources noted herein, data includes contact information, education and degrees, awards and recognitions, professional affiliations and memberships, and other career details.

Other Sources to Consider

14.49   *The Health Care 1500.* Washington, DC: Faulkner and Gray's Healthcare Information Center, 1995.

14.50   *Modern Healthcare.* Available: http://www.modernhealthcare.com/.

Although not updated, *The Health Care 1500*, published in 1995, offers an interesting snapshot of the state of medicine and health-care policy with profiles of influential people at the time. *Modern Healthcare*, a trade publication, prints an annual ranking of the 100 most influential people in health care, and includes biographical profiles of those selected. These resources, which have a decidedly commercial bent, could be considered less authoritative than some others; nevertheless, they can provide some details that might not be found from other sources.

Final Considerations

In instances where the previous resources do not provide an answer to a reference question or research query, thinking outside the ready-reference information box can be helpful. Biographical research is incomplete without consultation of Internet resources, though these require more care and evaluation. Most users will begin a search with Google or another search engine that may potentially lead them to un-reviewed but nevertheless helpful sources such as Wikipedia (as mentioned previously); university, hospital, or corporate employee websites; association membership directories; author book announcements; library records available via WorldCat; library subject guides or LibGuides; etc. Sources such as these should be verified by cross-checking what information is found, but they can act as helpful pointers.

Searching for relevant directories using natural language via Google; or meta-directories such as the Yahoo! Directory of organizations (Directory > Health > Medicine > Organizations) or the Internet Public Library resources by subject; or other curated resource lists, such as those found from other libraries or LibGuides can also be productive. For currently active professionals, a search of such widely used directories as LinkedIn or even Facebook can be useful in providing self-produced information about a biographical research subject, just as it is in an employee search.

Consultations with colleagues or other researchers, especially those who may have a professional or personal interest in a particular subject, can be particularly enlightening when the usual resources are insufficient. Serendipity should not be discounted either; those happy accidents uncovering a potential information source when looking for unrelated items that are mentally filed away for later can be invaluable.

CHAPTER 15

Grant Sources

JOHN D. JONES JR.

Are grants important to the success of one's institution? The need for increased grant and charitable funding continues to grow as a part of academic institutions' overall budgets. State-funded institutions are seeing more budget cuts than growth. Tuition in the public or private sectors can only increase so much. University administrators are expecting their schools, departments, and programs to find grant funding to not only take up slack but to grow existing or add new educational programs, curriculum, or degrees. Grants can fund travel, major construction, fellowships, internships, conferences, community outreach, and research. The more librarians are familiar with how grants work and which grant information sources are available, the more help they can provide to their users and their institutions. The bigger the organization the more coordination and collaboration is required.

Grants come predominately from government agencies, private business, and nonprofit organizations and foundations. The research tools leading to these groups typically set inclusion and exclusion criteria around dimensions such as funding sector, comprehensiveness, level of specificity, format, disciplines, and update frequency. Knowing and understanding the trade-offs within these dimensions will help librarians direct users to the best tools. Grant seekers have a specific purpose for which they require financial assistance. Matching their need to the best tool available is the librarian's goal. Finding the right grant may mean searching relevant government programs and moving to the corporate, nonprofit, or foundation sectors to identify matching funder interests or award-granting patterns.

In the realm of grant-finding tools, the digital revolution continues to overtake traditional print resources, especially regarding search capability, information updating, and ease of use. While print directories are still produced (and represented in this chapter), any institution really wishing to bolster current funding or pursue new funding on anything other than a small scale should be using online grant resources. If used, online grant resources are affordable. The next-generation tools will be (are) much more expensive but are expected to pay for themselves as an institution acquires more grant funds and awards.

Grant-finding resources are becoming more and more similar. One sees that many of the directories provide the same information fields. The publishers and producers of these resources still hand-search print journals or newsletters as well as online databases to identify grants to include but many can also access public Internal Revenue Service filings of 990 or 990PF documents to identify corporations and nonprofits providing charitable and grant funding.

Guides to writing grants, directories, and indexes are the most useful tools for those pursuing grants. This chapter focuses on directory-type resources for the grant seeker.

Multisector Funding

Multisector directories compile grant information from government, corporate, nonprofit, and foundation organizations. While they may cover much breadth and depth, they may be overwhelming to the beginning grant seeker unless given guidance by librarians or experienced grant seekers.

15.1   *Annual Register of Grant Support.* 46th ed. Medford, NJ: Information
        Today, 2013. Available: http://www.infotoday.com/.

Still one of the best first places to start looking for research endowments and grants, this edition offers introductions to more than 3,100 grant-offering organizations. While not restricted to the health sciences, this multidisciplinary resource covers public and private funding programs from government agencies, foundations, corporations, trusts, unions, professional associations, and special interest groups. The eleven major subject areas have more than sixty-one subcategories and four indexes: subject, organization and program, geographic, and personnel. Each grant program entry includes eligibility requirements, restrictions, application procedures, deadlines, grant size or range, and contact information.

While the Life Sciences section includes medicine and other health sciences specialty chapters, one must be imaginative in one's thinking and approach to finding grants by considering other content sections that might meet funding needs. For instance, the Education section has a Higher Education Projects and Research chapter; the International Affairs and Area Studies section has a chapter for International Studies and Research Abroad; and the Urban and Regional Affairs section has a Public Health chapter. Finding a grant to meet a specific need requires a certain amount of creativity.

15.2   *Directory of Research Grants.* 35th ed. West Lafayette, IN: Schoolhouse Partners, 2012. Available: http://www.schoolhousepartners.net/.

This annual multinational multidisciplinary funding directory, produced by Schoolhouse Partners, offers insight into more than 6,100 programs from more than 2,500 sponsors. This resource includes foundation, corporation, and government agency prospects. The Grant Program section is an alphabetical listing of grant programs where each entry includes an annotated description, requirements, restrictions, funding levels, application due and renewal dates, the *Catalog of Federal Domestic Assistance* program number, sponsor information, contact information, and Internet address. There are three indexes: the Subject Index, the Grants by Program Type Index, and the Geographic Index. The Subject Index covers a wide range of topics including health sciences such as diabetes, internal medicine, and nursing/nursing education. The Grants by Program Type Index breaks the different offerings down by categories leading to groups of grants supporting things such as symposia, conferences, workshops, and seminars; graduate assistantships; or exhibitions, collections, performances, and video/film production. The Geographic Index begins with the United States, moves to Canadian programs, and ends with other countries arranged alphabetically. Each index then lists the grant program title and accession number for the corresponding entries.

15.3   *Directory of Biomedical and Health Care Grants.* 23rd ed. West Lafayette, IN: Schoolhouse Partners, 2012. Available: http://www.schoolhousepartners.net/.

This Schoolhouse Partners annual health and biomedical-focused multisector grant directory covers more than 4,700 potential funding sources. The organization of the information is same as the *Directory of Research Grants* (see 15.2) with two main exceptions. Many of the Program Index listings offer examples of funded grants providing grant seekers with an indication of the sponsor's funding priorities. A fourth index, Sponsoring Organizations Index, aggregates the different grant opportunities for each sponsor allowing grant seekers to see the breadth of a sponsor's funding offerings and pursue parallel or similar prospects. The Directory of Biomedical and Health Care Grants offers an introductory section on proposal planning and writing.

15.4   GrantSelect. West Lafayette, IN: Schoolhouse Partners. Available: http://www.grantselect.com/.

GrantSelect is the online equivalent of the *Directory of Research Grants*, the *Directory of Biomedical and Health Care Grants* and several other grant directories published by Schoolhouse Partners. Using the Quick Search or Advanced Search, the database allows the user to see all of the Grant Program information as well as the information provided by the different indexes mentioned previously but in an online searchable environment with daily updating and e-mail alerting. Individual, institutional, and consortia subscriptions are available.

15.5   Grant Forward. Champaign, IL: Cazoodle. Available: http://www.grantforward.com/.

The online database, Grant Forward, contains more than 8,000 funding opportunities in the sciences, social sciences, arts, and humanities from government, private, and nonprofit organizations. Offers can be reviewed across thirty-nine subject areas containing more than 2,009 subcategories. The basic search works similarly to Web search engines—users type in what they want and review the results. The advanced search provides a set of fields for specific queries. In advanced search, specify general keywords, categories with subcategories, sponsors, and deadlines. Limit to grant types such as awards, fellowships, internships, research, training, travel, workshops, or conferences. Use these fields in combination to fully customize a query. After a search is run, filters or facets for sponsor, type of grant, type of submission, or grant deadline are generated to allow users to further refine their results. Save searches and create alerts based on the search strategy. In the results, each offering includes the description, sponsor, deadlines, amount, eligibility, submission information, and categories. When possible, Grant Forward links to the grant information source and application form. After taking the time to devise a thorough search strategy, save that search or create alerts to be notified of new funding opportunities. Grant Forward offers an administrative console, which may be of use to the institutional "Office of Research," but it also provides use statistics for the subscription. Grant Forward has replaced IRIS: the Illinois Researcher Information Service. Not available to individual subscribers, an institutional or organizational subscription is required to access Grant Forward.

15.6   SPIN—Sponsored Programs Information Network. Albany, NY: infoEd Global Available: http://infoedglobal.com/.

With more than 40,000 grant opportunities from more than 10,000 global sponsors, the online SPIN database allows users to configure and retain a variety of settings from one session to the next. Users can bookmark and share funding opportunities within SPIN or by e-mail. Signed-in users can save searches so the search can be re-run at any time in the future. Available category filters include applicant location, applicant type, project type, and project location. Search Options allows users to set search parameters like *Expand Search Terms via Thesaurus*, include and exclude different grant opportunities, and display award amounts in different currencies. SPIN covers government, private, and nonprofit offerings running the full range from million-dollar NIH grants to fellowship awards and travel fellowships. The vendor has provided a nice selection of fourteen short videos to help searchers make better use of the data. Not available to individual subscribers, an institutional or organizational subscription is required to access SPIN.

Federal Funding

First-time or novice grant seekers may not be aware that corporate and nonprofit foundations generally avoid duplicating federal, state, and local government grant offerings. As a rule of thumb, explore public government funding before moving on to private monies. Federal funding application processes typically have standardized forms. Government offerings follow public policy announcement procedures so grants are easier to hear about, follow, and find. Whichever source is used to identify opportunities, keep in mind that government programs are in a constant state of flux. The disparate budget processes cause changes in funding levels, program statuses, and application procedures. Be sure to check the website and contacts of the actual grant-making agencies for supplemental information regarding the offerings. One should consider consulting commercially produced sources on government funding, but be aware that some of these will be helpful and build on or add to one's understanding of the government playing field while others simply repackage government-produced information with little or no added value.

15.7   NIH Guide for Grants and Contracts. Washington, DC: National Institutes of Health. Available: http://grants.nih.gov/grants/oer.htm.

The National Institutes of Health (NIH) Guide for Grants and Contracts is not only the premier resource for finding federal medical and behavioral research grants, it is the official announcement tool for NIH and many other Health and Human Services agencies. The NIH Guide serves in lieu of the *Federal Register*. Online NIH Guide use is really the best way to keep up with the fast pace of announcements, change notices, and applications deadlines. Program Announcements, Request for Applications, and Notices are published daily. Subscribers to the free NIH Guide LISTSERV can receive a weekly update of published announcements or take advantage of the NIH Funding Opportunities RSS feed. The website also offers a wide variety of guidance and support concerning grants, grant processes, required and supplemental forms, and searching tutorials/videos. With basic and advanced searching, a searcher can quickly find potential monetary resources. Researchers can only benefit from reviewing this website, even if they are not applying for an NIH-funding opportunity.

15.8   NIH RePORTER—Research Portfolio Online Reporting Tools Expenditures and Results. Washington, DC: National Institutes of Health. Available: http://projectreporter.nih.gov/reporter.cfm.

NIH RePORTER (Research Portfolio Online Reporting Tools Expenditures and Results) is an electronic tool allowing users to search an NIH-funded research projects repository and access publications and patents resulting from NIH funding. Use RePORTER to find out if funding has already been provided for similar ideas and find out what kinds of grants have provided the funding. Is the field of competition for funding too large or too small? Discern areas of research with high potential and track funding trends to see where resources have increased or are dwindling. The RePORTER interface provides for searching across a huge number of dimensions (e.g., text string, award type, funding mechanism, deadline and application dates, principal investigator, NIH Spending Category, Congressional District, and more). A very comprehensive Frequently Asked Questions on the website covers almost any other questions one might have about what this database does and how one can use it.

RePORTER replaced CRISP (Computer Retrieval of Information on Scientific Projects), which was taken offline in December 2009. The CRISP data is available for download when more historical data is desired.

15.9   Grants.gov. Washington, DC: U.S. Department of Health and Human Services. Available: http://grants.gov/.

Managed by the U.S. Department of Health and Human Services, Grants.gov is a central repository for information on more than 1,000 grant programs to access approximately $500 billion in federal financial awards. Grants.gov allows one to search the discretionary grant offerings of twenty-six federal agencies (e.g., the Departments of Agriculture, Commerce, Defense, Veteran Affairs, and the National Science Foundation). An account to apply for grants is not needed in order to search for grant opportunities but will help when one is ready to use the online application system. Grants.gov offers a variety of subscription methods, including RSS feeds and customized search criteria, to receive automatic notifications of grant prospects and other updates. Users may browse by agency and category or search with the basic or advanced search options. A Search Grant Opportunities guide in PDF offers helpful strategies and tips to learn more about searching Grants.gov.

15.10   HHS Grants Forecast. Washington, DC: U.S. Department of Health and Human Services. Available: http://www.acf.hhs.gov/hhsgrantsforecast/.

A tool that may help in planning for future grant applications, the HHS Grants Forecast allows users to search the planned and proposed grant opportunities from

HHS agencies. Each forecast record estimates dates and funding levels for each proposed opportunity. Enactment of congressional appropriations ultimately denies or
affirms these proposed funding sources. Once funding is actually available, notices
are posted via Grants.gov and the NIH Guide for Grants and Contracts.

Foundation Funding

Private foundations are nongovernmental, nonprofit organizations receiving funding from single sources—usually individuals, families, or corporations. Directors
and trustees manage the monies according to foundation governance documents
and guidelines. Private foundations fall into four basic categories: independent,
company-sponsored, operating, and community. Geographic or subject area is
not always a deciding consideration with private foundations whereas company-
sponsored foundations are more likely to consider requests that have direct benefits in their own immediate neighborhood or community. Operating foundations use
their funds to conduct their own social welfare programs and research. Community
foundations typically make awards to charitable organizations that improve the local
community. The information regarding offerings from foundations is not aggregated
in a publicly free source. Lists of the overall opportunities are not generated and distributed. The vendors who offer online and print resources regarding private monies may find many of those private offerings through public tax records and other
required government filings but are often required to track down by hand much of
the details provided in foundation directories and databases. In order to promote the
offerings' visibility, some organizations upload or create their own profile information for these vendors.

When applying for funds, foundations tend to provide the grant writer with
general application guidelines allowing a high level of flexibility in the author's
approach to a proposal or request but offer very little guidance to help win the
award. Often, tracking down additional print or online material concerning a foundation or corporate award or awarding patterns may be difficult if not impossible.

15.11   Foundation Directory Online. New York: Foundation Center. Available:
         http://fconline.foundationcenter.org/.

Updated weekly, the Foundation Directory Online allows users to purchase access
to grantmakers' information at several levels. Choose "Basic" and access the top
10,000 U.S. foundations by total giving with the ability to search via keywords and
sixteen search fields. Move up to "Plus" where users can also search more than 2.4
million grants in addition to the top 10,000 foundations accessible with "Basic."
Advance to the highest level, "Professional," and access more than 108,000 foundations, corporate donors, and grant-offering charities with the ability to search via

keyword, thirty-one search fields, and more than 3 million grants. The Foundation Directory Online is brought together from foundations' Internal Revenue Service tax returns, grantmaker websites, annual reports, printed application guidelines, the philanthropic press, and various other sources. With Help files, tutorials, and FAQs, subscribers can help themselves or they can get phone or e-mail support from customer service. Individual, institutional, and consortia subscriptions are available.

15.12   *Foundation Directory.* New York: Foundation Center, 2012. Available: http://foundationcenter.org/.

The print edition of the *Foundation Directory* provides information on the 10,000 U.S. foundations providing the most funding. Learn about these foundations' fields of interest, financial information, decision makers, and contact information. The directory also includes information from more than 55,000 awarded grants which may help to illustrate a foundation's giving pattern. The *Foundation Directory* has seven indexes: Geographic, International Giving, Types of Support, Subject, Foundations New to the Edition, Foundation Name, and the Index to Donors-Officers-Trustees. Purchasing the Foundation Directory Part 2 provides the same content and information organization for the next 10,000 largest funders.

Corporate Funding

Since 1935, the Internal Revenue Service has allowed a charitable contribution of up to 5 percent of a corporation's net income. Corporate giving can include non-monetary and corporate sponsorship programs, matching gift and corporate volunteer programs, as well as traditional cash awards. Discovering corporate funding awards is frequently more difficult than identifying foundation awards. Not only are lists of opportunities seldom published or distributed, often company giving programs lack well-defined objectives and procedures. Business sector grant awards rely heavily on personal contact. Applicants for this funding type should expect to demonstrate how the project is related to the company's products or services or how it will benefit the company's customers, employees, or the company's public image.

15.13   *National Directory of Corporate Giving.* 17th ed. New York: Foundation Center, 2012. Available: http://foundationcenter.org/.

The *National Directory of Corporate Giving* provides profiles for more than 3,300 company-sponsored foundations and almost 1,700 corporate giving programs. This easy-to-use, fully indexed directory includes the typical contact and financial information but also includes fields for Giving Limitations, Types of Support, Fields of Interest, and Selected Grants. The directory includes indexes for Geographic Focus,

International Focus, Types of Support, Subject, Industry, Grantmaker/Company Name, and, finally, Donors, Trustees, and Administrators.

15.14   *Corporate Giving Directory.* 34th ed. Medford, NJ: Information Today, 2012. Available: http://www.infotoday.com/.

The *Corporate Giving Directory* provides access to the giving program priorities, giving preferences, evaluation criteria, contact information, and other data to help locate appropriate sources for corporate donations. Gain insight into more than 1,000 corporate foundations/giving programs. The listings include information regarding application procedures, restrictions, and specific grants given.

International Funding

Canadian Funding

Many of the multisector funding sources provide some international coverage. Use the geographical indexes to review the Canadian resources those directories have available. These resources are highly focused on the health sciences but are just a few of the overall Canadian resources that are available across all fields and disciplines. Many of the following Canadian resources cross-reference other potentially applicable government and foundation sites.

15.15   Canadian Institutes of Health Research (CIHR)/Instituts de recherche en santé du Canada (IRSC). Ottawa, ON: CIHR. Available: http://www.cihr-irsc.gc.ca/.

As the leading health research funder in Canada, the Canadian Institutes of Health Research provides funding opportunities around four thematic areas: biomedical, clinical, health systems services, and social, cultural, environmental, and population health. The CIHR Grants and Awards Guide provides detailed information on the application and grant management processes. The website provides information on agency funding policies and the peer-review process. The Find Funding section of the website allows the searching of opportunities, the viewing of all current opportunities, the browsing of current opportunities, and the browsing of archived opportunities. The search allows for keywords and phrases, limits by institute within the CIHR, program type, and applicant. Users may choose to include the archived opportunities as well as limit by launch date or application deadline. All information is provided in French and English.

15.16   Natural Sciences and Engineering Research Council (NSERC)/Conseil de recherches en sciences naturelles et en génie du Canada (CRSNG). Ottawa, ON: NSERC. Available: http://www.nserc-crsng.gc.ca/.

The NSERC offers a large number of funding opportunities to faculty and student researchers. By encouraging private companies to participate and invest in research projects, the NSERC hopes to make Canada a country of discoverers and innovators. Their website provides grant program descriptions, explanations of support for faculty versus students, eligibility guidelines, and frequently asked questions concerning the overall and individual processes. Giving great insight into funding patterns, NSERC provides an excellent search interface for reviewing previously awarded grants and scholarships. Users must register for a free On-Line System Login in order to apply for any of the awards.

15.17   Canadian Cancer Society (CCS)/Société canadienne du cancer. Toronto: CCS. Available: http://www.cancer.ca/.

A national community-based organization, the CCS acknowledges the high cost of conducting cancer research and attempts to cover or offset those expenses as it is able. Researchers from hospitals, universities, and research centers apply for CCS Research Institute funds annually. Subject to a strict national review process, the CCS is able to fund approximately 25 percent of the projects judged worthy. Grant seekers can review all grants and awards funded since 1999, which may reveal the organizations funding interest patterns.

15.18   Grant Connect. Toronto: Imagine Canada. Available: http://grantconnect.ca/.

Formerly known as the Canadian Directory to Foundations and Corporations, Grant Connect is an online subscription service from Imagine Canada with detailed searchable information to connect researchers with funders. Grant Connect includes funding opportunities from Canadian foundations, investment programs, and government agencies as well as American foundations willing to fund Canadian charities. To ensure high quality and currency, all of the information included in Grant Connect is researched, verified, and vetted by the staff. Specific search criteria include options for search by cause, type of support, and geography. Limit or filter results by deadline, gift amount, keywords, and preferred language. As a nonprofit, any revenue from Grant Connect subscription fees goes back into the charitable mission of Imagine Canada.

Other International Funding

As many institutions engage or experiment in global collaboration, it is easy to recognize that this important work still comes at a cost. There are foundations, trusts, and charitable and grant-making organizations around the globe willing to put forward assistance to those traveling and working abroad for a better global future. These resources offer insight into potential third-sector funding activity on a global scale.

15.19   *Guide to Funding for International and Foreign Programs.* 11th ed. New York: Foundation Center, 2012. Available: http://foundationcenter.org/.

The *Guide to Funding for International and Foreign Programs* provides foundations and giving programs willing to fund international efforts and research. Some of the types of giving are for international relief, disaster assistance, human rights, civil liberties, community development, education, and conferences. With more than 1,900 listings, searchers can review the contact information, financial data, giving priorities, and applications procedures of prospective funding sources. Examples of recently awarded grants help to reveal giving patterns. The guide provides indexes for subject, geographic area, and types of grant. A digital version is available for purchase but the licensing for campus- or institution-wide access would need to be reviewed.

15.20   *Europa International Foundation Directory.* 21st ed. New York: Routledge/ Taylor and Francis Group, 2012. Available: http://www.routledge.com/.

Listing global funding opportunities and international initiatives, the *Europa International Foundation Directory* connects people to more than 2,550 institutions around the world. The directory provides grantmaking information from foundations, trusts, and charitable and nongovernmental organizations. It covers offerings for nonprofit and profit-based organizations. Directory entries include contact information, organization aims, activities, and financial information. Indexes include Name, Area of Activity, and Geographical Area.

15.21   *World Guide to Foundations 2013.* Dublin, Ireland: Research and Markets, 2013. Available: http://www.researchandmarkets.com/.

Spanning 115 countries over six continents, the *World Guide to Foundations 2013* provides overviews and aims of grantmaking organizations worldwide. The entries are grouped by country and then arranged alphabetically within the countries. Each listing contains the name, abbreviation/acronym, contact information, year of establishment, grant areas supported, and grant restrictions. The publisher offers print and CD-ROM versions of this report.

15.22   Professional Research. London: ResearchResearch. Available: http://www .researchresearch.com/.

An online database originating in the United Kingdom, the scope and coverage of this resource has grown to include grant offerings worldwide. This resource's offerings range from large research councils to small private charities including travel grants to fellowships. Using a controlled thesaurus, identify searchable discipline terms to quickly locate funding opportunities within very specific research areas. While there is a decidedly European focus to their coverage, the database does cover North America (including NIH, NSF, and other federal agencies) and they list funding opportunities open to researchers worldwide. Professional Research includes access to a corresponding source of online news and analysis of research funding and policy which identifies every funding opportunity open to readers, listing pertinent entry information such as submission deadlines, funding amounts, research areas, eligibility, contact details, and more. Professional Research and the newsletter, *Research USA*, are only available via an institutional subscription. Free database trials are available. Newsletter editions cover the United Kingdom, Europe, Ireland, Netherlands, Africa, United States, Caribbean, and Australia/New Zealand. Not available to individual subscribers, an institutional or organizational subscription is required to access Professional Research.

Grants to Individuals

15.23   *Foundation Grants to Individuals.* 21st ed. New York: Foundation Center, 2012. Available: http://foundationcenter.org/.

Foundation Grants to Individuals includes more than 9,600 foundation and charity programs that fund researchers, students, and other individual grant seekers. Funding types cover a wide range of offerings that includes educational support, residencies, scholarships, fellowships, loans, research, and professional support. The directory includes basic information on the grant-offering organizations, the funding programs' scope and nature, and the grant-maker information availability. Where possible, listings include a purpose and activities statement, fields of interest, geographic focus, and funder limitations. Listings may include application procedures, financial data, and recently awarded grants. The directory includes the following indexes: foundation, locations, fields of interest, support type, geographic, and more. This resource is available as a print publication and as an online database.

15.24   RSP FundingFinder. El Dorado Hills, CA: Reference Service Press. Available: http://www.rspfundingfinder.com/.

RSP FundingFinder offers three different databases—RSP Funding for Undergraduates, RSP Funding for Graduate Students, and RSP Funding for Professionals and Post-doctorates—to help individuals find money to help pay for study, training, research, creative projects, professional development, and professional travel. These opportunities include scholarships, fellowships, loans, grants, awards, and internships. Information for funding programs may include sponsoring organization, program title, eligibility qualifications, amount and type of award, length of funding time and renewal applicability, number of awards granted, deadlines, and award subject focus. Information that cannot be verified or has not been updated by the grant maker in the past twelve months is withdrawn from the database. Reference Service Press offers a variety of print publications broken down by disciplines and by minority/ ethnicities—*Money for Graduate Students in the Health Sciences*, *How to Pay for Your Degree in Nursing*, or *Financial Aid for Hispanic Americans*.

15.25 *The Grants Register 2013: The Complete Guide to Postgraduate Funding Worldwide.* New York: Palgrave Macmillan, 2013. Available: http:// us.macmillan.com/.

The *Grants Register* points to more than 1,100 grant-funding organizations in more than forty-nine countries providing a gateway to more than 4,000 different awards. This annually updated directory has full contact information, subjects, eligibility, level of study, type of award, award value, award frequency, source of funding, important dates, and application procedures. The directory is arranged alphabetically by awarding body with a full list of awards from each organization. To help sort through and find what is needed, the directory includes three indexes—Index of Awards, Index of Discounted Awards, and Index of Awarding Organizations.

Next-Generation Tools

Sources for funding will shrink rather than grow. Competition for funding will grow rather than shrink. The next-generation tools will match funding opportunities to those researchers best placed to win the awards and make identifying collaboration partners quicker and easier. These tools will make it faster and simpler to apply for identified grants. The next-generation tools will be "smart" enough to find, follow, and track published research from an institution and its individual researchers to build and grow profiles for matching research interests to funding opportunities. No one system may do all of this yet but these tools are evolving now.

15.26 Pivot. Bethesda, MD: ProQuest. Available: http://pivot.cos.com/.

Pivot helps to quickly discover funding opportunities and match that funding to the best collaborative faculty and researchers to improve the chance of winning the award. It focuses on connecting faculty to each other and then to funding opportunities. Building from the Community of Science and Community of Scholars profiles, users can search for grants and instantly identify potential internal and external collaboration partners. The reverse is also true. Users can identify a specific researcher and have funding offerings that match the researcher's profile fed directly to them. Pivot includes federal, private, and international funding opportunities in multi-disciplines supporting research, collaborations, travel, curriculum development, conferences, and fellowships and is updated daily. Pivot is only available by institutional/

organizational subscription. Pivot has replaced the ProQuest Community of Science profile match to funding system.

15.27   SMARTS—SPIN Matching and Research Transmittal Service. Albany, NY: infoEd Global. Available: http://infoedglobal.com/.

GENIUS is infoEd Global's proprietary central expertise profile database built by capturing institutional faculty and researcher curriculum vitae details. SMARTS takes GENIUS, combines it with the SPIN funding database, and automatically over-lays and matches key information to generate and deliver relevant, targeted, spon-sored program options. Administrators and researchers can review these matches and weigh the value of applying for the funding opportunities.

Things to Consider: Issues, Concerns, and Comments

Finding external funding on a bigger and bigger scale is increasingly important. Seeking and receiving grants raises the profile of the library—with researchers in general and institutional administrators specifically. Librarians who can help their programs, departments, schools, and institution find external funding elevate the sta-tus of the library. Librarians working at institutions or hospitals with active research-ers should probably pursue the Collaborative Institutional Training Initiative, more commonly referred to as CITI training. CITI offers training concerning a number of research issues but is highly known for the human subjects research and the Responsible Conduct of Research preparation courses. Most institutional review boards require some form of this training before one may submit proposals as a pri-mary investigator or be listed as a co-primary investigator. Completing this training can help show that the library is positioned to be an active partner or collaborator promoting the institution's research objectives.

As more institutions move to the next-generation tools to maximize grant awards across the institution, the "Offices of Research" are likely to play an even bigger role in the pursuit of grant funding. If systems to match funding opportuni-ties with those most likely to win an award to conduct that research are to work at optimum levels, researchers will be expected to be more collaborative and forth-coming about their research interests. Managing their profiles or portfolios in order to best support their own research and the institutional direction will also be highly expected. Sharing information instead of hoarding or secreting away viable research topics will be the way that institutions earn more and varied grant funding. Grant funding is incredibly fast paced. The next-generation systems should give institu-tions the flexibility they need to respond quickly and thoroughly. That flexibility and speed was sorely tested when Congress passed the American Recovery and

Reinvestment Act of 2009. The turnaround time to respond to these high-stake grant announcements was short and those who could not maneuver the course failed to garner those dollars.

As library acquisition dollars shrink, many of these paper directory subscriptions are cancelled or only purchased every two or three years. Simply perusing the holdings in WorldCAT helps to show the demise of the print directory. Is the "Office of Research" already paying for online or print resources that are being underutilized? The online tools are getting more sophisticated and much easier to use. Libraries need to consider the best way to support their institution's need for grant resource tools—especially in the wake of decreased public and deflated tuition funding.

For years now, it has been said that librarians can play a major institutional role by better supporting the pursuit of external funding. There are pockets of librarians out there doing just that but overall, grant resources are shunned as too difficult, too complicated, or beyond the scope of the job. Consider carefully the ramifications of having others in one's institution take on these roles. Did the library dodge a bullet or miss the greatest opportunity?

CHAPTER 16

Point-of-Care and Clinical Decision Support Resources

SUSAN SWOGGER

One of the most vital and also most unique health sciences information needs is for accurate information at the point of care—at the bedside or examination table. A point-of-care (POC) resource is one intended for use by health-care practitioners in the clinic or hospital.

Point-of-care resources must provide reliable and current information both quickly and easily—immediacy and accuracy of information can literally be of life-or-death importance in medical situations. One oft-cited study reported that only 30 percent of physicians' point-of-care information needs were being met in 1985, largely due to inadequacy of content and slowness of access to available information sources.[1] In the period since that study was completed, this area has developed rapidly in response to opportunities provided by paradigm shifts to evidence-based medicine and to electronic information resources.

This chapter discusses the basic categories and qualities of POC resources, some of the reasons for their recent rise in prominence, and the reference librarian's role in their use. See chapter 5 (Indexing, Abstracting, and Digital Database Resources) for a discussion of additional electronic resources that are of secondary but still important use at the point of care.

Evidence-Based Practice and Information Needs of Clinical Professionals

Clinicians and other health-care practitioners have always kept books and journals ready to assist with difficult consultations, so much so that a shelf of such materials is nearly always present in any artistic depiction of the professions, but two cultural shifts sparked a major change over the past decade—the growing use of the Internet to find every kind of information and the widespread adoption of the concept of evidence-based practice.

As discussed in chapter 5, the Internet provides access to vast amounts of information in a format that can be very quickly reviewed and synthesized, meaning that the majority of such resources are online. The need for both speed and a solid, broad evidence basis for clinical decision making has resulted in the rapid growth of specific POC resources intended to provide instant access to the required evidence. Clinicians will seek out information online, whether within a POC resource or outside it, and studies show that searches using POC resources are more likely to be both swift and correct than when performed with other Internet sources, PubMed, or academic databases.[2-3] As these other resources are likely to be both familiar and available to clinicians, online resources specifically intended for use at the point of care should be acquired and promoted.

A core concept in the design of most POC resources is the need to support evidence-based practice (EBP). The concepts of evidence-based practice and evidence-based medicine have spread rapidly through many fields of health and social care professions since the early 1990s, and they have become widely acknowledged as a dominant medical paradigm. The central tenet of EBP is that practitioners will "use the best evidence possible, i.e., the most appropriate information available, to make clinical decisions for individual patients"—or for nearly any other undertaking appropriate to a field.[4]

The "best evidence possible" is usually described as current evidence derived from the careful examination, evaluation, and synthesis of multiple peer-reviewed research studies. The Association of American Medical Colleges (AAMC) lists as an objective a requirement that medical students be "skillful," defined in part as being able to understand the scientific basis and evidence of effectiveness for therapeutic actions, but this does not mean that every clinician will perform his or her own complete evaluation of the best evidence for every action taken.[5] It does mean that every clinician is likely to need to refer to trustworthy sources that *have* reviewed the evidence while creating treatment protocols and recommendations.

Point-of-care resources are assumed to be such sources by most clinicians and are trusted as such—numerous studies show that recommendations from POC resources are likely to affect clinical decision making.[6-8] It is important that such influential resources are well chosen by the providing institution in order to meet this assumption and provide good, evidence-based information to clinical users. Recent political mandates have ensured that online POC resources will only rise in influence.

The HITECH Act and Clinical Decision Support Systems

The Health Information Technology for Economic and Clinical Health Act (HITECH Act), included as part of the American Recovery and Reinvestment Act of 2009, mandates that hospitals must have information technology that makes "meaningful use" of electronic medical records (EMRs) or face what are effectively reductions in Medicare and Medicaid payments in comparison to their peers.[9] Although there is still some debate about the correct interpretation of meaningful use, the United States Department of Health and Human Services has stated that it must include the use of electronic tools for Clinical Decision Support (CDS), meaning that clinicians should be able to search and access an evidence-based clinical knowledge base while within individual patient health records.[10]

Though this phrase is often used to describe nearly any POC resource, by definition, a true Clinical Decision Support System (CDSS) is able to accept and return a search based on inputted patient data for an individual case and is intended to aid in diagnosis and decision making rather than act strictly as a reference tool.[11] A CDSS that meets the aims of the HITECH Act must be fully integrated into an EMR system. While many specialty CDSSs exist, those capable of EMR integration most commonly support multiple clinical specialties, often with a focus on diseases, conditions, and pharmaceuticals. This is an area of rapid development and change and is likely to become even more prominent in the near future.

Many POC publishers and EMR developers either already offer or have begun to develop means to integrate POC resources and EMR systems. Most of these are at varying stages of adopting the HL7 infobutton standard, developed to standardize and thus facilitate the integration between POC and EMR systems.[12] The HL7 standard requires that an EMR interact with a POC resource to produce "infobuttons" specific to an individual record that may be clicked to pull relevant information from the POC knowledge base.[13] This will permit a much greater number of resources to act as HITECH CDSS than is currently the case.

Librarians and Point-of-Care Resources

Although on the surface a resource designed for easy and intuitive usability that is likely to be integrated within an EMR may not display a need for the assistance of a librarian, there are a number of reasons why reference librarians should be knowledgeable about such resources. It is common for the library to be involved with the selection of such resources when subscribed institutionally, thus requiring knowledge of a wide variety of resources. Some hospitals support individual subscriptions to specialty resources for clinicians involved in particular areas of practice, which may fall to the librarian to manage and support. Once such a resource is chosen and in place, regardless of whether it is available institution-wide or is institutionally supported for individual users, there must be continuing and sustained librarian involvement in a number of roles.

Librarians usually serve as the first point of contact for most hospital and student users who need assistance with any online resource and will receive questions requiring a good understanding of both their content and use—POC resources are no different in this respect. POC resources are also by design somewhat superficial; if a clinician encounters an unusual or confusing case, he or she may not be able to provide an adequate answer. If a librarian is to most effectively assist in going beyond the POC resource, he or she must have a good understanding of both its limitations and what the clinician is likely to have already found on his or her own. This is true for both academic and hospital librarians—while POC resources are designed to meet the needs of clinicians in practice, they are also popular with student users. Health sciences students who have them available often find them useful as a starting point in understanding new topics—although they may need some assistance in realizing that they are best used as starting points and not as complete coverage for a new learner.

Librarians are often expected to provide or arrange training for the use of POC resources, just as with other online resources. This could include anything from arranging for the visit of a vendor-provided trainer, offering individual training, teaching classes to new cohorts of residents, or creating detailed online tutorials. Each of these options requires close and current knowledge of each resource. If a POC resource is available to every user on a campus IP range, it is also possible that campus users outside of the health sciences may encounter them and have questions, possibly requiring the health sciences librarian to assist. For example, many people have questions about prescription medications: Kinesiology students or athletes may seek out practical orthopedic information, and law students may try to find information to understand malpractice issues.

Hospital librarians may also find themselves supporting clinicians in other ways. Many may go along on hospital Grand Rounds, or the presentation of patients to groups of clinicians and clinicians in training, to provide expert searching assistance. In some cases, they may be responsible for managing the Continuing Medical Education (CME) functions provided by many POC resources. Many POC resources offer an option for recording and reporting CME or Continuing Education (CE) credits for clinicians who create personal logins for the resource and perform searches.

The American Medical Association (AMA) and other professional associations offer some CME credits for recorded searches, which can be very useful for clinicians These resources typically require a core administrator—who may be a librarian or require a librarian's support—in order to manage and track credits for all of the users of a particular resource.

Qualities and Formats of Point-of-Care Resources

As discussed previously, POC resources have several important qualities that are universally important because of their specific purpose, regardless of topic coverage. Their clinical content must be evidence-based and relevant to practice. Many tout their own skill at the evaluation of evidence and creation of reviews and recommendations—their process should be transparent and performed by respected reviewers. They must be regularly and frequently updated. They must be easy to search, understandable to read, swift to use, and free of unnecessary clutter. Finally, they must be available readily and in a format that is possible to use in the necessary location, which may range from a hospital lab to a clinical examination table to an ICU bedside.

Format can have a strong effect on whether a particular POC resource displays these qualities. It is also common for one POC resource to be available in multiple formats to meet different requirements, sometimes with unique content within each different manifestation depending on relevancy to intended uses. In this situation, it is not unlikely that a library or hospital may have multiple subscriptions to different forms of the same resource. For example, the author's home library once had access to a particular drug database in four different formats: It provided the hospital formulary, separately provided the drug content within a multi-specialty clinical POC database, was subscribed as an independent academic database, and was made available as a mobile application to a small group of faculty.

The variety of formats is changing rapidly and it is likely that this list will have been augmented by the time it is read; however, the following are the current most prominent options.

Individual Print or Electronic Books

Typically available in both print and downloadable e-book formats, these often have a long history of multiple editions. Most are in outline or handbook format and serve as quick reference for such topics as disorders and conditions, diagnostic algorithms, and prescriber's guides. This chapter will not further address these titles, but the subscription health sciences book review service *Doody's Core Titles* is an excellent source of further information (available at http://www.doody.com/dct/).[14]

Note: These are distinct from "enhanced" e-books databases, which may have begun their histories as print books but are now available as databases that include a large amount of additional multimedia or interactive content to supplement the original text.

Stand-Alone or Clinical Decision Support System Databases

These are the resources currently most and least likely to be used by health sciences librarians, as this category includes both POC databases and CDSS resources fully integrated into hospital EMRs. They include content such as but not limited to original monographs, image libraries, special journal article collections, decision trees, clinical books, vaccination schedules, calculators, streaming procedural videos, prescription guides, interaction checkers, and more. Some draw content from multiple publishers; others focus on content from one publisher. Some address multiple clinical specialties; others include just one. They can typically (barring some CDSS) be used independently of other resources even if capable of EMR integration, and are subscribed by academic as often as hospital libraries.

Note: Many of these databases may be searched or used with other databases both academic and clinical when subscribed on the same platform or when a partner agreement exists; this may be customized to best suit the needs of an institution. For example, subscribers of EBSCO's Dynamed may also subscribe to and integrate content from several others of its many POC databases and from the MEDLINE portion of PubMed and/or choose to integrate content from select other providers including Lexicomp and ZynxHealth. Each of these is further described below.

Note: Hospitals are highly likely to also have subscriptions to *formulary databases* containing prescribing and pricing information about drugs used specifically by the hospital or supported by particular insurance plans. It is unlikely that librarians will use or have access to these, but they may provide support for resources used by those who manage the formulary. It is also fairly common to have separate library subscriptions to the same databases used for the hospital formulary, albeit in a different format. It is important to be aware of any such overlap, as there may be confusion when discussing said resources with users or billing managers who are familiar with both but do not realize that they are separate subscriptions or installations.

Mobile Applications

Mobile resources are becoming increasingly widely used by clinicians and health sciences students just as is true of the general population. While the majority of these resources require a constant WiFi connection, some permit users to download significant or all content for use offline. This is highly desirable for many groups of users—students away on rotation or doing research, clinicians providing care outside of the hospital, any users dealing with very restrictive limitations on Internet use (common in hospitals), any users in older buildings with poor WiFi connections. Most of this type of downloaded content requires the user to maintain an affiliation with the subscribing institution, which may be managed manually by requiring individual annual renewals or automatically by using the resource via WiFi connection within the hospital or university IP range.

There are presently four mobile access types of major relevance to health sciences libraries:

1. Increasingly, stand-alone POC databases of the type described previously are releasing mobile applications available to institutional subscribers as part of a subscription. Health sciences librarians will often need to make sure that users are able to access and use the ones they are entitled to use. Some release only limited numbers of licenses for mobile applications. Typically these each require annual renewal to ensure that users can still prove affiliation with the institution, which inevitably falls to the librarian to manage, but this is becoming less common.

2. Many databases also provide *mobile optimization*; that is, while not a specific application, they will recognize and reformat specifically for smartphone or tablet access. Any further mention of "mobile" options in this chapter will not refer to this form of mobile access, but instead to downloadable mobile applications for smartphones or tablets (apps).

3. Some POC mobile applications are available as institutional subscriptions; libraries or hospitals may subscribe and give their entire user base the right to download and use the app. Some of these permit customization of included content.

4. Many POC resources of varying quality are available solely as individual mobile applications for smartphones or tablets. It is common for residents or interns to use these and request advice or assistance, but they are rarely financially supported by libraries and will not be included here.

Sources of POC Resource Information and Reviews

Most of these resources, and the issues surrounding their further utilization and development, are regularly reviewed and discussed in a wide variety of publications and forums. For more information, please search the following resources:

PubMed, http://www.ncbi.nlm.nih.gov/PubMed. PubMed is an excellent source of information about POC resources; many researchers, librarians, and practitioners write about them in different contexts.

Journal of the Medical Library Association (*JMLA*), Medical Library Association, http://www.ncbi.nlm.nih.gov/pmc/journals/93/latest/. JMLA often has articles about a wide variety of POC support-related topics, but most important, includes a regular section of electronic resource reviews that often covers POC resources.

Journal of Electronic Resources in Medical Libraries, Routledge, http://www.tandfonline.com/toc/werm20/current. This journal often includes reviews and discussions of POC resources.

Point-of-Care Databases by Content and Format

Multiple-Specialty Clinical Databases

The following databases include content to support multiple areas of practice. Many of them are available in multiple formats, and many are also in various stages of HL7 infobutton standard implementation in attempts to become true HITECH Act–qualified CDSSs. Many if not most of them also provide CME or CE credits to users. As these features are all undergoing rapid change and development, please see each resource directly for more information.

It is nearly as common for academic libraries as hospital libraries to subscribe to these, as they are often used in instruction or to support students starting their clinical studies. This type of resource is also commonly designed to suit the needs of one particular audience—physicians, nurses, hospital staff—but will also be used by others in the hospital or university, so librarians should be aware of any possible assistance that may be needed to make them most useful for a particular audience. Another important issue for academic librarians is that most such resources, if they include journal- or book-based content, will only include materials from a limited and rolling span of years, as they are intended to be very current. If the library requires perpetual access to included materials, it must make separate purchase or subscription of them. These resources very often provide valuable supplemental resources for an academic program, but are by design more superficial than is optimal for students and certainly for researchers.

This list includes some of the more prominent POC resources at the time of publication, with more attention paid to those most widely discussed among health sciences librarians. These resources are all capable of being used independently of EMRs, with one exception that can nevertheless interact with other subscribed library resources. Please see the resources suggested above to seek out the most current information, or information about resources only usable within an EMR.

16.1   Dynamed. Ipswich, MA: EBSCO. Available: http://dynamed.ebscohost.com/.

- Platform availability: Dynamed site, Mobile, EMR
- Subscription options: Individual or Institutional
- Scope and description: Dynamed is an evidence-based database of "clinically organized summaries" for more than 3,200 clinical topics, and is intended for use primarily by physicians. Its daily updates are supported by editors monitoring more than 500 medical journals for new evidence; each article is evaluated and then integrated or rejected using their seven-step "Systematic Literature Surveillance" process. Chosen articles are then linked directly to its summaries. It can include content from many of EBSCO Publishing's other databases or be used as a stand-alone resource, and is very widely subscribed by hospitals and universities. It can also integrate content from the POC resources Lexicomp and ZynxEvidence, both from other publishers.

16.2   UpToDate. Waltham, MA: UpToDate, Wolters Kluwer. Available: http://www.uptodate.com/.

- Platform availability: UpToDate site, OvidMD site, Mobile (forthcoming), EMR
- Subscription options: Individual or Institutional
- Scope and description: UpToDate is widely used both individually and in hospitals; it provides original review articles written by experts on more than 10,000 clinical topics across twenty specialties (and expanding), numerous patient information resources, medical calculators, images, and more. Its drug and drug interaction information derives from the pharmaceutical POC resource Lexicomp, also partially owned by Wolters Kluwer. If a library or hospital also subscribes to the image-focused POC resource VisualDx, it can be integrated into UpToDate's search engine and results. UpToDate itself can be integrated into OvidMD if a library subscribes to it, or used independently, or via an EMR.

16.3   ClinicalKey. Amsterdam: Elsevier B.V. Available: http://www.clinicalkey.com/.

- Platform availability: ClinicalKey site, Mobile (forthcoming), EMR
- Subscription options: Institutional
- Scope and description: ClinicalKey is a new resource, taking the place of the now defunct but nearly universal MD Consult and is designed to present all of Elsevier's current medical content in one resource designed to meet the needs of working clinicians. It includes all of the content from Elsevier's older POC resource, First Consult; all of its journals, medical textbooks, and medical reference books; all of the videos and images from Elsevier's books; the drug monographs from Clinical Pharmacology/Gold

Standard; the videos from the video methods resource Procedures Consult; an integrated search of PubMed; etc.

16.4   Essential Evidence Plus. Hoboken, NJ: Wiley-Blackwell. Available: http://www.essentialevidenceplus.com/index.cfm.

- Previously known as: InfoPOEMS
- Platform availability: Essential Evidence Plus site, Mobile
- Subscription options: Individual or Institutional
- Scope and description: This resource is designed to support physicians and nurses, as well as other clinical staff. It includes more than 13,000 topics, tools, images, drug safety information, weekly podcasts, etc. If a library has a subscription to Cochrane Systematic Reviews, it will link full text to it; if not, it will offer abstracts.

16.5   BMJ Best Practice/Clinical Evidence. London: British Medical Journal.

- Platform availability: BMJ Evidence Centre site, Unbound Medicine (Mobile platform), Mobile
- Subscription options: Individual or Institutional
- Scope and description: This British resource is designed to make BMJ's Clinical Evidence reviews as well as treatment guidelines from the UK's National Institute for Health and Clinical Excellence (NICE) usable at the point of care. It includes original topic reviews and monographs, calculators, images, practice guidelines, integrated reference texts, etc. It is available on Unbound Medicine's mobile platform as well as directly from BMJ.

16.6   OvidMD. New York: Ovid, Wolters Kluwer. Available: http://ovidmd.ovid.com/.

- Platform availability: OvidMD site
- Subscription options: Institutional
- Scope and description: OvidMD is designed to be a physician-specific interface for use with Wolters Kluwer/Ovid content for clinicians at the point of care, as opposed to the research-oriented OvidSP interface. More library friendly than some POC resources, its basic subscription includes the ability to link out to library catalogs and library link resolvers, access to Ovid MEDLINE, some of Lippincott Williams and Wilkin's Current Opinions journals, evidence-based guidelines, drug monographs from the POC resource Facts and Comparisons, patient handouts, etc. It can include most other Ovid subscriptions as well as many offered by the parent company Wolters Kluwer, if they are concurrently subscribed—the POC resource UpToDate, the Cochrane Reviews, assorted e-book collections, journal collections, etc.

16.7   Micromedex. Ann Arbor, MI: Truven Health Analytics. Available: http://www.micromedex.com/.

- Platform availability: Micromedex site, Mobile, Formulary, EMR
- Subscription options: Institutional
- Scope and description: This hospital POC resource has a long history as a core pharmaceutical product and is becoming established as a broader CDSS. Its 2.0 version includes more disease and condition information as well as its traditional toxicology, prescribing, and pharmacy information. It can include and integrate a number of additional specialty databases beyond its base if applicable for a particular hospital. Knowledge and use of it is considered critical for pharmacy students.

16.8   AccessMedicine. Columbus, OH: McGraw-Hill Education. Available: http://accessmedicine.com/.

- Platform availability: AccessMedicine site, Mobile
- Subscription options: Institutional or Individual
- Scope and description: AccessMedicine centers on some of McGraw-Hill's many long-respected medical reference books and textbooks, including the nearly universally used *Harrison's Principles of Internal Medicine*. These are supplemented with image libraries, guidelines, case files, drugs, quick reference, podcasts, real-time updates, resources for clerkships and study, etc. This resource is perhaps more widely used as an academic resource but can serve both purposes.
- Additional resources: Similar Access specialty platforms from McGraw-Hill include AccessPharmacy, AccessEmergency Medicine, AccessPediatrics, AccessSurgery, AccessAnesthesiology, AccessPhysiotherapy.

16.9   PEPID. Evanston, IL: Pepid. Available: http://www.pepid.com/.

- Platform availability: PEPID site, Mobile, EMR
- Subscription options: Institutional
- Scope and description: Unlike most of the other resources on this list, PEPID was designed as a mobile resource first for Personal Data Assistants (PDAs) and then moved online. PEPID also offers a number of different practice-specific options—physician, nurse, physician assistant, etc. It also offers number of student-specific resources for the beginnings of clinical training. It includes clinical topic reviews, drug resources, differential diagnosis tools, assorted drug checkers, other calculators, images, etc.; there is optional specific content for different modules.

16.10   ZynxEvidence. Los Angeles, CA: ZynxHealth, Hearst Corporation. Available: http://www.zynx.com/.

- Platform availability: EMR
- Subscription options: Institutional
- Scope and description: ZynxEvidence is available primarily within an EMR, though hospitals with subscriptions can provide access to some content outside of it. It is intended to serve as the knowledge bank for a number of other Zynx clinical resources. It includes over 145 modules offering original clinical topics, drug resources, differential diagnosis tools, assorted drug checkers, other calculators, images, etc. ZynxEvidence can include links to relevant searches in a large number of other databases if subscribed, including content from EBSCO, Truven Health Analytics, Elsevier, and others.

Specialty Stand-Alone Databases

In addition to the broader resources that are intended to support the range of specialties in one package, there are many specialist resources that focus more in depth on one area of practice. This may allow more detail, or a specialized format or tools best suited to one area of practice, or may simply be intended to allow subscription only to the most necessary content. In many cases, some combination of specialist databases with or without a broader one will best suit the needs of the hospital, practice, or library. The following list is not intended to be exhaustive, as this is an area of very rapid growth and development.

16.11 VisualDx. Rochester, NY: Logical Images. Available: http://www.visualdx.com/.

- Platform availability: VisualDx site, Mobile, UpToDate site, EMR
- Subscription options: Individual or Institutional
- Scope and description: VisualDx is a CDSS that provides very detailed images of dermatological conditions and infections, drug reactions, eye disorders, oral disorders and infections, pulmonary problems, etc.— visually diagnosable conditions that can be searched by specific patient symptoms and characteristics. It provides all institutional subscribers access to a downloadable mobile app. If a Library or Hospital also subscribes to UpToDate, its records can be integrated into the UpToDate search results.

16.12 Pediatric Care Online (PCO). Elk Grove Village, IL: American Academy of Pediatrics. Available: http://www.pediatriccareonline.org/.

- Platform availability: Pediatric Care Online site, Mobile
- Subscription options: Individual or Institutional
- Scope and description: Pediatric Care Online provides access to a collection of widely used textbooks from the American Academy of Pediatrics (AAP), including the *Red Book*, *Bright Futures*, and the *AAP Textbook of Pediatric Care* as well as pediatric drug and vaccination information, a library of

pediatric images, an assortment of clinical calculators and algorithms, patient handouts, etc.

16.13   PEMSoft. Ipswich, MA: EBSCO. Available: http://www.pemsoft.com/.

- Platform availability: PEMSoft site
- Subscription options: Individual or Institutional
- Scope and description: PEMSoft offers fifty basic emergency and fifty top primary care topics, thousands of video and images, a pediatric formulary with links to the relevant topics, assorted calculators and algorithms, a triage section, quick reference, and a toxicology section. At the time of this writing, it has recently been purchased by EBSCO, and it is likely that changes in platform availability and possibly content will occur in the near future.

16.14   Mosby's Nursing Consult. Amsterdam: Elsevier B.V. Available: http://www. nursingconsult.com/nursing/index.

- Platform availability: Mosby's Nursing Consult site, Mosby's Nursing Suite site
- Subscription options: Institutional
- Scope and description: Mosby's Nursing Consult offers a number of Elsevier's nursing textbooks and references, nursing journals, drug information, patient education materials, evidence-based nursing resources, and nursing calculators. It provides the option to create and upload organization-specific materials for use within a subscribing hospital or university. It can be subscribed to independently or can be integrated with the additional nursing resources of Mosby's Nursing Suite, which support research, continuing education, and skills growth.

16.15   Nursing Central. Charlottesville, VA: Unbound Medicine. Available: http:// nursing.unboundmedicine.com/nursingcentral/ub.

- Platform availability: Mobile within the Unbound Medicine app platform
- Subscription options: Institutional or Individual
- Scoped and description: Nursing Central is a mobile app that provides a specialized search of MEDLINE, mobile access to a number of nursing point-of-care e-books and textbooks, and customizable access to PubMed Central or institutionally subscribed journals. It can be subscribed individually or institutionally and is designed for both practicing and student nurses. If a library or hospital subscribes to multiple resources from UnBound Medicine, it can be used independently or as part of a package. Unbound also offers a number of familiar POC book resources as add-on modules that can be customized. Its included books can be downloaded to a mobile phone and do not require ongoing WiFi access, allowing them to be used in hospitals or distant locations with poor connectivity.

16.16   Nursing@Ovid. New York: Ovid, Wolters Kluwer. Available: http://
        resourcecenter.ovid.com/site/resources/index_nursing.jsp.

   • Platform availability: Nursing@Ovid site

   • Subscription options: Institutional

   • Scope and description: Nursing@Ovid uses OvidSP's platform and tool suite
     and proprietary nursing subject thesaurus to provide full-text access to a
     collection of Lippincott Williams and Wilkins and other journals for nursing
     and allied health, in addition to bibliographic records for a specialized
     international collection of other nursing journals and a collection of nursing
     tools. It can be used in concert with other Ovid databases both point-of-
     care and research-focused, if subscribed.

16.17   Nursing Reference Center. Ipswich, MA: EBSCO. Available:
        http://www.ebscohost.com/nursing/products/nursing-reference-center.

   • Platform availability: EBSCOhost site, Mobile, EMR

   • Subscription options: Institutional

   • Scope and description: One of several EBSCO Reference Centers, this one
     includes "quick lesson" topic reviews, evidence-based care guidelines, a
     focus on cultural competencies, drug resources, patient education materials,
     the text of an assortment of nursing reference handbooks, a collection of
     relevant legal cases, clinical assessment tools, and CE modules. If a library
     subscribes to other EBSCOhost health databases, many of those relevant
     can be searched or browsed within Nursing Reference Center.

   • Additional resources: Similar Reference Centers from EBSCO include Re-
     habilitation Reference Center (occupational, speech, and physical therapies),
     Patient Education Reference Center, and Health Policy Reference Center
     (of use to hospital administration).

16.18   Lexicomp. Hudson, OH: Lexi-Comp, Wolters Kluwer. Available:
        http://www.lexi.com/.

   • Platform availability: Lexicomp site, Formulary, Mobile, EMR

   • Subscription options: Individual or Institutional

   • Scope and description: This pharmaceutical resource offers toxicological,
     pharmaceutical, prescribing, and drug interaction information, some of
     which it still co-produces as print prescription guides. Nearly uniquely,
     it offers a specialized module and interface for dentistry and oral drug
     reaction information. It offers some other optional add-on modules,
     including some for clinical information beyond the pharmaceutical,
     and is widely used to provide formulary management. Lexicomp also
     provides the content for the drug monographs and information to be
     found in UpToDate.

16.19   Natural Standard. Somerville, MA: Natural Standard. Available: http://www.naturalstandard.com/contact.asp.

- Platform availability: Natural Standard site, Mobile
- Subscription options: Individual (via Skyscape) or Institutional
- Scope and description: Natural Standard offers graded, evidence-based information about complementary and alternative medicine, including but not limited to functional foods, dietary supplements, diets, exercises, and integrative therapies. It also provides calculators, interaction checkers, and continuing education.

16.20   *Natural Medicines Comprehensive Database (NMCD)*. Stockton, CA: Therapeutic Research Faculty. Available: http://naturaldatabase .therapeuticresearch.com/.

- Platform availability: *NMCD* site, Mobile, Print
- Subscription options: Individual or Institutional
- Scope and description: This resource offers graded, evidence-based information about complementary and alternative medicine, including but not limited to dietary supplements and integrative therapies. It also provides calculators, interaction checkers, patient education resources, effectiveness checkers, and a brand product report database. *NMCD* also has a consumer version of the professional site produced to be accessible and usable by patients and the general public. It regularly publishes a print edition of its database content that can be used to supplement a print reference collection.

Book-Based Specialty Databases

Early print POC resources were nearly all book-based, and many prominent ones are still widely used, as discussed earlier. While most are still available as simple text, it is becoming increasingly common for publishers to repackage them as databases. These usually include the original text serving as the center of a group of related images, calculators, schedules, and other resources. Quite often, they are available either as enhanced databases from their publishers or as static text-based e-books from a number of other sources. The best of the publisher databases take advantage of the fluidity of an online format to provide regular updates in between new print editions, making them more effective as a POC resource, as well as extensive supplementary content impossible to include in a print book. In some cases, a library may find it useful to have both formats to meet different needs for the same content, or in order to ensure access to at least some content in case of power outages. The following are two of many examples.

16.21   5 Minute Consult. Philadelphia: Lippincott Williams and Wilkins, Wolters Kluwer. Available: http://5minuteconsult.com/.

- Platform availability: Ovid site, Unbound Medicine Mobile Platform, 5 Minute Consult site, Mobile, Print

- Subscription options: Individual or Institutional

- Scope and description: Drawing from the many books in the *5-Minute Consult* series (*Clinical Consult 2013, Urology, AHA Cardiology, Orthopaedic*, etc.), this resource provides brief synopses of diseases and conditions, diagnostic algorithms, images, lab test information, patient handouts, etc. Some of its many sources are available as text-based e-books from several platforms in addition to the 5 Minute Consult site.

- Additional resources: 5 Minute Pediatric Consult

16.22   *Red Book Online.* Elk Grove Village, IL: American Academy of Pediatrics. Available: http://aapredbook.aappublications.org/.

- Platform availability: *Red Book Online* site, Assorted e-Book sites, Print, Mobile

- Subscription options: Individual or Institutional

- Scope and description: While there are a number of major print resources known as the Red Book, this one is the *Red Book: 2012 Report of the Committee on Infectious Diseases*. This resource is a core reference for pediatric infectious diseases, and has frequent new editions. The database version from the publisher includes a large image library, an assortment of calculators, vaccine information, and regular updates. The simple text version is available on several other platforms, and it is still published in print.

References

1.   Covell, D. G., G. C. Uman, and P. R. Manning. "Information Needs in Office Practice: Are They Being Met?" *Annals of Internal Medicine* 103, no. 4 (1985): 596–99.
2.   Thiele, R. H., N. C. Poiro, D. C. Scalzo, and E. C. Nemerqut. "Speed, Accuracy, and Confidence in Google, Ovid, PubMed, and UpToDate: Results of a Randomised Trial." *Postgraduate Medical Journal.* 86, no. 1018 (2010): 459–65.
3.   Alper, B. S., D. S. White, and B. Ge. "Physicians Answer More Clinical Questions and Change Clinical Decisions More Often with Synthesized Evidence: A Randomized Trial in Primary Care." *Annals of Family Medicine* 3, no. 6 (2005).
4.   McKibbon, K. A. "Evidence-Based Practice." *Bulletin of the Medical Library Association* 86, no. 3 (1998): 396-401.

5. "Learning Objectives for Medical Student Education—Guidelines for Medical Schools: Report I of the Medical Schools Objectives Project." *Academic Medicine* 74, no. 1 (1999): 13–18.

6. Dreiseitl, Stephan, and Michael Binder. "Do Physicians Value Decision Support? A Look at the Effect of Decision Support Systems on Physician Opinion." *Artificial Intelligence in Medicine* 33, no. 1 (2005): 25–30.

7. Kawamoto, K., and D. F. Lobach. "Clinical Decision Support Provided within Physician Order Entry Systems: A Systematic Review of Features Effective for Changing Clinician Behavior." *AMIA Annual Symposium Proceedings* (2003): 361–65.

8. Mollon, B., et al. "Features Predicting the Success of Computerized Decision Support for Prescribing: A Systematic Review of Randomized Controlled Trials." *BMC Medical Informatics and Decision Making* 9, no. 1 (2009): 11.

9. Blumenthal, D., and M. Tavenner. "The 'Meaningful Use' Regulation for Electronic Health Records." *The New England Journal of Medicine* 363, no. 6 (2010): 501–4.

10. Ibid.

11. Berner, Eta S. "Clinical Decision Support Systems: State of the Art." AHRQ Publication No. 09-0069-Ef. Rockville, MD: Agency for Healthcare Research and Quality. Last modified June, 2009. http://nmhealth.org/erd/antibiotics/AHRQ%20CDSS%20Review.pdf.

12. Del Fiol, G., V. Huser, H. R. Strasberg, S. M. Maviglia, C. Curtis, and J. J. Cimino. "Implementations of the Hl7 Context-Aware Knowledge Retrieval (Infobutton) Standard: Challenges, Strengths, Limitations, and Uptake." *Journal of Biomedical Informatics* 45, no. 4 (2012): 726–35.

13. Ibid.

14. *Doody's Core Titles in the Health Sciences*. Chicago: Doody Enterprises, 2012. Print.

CHAPTER 17

Global Health Sources

MEGAN VON ISENBURG and MELLANYE LACKEY

The phrase *global health* refers to "health problems, issues, and concerns that transcend national boundaries, may be influenced by circumstances or experiences in other countries, and are best addressed by cooperative actions and solutions."[1] It is a relatively new label for international health and tropical medicine and includes several factors: an increased globalization in education, an "international connectedness," a greater awareness of "common vulnerabilities" in communicable diseases, and a "discomfort" with health disparities in the disease burden of rich and poor countries.[2] Further, different institutions define and contextualize global health to meet their own goals. For example, some institutions may stress the interdisciplinarity of research, or the inclusion of local communities to solve health disparities, while others may have a stronger clinical or educational focus.

Interest in global health is increasing, and global health academic programs, institutes, centers, and partnerships are on the rise. A review of accredited, MD-granting U.S. medical schools found that nearly half boast some kind of global health program or office, and this number is surely higher today than when the review was done five years ago.[3] A recent count of members of the Consortium of Universities for Global Health includes seventy-four North American members and twenty-nine international (developing world) members.[4] A new European association, the European Academic Global Health Alliance has fifty-five full, associate, or affiliated members with partnerships in seventy-one developing world countries.[5]

Librarians are supporting the growing number of students and faculty in global health subject areas in both traditional and innovative ways. Informally, our colleagues at academic health sciences libraries attest to more reference questions and consultation requests in global health topics. Librarians are also partnering with global health researchers through embedded librarianship, work on grants, service projects, and international partnerships.

In this chapter, we address considerations for providing global health reference services. We also describe reference sources for working with researchers and students who are teaching, studying, and researching global health issues in the developed world. Because of the growth of international partnerships between developed and developing world institutions, we highlight resources for working with researchers and information professionals in both the developed and developing worlds.

Providing Reference Services in Global Health Contexts

Librarians can support global health research, education, and clinical efforts in a number of ways, from locating a statistic for a paper to traveling with a medical mission team to international locations. Given the increasing need for transparency, accountability, and evaluation to demonstrate the value of libraries and librarians to an organization, it is critical to consider how to measure the success and impact of any service or interaction. Librarians may need to justify supporting reference questions from global patrons, as opposed to those from one's home institution.

Supporting Global Health from the Home Institution

VIRTUAL REFERENCE SERVICE

Many libraries have virtual reference services that include e-mail and chat reference. This service can also assist patrons who are traveling, even while the librarian remains at the home institution. Time differences may make synchronous reference assistance difficult, but e-mail can certainly bridge the divide. If synchronous reference service is possible, consider using Skype or Google Hangout for free or low-cost phone, video, and desktop sharing. Some institutions may have Elluminate or other technologies that they prefer to use because of firewall and security issues.

Librarians may also want to offer additional services such as free scanning of print articles or book chapters from the library collections to patrons who are working in the field and cannot access the library's physical materials. The librarian could scan chapters or articles into a PDF which can be e-mailed to the user.

Measuring the success and impact of a virtual reference service for global health can follow the metrics for a library's other reference services. Traditionally this includes statistics, but could also include patron testimonials. Be sure to clarify how services using new technologies, such as online synchronous desktop sharing, should be counted in statistics collection.

SUBJECT GUIDES/LIBGUIDES

One of the most familiar ways in which librarians can simplify research for a group or specific discipline is to create a subject guide highlighting the most important and commonly used resources. In global health, subject guides should include key literature databases and statistical sources, and may also include information to support field research, such as research methodology or even language learning. The Health Sciences Library at the University of North Carolina at Chapel Hill has created a Global Health Toolkit (http://guides.lib.unc.edu/globalhealthtoolkit). The toolkit focuses on supporting the research of faculty and students working in global settings with pointers to helpful databases, datasets, and selected resources by topic. The guide does list some free or low-cost resources for global partners without institutional access. The toolkit also highlights creative and innovative ways that librarians can partner with researchers to improve global health.

Additionally, subject guides can also support the international partners of the home institution. For example, at Duke University Medical Center Library, the "Global Health International Partners" subject guide (http://guides.mclibrary.duke.edu/internationalpartners) highlights freely available resources (including most of those detailed in this chapter's final section, Working with Health Librarians and Researchers in the Developing World). It features site-specific information for the largest partner projects, based on feedback from both Duke and international faculty. This guide seeks to decrease the digital divide when Duke faculty and students are working side by side in the field with their international partners who do not have access to the Duke library collections.

Subject guides offer Web analytics to enable librarians to monitor the number of page views, hits, broken links, and popular links. LibGuides software, available from Springshare, offers built-in statistics that can simplify measuring the impact of the guide. Although it may be difficult to establish what number of clicks constitutes a successful guide, tracking usage patterns and popular links can help librarians keep the guide relevant.

OUTREACH

Most reference librarians participate in outreach activities to their institutions or liaison groups. Outreach activities typically take the perspective of the patrons rather than the library and can include holding office hours outside the library, sending e-mail updates with discipline-specific library news or table of contents alerts, and participating in discipline-specific activities.

In global health, additional outreach opportunities may include joining institutional global health interest groups, volunteering in activities to send medical
supplies overseas, and monitoring and sending out notice of funding opportunities.
Major sources of global health research funding include the Fogarty International
Center (http://www.fic.nih.gov/) at the National Institutes of Health, the Bill
and Melinda Gates Foundation Global Libraries program (http://www.gates
foundation.org/libraries/Pages/global-libraries.aspx) or the Elsevier Foundation
Innovative Libraries in Developing Countries (http://www.elsevierfoundation.org/
innovative-libraries).

Measuring the impact of outreach activities and virtual reference can be difficult. In addition to capturing simple metrics on numbers of e-mails sent, etc., one
may also want to investigate whether outreach leads to increased consultations,
instruction opportunities, new partnerships, or other requests for library help. A pre/
postsurvey of awareness of library services may enable some quantitative measurement of the outreach activities.

PURCHASING SPECIALIZED MATERIALS

Global health activities may benefit from the library's selection and purchase of
specialized collections of materials. For example, if the home institution develops
a field site in a foreign country, there may be numerous faculty, staff, and students
looking for language instruction books, CDs, or software. Books or other materials
on specific cultures or about cultural diversity in general may also prove helpful to
those working with international partners, whether home or abroad.

Global health resource collections can be evaluated for strength and utility
of collection using similar methods to most other collections. Resources should
be evaluated for currency, applicability to specific situations, cultural relevance,
and usability to judge collection strength. These particular qualities are especially
important if the physical collection consists largely of donated print or media materials, as it is very common for overenthusiastic donors to gift outdated or irrelevant
books. Usability and utility can be evaluated by considering any print circulation
or internal use, interlibrary loan or online usage statistics if available, and library
user feedback. As global health collections can vary from being part of a large academic library in the developed world to small collections of books and pamphlets
in a clinic in the developing world, useful and appropriate metrics will vary widely.

PRETRAVEL INSTRUCTION

"Preflight" workshops for faculty, health-care practitioners, and students traveling internationally can preemptively solve many potential problems that patrons
may encounter in the field. Workshops could include help on how to connect to the
library's resources from off campus and tips on searching for articles in the project's

research areas, if applicable. Librarians have also conducted specialized searches on very specific topics to give users PDFs of articles to save on their computers. Another option is to save PDFs in the cloud using document storage applications (like Dropbox.com which has offline usage options) before researchers go into the field. The advantage of saving PDFs in these spaces is that the researchers can still access them in locations with low or no Internet connectivity (or during long plane rides!).

Additionally, librarians can also offer information on HINARI, an online digital library available through the World Health Organization (WHO) to qualifying countries (described in 17.23), or other free resources mentioned in the next two sections of this chapter. This training allows the traveling patron to become something of an ambassador for the resources to which his or her international partners will have access.

Patrons planning international field work may also have questions about what vaccinations they need. This information could be part of a preflight workshop or provided to the departments or individuals as needed. Here are some recommended sites for this information:

The U.S. Centers for Disease Control (CDC) keeps an active list of travel vaccinations needed for visiting many countries. The page also addresses special health concerns such as pregnancy or traveling with children. An interactive map details vaccination requirements (http://wwwnc.cdc.gov/travel/page/vaccinations.htm).

Vaccinations for travel abroad are available at specialized travel clinics. The CDC lists some (http://wwwnc.cdc.gov/travel/page/travel-clinics.htm), including these:

- The International Society for Travel Medicine (http://www.istm.org/) has a searchable database of clinics. Click the global travel clinic link and then enter a specific geographic location to get a list of nearby clinics.
- Another option is the American Society of Tropical Medicine and Hygiene (http://www.astmh.org/source/ClinicalDirectory/), which provides lists of physicians who offer vaccinations and travel medicine consults.

To evaluate these workshops, maintain attendance records and follow up with patrons after they return from the field to determine how the workshop helped them and what additional information they may need.

Supporting Global Health from the Field

Is there a role for librarians out in the field? Based on an increasing number of recent conference presentations from librarians who have participated in global health field work, our answer is, "Yes! There are many roles for librarians in the field." Librarians have traveled with physicians to Uganda, Ghana, and other countries.

While overseas, many librarians lead training sessions on HINARI, PubMed, or other databases and search portals. Taking the HINARI "Train the Trainers" online course offered by the Medical Library Association (MLA) and taught by Lenny Rhine is excellent preparation for teaching a HINARI session. Course materials and talking points are available (http://www.mlanet.org/resources/global/lwb_trainthet rainers_ce.html) to help in getting started.

Librarians have also conducted information, education, and library needs assessments at international partner institutions. Findings of the assessments can suggest and help plan improvements for the institution's library and knowledge management services if one exists. If a library does not exist, these assessments can help determine if a library should be established at the global site. The authors suggest taking an approach that recognizes the assets of the current environment such as appreciative inquiry or strengths-based assessment.

CONNECTIVITY

Continuous electricity may not be available in global health field sites. In sub-Saharan Africa, for example, only 24 percent of the population has access to electricity, and industry experiences an average of fifty-six days without electricity.[6] Anecdotally, in Tanzania and Uganda, the authors have experienced daily brownouts where power was cut off regularly for several hours at a time. Political unrest can also impact the availability of electricity.

Similarly, Internet connectivity is not always available. WiFi access at institutions is sometimes accessible in common areas, such as libraries, but is dependent on electricity. Many individuals use USB modems to connect to the Internet, thus providing individual Internet access that runs off a laptop battery. This is a good solution for librarians working in the field, as it provides some computing and Internet access even when power and Internet are not available. These modems are available for purchase such that a certain number of gigabytes of data are available for a specific amount of money.

Apart from service disruptions, bandwidth is often low and variable, and that can result in delays to e-mails and lost connections during database searches. If planning to teach a session, it's always a good idea to bring backup slides with screenshots as a potential substitute to conducting live searches. When we as librarians create subject guides with links to PDFs, streaming tutorials on how to search, or other dynamic content, we must accommodate for these limitations. PDFs can sometimes take hours to load. Drop-down boxes that fill in as users type may not auto fill when the connection is too slow. Streaming videos are often unusable altogether. Low-bandwidth alternatives include providing transcripts of the tutorials, simple HTML webpages, and links to HTML rather than PDFs if possible. IT specialists or librarians in partner countries may be able to recommend alternative formats that are suitable for low-bandwidth computing environments.

The following three websites can help when designing webpages for areas with low bandwidth: Web Design Guidelines (http://www.aptivate.org/webguidelines/Home.html) offers practical tips on how to make webpages more usable in low-bandwidth environments. The Web Page Analyzer (http://www.websiteoptimization.com/services/analyze) will calculate the size of a page and the sizes of specific components of a page. After it analyzes a page, the site will offer suggestions for improving the load time. Finally, the Low Bandwidth Simulator (http://www.loband.org/loband/simulator.jsp) will load a page at the same speed as it would in a low-bandwidth environment, then tell the amount of time the page took to load (in case one wasn't keeping track). The wait can seem maddening, but it really helps to understand what users in low-bandwidth settings experience as they surf the Internet.

We speak broadly of connectivity issues here. Not all locations will have slow Internet connections. And, just because a site is not in the developed world, does not mean that it will not have fast Internet. Connectivity also varies between rural and urban settings.

Mobile devices, including feature phones, are on the rise in emerging markets, especially sub-Saharan Africa.[7] Feature phones can send text messages and can connect to the Internet, but without the display touchscreen and expensive data plans of smartphones. Librarians might leverage the widespread use of feature phones to provide reference services via text. In fact, the Ask-a-Librarian service offered through Springshare's LibGuides product offers a text service, helpful for answering users' reference questions.

TIME ZONE DIFFERENCES

Librarians who support global health researchers working in different time zones should expect time delays in responses to e-mails or text messages. For example, the end of the work day for researchers working in sub-Saharan Africa, India, or Asia may fall in the middle of the night or at the start of the day for a librarian in the Western Hemisphere. This may not be the case for librarians in Europe, nor for librarians in the Western Hemisphere supporting their users in South and Central America. Regardless of where the librarian works, he or she should be mindful of the time zones of the researcher and how that may affect communications.

CULTURAL CONSIDERATIONS

In the months and days leading up to a site visit in another country, there are many tasks to complete. We highly recommend that all travelers take time to educate themselves about some of the cultural practices and courtesies of the places they will visit.

In fact, a very useful role of the librarian is to collect information about the culture of the place where the team will visit. Knowing about the place, the habits, and the motivations of a group of people can impact the success of conversations and collaborations. Seemingly simple questions such as, "What do you specifically need from us?" and "Can you show me how your group has spent the money from the grant?" may offend, fall flat, and cause misunderstandings between the parties. Time spent learning about the cultural practices of a place can greatly boost the potential for success of a project.

Resources for Global Health Information and Research

This section details some of the resources that include global health or international health information. The list includes peer-reviewed, scholarly databases, datasets and statistical sources, and grey literature sources.

Scholarly, Peer-Reviewed Databases

17.1   Global Health. Wallingford, Oxfordshire, UK: Centre for Agriculture and Biosciences International (CABI). Available: http://www.cabi.org/default .aspx?site=170&page=1016&pid=328 via CAB Direct, OvidSP, EBSCOhost, Thomson Web of Knowledge.

Global Health is a public health database containing information from serials, books, conferences, patents, theses, and electronic publications from more than 150 countries. Subject coverage includes international health, biomedical life sciences, noncommunicable diseases, public health nutrition, food safety and hygiene, occupational health, toxicology, health services, and maternal/child health. This database offers global coverage of both the developing and developed world with more than fifty languages translated into English. (Subscription)

17.2   Global Health Archive. Wallingford, Oxfordshire, UK: Centre for Agriculture and Biosciences International (CABI). Available: http://www.cabi.org/ default.aspx?site=170&page=1016&pid=2221 via CAB Direct, OvidSP, EBSCOhost, Thomson Web of Knowledge.

Global Health Archive is fully compatible with the Global Health database (see 17.1) and can be searched alongside it for records from 1910 to the present day. Together they provide a global, historical picture of international health research. (Subscription)

17.3   MEDLINE. Bethesda, MD: U.S. National Library of Medicine. Available: http://www.ncbi.nlm.nih.gov/pubmed via PubMed, OvidSP, EBSCOhost, and many others.

MEDLINE offers access to high-quality health research. MEDLINE is a bibliographic database with citations and links to an ever-increasing number of full-text articles in a variety of subjects, including global health. Citations may include links to full-text content from PubMed Central and/or publisher websites. (Free or subscription, depending on vendor)

17.4   Embase. New York: Elsevier. Available: http://www.embase.com/ via Elsevier, OvidSP, and Dialog.

Embase is strong in a variety of health topics including drug research, public health, and clinical medicine, among others. Some content in Embase overlaps with that in MEDLINE, but Embase does contain about 30 percent unique material. The advanced search option allows users to eliminate MEDLINE-only records, reducing the number of duplicates. (Subscription)

All of the previous databases use controlled vocabularies and subject thesauri to assist searchers in finding information. Help using these thesauri is available from each database.

17.5   Global Infectious Diseases and Epidemiology Network (GIDEON). Los Angeles: GIDEON Informatics. Available: http://www.gideononline.com/ via EBSCOhost.

GIDEON focuses on infectious diseases, microbiology, epidemiology, and toxicology. The database contains diagnostic tools to help identify more than 300 tropical diseases and travelers' illnesses. GIDEON also contains information on drugs used to treat the illnesses, vector and vehicle listings, and e-books on the diseases. An interactive map highlights what is available for countries around the world. (Subscription)

As global health librarians ourselves, we find that many researchers want information on a particular topic in any developing country setting. To this end, we refer to a search hedge that contains the names of all the developing countries in the world as well as synonyms for the term "developing country" to use in searches. This list is on the UNC HSL's Global Health Toolkit (http://guides.lib.unc.edu/globalhealthtool kit). We've found it helpful, and we'd like to share with librarians assisting global health researchers.

17.6   Google Scholar. Mountain View, CA: Google. Available: http://scholar.google.com/.

Google Scholar searches specifically for scholarly literature, though "scholar" is a loosely defined term in this database. Items in Google Scholar include citations to peer-reviewed journal articles, white papers, theses, books, preprints, abstracts, and technical reports from all areas of research, including global health. Unlike other databases, Google Scholar searches the full text of items when available. This feature could aid researchers whose global health topics do not fit within a controlled vocabulary. The full-text searching also aids discovery of information on topics that are tangentially discussed in an article, but not enough that search terms would be included in the title, abstract, or descriptors. Google Scholar has reports from some global health agencies like the World Health Organization (WHO), and it complements the other resources in this chapter. (Free to search, with some free, full text; other full text subscription based, with institutional subscriptions determining access)

Subject-specific databases such as Popline (population health, http://www.popline.org/), Ethnomed (immigrant health in the United States, http://ethnomed.org/), Agricola (agriculture, http://agricola.nal.usda.gov/) or Abstracts in Anthropology (http://anthropology.metapress.com/), to name a few, may also have global health content. Likewise, interdisciplinary databases such as Academic Search Complete or ISI Web of Science will include global health information, even though global health is not the primary focus of those databases.

Datasets and Statistical Resources

For the purposes of this chapter, we felt that free datasets and statistical resources would be the most beneficial. Therefore, all of the sources listed in the next section are available at no cost.

17.7   WHO Global Health Observatory. Geneva: World Health Organization. Available: http://apps.who.int/gho/data/.

The Global Health Observatory (GHO) is a repository with access to data and analyses for monitoring the global health situation. The observatory covers key health themes such as mortality and burden of diseases, maternal and reproductive health, immunization, HIV/AIDS, tuberculosis, malaria, neglected diseases, water and sanitation, noncommunicable diseases and risk factors, epidemic-prone diseases, health systems, environmental health, violence, and injuries. The GHO also offers electronic access to annual health summaries and statistics of the 194 member countries. (Free)

17.8   MEASURE Demographic and Health Survey. Calverton, MD: ICF International. Available: http://www.measuredhs.com/data/available-datasets.cfm.

MEASURE DHHS strives to provide high-quality data about the health of countries for meaningful analysis. The datasets cover family planning, maternal and child health, child survival, HIV, AIDS, and other sexually transmitted infections, infectious diseases, reproductive health, and nutrition at the country and sub-country level. Sample surveys and questionnaires are also available, as are suggestions for how to use the data. (Free)

17.9   Organisation for Economic Co-operation and Development (OECD) iLibrary Statistics. Washington, DC: OECD. Available: http://www.oecd-ilibrary.org/statistics;jsessionid=6nhf52ejnet9q.x-oecd-live-02.

The iLibrary is the OECD's source for online statistics. It doubles as the gateway to OECD's analysis and data. The OECD offers evidence-based and independent analyses for topics such as agriculture, development, education, the environment, science, and technology, all of which affect the overall health of a country. (Free)

17.10   Global Health Data Exchange (GHDx). Seattle: Institute for Health Metrics and Evaluation. Available: http://www.healthmetricsandevaluation.org/ghdx.

The GHDx aggregates world population census data, surveys, registries, indicators and estimates, administrative health data, and financial data. The GHDx catalogs and lists microdata, aggregated data, and research results. (Free)

17.11   Global Health Facts. Menlo Park, CA: Kaiser Family Foundation. Available: http://www.globalhealthfacts.org/.

Country-level data on key health issues such as HIV/AIDS, tuberculosis, malaria, and health workforce capacity. The data also allow for comparing topics across several countries. This project of the Henry J. Kaiser Family Foundation has a focus on the U.S. role in global health. (Free)

17.12   UNdata. New York: United Nations Statistics Division. Available: http://data.un.org/.

UNdata is a gateway to all the statistical databases of the United Nations. The collection gives free access to global statistics for evidence-based policy and decision making. This single point of entry brings to light many statistics that would otherwise remain hidden in proprietary databases. Of particular interest to global health audiences are sections on crime, education, energy, environment, food and agriculture, gender, health, HIV/AIDS, Information and Communication Technology (ICT), population, refugees, and trade. (Free)

17.13   UN International Human Development Indicators. New York: United Nations Development Programme. Available: http://hdr.undp.org/en/statistics/.

The indicators contain datasets that informed the preparation of the Human Development Index (HDI). The HDI combines life expectancy, income, and education to create a single statistic with which to compare social and economic development of countries. The site also offers reports on gender inequality, poverty, and other inequalities which impact the overall health of a country. (Free)

17.14   UN Millennium Development Goals Indicators Data. New York: United Nations Statistics Division. Available: http://unstats.un.org/unsd/mdg/Data.aspx.

The Millennium Development Goals (MDGs) are eight targets to improve the world's health by 2015. All nations under the auspices of the UN agreed to the

MDGs, and the UN Statistics Division measures countries' progress toward meeting the MDGs through publications and data for sixty+ indicators. (Free)

17.15   United Nations Children's Fund (UNICEF) Core Indicators. New York: United Nations Children's Fund. Available: http://www.unicef.org/statistics/index_24296.html.

The core indicators monitor the status of the health of children and women globally. The data come from an array of UNICEF field offices and updates occur annually. Global health topics include child survival and health, nutrition, maternal health, newborn health, education, sanitation, and HIV/AIDS. (Free)

17.16   World Bank Open Health Data. Washington, DC: World Bank. Available: http://data.worldbank.org/topic/health.

In an effort to show transparency and accountability, the World Bank created the Open Data Initiative with access to more than 2,000 indicators from World Bank data sources. World Bank datasets, databases, pre-formatted tables, reports, and other health resources are available. (Free)

17.17   WHO Global Atlas of Infectious Diseases. Geneva: World Health Organization. Available: http://gamapserver.who.int/GlobalAtlas/home.asp.

The Global Atlas of Infectious Diseases offers global, regional, and country-level data and statistics in standardized form for infectious diseases. The atlas contains epidemiologic information and links to the Global Outbreak Alert and Response Network, as well as links to essential support services and health centers. In addition to providing data, the page features interactive maps, surveillance information, and response reports. (Free)

17.18   CANCERMondial. Lyon, France: International Agency for Research on Cancer. Available: http://www-dep.iarc.fr/dephome.htm.

This site compiles cancer registries from around the world, and it provides data on cancer incidence, prevalence, mortality, and disability-adjusted life years (DALYs)[8] when the information is available. The Cancer Information Section of WHO's International Agency for Research on Cancer maintains the page. (Free)

Grey Literature

The term *grey literature* (or *gray literature*) describes written materials that are not published journal articles in peer-reviewed journals but still contain valuable and authoritative information on a topic. Why should researchers (and librarians) seek out grey literature for searches? Sometimes it is the only source of information available if the topic of interest emerges faster than the research and publication process.

Grey literature is often original and recent. Grey literature is an invaluable comple-ment to the scholarly published literature, especially in global health as important sources of information reside outside of the traditional journal literature. Including grey literature is especially important when conducting systematic reviews when a researcher attempts to find all the available information on a specific topic.

Specific examples of grey literature sources for global health include publi-cations from the World Health Organization (http://www.who.int/en), the Kaiser Family Foundation (http://globalhealth.kff.org/) or the United States Agency for International Development (USAID) (http://www.usaid.gov/). Other sources include proceedings from the International AIDS Conference, monitoring and evalua-tion reports, or policy documents from a particular country's Ministry of Health. Technical reports, patents, doctoral dissertations, white papers, or interviews with subject matter experts are more examples of grey literature.

Because grey literature is often hard to locate through scholarly, peer-reviewed databases like those listed in the beginning of this section, researchers must turn elsewhere to find the information. Grey literature repositories, conference archives, association or foundation websites, or even conventional search engines will help them find the information they seek. Sometimes these resources are freely available while others may be available for a fee. Some professional associations offer access to their publications to members only, or by special request. Each resource will have different access. While some websites aim to pull together collections of grey litera-ture for a specific topic or region, there is no one source for all grey literature in all areas of global health. Rather, the information resides in many disparate locations. Some sources that collect grey literature in global health follow.

17.19   OpenGrey. Vandœuvre-lès-Nancy, France: System for Information on Grey Literature in Europe. Available: http://www.opengrey.eu/.

OpenGrey combines multiple sources of grey literature from Europe. The repos-itory classifies documents according to SIGLE indexing (System for Indexing the Grey Literature on Europe). Users can search for topics or browse items in categories such as biomedicine or health policy. (Free)

17.20   Grey Literature Report. New York: New York Academy of Medicine. Available: http://www.greylit.org/.

From the New York Academy of Medicine Library, this bi-monthly report high-lights new publications in grey literature that discuss health services research and selected public health topics. Users can search for topics or browse items in catego-ries such as world health or eliminating health disparities. (Free)

17.21   WorldWideScience.org. Oak Ridge, TN: U.S. Department of Energy. Available: http://worldwidescience.org/.

This site from the United States government culls reports from country level and global scientific databases and portals. The gateway also translates search results into ten different languages and deep searches scientific reports and portals to facilitate scientific discovery across boundaries and languages. (Free)

17.22   Human Resources for Health Global Resource Center. Chapel
        Hill, NC: Capacity Plus, IntraHealth International. Available:
        http://www.hrhresourcecenter.org/.

The HRH Global Resource Center focuses strengthening health systems and improving skills of the health workforces in developing countries. The Center is a global library with publications, free e-Learning classes, and a health policy toolkit. Users can browse by subject, geographic focus, or publication type. Subject guides explain basic concepts concerning the global health workforce and link users to recommended readings for each subject. (Free)

Working with Health Librarians and Researchers in the Developing World

Increasingly, librarians at U.S. and other developed world institutions are becoming involved with global health efforts through their institutions or through other international partnerships like sister countries. In this context, librarians are frequently asked to make the institution's collections available to international partners. Since publisher licenses rarely extend to international partners, librarians may assist their international partners either by collection-building or by referring them to existing programs and materials.

This section identifies key resources for librarians working with health sciences librarians and researchers in the developing world. Most are free or very low cost.

Free or Low-Cost, Full-Text Digital Library Collections

RESEARCH4LIFE PROGRAMS

Research4Life (http://www.research4life.org/) is the collective name for four programs that provide access to the scientific literature for developing countries. It comprises a public-private partnership of the WHO, FAO, UNEP, WIPO, Cornell and Yale Universities, and the International Association of Scientific, Technical, and Medical Publishers. All portals are Internet-based. The four programs are HINARI (health), AGORA (agriculture), OARE (environment), and ARDI (science and technology). A description and access information for each program follows:

17.23 HINARI. Geneva: World Health Organization. Available:
http://www.who.int/hinari/en/.

The HINARI Access to Research in Health Programme offers a free or very low-cost digital library of electronic journals, books, and databases to countries in the developing world. In 2002, the World Health Organization (WHO) launched the program with six major publishers, including Blackwell, Elsevier Science, Harcourt Worldwide STM Group, Wolters Kluwer International Health and Science, Springer Verlag, and John Wiley. In 2012, more than 150 publisher partners offer more than 15,000 information resources through HINARI. Today, WHO partners with Yale University Library and publishers to manage HINARI.

Through the program, not-for-profit institutions in eligible developing countries can register for HINARI. Three international measures of national income and development determine a country's eligibility. Eligible countries either fit under Group A, which offers free access to HINARI, or Group B, which offers low-cost access. Once Research4Life grants access and registers the institution, all permanent and visiting faculty, staff, and students can access HINARI through their institution's username and password, which is generally maintained by the librarian. As there are strict rules about accessing HINARI, the institution must educate its users on the appropriate use of the password when promoting HINARI.

The HINARI portal functions like a digital library, offering A–Z lists of electronic journals and books, lists of reference sources, databases, and free collections. It also features a link to a special version of PubMed that displays HINARI and free full-text filters and buttons for accessing HINARI content from individual PubMed abstracts. The program provides access to information resources in medicine, nursing, health, and related social sciences.

HINARI promotional and training materials are available for end users (http://hinaritraining.org/). Information about training for librarians on using HINARI is at the end of this section, before the chapter's conclusion. HINARI is an excellent solution for institutions in eligible countries with stable Internet access. (Institutional registration required, eligible institutions in eligible countries only; free for Group A countries, fee-based for Group B countries)

17.24 AGORA. Rome, Italy: Food and Agriculture Organization, United Nations.
Available: http://www.aginternetwork.org/en/.

AGORA stands for Access to Global Online Research in Agriculture. Managed by the Food and Agriculture Organization (FAO) in partnership with Cornell University and publishers, AGORA provides access to information resources in agriculture, fisheries, food, nutrition, veterinary science, and related biological, environmental, and social sciences.

17.25   OARE. New Haven, CT: Yale University and Nairobi, Kenya: United
        Nations Environment Programme. Available: http://www.unep.org/
        oare/en/index.html.

OARE stands for Online Access to Research in the Environment. Managed by the
United Nations Environment Programme (UNEP) in partnership with Yale University
and publishers, OARE provides access to information resources in environmental sciences, including zoology, botany, ecology, geology, climatology, geography, environmental toxicology, pollution, economics, law, policy, engineering, and chemistry.

17.26   ARDI. Geneva: World Intellectual Property Organization. Available:
        http://www.wipo.int/ardi/en/.

ARDI stands for Access to Research for Development and Innovation. Coordinated by the World Intellectual Property Organization in partnership with publishers,
ARDI provides access to scholarly literature in interdisciplinary science and technology in an effort to promote research innovations in developing countries. (Institutional
registration required, eligible institutions in eligible countries only; free for Group A
countries, fee-based for Group B countries)

OTHER PROGRAMS

Other resources outside of the Research4Life umbrella also provide access to global
health information for developing countries.

17.27   PERii. Oxford, UK: International Network for the Availability of Scientific
        Publications. Available: http://www.inasp.info/file/5f65fc9017860338882881
        402dc594e4/perii.html.

PERii stands for the Programme for the Enhancement of Research Information
and is a project of INASP, the International Network for the Availability of Scientific
Publications. PERii focuses on developing and emerging countries by making international scholarly journals more widely available, helping develop digital libraries,
and supporting publication of research from these countries.

INASP comprises a partnership of twenty-three countries and eighty network
countries, and it negotiates with publishers for deeply discounted prices on journal packages to create a countrywide license. Generally, a national consortium will
choose which titles to license based on budget and research priorities. Individual
institutions should work with their national consortium or contact INASP to determine which digital library offerings are available to them via PERii and at what price.

PERii also offers training to librarians (http://www.inasp.info/file/d823e4728f59
bedea7b975aba08e66cd/perii-library-development.html) and ICT professionals (http://
www.inaspinfo/file/5e463a8d94f31641096b23351cd4e8b7/perii-ict-training.html).

17.28   eGranary. Chapel Hill, NC: The WiderNet Project. Available:
         http://www.widernet.org/egranary/.

Designed for institutions with little or no Internet access and calling itself the
"Internet in a box," eGranary seeks to provide access to online information in an offline
environment. With permission from the copyright owners, eGranary copies educational
and information-rich websites and re-packages them for either a local area network
(LAN) or stand-alone USB drive. Because the information in eGranary exists offline,
searching and browsing is faster than using real-time Internet connections. Subscribers
can also create or upload their own resources to add to their local eGranary.

eGranary includes websites, books, videos, pictures, and audio in medicine,
nursing, public health, languages, teaching, and other areas. It even includes MIT's
Open CourseWare package of MIT lectures, exams, and videos. eGranary has a menu
of pricing ranging from a single external USB drive ($1,800 plus shipping as of
November 2012) to multiple institution computer labs ($130,000 as of November
2012), which includes computers, a server, installation, and training. Updates are
available two to three times per year via a pocket-sized hard drive.

eGranary was founded in 2001 and is developed by the WiderNet Project. It is
affiliated with the University of North Carolina at Chapel Hill. (Subscription-based)

Free Book and Journal Directories

There are numerous lists of free, high-quality health information sites. The following includes the most comprehensive and most reliable.

17.29   FreeBooks4Doctors. [Online]: Flying Publisher. Available:
         http://www.freebooks4doctors.com/.

17.30   Free Medical Journals. [Online]: Flying Publisher. Available:
         http://www.freemedicaljournals.com/.

The FreeBooks4Doctors and Free Medical Journals sites both offer lists of
medical and health-related content. The interfaces are available in English, French,
Spanish, and Portuguese, though content in the journals and books is not translated.

The books include more than 300 freely available books and book-like websites
such as the *Merck Manual of Diagnosis and Therapy*, society and institution publications, free content from publishers, and some books published by the site's parent
company, Flying Publisher.

The journals page lists more than 3,000 journals, and all offer some free content. Journals such as *New England Journal of Medicine* and *JAMA* are available,
even though they embargo current content. Manuel Montenegro, a librarian at the

Virtual Library of the University of Porto—Portugal, and Bernd Sebastian Kamps, the founder of Flying Publisher, regularly update the sites.

Additionally, Flying Publisher offers a free subscription and personalization service, Amedeo. The service allows individuals to subscribe to receive free weekly literature newsletters, highlights new articles in personalized journal subsets, and alerts of new book publications.

Flying Publisher publishes their own free, concise topic guides on the FreeBooks 4Doctors site and offers these same publications for sale in print. More information on the publishing model is available on their site (http://www.amedeo.com/TheGuides/index.php). (Free)

17.31   Free Medical Journals List. Geneva: Geneva Foundation for Medical Education and Research. Available: http://www.gfmer.ch/Medical_journals/Free_medical.php.

The Geneva Foundation for Medical Education and Research (GFMER) maintains a list of free medical journals organized by subject area, including journals in many languages. Notes indicate the years of free access or when the journal includes only "some free papers." There are likely redundancies with the titles included on Free Medical Journals, but there may be some unique content as well. (Free)

Open-Access Collections and Publishing Models

Disparities in access to health information are a compelling reason for open-access publishing. While there are many open-access publishers, due to their high quality, relevance to global health, and depth of content, two platforms stand out as particularly useful for libraries and researchers in developing countries.

17.32   SciELO. São Paulo, Brazil: SciELO. Available: http://www.scielo.org/php/index.php?lang=en.

SciELO (Scientific Electronic Library Online) is an open-access, cooperative platform for publishing electronic scientific journals based in and focusing on South American, Latin American, and Caribbean countries. The goal is not only to provide access to scientific journals, but also to highlight research coming out of the region.

Users can search or browse SciELO alphabetically or by subject. Content portals are available for two subjects (public health and social sciences) and for numerous countries in Latin America, South America, and the Caribbean. Portals primarily offer journal articles, though there is also a book collection for Brazil. Interfaces are available in English, Spanish, and Portuguese.

SciELO was founded in 1997 in Brazil by FAPESP (the State of São Paulo Science Foundation) and BIREME (the Latin America and Caribbean Center on Health Sciences Information). Strict quality requirements govern journal inclusion in SciELO. (Free)

17.33   BioMed Central. London: Springer Science+Business Media. Available: http://www.biomedcentral.com/.

BioMed Central publishes more than 200 peer-reviewed, scientific journals. All research articles are accessible online immediately, freely, and permanently. Instant access is possible because BioMed Central charges authors a fee upon publication. Institutions can negotiate a fee reduction for its authors through membership. Biomed Central also offers a fee waiver to authors from developing countries to encourage research and publication.

Many, if not most, BioMed Central journals are generally indexed in MEDLINE; however, the BioMed Central site also offers users the ability to search and browse content directly. The homepage highlights new and popular research articles, and *Gateways* offer users the ability to see only content in their own discipline, such as Global Health, Nursing, Microbiology, and Infectious Diseases. (Free)

Other Key Free Resources

These subject- or organization-specific sites offer high-quality information for free. Consider including them when conducting reference work or helping to highlight accessible resources in global health contexts.

17.34   Médecins Sans Frontières Reference Books. Geneva: Médecins Sans Frontières. Available: http://www.refbooks.msf.org/.

Médecins Sans Frontières, also known as MSF or Doctors Without Borders, is an international organization that offers health care to people affected by natural disasters, conflict, or health-care exclusion. They publish a set of eight reference books, all in English and some in French and/or Spanish as well. Books include *Essential Drugs* (2010); *Clinical Guidelines* (2010); *Public Health Engineering* (2010); *Tuberculosis* (2010); *Management of Epidemic Meningococcal Meningitis* (2008); *Obstetrics in Remote Settings* (2007); *Rapid Assessment of Refugee or Displaced Populations* (2006); and *Refugee Health* (1997). Books are available as PDF downloads that work on multiple devices, making them useful in settings in which no Internet access is available.

At the time of publication, some but not all MSF books were also in the list of FreeBooks4Doctors. (Free)

17.35   Global Library of Women's Medicine. London: The Foundation for the
        Global Library of Women's Medicine. Available: http://www.glowm.com/.

The Global Library of Women's Medicine is a free website developed from the textbook *Gynecology and Obstetrics* by John J. Sciarra, MD, PhD, at Northwestern University. The site consists of more than 400 expert and peer-reviewed chapters on women's health, including topics in gynecology, obstetrics, maternal-fetal medicine, gynecologic oncology, reproductive endocrinology and infertility, fertility regulation, genetics, and human sexuality, behavioral, and psychosomatic issues. There is also a section dedicated to Safer Motherhood, which includes extensive coverage on postpartum hemorrhage, and fistula surgery, two major health issues in the developing world.

Some of the book content is available as PDFs, which can be useful in settings without Internet connectivity, while others are online and thus require an Internet connection. In addition to book chapters, the site also includes patient leaflets and surgical videos. Presented without advertising, this material is invaluable to settings that teach women's health or treat female patients. (Free)

17.36   Medscape. New York: WebMD. Available: http://www.medscape.com/.

Sometimes referred to as the free UpToDate, Medscape offers background topic reviews on numerous diseases and treatments. Medscape highlights recent articles and specialty sites for specific disciplines. The site requires individual registration, though it's free to do so. Medscape contains numerous advertisements. (Free, individual registration required)

Regional and Local Resources

International databases like those listed previously may not index local and regional health information. It is important to consider the additional benefit that local resources can bring when working with librarians and researchers in developing countries. Be sure to check for national publications from the country's ministry of health, which may include clinical guidelines specific to the country or reports of global monitoring and evaluation projects, to name a few benefits.

17.37   Global Health Library. Geneva: World Health Organization. Available: http://
        www.globalhealthlibrary.net/.

The WHO serves member states through Regional Offices (Africa, the Americas, the Eastern Mediterranean, Europe, South-East Asia, and the Western Pacific), many of which maintain their own libraries and documentation centers. These centers can be excellent sources for regional health information, publications, and statistics.

WHO Regional Offices publish regional medical indexes for various regions of the world. Each of these indexes provides access to bibliographic information about locally published health material, mostly journal articles. Users can search all the indexes simultaneously through the Global Health Library or separately through the regional site. The indexes published by WHO and included in the Global Health Library are:

17.38   African Index Medicus (AIM)

17.39   Index Medicus for the WHO Eastern Mediterranean Region (IMEMR)

17.40   Virtual Health Library LILACS for Latin America and the Caribbean (VHL)

17.41   Index Medicus for South-East Asia Region (IMSEAR)

17.42   Western Pacific Region Index Medicus (WPRIM)

The Global Health Library also includes MEDLINE, WHOLIS (WHO's database of WHO publications), and SciELO. The interface is available in English, French, Portuguese, and Spanish. (Free)

Print Materials

Many institutions and areas do not have Internet access or sufficient electrical power to rely on fully electronic, online collections. Print materials remain both reliable and relevant in these settings, and a core textbook collection could equal a very good reference collection. Here are some programs that provide print materials to institutions in developing countries at free or low cost.

17.43   WHO Blue Trunk Library. Geneva: World Health Organization. More
        information is available at http://www.who.int/ghl/mobile_libraries/
        bluetrunk/en/index.html.

Developed by WHO Library, Blue Trunk libraries are designed specifically for district health centers in Africa and contain more than 100 books on medicine and public health. Books are available in four languages and are shipped and stored in a blue trunk. Each Blue Trunk Library costs $2,000.

Shipping Books: Sister Libraries, Sister Countries, and Other Programs to Mail Books to Developing Countries

Many libraries maintain sister library status with libraries around the world. This arrangement frequently entails free document delivery, and may include mailing either new or discarded books to the developing world library. Other "sister" programs can include states, institutions, or even countries. When considering mailing books, be sure to consider the age, relevance, and accuracy of the information within the books. Simply having a newer, but still very old, version of a book is not necessarily a gift to the library in a developing country. It is worth asking the librarian(s) at the sister libraries if they have requests for specific titles or subjects, or if they want books at all. Also be sure to consider shipping and customs charges. In many countries, the package recipient must pay a fee to retrieve the package from customs. A well-intentioned gift may not be worth the hassle and cost.

Libraries interested in shipping printed material may want to explore a special service from the U.S. Postal Service (https://www.usps.com/send/airmail-mbags.htm).

Free Book Services

Libraries in developing countries are sometimes offered free books by services or publishers. Similarly, libraries in developed countries may prefer to donate books to a book service rather than distribute the books themselves. Free book services do fill a need for numerous libraries around the world. Ideally, libraries that receive books should be able to request specific titles or subject areas to be sure that the free books are relevant for the academic and clinical needs of the institution. Some specific services include the following:

17.44   Operation Medical Libraries (http://opmedlibs.medalumni.ucla.edu/): Based at UCLA, the grassroots group collects current medical textbooks and journals and distributes them to war-torn countries through partnerships with the U.S. military.

17.45   Book Aid International (http://www.bookaid.org/): Based in London, this organization sends books to sub-Saharan African countries.

17.46   Books for Africa (http://www.booksforafrica.org/): This organization receives books donated by libraries, schools, and publishers and sends them to libraries and schools in African countries.

17.47   Darien Book Aid Plan (http://www.darienbookaid.org/): Darien Book Aid distributes free books in response to specific requests from libraries, schools, and Peace Corps volunteers around the world.

17.48   Imagine Asia (http://www.imagine-asia.org///#/what-we-do/medical-textbooks): Imagine Asia collects and sends medical textbooks to Afghanistan and Pakistan.

17.49   International Book Project (http://www.intlbookproject.org/): Based in Kentucky, this nonprofit group sends books to libraries, schools, and Peace Corps volunteers around the world and within the United States. The organization accepts both book and monetary donations.

17.50   United States Book Exchange (http://www.usbe.com/): This company supplies back issues of scholarly journals and other periodicals to libraries worldwide. Some periodicals are specifically for free donation to libraries in developing countries.

Additional lists of book services are available online from the Africana Librarians Council (ALC, http://www.albany.edu/~dlafonde/Global/bookdona tion.htm) and the Humanitarian Efforts program of the American Academy of Otolaryngology—Head and Neck Surgery Foundation (http://www.entnet.org/Community/public/loader.cfm?csModule=security/getfile&pageid=39565).

Beyond providing awareness of (and potentially access to) these resources, another way librarians can partner across international boundaries is through professional, collegial training. HINARI promotional and training materials are available for librarians or other trainers on the HINARI website (http://www.who.int/hinari/training/en/). There is also a HINARI trainer e-mail discussion list. To join, send an e-mail to hinari@who.int. Librarians Without Borders, a Medical Library Association initiative, offers online HINARI training as well as some in-person, in-country training opportunities.

Additionally, there are several international medical librarian conferences such as the International Congress on Medical Librarianship (ICML) and the International Clinical Librarian Conference (ICLC). Many regions also have their own medical or health sciences librarian associations that meet regularly and offer conferences, networking opportunities, or other training.

Conclusion

Performing global health reference work may take place in one's library or even in the field, and communications may transpire through synchronous or asynchronous technologies. The scope of work may include serving one's institution's patrons, international partners, and even unaffiliated researchers, students, and librarians. Serving these different patron groups may require balance and setting priorities, as any one group's needs could blossom from a side project to become a full-time job. Librarians may wish to create a policy or model for how to structure their global health reference services. One example comes from a white paper written by the UNC-CH Health Sciences Library Global Health Task Force.[9] The group developed a clientele model to guide their decision making for outreach and support for global health at the library. The model prioritizes global health projects with close involvement by UNC researchers at the center of their outreach strategy and service plan. Other projects with less connection to the university's global health efforts fall into larger, concentric circles and may be less of a priority for the library.

Global health is interdisciplinary, encompassing, and affected by subjects as diverse as economics, engineering, epidemiology, and clinical sciences. Like many interdisciplinary subjects, global health is continually evolving. Fortunately, the authors have found that there exists a community of global health information providers, from librarians to professionals in nongovernmental organizations. This community can be incredibly helpful in finding the right information source or expert when needed. To stay involved, join an international library association, such as IFLA (International Federation of Library Associations and Institutions, http://www.ifla.org/) or the International Cooperation Section of the Medical Library Association (http://ics.mlanet.org/). Also, most countries or regions have library associations for health information like AHILA (the Association for Health Information and Libraries in Africa, http://www.ahila.org/), or EAHIL (the European Association for Health Information and Libraries, http://www.eahil.net/). Finally, there are numerous projects between developing and developed countries that could provide global health librarians assistance but also could benefit from their expertise and time. Two examples are MLA's Librarians Without Borders (http://www.mlanet.org/resources/global/) and Partners in Health Information (http://www.partnershipsinhealthinformation.org.uk/).

References

1. Institute of Medicine, Board on International Health. *America's Vital Interest in Global Health: Protecting Our People, Enhancing Our Economy, and Advancing Our International Interests*. Washington, DC: National Academy Press, 1997.
2. Macfarlane, S. B., M. Jacobs, and E. E. Kaaya. "In the Name of Global Health: Trends in Academic Institutions." *Journal of Public Health Policy* 29, no. 4 (2008): 383–401.
3. Crump, J. A., and J. Sugarman. "Ethical Considerations for Short-Term Experiences by Trainees in Global Health." *JAMA* 300, no. 12 (2008): 1456–58.
4. "Consortium of Universities for Global Health." Accessed November 12, 2012. http://www.cugh.org/membership/members.
5. "The European Academic Global Health Alliance." Accessed November 12, 2012. http://www.eagha.org/.
6. "Fact Sheet: The World Bank and Energy in Africa." Washington, DC: The World Bank Group. Accessed November 12, 2012. http://go.worldbank.org/8VI6E7MRU0.
7. Butcher, Mike. "Smartphones Not Required—Mobile Money on Feature Phones Is Hot in Emerging Markets." *TechCrunch,* October 22, 2012. http://techcrunch.com/2012/10/22/smartphones-not-required-mobile-money-on-feature-phones-is-hot-in-emerging-markets/.
8. "WHO Metrics: Disability Adjusted Life Years." Accessed February 29, 2013. http://www.who.int/healthinfo/global_burden_disease/metrics_daly/en/.
9. Lackey, M., P. Chavez, K. Crowell, J. Mayer, K. McGraw, M. Moore, S. Swogger, E. Vardell, and C. Jenkins. "White Paper for a Health Sciences Library Global Office." Last modified November 21, 2012; accessed March 12, 2013. http://www.hsl.unc.edu/global/whitepaper.pdf.

Contributors

LAURA ABATE
Electronic Resources and Instructional
    Librarian
Himmelfarb Health Sciences Library
George Washington University
Washington, DC
(Chapter 5)

MELODY ALLISON
Assistant Biology Librarian and Assistant
    Professor of Library Administration
Biology Library
University of Illinois at Urbana-Champaign
Urbana, IL
(Chapter 6)

PENNY COPPERNOLL-BLACH
Reference Coordinator
UCSD Biomedical Library
University of California at San Diego
La Jolla, CA
(Chapter 10)

JEAN BLACKWELL
Reference Librarian
UNC Health Sciences Library
University of North Carolina at Chapel Hill
Chapel Hill, NC
(Chapter 2)

JENNIFER DARRAGH
Librarian for Data Services and
    Government Information
Sheridan Libraries
Johns Hopkins University
Baltimore, MD
(Chapter 12)

MICHAEL A. FLANNERY
Associate Director for Historical
    Collections
Lister Hill Library of the Health Sciences
University of Alabama at Birmingham
Birmingham, AL
(Chapter 13)

MARY L. GILLASPY
Manager
The Learning Center
Northwestern Memorial Hospital
Chicago, IL
(Chapter 11)

SHARON GIOVENALE
Library Liaison to Pharmacy and
    Nutritional Sciences
University of Connecticut Pharmacy
    Library
University of Connecticut
Storrs, CT
(Chapter 10)

BARRIE HAYES
Library Liaison for Bioinformatics
UNC Health Sciences Library
University of North Carolina at Chapel Hill
Chapel Hill, NC
(Chapter 12)

JEFFREY T. HUBER, PhD
Director and Professor
School of Library and Information Science
University of Kentucky
Lexington, KY
(Chapter 3)

J. DAVID JOHNSON
Professor
Department of Communication
University of Kentucky
Lexington, KY
(Chapter 1)

JOHN D. JONES JR.
Reference and Research Librarian
Health Sciences Library
Anschutz Medical Campus
University of Colorado
Aurora, CO
(Chapter 15)

MELLANYE LACKEY
Library Liaison for the School of Public
    Health
UNC Health Sciences Library
University of North Carolina at Chapel Hill
Chapel Hill, NC
(Chapter 17)

LUCRETIA W. McCLURE, AHIP, FMLA
Rochester, NY
(Chapter 13)

MARY O'CONNOR PRANICA
Consumer Health Information Specialist
The Learning Center
Northwestern Memorial Hospital
Chicago, IL
(Chapter 11)

KATHERINE SCHILLING, EdD, AHIP
Associate Professor
School of Library and Information Science
Indiana University
Indianapolis, IN
(Chapter 9)

TRACY SHIELDS
Librarian
Eskind Biomedical Library/Knowledge
    Management
Vanderbilt University Medical Center
Nashville, TN
(Chapter 14)

SUSAN SWOGGER
Collections Development Librarian
UNC Health Sciences Library
University of North Carolina at Chapel Hill
Chapel Hill, NC
(Chapter16)

ANNELIESE TAYLOR
Manager, Collection Development
Kalmanovitz Library and Center for
    Knowledge Management
University of California at San Francisco
San Francisco, CA
(Chapter 2)

FEILI TU-KEEFNER, PhD
Associate Professor
School of Library and Information Science
University of South Carolina
Columbia, South Carolina
(Chapter 4)

BEATRIZ VARMAN
Assistant Director for Public Affairs and
    Information Services Librarian
Houston Academy of Medicine–Texas
    Medical Center Library
Houston, TX
(Chapter 7)

MEGAN VON ISENBURG
Associate Director, Public Services
Medical Center Library
Duke University
Durham, NC
(Chapter 17)

MICHELLE L. ZAFRON
Senior Assistant Librarian
Health Sciences Library
University of Buffalo
Buffalo, NY
(Chapter 8)

Index